NUCLEAR
DETERRENCE

NUCLEAR DETERRENCE
ETHICS AND STRATEGY

EDITED BY RUSSELL HARDIN, JOHN J. MEARSHEIMER,
GERALD DWORKIN, AND ROBERT E. GOODIN

The University of Chicago Press
Chicago and London

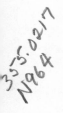

The essays in this volume originally appeared in *Ethics* 73 (January 1963), 94 (April 1984), and 95 (April 1985).

The University of Chicago Press, Chicago 60637
The University of Chicago Press, Ltd., London

Library of Congress Cataloging in Publication Data

Main entry under title:

Nuclear deterrence.

  Bibliography: p.
  Includes index.
  1. Deterrence (Strategy)—Congresses.   2. Deterrence
(Strategy)—Moral and ethical aspects—Congresses.
3. Nuclear warfare—Congresses.   4. Nuclear warfare—
Moral and ethical aspects—Congresses.   I. Hardin,
Russell, 1940–
U162.6.N818   1985   355′.0217   85-8423
ISBN 0-226-31702-1
ISBN 0-226-31704-8 (pbk.)

CONTENTS

ACKNOWLEDGMENTS

The papers in this volume were all originally published in *Ethics: An International Journal of Social, Political and Legal Philosophy*. Most were included in the April 1985 special issue on ethics and nuclear deterrence. The paper by David Gauthier was published in April 1984 and that by Theodore Roszak in January 1963. Publication of this volume and of the special issue of *Ethics* were made possible by generous grants from the Ford Foundation and the Exxon Education Foundation, which also sponsored a conference at the Aspen Institute, in Aspen, Colorado, where drafts of most of the papers were presented and discussed. We are grateful to the Ford Foundation, the Exxon Education Foundation, and the Aspen Institute for their contributions to this enterprise.

In addition to those who are represented in this volume, we wish to thank the several commentators who stimulated discussion in Aspen and who provoked revisions in the papers. These include Avner Cohen, David Hendrickson, Carey Joynt, Catherine Kelleher, Tony Kronman, Douglas P. Lackey, Steven Miller, Henry Shue, Duncal Snidal, Jack L. Snyder, Stephen Van Evera, Steven Walt, and Richard Werner. Charles Silver, formerly managing editor of *Ethics*, deserves credit for making the whole project succeed with his management of the conference and of the lives of all of us who participated in it. His successor, Thomas Christiano, and Erik Rieselbach have done yeomanly editorial work on the volume.

Introduction

Most of the papers in this volume were first presented at an Aspen conference that was organized to bring together two groups, philosophers and strategists, concerned with nuclear weapons, especially with the ethics of nuclear weapons policies. A striking feature of the conference was the extent to which the philosophers and the strategists, at least at the outset, each viewed the other group as monolithic in its beliefs. This is perhaps not surprising in light of the unfortunate fact that the two groups have had little contact with one another. At the same time, however, each group saw its own members as having quite diverse positions. As the conference progressed it became apparent that there is some truth in both these somewhat contradictory observations. There is considerable diversity within each group, but there are also marked similarities in the ways members of each community approach and answer certain fundamental questions.

These differences and similarities are naturally reflected in the following articles. The purpose of this brief introduction is to put those articles into a broader context: first, by outlining those themes that unite philosophers and those that unite strategists while also paying careful attention to differences between the two communities and, second, by describing the variety of views within each community.

UNIFYING THEMES

The theme that most unites strategists is that they are "realists" as this term is used in the literature of international relations. In philosophers' jargon, they view the world of nation-states as essentially a Hobbesian state of nature. This view is so widely taken for granted that it is seldom made explicit. It is a view defended here by a philosopher, Christopher Morris, and a strategist, Robert Tucker, but it is held by virtually all strategists. The view underlies the claim that deterrence is necessary for reasons of state or of survival. It is sometimes defended in other than Morris's Hobbesian terms with the claim that, after all, the state in our time is the condition for the pursuit of most moral values: hence the state must be defended. For example, if one is concerned with nuclear weapons because their threatened use violates the autonomy of innocents who are held hostage as a means to the end of protecting one's fellow citizens, then one must also grant that failure to defend one's state will lead to the violation of the autonomy of these fellow citizens. This argument is met by the contrary observation that the form of the defense of the state may well undercut some of the most important moral values that are supposedly supported by the state, as Sissela Bok and Richard Ullman argue.

A second theme that unites virtually all strategists is the belief that the Soviet Union is a formidable adversary that will exploit every foreign-policy opportunity presented to it. It cannot be trusted as, say, Canada or France can be. Hence, the United States must confront the Soviet Union with a strong defense. The intensity of this view, while held with varying degrees of strength among strategists, is seen by some philosophers as a *déformation professionelle* of the strategic community. But it is also true, and necessary to their belief in deterrence, that most strategists are inclined to think that a strong defense posture will force Soviet leaders to act less aggressively because these leaders are assumed to be rational, even cautious, in their pursuit of foreign-policy interests. There is little disagreement with Freeman Dyson's assertion that the "feasibility of influencing Soviet nuclear policies does not depend crucially on whether" a particularly hostile or a milder view of Soviet political character is right.[1]

The theme that most nearly unifies philosophers who write on nuclear deterrence is their concern with the question whether we may do—or threaten—evil that good may come. Is it permissible to threaten a nuclear holocaust, even if such a threat is very likely to deter the other side from ever starting a nuclear war? One strategist at the Aspen conference said that, in the hundreds of hours he had spent at other conferences on nuclear strategy, this question had never been raised. Philosophers of a utilitarian persuasion are not generally inclined to formulate such a question either since they generally weigh gains and losses that result from specific actions and then choose that action or policy that can be expected to produce the greatest net good. They do not judge kinds of action to be inherently bad independently of such a weighing. But it is a peculiarity of nuclear deterrence that the enormity of what it threatens forces even utilitarians to worry about this question to some extent because it challenges them to see how far they are willing to push their utilitarian principles. Hence, it is a, often the, central question motivating philosophical discussion of nuclear weapons, which seem to pose the ultimate test of any answer to the question whether we may do evil that good may come.

The strategists, as realists, simply ask what is the best deterrent strategy. They have moralized Machiavelli's concern with the narrow interests of the prince into the view that national leaders in the modern state should defend the interests of their peoples. Although the scope of this latter view is narrower than contemporary moral theorists would want, it is radically broader than Machiavelli's view of the prince's simple egoism. And it is broader than the strategists' stated concern with "prudence" suggests: they see national leaders as prudent not in the sense

---

1. Freeman Dyson, *Weapons and Hope* (New York: Harper & Row, 1984), p. 11.

that individuals may be prudent in seeking their own narrow interests but rather in the sense of doing their best to serve the interests of their people.

The ends of strategists are fundamentally normative and other regarding. They are concerned not with the well-being of all others, of course, but primarily with that of Americans and their allies. They are consequentialists, indeed, they are essentially utilitarians with limits. And, unlike the philosophers represented here, they are in very nearly complete agreement about what their ends are. They think that the prevention of war is a clear-cut moral imperative of our time. They differ only on their assessments of what are the most effective means to this end, although there appears to be considerable agreement that nuclear weapons provide an effective deterrent. Some strategists, including Robert Art, Josef Joffe, and George Quester, think that the nuclear deterrent is so effective that it may finally be a good thing. One could read their arguments to say that we are fortunate to have created nuclear weapons because, without them, it is likely that the world would be a more dangerous place. This is a position that seems not to have appealed to philosophers, not even to utilitarian philosophers, although, if utilitarians agreed with these strategists' analysis of the benefits of deterrence, they would presumably agree that the weapons are beneficial.

As moral theorists, the philosophers do not generally even address the strategists' policy question about effective means but ask rather whether our deterrent strategy is morally right. And here the focus is almost exclusively on a deterrent posture predicated on the threat of massive retaliation or what is commonly called "assured destruction." Philosophers typically are concerned with limited nuclear exchanges only insofar as they might be expected to increase the risks of a massive strategic exchange. This focus is arguably justified by the view of many strategists that we do not really know what would happen if there were a limited nuclear exchange or even a conventional war between the United States and the Soviet Union. Such confrontations might escalate in unexpected ways to all-out nuclear war.[2] Many philosophers are bothered by the argument articulated by Thomas Schelling and widely accepted among strategists that nuclear weapons deter even lesser acts of aggression because of uncertainty whether a limited war might escalate to all-out war.[3] In any confrontation with the Soviet Union, Schelling says, the perils that we face are "not as straightforward as suicide [implicit in a spasm war of mutual annihilation], but more like Russian roulette."[4]

2. See inter alia Desmond Ball, *Can Nuclear War Be Controlled?* Adelphi Papers, no. 169 (London: International Institute for Strategic Studies, Autumn 1981); Paul Bracken, *The Command and Control of Nuclear Forces* (New Haven, Conn.: Yale University Press, 1983); and Barry R. Posen, "Inadvertent Nuclear War? Escalation and NATO's Northern Flank," *International Security* 7 (1982): 28–54.

3. Thomas C. Schelling, *Arms and Influence* (New Haven, Conn.: Yale University Press, 1966), chap. 3.

4. Ibid., p. 94.

One philosopher who does seem to think that nuclear weapons are beneficial because of the deterrence they offer is David Gauthier. He asks whether one can rationally—that is to say, in one's own interest—carry out the threat of a nuclear counterattack once the threat has failed to deter. He is concerned with the problem of the coherence of relevant intentions, with whether one can rationally precommit oneself to do what would seem to be irrational when the time came. He thinks one can. This is an issue that strategists occasionally address when they wonder whether an American president, on learning that the West lay in ruins, would bother to respond by devastating the Soviet Union. Many strategists, and organizational decision theorists more generally, suppose that the relevant precommitment is achieved not by a particular individual but by an organization that is largely beyond the control of any one individual.

Robert Goodin supposes that to have the possibility of mutual assured destruction in the background is to take a risk that, no matter how small the probability that we will experience the final disaster, is plainly immoral. Most philosophers of a deontological bent—such as Thomas Donaldson and Gerald Dworkin—generally agree with him because they think it wrong under any circumstances intentionally to risk killing massive numbers of innocents. Since the only way we can avoid such a risk altogether is to dispose of our nuclear weapons, Goodin thinks we must therefore disarm. This seems to be the inescapable conclusion of any strong deontological argument against the killing of innocents, with the only caveat that purely defensive weapons might possibly be retained.

Finally, we should note here a supposedly moral position that is often taken on this issue, that may even be the popular view, which is that we have the right under some principle of reciprocity to strike back at Soviet cities if the Soviet Union destroys American cities. This position was actually stated in discussions at Aspen, by at least one strategist and at least one philosopher. But most moral philosophers reject it as incoherent on the ground that there can be no sense in which many—perhaps the vast majority—of the residents of the Soviet cities we might destroy could plausibly be held responsible for the destruction of American cities.

No matter what disagreements we may have on the issues of nuclear weapons, Gerald Dworkin and Richard Wasserstrom note, surely we must agree that no credible position on collective responsibility can include young children. Hence, any attack on Soviet cities must of necessity involve the wholesale killing of innocents. Without a relevant notion of collective responsibility, the justification from reciprocity can only be a morally flawed justification. It is a justification that may be rooted in the typically individual focus of most ethical argument. But one must be careful in jumping from individual-level to group-level claims. As Thomas Donaldson argues, the so-called domestic analogy—that I may rightly use force against someone who harms or threatens my family—simply does not fit the system of nuclear deterrence through the threat to destroy cities because many of those in the threatened cities cannot meaningfully be said to threaten or harm us.

Those who are given to justifying deterrence on the grounds of reciprocity should rather claim that the policy is utilitarian on either a general view (that counts the interests of all people equally) or a limited view (that weights the interests of Americans and their allies especially heavily). As noted above, the position of many strategists seems typically to be utilitarian on a limited view. But they seem to think it necessary to justify taking a limited rather than a general view, and the crude and largely misdirected argument from reciprocity may be brought in for that justification. The alternative is simply to assert the limited view, as many realists implicitly do when they refer to reasons of state. If one is to justify attacking Soviet cities nonetheless, the ground will have to be that other considerations are overriding, as Steven Lee argues and as would be assumed in a utilitarian argument for deterrence, or that morality is forfeit after a nuclear attack, as Christopher Morris and, by implication, Robert Tucker argue. Deterrence that threatens children may be morally right as a device to produce the better result overall, but this is not to say that to retaliate would be right as a matter of reciprocity unless the retaliation is directed at only those responsible for attacking us.

Perhaps this is the most important lesson moral philosophers offer for the debate over nuclear policy: the popular view of the Soviet-American conflict as us against them and of nuclear retaliation as an act of vengeance cannot be squared with the threat of immolating tens of millions of children. If Medea had merely killed Jason out of vengeance, Euripides would have had no subject for his play. That she killed her children to revenge Jason—"this is the best way to wound my husband"—made her a moral monster.[5] To justify the immolation of a generation of Soviet children simply by right is to sink to the level of Medea's moral depravity or to be incoherent.

THE DIVERSITY OF POSITIONS

What most divides strategists is their varied assessments of the objective facts of deterrence, of what weapons and what strategies for employing those weapons best serve deterrence. The most important question here is whether our current strategic doctrine and the weapons that support it are adequate for deterrence. The range of opinion on this matter is impressive, although one can identify three broad positions:

1. The first position, as articulated by Robert Art, expresses considerable satisfaction with the status quo. First, Art argues that the system of deterrence as it is presently constituted is extremely stable, that the so-called balance of terror is not delicate, and that it is not likely to be significantly affected by changes in the level of armament in either direction for the foreseeable future. Second, he maintains that, because nuclear weapons are so awful in what

5. Euripides, *Medea* 817, trans. Rex Warner, in *The Complete Greek Tragedies*, ed. David Grene and Richard Lattimore, 4 vols. (Chicago: University of Chicago Press, 1955), vol. 3, p. 87.

they threaten, they have made leaders on both sides very cautious and thus have significantly reduced the likelihood of any kind of war between the superpowers.

2. The second position, as articulated by Colin Gray, reflects considerable dissatisfaction with the status quo. First, Gray believes that it is morally untenable to base deterrence on the threat to destroy large portions of each side's population. He argues that we have a moral responsibility to defend our population. Second, Gray believes that it is strategically desirable for the United States to have the capability to fight and win a nuclear war. Thus, he favors fundamentally altering our strategic-force posture by developing counterforce weapons and strategic defensive systems. He wants to transcend the balance of terror and develop what strategists call a war-fighting, damage-limiting capability.[6]

3. A third position, represented by Richard Ullman, is also characterized by dissatisfaction with the status quo. Although Ullman thinks it is not possible completely to eliminate nuclear weapons, he favors substantially denuclearizing international politics. He wants significantly to reduce the size of the superpowers' nuclear arsenals and, especially, to eliminate counterforce weapons, which he considers highly destabilizing. Unlike Art, he is not convinced that the present nuclear balance is very stable. Moreover, he questions the belief that nuclear weapons have deterrent value that goes beyond simply deterring the other side from using its nuclear weapons.

Ullman does not go all the way and argue for complete disarmament because he is convinced, as is almost everyone who writes on this topic, of what Thomas Donaldson calls the "technological recalcitrance" of nuclear weapons: they cannot be disinvented, and, hence, one way or another we will have to deal with them. Ullman's argument for a reduction in nuclear armaments is a conclusion with which many philosophers agree (see the essays by Jan Narveson and Steven Lee); indeed, perhaps the large majority of philosophers writing on this topic would agree that substantial arms reductions would be morally preferable to the current state of affairs and to a continued arms race. Although most philosophers seem to agree with Ullman's call for significantly reducing the size of the strategic retaliatory forces of the superpowers, some of them add a fourth position to those of the strategists: unilateral disarmament by the United States (see Robert Goodin's essay). This position enjoys only limited support among philosophers and none at all among strategists.

It should be clear already from this discussion that philosophers are no more united in their views than are strategists. Christopher Morris supports the American system of nuclear deterrence on the ground that notions of morality are forfeit once one's nation has been attacked in an international system that is basically a Hobbesian state of nature. Jan Narveson also supports it but on the more or less utilitarian ground that

---

6. See also Colin Gray, "Nuclear Strategy: The Case for a Theory of Victory," *International Security* 4 (1979): 54–87.

a system of nuclear deterrence produces the best outcome on the whole. Others object to deterrence based on the threat of killing massive numbers of innocents in cities but think that at least purely defensive and certain counterforce weapons are legitimate insofar as these do not disproportionately threaten innocents (see the essays by Gerald Dworkin, Gregory Kavka, and Jeff McMahan). While these philosophers have major disagreements with Gray's position on war fighting, they share his view that it is morally preferable to defend against deaths in the West by defending against weapons than to prevent the use of the weapons by threatening retaliation. In the jargon of the strategic community, they prefer deterrence by denial to deterrence by punishment.[7]

Yet it should be clear that the diverse conclusions of philosophers, unlike those of the strategists, are not principally determined by differences in their objective assessments of what systems would work best for deterrence. Rather, what most divides philosophers on the issue of which nuclear policy should be adopted are basic assumptions of moral theory. In rough outline, the two principal positions are deontological and utilitarian. Deontologists are concerned with the nature of actions, including the nature of threatened actions. Utilitarians are concerned with likely outcomes of actions, as, of course, are strategists. Most philosophers who are inclined to defend the morality of nuclear deterrence through the threat of massive retaliation even against innocents are utilitarians, who share with strategists the view that the world with nuclear deterrence is likely to be better than the world without it.[8] Nevertheless, one might argue, even on utilitarian grounds, that nuclear deterrence is immoral just because one thinks it will lead to worse disasters on the whole—as defined by the number of expected deaths that will result from the policy—than will nuclear disarmament, even if this must be unilateral. This is a position defended elsewhere by Douglas Lackey.[9]

Deontologists generally are far less ready than utilitarians are to concede that we may threaten evil (the evil of destroying innocent civilians in the Soviet Union) in order that good may come. However, very few deontologists, if any, would insist that the only considerations that determine the morality of an action are abstract characteristics of the action. In particular, the likely results of an action may also be taken into account, and when these are grievous, they may override the prima facie strictures against an action of a certain kind. Hence a deontologist might suppose that, in the case of nuclear deterrence, the good of the protection of Americans and others from various evil prospects finally outweighs deon-

7. For discussion of this classic distinction between denial and punishment, see Schelling, chap. 1; and Glenn Snyder, *Deterrence and Defense* (Princeton, N.J.: Princeton University Press, 1961), chap. 1.

8. There are other positions, of course, as represented by Christopher Morris's view that in the state of nature that characterizes international politics notions of justice and right have no meaning, so that states may do what they must to survive.

9. Douglas Lackey, "Missiles and Morals: A Utilitarian Look at Nuclear Deterrence," *Philosophy & Public Affairs* 11 (1982): 189–231.

tological concern with the nature of the threat of killing millions of innocents, as Steven Lee concludes.

Discussion among philosophers often stops at the point of fundamental disagreement over moral principles, just as discussion among strategists often stops at the point of disagreement over hypothetical assertions about deterrence. But most moral theorists—and all utilitarians—also require consideration of hypothetical assertions to reach their conclusions, although they are typically even less adept at objective, causal argument than are strategists, who are themselves often quite casual with their social scientific claims. Even if one wishes to argue principally from deontological principles, one must have some confidence in one's social scientific expectations to decide whether consequences might not in this instance be overriding. Only a deontologist who held the extraordinary position that consequences never matter could easily reach a conclusion on nuclear weapons without considering the quality of various outcomes. Alas, on this dreadful issue good causal arguments are desperately needed, as Marc Trachtenberg forcefully argues.

ALTERNATIVES TO MUTUAL ASSURED DESTRUCTION

As noted in the previous section, there are many critics of the present American deterrent policy, which emphasizes mutual assured destruction and which relies, in part, on nuclear weapons to deter conventional wars in areas such as Europe and Korea.[10] Criticism, of course, comes from both philosophers and strategists. Let us take a closer look at the principal alternatives to the present policy: placing much greater emphasis on counterforce and defensive weaponry and "denuclearizing" international relations.

Perhaps the largest body of argument against a policy of massive retaliation is based on the so-called just war tradition.[11] As Theodore Roszak notes, the chief element of this varied tradition "is expressed in the single provision of civilian immunity from *direct* attack." Just war theorists are invariably disturbed by the policy of mutual assured destruction since it is predicated on the threat to kill massive numbers of innocent

10. It is important to emphasize that although the United States has adopted a policy of mutual assured destruction, it still maintains a significant counterforce capability. It does not, however, have counterforce capability adequate to threaten the Soviet Union's assured destruction capability or to "fight and prevail" in a nuclear war with the Soviet Union. Developing such capabilities is what the counterforce debate is all about.

11. Useful recent works on the application of just war thinking to nuclear weapons include David Hollenbach, S.J., *Nuclear Ethics: A Christian Moral Argument* (New York: Paulist Press, 1983); and John Howard Yoder, *When War Is Unjust: Being Honest in Just-War Thinking* (Minneapolis: Augsburg Publishing House, 1984). The standard history of the just war tradition is James Turner Johnson, *Just War Tradition and the Restraint of War: A Moral and Historical Inquiry* (Princeton, N.J.: Princeton University Press, 1981). Perhaps the most important contribution to just war debate in our time is the 1983 pastoral letter by the National Conference of Catholic Bishops, *The Challenge to Peace: God's Promise and Our Response,* which has been widely published, e.g., as a special supplement to the *Chicago Catholic* (June 24, July 1, 1983). Also see Albert Wohlstetter, "Bishops, Statesmen, and Other Strategists on the Bombing of Innocents," *Commentary* (June 1983): 15–35.

civilians. Some advocates of this tradition maintain that there is an alternative: a satisfactory deterrent posture can instead be built around counterforce and defensive weapons, which, so it is argued, can be used without killing large numbers of civilian innocents and certainly without the intention to kill innocents. Hence, as Paul Ramsey and others have argued, such weapons are permissible under the so-called principle of discrimination of the just war tradition insofar as they are used against military targets without indiscriminately killing noncombatants.[12] For example, it has been supposed that the cruise missile, which can be used discriminately because of its great accuracy, represents a moral advance over weapons aimed at cities.[13] (Of course, the cruise missile could also be used against cities.) Unfortunately, as Roszak notes, military targets are too often near urban areas for a counterforce deterrence policy to be effective unless it involves massive losses of civilians. Hence, "the moral satisfaction to be taken in this strategy is not that it will spare civilian lives, but rather that the colossal human carnage the strategy may produce is 'incidental' or 'indirect.'"

The support for counterforce and defensive weapons that some just war theorists draw from the principle of discrimination is openly rejected by many strategists. This position is based on two considerations. First, many strategists believe that these weapons are destabilizing. They produce crisis instability, so the argument goes, by threatening the Soviet Union's assured destruction capability. This gives Soviet leaders strong incentive in a crisis to launch their nuclear forces quickly, before they can be eliminated by our counterforce weapons. In effect, the Soviet Union is placed in what is sometimes referred to as a "use them or lose them" situation. Also, because these weapons are likely to make nuclear war seem less horrible to decision makers (the principal attraction, of course, to just war theorists), they will have the effect of making war more likely. Second, many strategists do not believe that it is possible to fight in a discriminating manner with nuclear weapons. The potential for escalation is so great, they believe, that it makes no sense to talk in terms of a limited nuclear war. The consequentialism of these strategists thus brings them, as it does many utilitarian philosophers, into opposition to this just war principle.

Nevertheless, not all strategists are opposed to pursuing a counterforce strategy. Some, like Colin Gray, feel that there are good moral as well as sound strategic reasons for doing so. The moral argument offered by these strategists is that of the just war tradition. The strategic rationale, on the other hand, is usually of three kinds. First, the case is often made that the Soviet Union is developing a formidable counterforce capability of its own and that the United States must move to check this development by deploying its own counterforce capability. Second, there are some who believe that the United States would gain significant political advantage

12. Paul Ramsey, *War and the Christian Conscience: How Shall Modern War Be Conducted Justly?* (Durham, N.C.: Duke University Press, 1961).

13. James Turner Johnson, *Can Modern War Be Just?* (New Haven, Conn.: Yale University Press, 1984), p. 124.

over the Soviet Union if it had a marked advantage in counterforce capabilities. In effect, proponents of this view answer yes to the question, Does nuclear superiority matter? Third, and related to the previous point, advocates of counterforce feel that, if the United States is going to rely on its strategic nuclear forces to deter conventional wars in places such as Europe and Korea, then it is necessary to have the capability to wage and to prevail in a nuclear war. This discussion points up quite clearly that there is no agreement among either philosophers or strategists on the question of the counterforce option. In fact, strategists and philosophers are found on both sides of the issue, making it difficult to generalize about the positions of the two communities.

The second alternative to mutual assured destruction calls for significantly deemphasizing our reliance on nuclear weapons and placing greater reliance on our conventional forces. In the strategists' vocabulary, this is referred to as a "finite deterrent." One only needs to maintain enough nuclear weapons to destroy a large fraction of the opponent's population. A key assumption underlying this school of thought is that nuclear weapons are only effective at deterring one's adversary from making a direct attack on one's homeland. Nuclear weapons are not capable of deterring attacks against one's allies in other areas of the world. In the strategist's jargon, the "extended deterrent value" of these weapons is minimal. Thus, one needs only a small number of nuclear weapons to deter a direct attack on the homeland.

It seems clear that virtually all of the philosophers represented in this volume favor substantial reductions of nuclear arms. This position does not enjoy widespread support among strategists, although there are a good number, Richard Ullman among them, who advocate this view. In general, most strategists believe that nuclear weapons have great deterrent value for which conventional forces cannot substitute. The issue takes its clearest form in the debate over whether NATO should adopt a "no first use" (NFU) policy. Ullman calls for adopting an NFU policy as part of his program for "denuclearizing" international politics. Josef Joffe and George Quester disagree. The case against NFU is built on the assumption that nuclear weapons, because they are so horrible, deter war in Europe. In other words, the best way to prevent war in Europe is to make both sides believe that any conflict there has some likelihood of escalating into a general thermonuclear war. Adopting an NFU policy, so the argument goes, has the effect of making Europe "safe" for a conventional war that would probably not involve direct attacks on the homelands of either superpower. War would be more likely to break out in a situation like this than it would be in one where both superpowers believed that it was very likely that a war in Europe would escalate to the nuclear level. Again, the issue is threatening evil that good may come or that greater evil may be avoided.[14]

14. Against Joffe's conclusion, Jeff McMahan and Arne Naess have argued that unilateral nuclear disarmament would provide the best protection of lives in at least the United

There is another dimension to the strategist's case against moving to denuclearize international relations. Many, Robert Art included, feel that the dangers associated with nuclear war are so great that the superpowers have been forced to behave in an extremely cautious manner when dealing with each other.[15] This caution, it is supposed, extends to minor conflicts in relatively remote areas of the globe. Basically, nuclear weapons have altered the way great powers behave toward each other. The clear implication is that relations between the United States and the Soviet Union would have been much different over the past forty years if there had been no nuclear weapons. McGeorge Bundy once referred to this effect of nuclear weapons as "existential deterrence."[16] Many strategists believe that this caution induced by nuclear weapons is a good thing and that efforts to denuclearize international relations would not serve the interests of world peace.

Of course, not all strategists agree with this line of argument. Robert McNamara, for example, believes that nuclear weapons in the arsenals of the superpowers have no deterrent value other than to deter an adversary from using nuclear weapons.[17] Because any use of nuclear weapons might escalate to involve direct attacks on the superpowers, we cannot sensibly threaten their use for lesser purposes such as the defense of Western Europe. In effect, he interprets the caution that attends nuclear weapons to mean that it is highly unlikely that either side will ever use them, thus greatly diminishing their deterrent value. Critics of NFU typically disagree with this supposition.

Perhaps the starkest way to pose the issue of denuclearization is to suppose that nuclear weapons had never been invented and to ask what our world would be like without them. Many strategists are inclined to think that we would have had disastrous war with the Soviet Union. One suspects that most philosophers concerned with nuclear weapons and at least some strategists would prefer the counterfactual world in which there were no such weapons. If Robert Art and many of his fellow strategists are right, this preference wants examination. Consequentialists of either a limited or a broadly utilitarian persuasion might suppose that a hundred million dead in a conventional war with high probability would

Kingdom and Scandinavia, in part because, they suppose, these countries could opt out of the larger East-West conflict by disarming unilaterally and thereby ceasing to threaten the Soviet Union. Jeff McMahan, *British Nuclear Weapons: For and Against* (London: Junction Books, 1981); Arne Naess, "The Consequences of an Absolute NO to Nuclear War," in *Nuclear Weapons and the Future of Humanity: The Fundamental Questions*, ed. Avner Cohen and Steven Lee (Totowa, N.J.: Rowman & Allanheld, 1984).

15. Also see McGeorge Bundy, "To Cap the Volcano," *Foreign Affairs* 49 (1969): 1–20; Robert Jervis, *The Illogic of American Nuclear Strategy* (Ithaca, N.Y.: Cornell University Press, 1984); and Kenneth Waltz, *The Spread of Nuclear Weapons: More May Be Better*, Adelphi Paper, no. 171 (London: International Institute for Strategic Studies, Autumn 1981).

16. See McGeorge Bundy, "The Bishops and the Bomb," *New York Review of Books* (June 10, 1983), p. 4.

17. Robert McNamara, "The Military Role of Nuclear Weapons: Perceptions and Misperceptions," *Foreign Affairs* 62 (1983): 59–80.

compare unfavorably to far more dead in a nuclear war with much lower probability. Deontologists have difficulty with moral conclusions drawn from such comparisons. But if the numbers are sufficiently stark, they must give even the staunchest deontologist pause.

OTHER ISSUES

There are two other broad issues associated with nuclear weapons that receive considerable attention in this volume: the impact of nuclear weapons on civic life and the matter of controlling military technology.

Sissela Bok and Richard Ullman argue that nuclear weapons are fundamentally incompatible with democratic government. Ullman is principally concerned with the fact that the ultimate decision to use nuclear weapons is placed in the hands of a small number of decision makers who would not have to consult the publics in whose name they would presume to act. Bok appears to be more concerned about the need for secrecy that surrounds nuclear weapons. She believes that this has a debilitating effect on the body politic and ultimately works to undermine democratic institutions.

As is often the case in the field of national security affairs, such effects may cut both ways. The system of control over nuclear weapons may have an adverse impact on democratic politics, but building substantially more powerful conventional forces as a substitute for our heavy reliance on nuclear weapons is likely to have even more corrosive effects on our democratic polity. If European history is any guide, it suggests that large standing armies are likely to be incompatible with democracy.[18] While the secrecy attending nuclear forces may pose special problems, it is nevertheless true that military secrecy has permeated public life since long before the nuclear era. In fact, one could probably make a convincing case that among states in the West there is now less secrecy about national security matters than there has been at any time in modern history.

Second, there is the matter of arms control or controlling military technology. Nuclear weapons and especially the systems we develop for delivering them against an opponent depend very heavily on the constant flow of new technologies. It is widely recognized that military technology is highly dynamic. More specifically, it is important to note that there is a feeling among many strategists that we are on the threshold of a revolution of sorts in the realm of nuclear technology. We can expect, it is widely supposed, great increases in missile accuracy and the development of effective strategic defensive systems. Gray and Ullman, who have quite different views on nuclear strategy, seem to agree that significant changes in the nuclear inventories are in the offing.

It would be beneficial if the superpowers were to control the development of military technology so that only those systems that enhanced

---

18. For the classic statement of this position, see Felix Gilbert, ed., *The Historical Essays of Otto Hintze* (New York: Oxford University Press, 1975), chaps. 4, 5.

deterrence were developed. Unfortunately, directing or restraining technological developments before they are transformed into military capability is a very difficult task. As Karl Lautenschläger argues, it is not a simple matter to separate military from nonmilitary technologies, and sometimes technologies that appear to be of a nonmilitary nature turn out to have significant military capability. Other times, technologies serve useful nonmilitary purposes as well as military ones. Thus, the society at large would pay a heavy price if the development of such technologies was thwarted. Finally, there is usually considerable disagreement among strategists over the desirability of various military technologies. Gray and Ullman, for example, would surely disagree about the desirability of almost all the new technologies that they see coming.

Lautenschläger argues that controlling military technology may do more harm than good. One could accept the logic of this argument as it applies to controlling technology at the early stages of the development process and still see some hope for arms control. It might be argued, for example, that the prospects for control are much better if one intervenes at the testing stage rather than at the level of basic research. This approach has been emphasized over the past fifteen years in arms control negotiations between the superpowers. Furthermore, the kinds of arms control that Ullman recommends are not terribly difficult to effect, although as he admits the payoffs from arms control measures that are easy to achieve are not particularly great. Whatever approach we take, arms control will still be plagued by questions about "good" and "bad" weapons.

Perhaps the best way to control military developments would be to influence the political forces that drive the arms race. If, as Bok believes, the postwar arms race is substantially a consequence of failed political will, then improving American-Soviet relations will have more impact on slowing down arms developments than direct efforts at controlling military technology will. It is an assumption of many in both the philosophical and strategic communities that the competition between the superpowers is largely a matter of ideological differences and that these differences can be ameliorated. Others, however, believe that the conflict grows out of geopolitical considerations that are independent of ideological differences. This view is certainly consistent with the realist interpretation of international relations so common to strategists. If this view is at least partly correct, direct efforts at arms control may hold more promise than more general efforts to alter significantly the general tenor of relations between the superpowers. This would be especially true if both sides were convinced that it served their economic interests to achieve controls. In sum, the policy we recommend depends on what we consider to be the motor that drives the competition between the great powers. And here there is little agreement.

Russell Hardin and John J. Mearsheimer

War, Nuclear War, and Nuclear Deterrence: Some Conceptual and Moral Issues

Richard Wasserstrom

One cannot think adequately about the moral issues of nuclear deterrence without thinking about the moral issues of nuclear war. That, at least, is both an assumption with which I begin and a claim I hope to make more plausible through the structure and argument of this paper. In it, I seek to do three things.

First, I want to detach ideas about war in general from the realities of what is misleadingly called "nuclear war." For the ways in which nuclear war differs from war have consequences for matters of political and constitutional theory as well as for the putatively more circumscribed issues concerning the practice of nuclear deterrence.

Second, I want, nonetheless, to connect nuclear war tightly with conventional war in one respect. For I shall argue that there is something important and right in the view that there are certain kinds of things that it is wrong to do even in a total, conventional war in the light of which nuclear war is always morally wrong—without the real possibility of overriding justification or excuse.

And third, I want to examine directly certain issues concerning the theory and morality of nuclear deterrence. The issues of theory concern similarities and dissimilarities between rather well understood deterrent theories of the criminal law and theories of nuclear deterrence which, in often unnoticed and problematic ways, borrow or rest on them. The moral issues have to do with the ways in which issues of the morality of nuclear deterrence are in fact harder to detach from those of the morality of nuclear war itself than may at first be thought.

I

What many persons surely have most in mind when they talk about, think about, and worry about nuclear war is the use by the two dominant nuclear powers—the United States and the Soviet Union—of some portion of their vast arsenal of nuclear weapons against the cities and missile sites of these countries at which they are presently targeted. This, too, is what I mean by "nuclear war," and in this section I seek to do two things: first, to delineate some of the central but less-noticed respects in which nuclear war, were it to occur, would be false to our ideas about what war is and, second, to explain why and for what reasons nuclear war, were it to occur, would be wrong.

In order to think adequately about either the conceptual or the moral issues of nuclear war it is important to have some understanding of the destructive power of individual nuclear weapons and of the number of such weapons possessed by the two dominant nuclear powers. Such an understanding bears on both sets of issues in related, but different, ways.

A single, one megaton nuclear bomb or warhead is one which possesses eighty times the explosive power of one of the two nuclear weapons ever used to date, the one dropped on Hiroshima. Were such to be detonated a mile or so above a large urban area, it would, in virtue of its explosive force, flatten virtually every structure within a radius of four miles, and it would heavily damage buildings within a radius of eight miles. Within two miles from the center of the explosion, winds of four hundred miles per hour would be produced, and four miles from the center they would still have a speed of one hundred eighty miles per hour. The fireball, which follows directly on the explosion, would produce at least third-degree burns on the body of any person out in the open and within a radius of nine miles from the center of the blast. Those closer to it would be incinerated if they were not otherwise killed by the force of the explosion, the ensuing winds, and the falling structures. Within a radius of eight miles, mass fires would soon occur, caused by the inflammable materials ignited by the heat of the fireball, and those within these fire storms would also be burned to death. And within the first twenty-four to forty-eight hours, the radioactive fallout from the detonation would deliver doses of radiation, well in excess of those that are lethal, to persons who were within an area of about two thousand square miles and exposed to it.[1]

It cannot be known that these figures are accurate, for a one megaton device has never been detonated above or on a city, and the estimates of what would happen vary with assumptions about the site of detonation, the climatic conditions, the kinds of structures involved, and the like. But there is rather little disagreement about the general scale of the devastation that would be involved. And the account just given makes no further conjectures about the longer-term, less-direct destructive consequences.[2]

Nor is there much disagreement about the size of the nuclear arsenals of the United States and the Soviet Union. The Soviet Union possesses approximately seven thousand nuclear warheads, which, were they all

1. Jonathan Schell, *The Fate of the Earth* (New York: Avon Books, 1982), pp. 47–50.
2. The uncertainties involved in such estimates, as well as those involved in effects that cannot even be estimated, are discussed in U.S. Congress, Office of Technology Assessment, *The Effects of Nuclear War* (Washington, D.C.: Government Printing Office, 1979).

to be launched and detonated, would probably yield something over ten thousand megatons of short-term, immediate destructive force—a force equivalent to that of the destructive power of eight hundred thousand bombs of the type dropped on Hiroshima. The United States possesses nine thousand nuclear warheads, which, were they all to be launched and detonated, would probably yield about 3,500 megatons of short-term, immediate destructive force—a force equivalent to that of the destructive power of three hundred thousand bombs of the type dropped on Hiroshima. Were either country to launch and detonate some substantial number of its nuclear warheads, most, if not all, of the persons living in the country so bombarded would be killed by the initial blasts, the ensuing massive fire storms, and the lethal radiation generated.[3] And it is possible, perhaps even probable, that, were either or both to do so, all forms of life existing on earth would be destroyed by the longer-term effects and consequences of the force, fire, and radiation unleashed.[4]

While we speak of such a use or exchange of nuclear weapons as nuclear war, it is important to notice the significant ways in which such an exchange or use of weapons is at odds with virtually our entire stock of ideas about what war is, no matter how total a conventional, nonnuclear war we may have in mind.

The first and most obvious thing has, of course, to do with the weapons, with the combination of the massiveness and the necessary indiscriminancy of the destructiveness that would result. There would be no identifiable battlegrounds or individuals doing battle—there could not be any, even residual, descriptive sense to a differentiation between combatants and noncombatants or between combat zones and military bases, on the one hand, and hospitals, schools, places of worship, and homes, on the other.

A second, related thing also has to do with the spatial scale. We take for granted in our thinking about war that countries and national boundaries remain in place. In war a country's borders can, of course, be crossed by the armed forces of another, and those countries not at war can be affected by a war going on elsewhere. But once a war begins, the countries

3. Schell, pp. 56–59. Douglas Lackey gives the total expected deaths, under two differing scenarios of nuclear strikes and counterstrikes between the United States and the Soviet Union, as in one case 150,000,000 and in the other 104,000,000 ("Missiles and Morals," *Philosophy & Public Affairs* 11 [1982]: 189–231, pp. 223–27). Lackey (p. 226, n. 31) also cites the much higher estimate of 133,000,000 American deaths within a two-month period from a 6,559 megaton attack on the United States given by Herbert Abrams and William von Kaenel in "Medical Problems of Survivors of Nuclear War," *New England Journal of Medicine* (November 12, 1981), pp. 1226–32. Comparable figures are also offered in Bruce Russett, *The Prisoners of Insecurity* (San Francisco: W. H. Freeman & Co., 1983), pp. 55–58; and still larger ones are cited in P. R. Ehrlich et al., "Long-Term Biological Consequences of Nuclear War," *Science* 222 (1983): 1293–1300, pp. 1293–94 and accompanying notes.

4. R. P. Turco et al., "Nuclear Winter: Global Consequences of Multiple Nuclear Explosions," *Science* 222 (1983): 1283–92; Ehrlich et al.

not at war can decide whether they will go to war too; and countries at war can choose whether or not to respect national boundaries and keep the war out of uninvolved or neutral countries. Nuclear war is different. Quite apart from the unknown changes in the biosphere that might well be wrought by nuclear explosions, it is apparent that nuclear radiation and fallout are not, and cannot be, respecters of national boundaries, confined in their direct and lethal effects to the inhabitants of the countries engaged in nuclear war. Whether the countries engaging in nuclear war intend it or not, nuclear war in part takes place wherever the winds of that war happen to be blowing at that time.

A third thing has to do with time. The standard case of a total conventional war, such as World War II, has appreciable duration. Once such a war begins, it is anything but over. A nuclear war has no comparable duration. Depending on the location and speed of the components of the delivery systems, the destructiveness would commence and its full short-term effects would be experienced between seven minutes and several days after the war commenced. Such a war would be an event, or a temporally compressed series of events, not a struggle persisting over time and composed of numerous raids, engagements, battles, mo-bilizations, and the like. There would be no meaningful, extended temporal interval within which the war occurred and within which it was fought and either won or lost.

Still another distinction is connected with several of those already identified. There would be few if any occasions within nuclear war for displays of the virtues and vices of war, few if any contexts for heroism and bravery, valor and self-sacrifice, comradeship and affection, or their ignominious opposites.

A fifth and particularly important difference concerns the altered place of individual decisions and actions and the diminution of the number of such decisions and actions. Wars, total or otherwise, can be (and some-times are) begun as a result of the decisions of comparatively few persons or even a single head of state. But the war that then ensues requires the decisions and actions of vast numbers of persons if the war is to be fought at all. Such, too, is not the case in nuclear war. To the extent to which the delivery systems of the United States and the Soviet Union utilize planes, land-based missiles, and submarines, the crews needed to make them work are still required. But the primary action constituting the entire war itself is intimately and firmly connected with the unitary decision of the individual or individuals having access to the unified command network necessary and sufficient to initiate the activation and launch of the nuclear weapons.

These differences make it impossible for a nuclear war to be either popular or unpopular in any meaningful sense with the citizens of the countries directly engaging in nuclear war. It is not merely that there is so little time or that most of them will die; it is also that there is nothing for them to do in the waging of the war. Less obvious, perhaps, but no less significant is the fact that all the decisions that individuals might want to make and all the actions they might want to take in respect to nuclear war have to be made and taken, if they are to be made and taken at all, before the war occurs. Just as conscientious objection does not have any meaning or place in a nuclear war, there are also no questions that any persons can ask or entertain about whether the war is being fought in the right or wrong way or for the right or wrong reasons. Once any conventional war commences, especially if it is a total war, those are very difficult questions to ask, answer, or act on—both because relevant, accurate information is very difficult to obtain and because individual action is typically constrained in so many special and unusual ways. With a conventional war, however, they are nonetheless possible; and the ways they are asked, answered, and acted on can have something intelligible to do with retrospective as well as contemporaneous judgments of responsibility and accountability for the war and the way it was fought and conducted. In nuclear war all issues such as these are foreclosed and, of necessity, relocated in an earlier time and context. That is why protest directed against nuclear war must occur before the war if it is to occur at all. That is why, too, the question of whether an individual behaves rightly or wrongly, culpably or permissibly, in participating in the design, manufacture, or maintenance of nuclear weapons and nuclear delivery systems is one that is an especially pressing, real, and timely one now, even though there is no nuclear war occurring.

The nuclear arms race, the time during which it continues to be just a race, is the only time within which persons can act in any way in the light of sound moral ideas about actual, massive nuclear destruction. The issues extend beyond those of individuals' causal contributions to and possible moral culpability for the production of nuclear weapons, delivery systems, and the plans for their use. They extend to such matters as whether allocations of political authority and power in respect to making and waging war can have the place that we may unreflectively think they have when we consider nuclear war. And if they do not, and they cannot, then this calls sharply into question—more so than in the case of conventional war—whether there is continuing sense to the idea that those individuals who constitute the members of a country can be identified in the various, familiar ways with the country that goes to, or engages in, nuclear war. That is one reason the nuclear arms race puts established ways of thought and conduct concerning the centrality of the nation-state into question, however else nation-states may be causally connected with the dangers so created. That is also a reason why there is a need, for example, to notice and to reexamine in respect to nuclear war the illusory authority vested in the Congress by article 1, section 8, of our constitution to decide whether or not to go to war by declaring war.[5]

5. This issue is addressed in Jeremy J. Stone, "Presidential First Use Is Unlawful," *Foreign Policy*, no. 56 (1984), pp. 94–112. Stone also argues that there is not a comparable

It is, therefore, for these as well as other reasons and in these as well as other ways, a pervasive and fundamental mistake of a conceptual or phenomenological sort to talk about and think about nuclear war as though it were essentially a war at all. Our ideas about war are rooted in contexts, situations, and meanings that have little if any application when it is the use of nuclear weapons to make nuclear war that is at issue. While the words remain the same, they are false, necessarily and misleadingly so, to the realities of the phenomenon being considered when questions of nuclear war are addressed. It is essential, therefore, to endeavor to keep in mind some, if not all, of the ways in which thought can be seriously led astray in and through what is said and assumed by talking about nuclear war and thereby in supposing that it would have the features of war at all.[6]

---

problem with the president's authority to use nuclear weapons in response to a nuclear attack on the United States in virtue of the inherent authority to act immediately to repel an attack on the United States. For the reasons given in Sec. II of this paper, I am doubtful that this is so since I am uncertain what, in many circumstances, such a responsive use could be plausibly thought to repel or otherwise accomplish.

6. It might here, as well as elsewhere in this paper, be objected that, while I have correctly described one kind of nuclear war—the worst kind—and identified ways in which it would be radically different from conventional war, there could be other, more "limited" kinds of nuclear wars that would possess many more of the usual characteristics of war and that these would, therefore, be subject to a moral assessment different from the one I provide. The claim that there could be other more limited kinds of nuclear wars might focus on one or both of two matters. The first has to do with how the weapons might be different in destructive range and effect. If tactical nuclear weapons are substantially different in these respects from the strategic ones of the sort I have described, then their use in battle against combatants may in itself be no different from (and be no more or less morally problematic than) the use of other familiar and deadly weapons of war. If this is so, then, e.g., what I say in the remainder of this section would not apply in a straightforward way to them, and the primary moral question would concern the possible or likely consequences of breaking the taboo, in place since 1945, on the use of all such weapons, in virtue of the fact that they are nuclear weapons. The second has to do with the idea of a nuclear war waged with strategic nuclear weapons but limited in that only some of the strategic nuclear weapons of mass destruction are used against their targets while others are held in reserve and are to be launched against their targets only if those used so far do not succeed in bringing the "limited" nuclear war to an end. I am very skeptical that one could draw an intelligible line between the kind of indiscriminate devastation that would result from the limited nuclear war imagined by these strategic scenarios and the kind, magnitude, and rapidity of devastation central to the kind of nuclear war which I have described thus far and which I consider further in the remainder of this paper. For the reasons given in the rest of this section I think that this kind of "limited" nuclear war is subject to the same moral criticisms there advanced. Nonetheless, to the extent to which this claim about different kinds of nuclear war, in either or both of its forms, does raise different questions, I do not consider them directly here. This is so because my primary concern is to delineate the discrepant features of an all-too-possible kind of nuclear war between the United States and the Soviet Union—one involving some substantial portion of the nuclear weapons now in place, aimed at targets in the other country, and launched and detonated by both sides in the initiation of or response to a real or perceived nuclear attack. This kind of nuclear war would, I believe, have all the features I have identified. I think it valuable and instructive to focus on this worst case, if that is what it is, so as to be as clear as possible

Despite these considerations and the distortions they give rise to, one primary moral issue concerning nuclear war remains tightly connected with thought about conventional war, namely, whether it could possibly be right for the United States, the Soviet Union, or any other country to use its nuclear weapons and thus go to or engage in nuclear war. I do not think that it could be right to do so, and the reasons have to do with ideas about the morality of killing in time of war and with the massiveness and the indiscriminancy of the killings that would be wrought. This may seem an obvious, quite unexceptionable conclusion to reach, but theories and ideas about the rightness and wrongness of killing in war are themselves controversial, uncertain, and contested and this conclusion anything but universally accepted. In addition, for reasons I endeavor to develop and defend in Section II, this conclusion has implications, not always sufficiently noticed and attended to, for an assessment of the morality of nuclear deterrence. Attending to the moral issues of nuclear war is one way to make explicit assumptions and lines of arguments concerning morality in war as well as to see what would be wrong with nuclear war and what is deeply problematic about nuclear deterrence.

Features internal to war itself can go a great distance toward justifying much of the deliberate killing of combatants by combatants that occurs in time of war. For if there is a war going on, the members of the armed forces—the combatants—of the countries at war are at least necessarily prepared to use deadly force in battle against the members of the armed forces of the opposing side. Familiar ideas about the justifiable use of deadly force in self-defense, appropriately relaxed because the context is war rather than civil society, work reciprocally to license the killing of the opposing combatants, once it is a war that they find themselves engaged in. Or so, at least, I am prepared to assume.[7]

The more difficult problems concern the deliberate killing of non-combatants. Here, two distinct lines of argument can be advanced in support of the view that much of the killing of persons who are ostensibly noncombatants is morally permissible. The first has to do, once again, with self-defense, the second with moral responsibility and culpability. The same arguments concerning self-defense, which most firmly support the killing of opposing combatants, can be plausibly extended to reach and include those noncombatants whose activities make a causal contribution of the requisite sort to the more direct and deadly activities of

---

about its characteristics and its defects. If they are as striking and as serious as I take them to be, one has, at least, a framework within which to locate and then consider claims about the conceptual and moral features of other kinds of nuclear war— if they would in fact be different. Thus when I refer throughout this paper to nuclear war, I have in mind the kind of nuclear war described thus far, and when later I discuss issues concerning the use of nuclear weapons, I am talking about the use of the strategic nuclear weapons possessed by the dominant nuclear powers.

7. I discuss this in somewhat greater detail in "On the Morality of War: A Preliminary Inquiry," *Stanford Law Review* 21 (1969): 1627–56, pp. 1627–36.

the combatants, for example, workers in munitions factories and the like. And ideas and arguments about moral responsibility and culpability can, perhaps, also be plausibly extended to include within the class of those permissibly killed those noncombatants whose commitments, beliefs, and actions with respect to the initiation and pursuit of the war make it appropriate to view them as either having themselves assumed the deadly risks of war or being culpable for the initiation or conduct of the war and for these reasons not wrongly killed. Or so, here too, I am prepared for purposes of argument to assume.

But no matter how either or both of these lines of argument may be exploited and extended to justify the deliberate killing of many noncombatants in war, they cannot support the intentional or knowing killing of those persons who are both unmistakably and unequivocally noncombatants in causal terms and also wholly innocent in all the morally relevant respects. Children, of whom there are many in all countries, are the clearest example of such persons. They are fully noncombatants in all the relevant causal respects, and clearly so. If they are reasonably young children, they literally cannot fight or engage in any of the other activities that might have the requisite causal connection with more direct war-making activities. Hence, to kill them intentionally or knowingly is not to use deadly force directed against either a culpable or a nonculpable deadly attacker, no matter how relaxed the relevant causal criteria may be thought to become in time of war. And they are innocent in each and every one of the senses in which it might be permissible to kill in the course of war those who are not. Given the way social, institutional, and political life is organized in all countries, they play no role in bringing about the war or in supporting it through their actions, commitments, and the like. Nor, typically, have they had any hand or choice in being wherever they happen to be once war begins, or as it continues, so that it can correctly be said that they assumed those risks of being killed that are known to be associated with the occurrence of war. They are, a large and indeterminate number of them, fully noncombatants and wholly innocent in all of the relevant senses. They are the clearest kind of case, but there are also many other individuals in all countries at war to whom these same descriptions and conclusions apply.

In conventional war, particularly when it becomes total war, persons easily, perhaps even naturally, tend to neglect or abuse these considerations. When they do, and kill in this way, they act wrongly, and this tendency is surely one thing that makes war itself wrong. But nuclear war is the limiting case because it unmistakably and irretrievably ignores all this, and necessarily so.

As has already been indicated, were the nuclear missiles and bombs of the Soviet Union, the United States, or both to be launched and detonated, there would not be, nor could there be, nor could there be thought to be, a differentiation either intended or expected among the individuals who would be killed by the explosions, the fires, and the radiation. I do not see, therefore, how their use in such circumstances could be anything but the deliberate wrongful killing—the murder—of vast numbers of wholly innocent persons on a scale and in a fashion that is barely comprehensible. I do not see how it could possibly be thought other than absolutely wrong to use them, given these known and clearly foreseeable results. To engage in nuclear war seems to me to be the morally worst and most despicable action conceivable.

To use nuclear weapons, in even the most plausible case, as a means of national self-defense against a wrongful, evil, murderous aggressor would still always be monstrously wrong and never in practice justifiable, even as a lesser of awesome and awful evils. For if our ideas about the permissible use of deadly force in national defense are to have any meaningful connection with our ideas about individual self-defense, the individuals against whom deadly force is used in a war of self-defense must have some causal, or closely analogous, connection with the danger at hand before they can rightly be deliberately killed by the weapons used in a war of self-defense. And if, as surely is the case, there are many such individuals in any country (no matter how aggressive) who have no such connections, then the use of weapons of indiscriminate mass destruction against them is not, and cannot be, founded on an intelligible or defensible recourse to ideas of legitimate, national self-defense.

One pervasive temptation, especially prominent in all talk and reflection about war, is created by the language used to identify and assess the relevant actors and their conduct. Because countries are in many senses the entities that make war, it is easy and common to think of the nation-state as a unitary entity that is neither morally nor in any other way reducible to the individual persons who are its members or who happen to reside within its borders. In conventional war, especially a total war, this temptation, though still dangerous and wrong, becomes most understandable because, as has been indicated, such a war does depend on the coordinated, continuing activities of so many of the persons living within the countries at war. But in respect to nuclear war, where even these features are wholly absent, to succumb to this temptation is especially inexcusable and pernicious. Yet, it is only by succumbing to it that one could thereby regard the children of the United States or the Soviet Union as appropriately subject to mass, indiscriminate slaughter in virtue of their unchosen relationships with their parents or their bare unchosen membership in these countries. No defensible moral and political theorizing and reasoning can sustain such a conclusion. And without it, I do not see how it could be thought right rather than wrong, better rather than worse, that, say, tens or hundreds of millions of the inhabitants of the Soviet Union—the children as well as the adults, the farmers as well as the commissars—be deliberately killed by a nuclear attack so that those of us in the United States and elsewhere should not be either dead or red, if that is in fact the only choice at hand.

Nor can it even be plausibly argued, I think, given the peculiar character of nuclear weapons and nuclear war, that going to nuclear war could be defensible, on balance, as the lesser of two great evils or wrongs. There may be some genuine plausibility to the view that, in cases of extraordinary emergency or peril on the national (or the individual) level, it is permissible to do what is wrong in order to prevent a still much greater wrong from occurring. If the differential magnitudes of innocent loss of life are great enough, for example, that may itself make the moral difference, making defensible the deliberate taking of innocent lives while still giving sense to the idea that something seriously wrong was thereby done. In this view, it is hard, and morally not very plausible, whatever one's worries about consequentialism, not to allow consequences at least to matter mightily in this way when circumstances come to this—especially when the calculations are concerned with magnitudes all having to do with innocent lives and their preservation. And even if such is not finally justifiable, it may come very close to being so because it is so easily and so understandably excusable. If the stakes are really high enough and the options really bleak enough, we can understand why otherwise innocent persons do act so as to save themselves rather than suffer death, even if they must kill other innocent persons to do so.

I am uncertain whether an argument of this kind can be rejected out of hand as resting on a fundamental and obvious moral or theoretical mistake. For despite the familiar and genuine difficulties with such a view, there is surely something plausible about this concern for saving innocent lives and even, perhaps, for preserving the character and being of existing, diverse forms of social and political life. And that plausibility increases as the differential magnitudes in terms of innocent lives or other comparable values become greater, the dangers more imminent, and the choices genuinely bleak and severely limited. But these considerations simply lack applicability in the case of nuclear war. To engage in nuclear war by being the first to devastate those living elsewhere would surely be to act too soon in light of the magnitude of the certain murderous slaughter of the innocent that the weapons would produce; to respond to a nuclear onslaught by launching nuclear weapons in return would be to act too late and in an equally murderous way in light of the danger that no longer can be averted. Whether consequences to the innocent can ever justify the murder of other innocent persons can here be left a theoretically open question because in nuclear war the relevant consequences are either too uncertain and anticipatory to license the certain, massive murder inescapably linked to a first nuclear attack or too fixed and already irremediably determined to license the certain, massive murder equally inescapably linked to a second responsive attack.

II

One very common view is that issues such as the ones just discussed are not the primary ones to be confronted in thinking about nuclear weapons because the fundamental issues have to do, not with nuclear war, but with how these weapons are most properly developed, positioned, armed, and aimed in furtherance of the practice of nuclear deterrence. As such, it is often assumed or maintained, the problems are very different in character from those of the use of nuclear weapons and the features of nuclear war, and far more tractable. I am less confident. I do not think that issues of nuclear deterrence are so easily separable from those of nuclear war, and the topic of nuclear deterrence seems to me to be a very difficult one, possessing elusive, puzzling, and deeply problematic aspects.

The nature of nuclear deterrence and the case for it can ostensibly be set out in simple, straightforward terms. Deterrence in this context consists in the adoption and maintenance of a policy by which one country threatens to use nuclear weapons against another in order to discourage that country from doing certain things that it might otherwise do— especially, but not exclusively, using its nuclear weapons first to devastate the other. Without such a policy, the argument goes, without such a threat and without the resulting belief that it will be subject to a nuclear attack, the Soviet Union might well decide that it is in its interests to use its nuclear weapons against the United States or to realize in some other fashion its wrongful, aggressive ambitions. However, by convincing the Soviet Union that a nuclear attack on it will occur should it do any of these things, the United States can lead the Soviet Union to decide that it is not in its interests so to act. The costs of such an attack on the Soviet Union by the United States simply have to be made perceptibly and decidedly greater than any benefits capable of being realized by the Soviet Union through action that would produce the threatened nuclear response. Thus the nuclear attacks or other aggressive acts by the Soviet Union that might otherwise have occurred are deterred and in that way prevented by the threatened response.

Furthermore, so the argument continues, because this is what is involved in adopting and maintaining a policy of nuclear deterrence, it is beside the point to concentrate on the question of whether it is wrong to use the kind of massive, indiscriminate deadly force that would be unleashed in actually employing the nuclear weapons that the United States has in place. Threats are, after all, one thing, and actions, the real things, quite another. Using nuclear weapons and thereby killing millions or hundreds of millions of citizens of the Soviet Union and other countries would be wrong even if threatening to use them is not. If the United States can prevent something as awful as nuclear devastation from occurring to its citizens (or to those of any other country) by threatening to use its nuclear weapons against the Soviet Union, it is surely a most fastidiously unattractive deontological morality that insists that the mere threat, by itself, is forbidden even when introduced to prevent such a morally wrong outcome. Policies of threats that work to prevent massive indiscriminate nuclear destruction are in such a context morally proper. Some such account constitutes much of the core of the case for nuclear deterrence and gives the practice of nuclear deterrence much of the plausibility that it seems, initially at least, to have.

Yet things are more complicated than this if for no other reason than that threats are, typically, more than just words. Real threats (as opposed to feigned or pretended ones) are words accompanied by an intention to act if certain things occur. Credible, as well as real, threats require the threatener to have the ability to act in accordance with that intention, for it is the belief that what is threatened will occur and the belief that that occurrence is to be avoided that succeed in deterring the undesired action. So, if and when threats are effective, they work by getting the threatened agent to behave in the way specified by the maker of the threat, and when threats work, the threatener never has to act in accordance with the conditional intent.

Is there something fundamentally wrong with deterrent threats to use nuclear weapons? I do not think that the question, when posed as a single one, makes full sense. Part of the problem has to do with establishing the appropriate context within which to understand and assess policies and practices of deterrent threats and then seeing what such a context requires. A second, related part of the problem has to do with whether we should concentrate on threats that are effective or on those that are ineffective. And a third, also related, part of the problem has to do with special issues concerning where the pursuit of successful nuclear deterrence seems apt, if not inexorably, to lead.

The appropriate and most instructive context within which to understand and assess policies and practices of deterrent threats is, I believe, that of the system of domestic criminal law. For this system is surely the most fully developed social institution in which deterrent threats can readily be understood to play a central role, and efforts to explain and justify it as a complex practice constituted of deterrent threats in the form of announced criminal sanctions are both many and familiar. An understanding of how these efforts can work to explain the criminal law as a system of deterrent threats sheds light on both the misleading and the plausible ways to think about nuclear deterrence; and an understanding of the requirements of any adequate deterrent theory of the criminal law can also help to make clear the requirements of any comparably adequate theory of the practice of nuclear deterrence.

The first thing that attention to the criminal law makes clear is that deterrent threats are not central to the typical situations having to do with self-defense and justifiable deadly force. For what constitutes the standard case of self-defense is the use of force against the aggressor; and it is the immediacy and seriousness of the danger that primarily justifies the application of force against the aggressor as the way to prevent the impending danger. Perhaps some, or many, would-be aggressors do not become actual ones because of their beliefs that sufficient force will be used directly against them. But that is surely an indirect (though welcome) benefit and not the central rationale for the legitimacy of using deadly force in self-defense. Thus it is the general system of criminal law, viewed as a system of deterrent threats, not particular situations concerning self-defense, that provides the appropriate context for understanding threats and their pivotal place in policies and practices of deterrence.

More important, if the criminal law is viewed as a system of deterrent threats, it is easy to see how it can plausibly be viewed as a system of threats which always works, so that attention to the very serious problem in the nuclear context of wholly unsuccessful threats never arises. The reason this problem of wholly unsuccessful threats is never a pressing or prominent one in respect to the criminal law is that it is reasonable here to suppose that the threats "behind" the prohibitions of the criminal law are always to some extent effective. To be sure, whenever a crime is committed, the threat did not work in that case, and this does create a real and a deep problem for theories that put deterrence at the center of things.[8] But the context for thinking about crime and punishment in terms of deterrence is still that of deterrence by threats which are effective. The fact that they did not work in the case of the actual offenders is not crucial because it is not actual offenders but potential ones on whom theories of general deterrence concentrate. Actual offenders are punished, so the theory goes, because that is the way to make the threat sufficiently credible to others—to potential offenders who would, in the absence of a sufficiently credible threat, become actual ones and who, when confronted with a sufficiently credible threat, do not. So attention can here solidly and continuously remain on deterrent threats that work. To think about deterrence in this way and in this context is to think about it as always systemically successful; to regard the criminal law as a system of threats in which the threats are justifiably acted on for reasons of general deterrence only makes sense because the criminal law can be understood to be a system which makes a continuing set of successful threats over time.

Tightly linking deterrent threats with success in this way is difficult to avoid because the linkage is so unproblematic in this setting. Yet to carry over assumptions about a comparable linkage to the case of nuclear deterrence is misleading and dangerous. Here, I believe, it is essential to pay full attention to an unfamiliar context, namely, one in which there is a wholly ineffective and unsuccessful deterrent threat. How is that kind of case to be thought about and properly understood? Suppose, that is, that a threat is made, that the requisite conditional intent is formed, announced, and communicated clearly, and that the threat does not work and the behavior sought to be deterred nonetheless occurs. What, then, is it reasonable or right for the threatener now to do? We do not, I believe, have much if any experience thinking about threats and deterrence

8. I have tried to identify and to discuss this problem and its ramifications for deterrent theories of punishment in "Punishment," in *Philosophy and Social Issues: Five Studies* (Notre Dame, Ind.: University of Notre Dame Press, 1980), pp. 112–51, pp. 130–35, and in "Capital Punishment as Punishment: Some Theoretical Issues and Objections," in *Midwest Studies in Philosophy* 7, ed. Peter A. French, Theodore E. Uehling, Jr., and Howard K. Wettstein (Minneapolis: University of Minnesota Press, 1982), pp. 473–92.

in this setting—either in the case of individuals or nations. Once the prospect, possibility, or fact of successful future deterrence is removed from the picture the terrain is different and unfamiliar.

Take, first, the case of an individual under direct and immediate threat of death at the hands of a wrongful aggressor who threatens the wrongful aggressor with death if the aggressor does not cease forthwith.[9] This is not, as has been indicated, the typical case of self-defense, but surely one can imagine it as a possibly real case. Suppose the deterrent threat is unsuccessful and the aggressor shoots first and kills the individual. There is then no question of acting in accordance with an unsuccessful deterrent threat. The threatener, the person under attack, cannot carry out what was threatened because he or she is now incapable of action.

The case can be changed slightly so as to preserve the question. Suppose that it is an individual other than the threatener whom the wrongful aggressor is about to kill. "Don't shoot that baby or I will kill you" is the deterrent threat now directed at the aggressor. Suppose the aggressor shoots the baby and kills it. What is the threatener now to do? Here we can still think about the appropriateness of shooting and killing the wrongful aggressor. It might be thought defensible to do so as a matter of self-defense, as a way actually to use deadly force to keep the aggressor from turning on and wrongfully killing the threatener. It might conceivably be thought right as a matter of indirect general deterrence: allowing persons to threaten deadly force and actually to use it when the threat fails is a way to deter other potential wrongful aggressors from becoming actual aggressors in comparable situations. It might even be thought right as a matter of summary, nonjudicial punishment—having wrongfully killed, that is what the aggressor now deserves. But take considerations such as these out of the picture, and what remains is a situation that is novel in any domestic context and never present within a system of criminal law. And once these considerations are removed, it is hard, if not impossible, to develop plausible and convincing reasons to explain how completing the threatened action could have been either sensible or right.

The issue is a pressing one in the nuclear context. For if what I argued earlier is correct, the use of nuclear weapons as the responsive feature of the announced threat is not justifiable either as a matter of forward-looking preventive or deterrent self-defense or as the summary punishment of only those who were culpable wrongdoers. Nor can it be plausible to rest the intelligibility or justifiability of this kind of indiscriminate deadly response on a redescription of the causal chain so as to make the real or primary cause of the response the wrongful action whose nonoccurrence was sought; nor can it be rested on a claim that, having sincerely threatened to so respond, one has undertaken a commitment

9. Notice that here "threat" does not refer to the kind of deterrent threat now being considered.

to do so and one is for that reason licensed, if not obligated, to act accordingly. One paradox of nuclear deterrence is that the carrying out of the threatened response, when the threat has been unsuccessful as a deterrent, lacks sense as well as justification, whatever may be said and thought about the sense and justifiability of making the threat in the first place. This is, I think, a genuinely stubborn and serious problem that is not fully addressed by focusing on the question of whether, and for what reasons, it might be wrong to formulate and maintain the requisite conditional intent so to act.[10] This context of wholly unsuccessful deterrence is one that must be attended to in respect to the circumstances of nuclear deterrence that now obtain. It is one crucial situation, if not the only one, that theories of nuclear deterrence must speak to and concerning which they must provide a defensible, coherent account. I do not think that they have or that they can.

There is, of course, the temptation here, too, to retreat immediately to the situation of successful deterrence in light of the fact that, if the missiles now in place are all launched, the result will be mutual assured destruction. The temptation is to shift to the setting of successful deterrence and to focus on how to make the threats sufficiently credible so that they never will have to be carried out. Here one can, I think, manage to remain within that setting while talking about risks of decisions and actions under conditions of uncertainty. For it is easy, still, to focus on

10. A number of issues concerning conditional intentions in the nuclear context are explored in Gregory Kavka, "Some Paradoxes of Deterrence," *Journal of Philosophy* 75 (1978): 285–302. For the reasons indicated here and in what follows I do not think there is a univocal, stable context within which to address the question of the morality of a conditional intention to use nuclear weapons. It is easy to assume, typically implicitly, that the context is one of successful deterrence by reasoning that a genuinely credible threat of nuclear response will surely be sufficient by itself to assure success. Unlike the criminal law, where the threats must be acted on to be credible, the threats of nuclear response, necessarily tied to the requisite conditional intention, can be counted on to do the job. Given this assumption, the force to the wrongness in forming and maintaining a conditional intention to use nuclear weapons and thereby becoming a person or a country prepared and willing to act in a way that is morally wrong and indefensible because murderous is deflected or vitiated by the counterbalancing certitude that the wrongness in question is restricted solely to matters concerning the having of the conditional intention per se. There is, doubtless, much to be said about the wrongness of such a conditional intention, considered purely as an intention, but I do not address this issue in this paper in part because I am very unclear about how to think about conditional intentions correctly once they are decisively severed from the action to which they are firmly conditionally attached and in part because of the illusion, as well as the change in the structure of the intention, that is wrought in assuming that the intention can be securely and coherently detached from the action through the implicit definition of the context as one of successful deterrence. Surely one real and pressing moral problem with forming and maintaining a genuine conditional intention to use nuclear weapons is with the necessary connection between that conditional intention and the commitment to action, which must result in attempted if not completed action should the threat fail to deter. Here, too, the context of unsuccessful nuclear deterrence must, I think, be attended to in an assessment of the rightness or wrongness of a conditional intention to use nuclear weapons, and in this context there is much more in the picture than the intention per se.

risks that might eventuate in harms but do not or on decisions and actions which, while made under conditions of uncertainty, prove to have been the right ones in the end. And within that context one can address, as well, questions of whether the United States and the Soviet Union have too many nuclear missiles and warheads—many more than are needed to practice successful deterrence.

Yet this recourse to the domain of successful nuclear deterrence depends for its intelligibility both on the conditional intent actually to employ the threatened nuclear weapons and on the assumption that they will not actually be employed. Given the special features of the nuclear situation, were these weapons actually to be employed, the situation could only be one of unsuccessful nuclear deterrence. While the assumption that the weapons will not actually be employed, because the threat will be successful, may make it comparatively easy to justify the formation of that conditional intent and the strategies attendant on it, the idea of unsuccessful nuclear deterrence requires confronting quite different matters and in a very different way. For in the nuclear context, success is an all-or-nothing matter. There is no third way, as there is in thinking about the system of criminal law and deterrence, of viewing it as systemically successful even while it fails in some particular cases. If it is not successful, it is wholly and irremediably unsuccessful, and there is nothing any longer to be achieved in terms of deterrence, other good consequences, or other morally relevant considerations that could be appealed to in this context to make action in accordance with an unsuccessful nuclear deterrent threat either intelligible or right.

One can, of course, insist that, even after the nuclear threat has failed to deter, there are other possible actions yet to be deterred by producing the threatened responses and thereby bringing home to the other side the awesome consequences to it of continuing to act in certain ways. But that is both to change the nature of the case under consideration and to see revealed something of the persistent allure of assumptions of success when it is nuclear deterrence that is under consideration. It is to refuse to consider directly the sense or rightness of action in accordance with the threat in this genuine, all-too-possible case of wholly unsuccessful deterrence.

One can also, I think, try two other responses, but neither is very adequate. On the one hand, one can claim that action in accordance with the threat makes sense and is justifiable as the way to prevent the country subject to the unsuccessful threat from surviving and thereby enjoying the benefits of the wrongful action sought unsuccessfully to be deterred. This seems to me to be a possibly intelligible explanation but not a morally adequate one. It appeals either to the devastation of the country subject to the threat as the means by which to render it incapable of further action or to the rightness of its devastation as deserved in light of the wrongfulness of what it has already done. Both approaches, however, fail morally because of the wrongness of using nuclear weapons indiscriminately either to kill those who happen to be within some national border in order to prevent that country, conceived now as a unitary entity, from prevailing or to punish those culpable individuals within that country for their wrongdoing by also killing those innocent persons who are wholly lacking in culpability for any wrongdoing.

On the other hand, one can claim that a deterrent threat can only be successful if there is the conditional intention to act accordingly and that this requires, therefore, action in accordance with that intention should the threat not succeed. In this view, an action of this kind, occasioned as it is by the threat's failure to be successful, is simply part of what is involved in endeavoring to threaten successfully. Because I do not see how such action could be justifiable in the nuclear context, I do not see how this claim advances matters at all. If using nuclear weapons, should deterrence fail, is required in order to promote successful deterrence, the two contexts of successful and unsuccessful deterrence are introduced within the same overall account, but only incoherently so. If deterrence is successful, the "use" that is required never occurs. If deterrence is unsuccessful, the use that does occur is no longer required (or even efficacious) and is instead murderous and profoundly wrong.

If I am right in thinking that our ideas about nuclear deterrence are all fixed within a context in which successful and effective threats are in one way or the other unreflectively presupposed, then there is a moral danger in neglecting this other, far less familiar context of wholly unsuccessful, ineffective threats; and if I am right about the wrongness of using nuclear weapons, it is wrong to act as the policies and practices of nuclear deterrence require because they are conceived, elaborated, and defended within the very different context of deterrent threats which are always to some extent successful. It is essential that thinking about nuclear deterrence be wrenched out of that central, familiar context in which success is somehow deeply embedded—presupposed as well as implied. Theories of nuclear deterrence, like theories of criminal deterrence, depend for their plausibility on this context of success, but while the latter do so appropriately, the former do not. Lacking such a stable context, theories of nuclear deterrence are incoherent and incapable of unitary assessment; once removed from the context of success they are manifestly and gravely wrong in what they are committed to bring about and will endeavor to bring about should deterrence fail.

Nor are the problems of theories of nuclear deterrence limited to those unusual, special ones of unsuccessful deterrence which are not central in the same way to theories of criminal deterrence. There are at least two others, both of which occur within the more general and usual context of successful deterrence. The first concerns some of the intellectual accoutrements necessary to any fully developed theory of nuclear deterrence—the same kinds of accoutrements required by any deterrent theory of the criminal law. There must, for one thing, be the analogue to the theory of human nature central to deterrent theories of the criminal law. A credible account of the nature of countries and their behavior on the international scale must be explicated and defended as part of ay theory of nuclear deterrence. That account may in part be one of the nature of countries generally and of their behaviors and in part be one concerning the nature of particular countries at particular times and how correctly to understand, explain, and predict their behaviors. In both cases, however, it is important that the view be made explicit, that the empirical evidence on which its distinctive claims are rested be subjected to careful critical examination, and that in the light of all of this the plausibility of the resulting claims and conclusions be assessed. To the degree to which this part of any theory of nuclear deterrence involves problematic and uncertain components, the overall reasoning assuming the success of nuclear deterrence is also less secure than is often supposed. Here one matter that seems to me crucial and insufficiently attended to is the degree to which the actual and expected behavior of countries in the nuclear age is produced by, rather than the reason for, the adoption of existing policies of nuclear deterrence and the nuclear weapons and delivery systems they seem to require. Also requiring examination and defense are the claims about nuclear blackmail as well as about the allegedly comparative evils of nuclear war and conquest or domination of the more familiar sort, both of which are often invoked and embraced by the accounts of national ambition and action ordinarily produced in this connection.

The second and final point has to do with the analogue to another part of deterrent theories of the criminal law. One fundamental part of those theories has to do directly with the evidence and arguments for thinking that the practice of making and acting on threats to impose criminal sanctions has worked and can be expected to continue to do so in the future. What is typically assumed, and what does seem relatively unproblematic in these theories of the criminal law, is that the future will be like the past in all sorts of essential ways. Not only is it assumed that human nature will remain unchanged in the relevant respects, but it is also supposed that the sanctions threatened and the policies and mechanisms for carrying out the threats remain essentially unchanged. There is an important equivalence within these theories between the conditions that hold when one looks to the past in order to extract evidence about the success of deterrence and the conditions that are assumed to continue to hold when one looks forward so as to justify a continuation of the threats on the expectation that the workings and the consequences will in the future be the same. These theories all benignly presuppose a kind of equilibrium between the force exerted by threats of various sanctions and the behaviors they will continue to induce and constrain—an equilibrium that is unaffected by whether one looks backward to what has been the case or forward to what will be the case.

The assumption of this kind of equilibrium and the resulting assumption about the equivalence between past and future conditions both seem to me to have been insufficiently attended to in theories of nuclear deterrence which rely on them to warrant the belief in the continuing success of nuclear deterrence. Reasoning about how to practice nuclear deterrence is strongly motivated by the search for ways to remain always and ever more securely within the realm of successful nuclear deterrence. The endeavor to assure this has led both the United States and the Soviet Union to adopt and implement policies aimed at eliminating the possibility of indecision or confusion about what the other will do if missiles are launched against it; and they have also implemented policies aimed at eliminating the possibilities that their missiles will be destroyed before they can be responsively launched by making it ever more certain that they can launch their missiles before the other's land and destroy them. I am not certain whether all thinking about genuinely successful nuclear deterrence has to go down this path, but it seems very unclear how the very natural focus on the assurance of successful deterrence can avoid it, and it certainly does not seem to have been avoided so far. And this leads, I believe, to an intellectual as well as a moral difficulty—perhaps a final, self-defeating trap of the worst sort. For to proceed in this way necessarily calls into question the correctness of the assumption of the similarity between past and future conditions concerning successful nuclear deterrence—an assumption which itself depends on the presupposition of a continuing equilibrium between the deterrent threats and the behaviors believed to be induced and constrained by them.

The foundational presupposition of equilibrium supposes that the relationship between nuclear deterrent threats and the nonrecourse to the use of nuclear weapons to date can be expected to continue because there will continue to be this kind of relationship between the threats and the nonuse of the weapons. Yet we know that in many contexts having nothing to do with threats such an inferential assumption can be foolish and wrong. We know, for example, that, were we continuously to increase the volume of a gas within a container such as a balloon, it would be extremely foolish to suppose that we could count on the balloon remaining intact just because it had not burst so far. The apparent equilibrium that had obtained to date would be only speciously assumed to be a genuine equilibrium which could be counted on to obtain in the future.

It seems to me that, given the way the pursuit of successful nuclear deterrence works, the correct assumption is that of nonequilibrium rather than that of equilibrium in certain key respects. And if this is so, the assumptions and the inferences made about nuclear deterrence continuing to be successful because it has been so far are both highly suspect and dangerous. The risks of accident or mistake, even given steady-state assumptions, are hard enough to calculate and awesome enough in so far as they can be calculated. But if the path which seems to lead to the increased assurance of successful deterrence is anything like the one I described, then the risks of accident or mistake, as well as of intentional "rational" calculation, resulting in action are continuously increasing as well. As the mechanisms of response to a perceived nuclear attack become ever more inflexible and certain in respect to response, and as the purposive pursuit of successful deterrence becomes ever more focused on the achievement of the ability to respond before one's weapons are destroyed, the forces necessarily operating on and within the policies, persons, and systems now in existence seem anything but constant, or steady, over time. The presuppositions of deterrent theories of the criminal law which give rise to and support defensible assumptions about the constancy of the conditions and forces necessarily operating on and within the policies, persons, and systems now in place within civil society do not have to be made explicit because, as has been indicated, they are not problematic in these ways.

When theories of successful nuclear deterrence borrow these pre-suppositions, even while the purposive pursuit of "rational" successful deterrence itself undermines them, it is essential, however, that they be made explicit so that they can be seen to be here unwarranted and hence inappropriately borrowed. This is, perhaps, another kind of paradox, peculiar to the domain of nuclear deterrence; whether paradoxical or not, these features are deeply embedded in all reasoning about nuclear deterrence and reliance on its continuing success.

Finally, because successful deterrence is not an all-or-nothing matter within the system of criminal law, mistakes and accidents can be readily anticipated within the theory of criminal deterrence, and they can be accommodated, tolerated, and explained as regrettable but inevitable features of human fallibility and error. The system can still be viewed as succeeding despite the failures of the threatened sanctions to deter some and despite the inevitable, mistaken imposition of the sanctions on others. But the nuclear context is radically different in this respect too. Given the structure and design of policies of nuclear deterrence, no mistakes or accidents are tolerable because one such failure—no matter what the cause—eradicates the system and all those individuals ostensibly served by it. If a mistake or accident occurs, all can, all too unfortunately, be certain of its absolute and irremediable catastrophic nature. If deterrence fails, there can be no opportunity to learn from the failure, to make amends for it, or to reconsider and revise the policies and practices accordingly. There will not and cannot be any second chance whatsoever. This is certain. Yet if, as seems to me the most plausible way to look at things, all of us have been extremely lucky that so far there has been no accident, mistake, or intentional, "rational" calculation dictating nuclear attack, and if the existing policies of nuclear deterrence make such an occurrence increasingly more, rather than less, likely over time, then their continuation is intellectual and moral madness of the absolutely most terrifying sort. I, at least, cannot comprehend how any theory defending the present practices of nuclear deterrence can make genuinely plausible and defensible the maintenance or pursuit of a state of affairs possessing these kinds of inherently disequilibrious and morally disastrous components and consequences.

None of the issues examined in this paper has, I realize, been dealt with in a wholly adequate way. They are, I readily concede, all difficult as well as awesome. But if even the general lines and directions of argument I have advanced are right, the truly fundamental issues, dangers, and mistakes have, I hope, been made somewhat clearer and in that small fashion rendered a tiny bit less ominous. The situation is perilous and the time, I fear, limited.

Nuclear Intentions*

Gerald Dworkin

A terrorist engages in violence in violation of law against people who do not understand themselves to be at war. The victims of terrorist attacks are unarmed, undefended, and unwary. The crucial point is that they conceive of themselves as civilians. They do not understand that they are regarded by the terrorist as belligerents in an ongoing war. Terrorist war is part of a total war, which sees the whole of society as the enemy and all the members of society as appropriate objects for violence.[1]

This is an essay on the relationship between the morality of the use of nuclear weapons and the morality of the threat to use such weapons under certain conditions, that is, the doctrine of nuclear deterrence. There are four possible positions that can be taken about the permissibility of use or the threat to use. One can claim that both the actual use and the threat to use are morally permissible. This is the view of Gauthier.[2] One can claim that although actual use is wrong the threat to use can be morally legitimate under certain conditions. This is the view of Kavka.[3] One can believe that neither the actual use of nor the threat to use nuclear weapons is morally permissible. This is the view I shall be defending in this essay. Finally, there is the view, held by nobody to my knowledge, that, although the actual use of nuclear weapons is morally legitimate, the threat to use is illegitimate.

In addition to the various substantive differences just mentioned there are differences in the logical relationships different philosophers use in their arguments. There are those, such as Kenny, who argue that because the actual use of nuclear weapons is impermissible so is the

* I wish to express my appreciation for comments on earlier drafts by Charles Chastain, John Deigh, Art Flemming, Robert Goodin, Russell Hardin, Chris Korsgaard, Richard Kraut, and Jeff McMahan. Versions of this paper were read at the Arms Control Seminar at the University of Chicago, April 8, 1984, the Aspen Conference on the Ethics of Nuclear Deterrence and Disarmament, September 2, 1984, Aspen, Colorado, and the University of Colorado.

1. Jeanne J. Kirkpatrick, *Harper's* (October 1984), p. 44.
2. David Gauthier, "Deterrence, Maximization, and Rationality," in this volume.
3. Gregory S. Kavka, "Some Paradoxes of Deterrence," in *Moral Issues,* ed. Jan Narveson (Oxford: Oxford University Press, 1983), pp. 72–87, p. 76.

threat to use.[4] There are those, such as Kavka and Lewis, who believe that the questions of use and threat are logically independent of one another.[5] And finally there are those such as Gauthier and I who focus on the permissibility of threatening and argue that if the threat is legitimate (rational for Gauthier) then one does not need a separate justification for carrying out the threat.

For some parts of my argument I shall be assuming that the actual use of nuclear weapons is morally and rationally forbidden. While this is, as I have already indicated, not a position which enjoys unanimous support, it is one which can be plausibly supported by a number of different considerations and by quite different normative positions.

Under the traditional just-war criteria the use of weapons which cannot be used in a manner so as to discriminate between combatants and noncombatants is forbidden. One can quibble about the exact definition of "noncombatant," but in any reasonable view the millions of children under the age of fifteen, the millions of women engaged in running households, the millions of persons in hospitals and nursing homes, are not combatants. Even if one has a very broad notion of collective responsibility so that any citizen of an aggressor nation is somehow implicated in the aggressive action of its leaders, the citizens of other countries who would be damaged by radioactive fallout or, if recent predictions are correct, by the consequences of nuclear winter would have to be considered noncombatants on even the broadest view of the distinction.

Those who disagree with my assumption may regard my argument as hypothetical in form. If the actual use of nuclear weapons is neither rational nor morally permissible, what follows about the morality of the possession, threat, or conditional intent to use such weapons?

I

Under a policy of nuclear deterrence we do many things now, for example, appropriate money for missiles, manufacture them, install them, maintain them, train personnel to fire them, make announcements about them, and negotiate about their dismantling. In addition to all these acts and policies those in positions of responsibility for making policy and implementing it form intentions for the future. We do all the above in the light of a decision to act in certain ways, under certain conditions. We can, of course, change our minds about what we are prepared to do. We can give up our intentions for the future. Or we can keep them, and the world may go in such a way that they are never carried out, either because the conditions for their implementation do not arise or because we cannot do what we set out to do. But to adopt or form an intention for the

4. Anthony Kenny, "Better Dead than Red," in *Objections to Nuclear Defense*, ed. Nigel Blake and Kay Pole (London: Routledge & Kegan Paul, 1984), pp. 12–27.

5. Kavka; D. Lewis, "Devil's Bargains and the Real World," in *The Security Gamble: Deterrence Dilemmas in the Nuclear Age*, ed. D. MacLean (Totowa, N.J.: Rowman & Allanheld, 1984).

future is to commit oneself in certain ways—to action, to belief, to values and purposes.

Future intentions are objects of moral evaluation and assessment. Insofar as the formation or adoption of an intention is an act of the agent, although indeed a mental act, it is subject to evaluation as an act. One's decisions, plans, resolutions, have effects both on oneself and on others and can be assessed morally in terms of those effects. In addition, just as certain overt acts are wrong because of the kind of act they are, so can the formation of an intention be wrong because of the kind of intention it is.

Future intentions can also be evaluated as evidence for, or as constitutive of, the character of the agent. What an agent decides to do, what she is prepared to do, what she is willing to do, tell us what kind of person she is. And insofar as future intentions result in future acts (with the appropriate causal connection) we assign responsibility in terms of those intentions.

II

The question, in its broadest form, may be put this way. What is wrong with (conditionally) intending evil? What is wrong with intending to do that which it is morally forbidden to do? It seems that the answer to this question cannot be independent of one's moral theory. For the theory specifies the features in terms of which something can be right or wrong. For example, in a divine-command ethical theory at least part of what is wrong in intending to do what is divinely forbidden is that one is disobedient to the will of God. For consequentialist moral theories what makes it wrong to intend to do what is forbidden is that such an intention makes it more likely that one will act in a manner which will be productive of the bad consequences that are forbidden. For the Kantian, to intend that which is forbidden is to be willing to act in a manner which is ruled out by the Categorical Imperative. The intent is wrong quite independent of its being linked to future effects. For most deontological systems there will be a special importance attached to what we do intentionally as opposed to what happens as a result of what we do. The choice of evil becomes the focus of moral appraisal.

I do not intend to settle matters of fundamental moral theory here. I shall not argue what the relative importance of consequentialist versus deontological considerations ought to be. Instead I want to look at various kinds of deterrent strategies and explore how consequentialist or deontological theories would assess the role and significance of a conditional intention (or its absence) to use nuclear weapons on the assumption that their use is wrong.

III

I am going to consider six possible options. They have been selected because of their usefulness for exploring the moral issues and not because they are the ones which strategists regard as the most realistic or practical options available to us at this point in time. Indeed, two of them are not technologically feasible currently.

1. *Deterrence.*—In this option the United States possesses a second strike capability and forms the conditional intention to use this capability to retaliate for any nuclear attack on the United States. It either announces this policy or makes the policy manifest in some other way. In either case it threatens an aggressor with retaliation under certain conditions.

2. *Bluff.*—This option is the same as deterrence except that we make a secret decision not to use the weapons under conceivable circumstances. We do not form the conditional intention to retaliate.

3. *Retaliation machine.*—Herman Kahn originated the idea of a Doomsday machine which was programmed so that if nuclear weapons were exploded over the United States a device would be automatically triggered that would destroy the earth. For our purposes suppose, instead of destroying all human life, it launches our missiles at the attacker's homeland.

4. *Mere possession.*—The United States would maintain exactly the same nuclear arsenal and delivery system as in deterrence but would form no intention one way or the other as to future use. For this option to be perceived as different from 1 or 2 it would have to be made clear, in some fashion, that we are neither bluffing nor threatening. We merely possess a capacity without any plans or decisions about future use. By this I mean not that we make it unclear whether we have plans but that we make it clear that we have no definite plans.

5. *Autoretaliator.*—This terminology is borrowed from Kavka, as is the following description of the device: "Imagine that the U.S. invents a radio device that fifty per cent of the time is able to deflect Soviet ballistic missiles in flight and send them to present targets. For purposes of deterrence, the U.S. programs Soviet cities instead of the oceans as targets, and announces this openly."[6] The point of the 50 percent limitation is that this is not a shield by which we can protect ourselves from harm but a way of inflicting harm on an aggressor.

6. *Bounce back.*—This is a form of shield which bounces back incoming missiles to wherever they are fired from. We do not have the capacity to target the deflected missiles. They simply return to wherever they are fired from. If they are fired from centers of population, they return to those centers. If they are fired from remote military bases, they return to those bases.[7] Let us suppose that we know that, in fact, many of the enemy missiles are located

6. Gregory S. Kavka, "Nuclear Deterrence: Some Moral Perplexities," in MacLean, ed.

7. Douglas Lackey called my attention to the existence of a similar device (in his "Nuclear Deterrence and the Deflection of Risks" [1984, typescript]). Richard Ullman suggested to me a variation of this device which would deflect missiles targeted at civilian centers back to civilian centers and missiles targeted at military sites back to military sites.

around centers of population. For purposes of keeping things constant I assume that as in case 5 there is a 50 percent limitation on effectiveness.

These examples are selected because the existence and nature of various intentions varies among them. At the same time other variables such as risk to innocents, foreseen consequences, and the announcement of threats vary as well. By examining the moral evaluation of the different cases by differing theories we may hope to gain a better understanding of the role of intention.

IV

In case 1—the standard case of deterrence—we have the intention to retaliate and hence, by our assumption, the intention to do what is morally impermissible. The argument for the permissibility of the threat is a consequentialist one. The presence of the intention is assumed to be necessary for the credibility of the threat to retaliate, which is assumed to lower the probability of enemy attack. If that initial probability is high enough, if the losses due to such an attack are great enough, if the lowering of the probability is large enough, then it is plausible to suppose that the expected utility of forming the intention to retaliate is greater than the expected utility of some other policy which does not involve forming such a conditional intention. Of course such a utility calculation has to take into account all the likely consequences of such a policy, including the dangers of accidental war, the psychological effects of threatening behavior on one's adversaries, the effect of making such threats on those who make them and are prepared to carry them out, et cetera. And as the recent discussion by Hardin and Lackey has shown, there may be great disagreement about the results of such calculations.[8] (Much such discussion has the appearance of somebody trying to figure out an answer to a mathematical question, but closer scrutiny almost always shows values being more or less arbitrarily assigned to both probabilities and utilities. As one State Department official put it in conversation about "real" defense calculations, "In all the years of talk about calculated risk I have never seen a calculation.") But the question I am interested in is what significance the presence or absence of conditional intentions plays in such a consequentialist assessment.

The answer must be, for such a theory, that the forming of the conditional intention to do *x* has causal consequences. Let us distinguish the consequences into the following classes. First, the probability of the agent doing *x* alters. For rational and noncompulsive agents what they wind up doing is some function of what they plan or intend to do. Other things being equal, it is more likely an agent will do what he intends to

8. Douglas Lackey, "Missiles and Morals: A Utilitarian Look at Nuclear Deterrence," *Philosophy & Public Affairs* 11 (1982): 189–231; Russell Hardin, "Unilateral versus Mutual Disarmament," *Philosophy & Public Affairs* 12 (1983): 236–54.

do than what he has no intention of doing. Second, the adoption of the conditional intention has what Kavka calls autonomous effects. It may, for example, make the subject more callous or more courageous. It may make others more fearful or more sanguine. Given that on consequentialist grounds the doing of x is ruled out, it would normally follow that an act which increases the probability of doing x is also ruled out. It is only because the act which increases the probability of doing x also increases the probability of other (good) consequences that the normal inference does not hold—or so Kavka argues. Since a consequentialist theory is concerned with the goodness or badness of states of affairs, the relevance of the forming of an intention is exhausted by its causal contribution to the production of one or another state of affairs. It makes no sense to assess the intention as being intrinsically wrong, although the willingness to adopt certain intentions may be good evidence about the moral character of an agent. In short, the relevance of intentions to do morally forbidden acts is exhausted by the increased risk of harmful consequences.

The difference between case 1 (deterrence) and case 2 (bluff) is exhausted, from the standpoint of evaluating intentions, by facts such as that under a bluffing policy there is no risk of doing the forbidden act, that there is a risk that the bluff may be exposed, that one will have to lie, and so forth.

Case 3 (retaliation machine) differs from 1 only in the fact that it is impossible to alter one's intentions. This, of course, affects the issue of risk in a complicated fashion. It decreases the risk of doing x since the threat to retaliate is made more credible, and this decreases the risk of attack. On the other hand it increases the risk of doing x since the option of changing one's mind, if attacked, is no longer present.

Lackey uses this case in an argument designed to show that Kavka is mistaken in supposing that it can ever be morally permissible to form the conditional intention to do x if x is itself morally impermissible: "To see that this is so, consider whether it would be permissible for the agent to construct a device such that, if C occurs, he cannot fail to do x. If it is not permissible to do x if C, it is not permissible to construct a device which will force him to do x if C if there is a real chance that C will occur."[9]

This obviously begs the question, for Kavka, if he is consistent, must believe that it is permissible, other things being equal, to construct such a machine. After all, he says that his agent is "willing, in order to prevent the offense, to accept a certain *risk* that in the end, he will apply the sanction."[10] This must be the correct view for a consequentialist like Kavka since the machine merely fixes some level of risk that is antecedently decided to be acceptable.

9. Douglas Lackey, "The Intentions of Deterrence," in *Nuclear Weapons and the Future of Humanity: The Fundamental Questions,* ed. Steven Lee and Avner Cohen (Totowa, N.J.: Rowman & Allanheld, 1984).

10. Kavka, "Some Paradoxes of Deterrence," p. 76.

Case 4 (mere possession) presents a level of risk, relative to intention, which is intermediate between cases 1 and 2. It is lower than 1 insofar as it is left open that we will not retaliate. It is higher than 2 insofar as it is left open that we will. Ignoring autonomous effects, we create less risk that we will do the forbidden act than we do by forming the intention. Therefore it is a superior policy relative to deterrence.

Case 5 presents an interesting twist for the consequentialist since the causal effects on the enemy of adopting this policy are (or could be, depending on various technological assumptions) identical to those in case 1. In both cases we arrange matters so that missiles fall on the enemy, and in particular on noncombatants. The difference is in whose missiles do the falling. In the case of deterrence we launch our missiles at the enemy. In case 5 we deflect their missiles to our targets. In either case it is the launching of their missiles which triggers the retaliation. The example has the additional feature that our losses are (probabilistically) cut in half so that total damage is likely to be less than under a policy of deterrence, but this is not the feature I want to focus on.

Traditional theories of self-defense would distinguish between these policies. If someone throws a hand grenade into my house, I am entitled to throw it back at him, but am I entitled to throw it into his neighbor's house?

Case 6 is also an interesting one from a consequentialist standpoint. For in such a case we may have exactly the same degree of risk imposition as in case 1 or 5 but without forming the conditional intention to impose such risk. We do not announce that we will launch missiles or drop bombs on the aggressor or even redirect his missiles to his cities. We simply arrange matters such that the aggressor's own weapons fall on his own cities if he launches them from those cities. We cannot deny that we increase the risk of death and destruction to noncombatants, but we can deny that we have any intention of retaliating. We need not even possess offensive weapons. On consequentialist grounds the presence or absence of such an intention is irrelevant. Case 6 is not morally more favorable than case 1 from the standpoint of forming an intention. It may, of course, be more favorable on other grounds such as being cheaper, reducing the risk of accidental war, being psychologically less threatening, et cetera.

Case 6 provides us with a test case for assessing the difference between consequentialist and nonconsequentialist views about the moral relevance of intention since it separates out the elements of risk and intention which normally go together.

V

I now want to consider these various cases from a nonconsequentialist standpoint, that is, one which denies that the right action is always to be defined in terms of the production of the best consequences. An action may be wrong because of the kind of action it is, or because it cannot be justified to those whom it adversely affects, or because it is not in accordance with a set of principles which would be consented to by all those affected by the action, or because it violates certain rights that individuals have. I leave unspecified the exact nature of the theory. For such views what is the significance of intending to do what it is wrong to do?

Roughly speaking, the significance is in terms of how the interests and welfare of other moral agents enter into our practical reasoning about what to do. Our values and our character are shown not by what comes about as a causal result of our actions but by the forms of reasoning we use in deciding how to act. Of course consequences count insofar as they must enter into our deliberations, but it is as intended or foreseen or negligently omitted from our deliberations that they enter. Let us look at cases 1 and 5 on the one hand and case 6 on the other from this standpoint.

It must be conceded that the installation of the bounce-back machine creates an increased risk of the same death and destruction to enemy noncombatants that a policy of deterrence does. If it is morally impermissible to impose such a risk intentionally, how can it be morally permissible to impose such a risk as a foreseen consequence of one's otherwise permissible acts? This, of course, is the issue usually discussed under the heading of double effect. I do not intend either to explicate or to defend that doctrine here. But I do intend to try and defend a view of the significance of intention which at least clears the way for defending the doctrine. For the initial conceptual obstacle seems to be the difficulty of seeing how the distinction between what one aims at as opposed to what one foresees can make any moral difference. There is an important difference between cases 1 and 5 and case 6 having to do with the form of practical reasoning we engage in when adopting one or another of the strategic policies. The difference between an agent who adopts a strategy of deterrence or autoretaliation on the one hand and one who adopts a strategy of a bounce back on the other is reflected in the means-ends relationships he is willing to countenance in order to attain his ends. In all cases I take the end to be that of preventing an unjust act of aggression, and I take that to be justified. In case 1 the agent imposes a risk of death and destruction on those who (by assumption) are not legitimate targets of such risk, and it is precisely by imposing such a risk that he believes his end will (causally) be obtained.

It, of course, does not follow that he desires to follow that causal path or that he would not prefer to obtain his ends in an alternative fashion. If, say, bluffing would work (almost) as well, he might prefer to bluff. But having made a determination that other causal paths would not work, he adopts this one. He uses threat and the imposition of risk to obtain his ends. In doing so he does more than show himself prepared or willing to risk the morally forbidden. He adopts a plan which makes the imposition and maintenance of such risk necessary (causally) to his being successful.

That this is so can be seen by considering the ways in which the agent must think and act in order to preserve the causal link between the unjust risk imposition and the end of successful deterrence. In both cases 1 and 5, if the potential aggressor were, say, to develop a successful antiballistic missile (ABM) defense, then we must seek to develop weapons which will defeat that defense. If the potential aggressor seeks to disperse the civilian population, then we must find ways of launching our own missiles or deflecting his so as to destroy those populations. The point is that, given our plan, the risks to the noncombatants must be maintained or increased. Their potential death and destruction is required for our plan to be successful. Otherwise our threats are empty.

And it is interesting to see that this is true of both cases 1 and 5. For both are based on the threat to inflict harm on noncombatants in order to deter. Whether there are other differences because of the fact that in one case it is our missiles that inflict the harm and in the other it is theirs I leave open. From the standpoint of intention the cases are parallel. In both we adopt a plan, and arrange causal relations, that requires the imposition of risk on those who (by hypothesis) are not the legitimate bearers of such a risk.

Whereas, in case 6, although we arrange matters in such a fashion that we may be able to foresee the same degree of injury, we do not require the imposition of such a risk in order for our plans to be successful.

If the enemy relocates his missiles far from population centers, we need not rearrange our strategy. Our end is not to be achieved through the imposition of risk on noncombatants, although we certainly foresee its occurrence. Of course if the enemy develops an ABM system, then, since our bounce back is only 50 percent effective, the absence of a deterrent system will leave us at a severe strategic disadvantage. But this is a separate point. All I am trying to show is that case 6 may be evaluated differently morally than case 5 and that the difference reflects what our intentions are.

I have claimed that the bounce-back case should be evaluated more favorably than the autoretaliator case and that it is permissible to employ it. There are, nevertheless, limits on what one can do even by way of simply deflecting threats. Here are two other cases for further reflection. First, suppose the bounce-back system deflected missiles onto the citizens of Switzerland. I am committed by my position to thinking this permissible since the noncombatants of the aggressor nation are no more responsible for the attack of their leaders than are the citizens of Switzerland. Second, suppose the incoming missile is targeted for a small city (80,000 population) but fired from a large one (8,000,000 population). Is it still permissible to deflect?

VI

Let us look at the differences between cases 1 and 2, deterrence and bluff. Jeff McMahan in his essay "Deterrence and Deontology" argues that the crucial moral element is the likelihood of using nuclear weapons, not the presence of a conditional intention.[11] In his discussion of the bluffing case he argues that the deontologist is committed to being opposed to bluffing since those in the military chain of command would have to be deceived about the policy in order to maintain the illusion of deterrence. They would have the conditional intention to retaliate, although the commander in chief knows that he will in no circumstances issue an order to them to fire the weapons. But if it is morally impermissible to form the conditional intention to use the weapons, then it must be similarly impermissible to implant that intention in the minds of others. So the deontologist is committed to denying that there is any difference between cases 1 and 2. This is absurd since it condemns equally a policy in which there is no possibility that possessing nuclear weapons will lead to their use and one that involves such a risk.

This argument assumes a position which is far stronger than the one I am defending here. It assumes a deontologist who holds that all morally forbidden acts are equally wrong and a position which works only with the categories of the morally forbidden, the morally permissible, and the morally obligatory. It is more plausible to argue from a position which claims that two acts which are morally impermissible may differ in their wrongness and that our appraisals of persons and their characters are related in a much more complex way to the aforementioned division of acts.

If we are judging the commander in chief, then the morally crucial feature of his policy is that he is not prepared or willing or intending to bring injury to innocent parties. And his policy is not one that involves using potential risk to those parties in order to achieve his ends. It is true that he lies to his subordinates, but this shows only that it is not always morally forbidden to lie. And this must be assumed for any policy that involves bluffing.

As to those further down in the chain of command, it is not the case that they have the conditional intention to retaliate. They have the conditional intention to obey the orders of their superiors. This, indeed, involves the abdication of a certain amount of autonomy, but that is a feature of all military (and many other) structures. Whatever corruption is involved in renouncing the right to think for oneself about what one does is not associated in any special way with the bluffing scenario.

Again, in my view it may be impermissible to form the conditional intention to use nuclear weapons, and it may be impermissible actually to use such weapons, but I am not committed to the view that they represent equal wrongs. For why may not both be above some threshold which rules them both out and yet one be, so to speak, more above the threshold than the other? To say that they are both impermissible is to say that there is no adequate justification for either, or that neither would be allowed by any set of principles that meets our criteria for an adequate

11. Jeff McMahan, "Deterrence and Deontology," in this volume.

moral theory, or whatever. But that still allows that one of the acts is more evil than the other, in the sense that more bad is produced, and also allows for the view that if one had to choose one or the other, in a situation of necessity, one ought to choose the less evil. Of course if one has to choose between risking a nuclear war and fighting one, it is preferable to choose risking. If one had to choose between firing a pistol with six bullets in the chamber at a baby and firing a pistol with five bullets, one would choose the latter. But both are morally impermissible.

VII

If one believes that cases 2 and 6 are permissible, that case 4 is problematic to the extent that one leaves it open that one will retaliate, and that the other cases are not permissible, and if the alternative hypothesis of increased risk to the innocent does not explain all these judgments, it seems as if the focus remains on the conditional intention to retaliate. I want to set out some significant features of deterrent intentions which are morally relevant.

The first feature is that since the intention is conditional the intention creates a risk of doing what is morally forbidden, depending on the likelihood of the condition's being satisfied. The intention is only carried out if certain conditions are fulfilled. Actually this is probably true of most intentions which are thought of as "categorical." My intention to repay a loan is often conditional on the loan's not being forgiven. The doctor's intention to lie to his terminally ill patient is conditional on his being asked for the information. My intention to write a paper for a conference is conditional on my children's not becoming dangerously ill. Almost all intentions have an other-things-being-equal character to the commitment to fulfill them, even when this is not explicit.

Still it would be a mistake to think of all intentions as "really" being conditional in nature. This would be like thinking my belief that my pet is a cat assumes that I won't discover its insides to be made of transistors. In both cases there is a context within which the formation of the intention (belief) takes place, but the context is not part of the structure of formation.

That one has a conditional intention is, as is the case of nonconditional intentions, shown partly by how one's actions are guided by the intention— whether one takes appropriate steps to insure that one will be in a position to do what is envisioned if the conditioning event occurs, whether one takes steps to be in a position to determine that the conditioning event occurs, and so forth. With many conditional intentions the carrying out of the intention (if the conditioning event occurs) is desired for its own sake (If I get a raise, I will go to Paris for a week) or as a means to some end the agent has (If the test shows a malignancy, I will have an operation). The forming of a conditional intention shows what the agent is prepared to do and therefore what values guide his decisions.

The peculiar feature of deterrent intentions is that it is believed that the formation and expression of the intention makes it less likely that the condition will occur. Since this is the point of forming the intention, it is part of the logic of deterrent intentions that one does not have to value the fulfillment of the intention, either as an end in itself or as a means to some other end one has. It is the forming of the conditional intention itself which reflects the agent's values by showing what he is prepared to do (under certain circumstances).

This last point is important and often misunderstood. For it is supposed that if deterrent intentions fail, that is, do not succeed in avoiding the occurrence of the condition, then the fulfillment of the intention must be viewed as a means to some other goal, the most usual one being future deterrence of the offender or others. But while this may be a reason for fulfilling the intention, it need not be. One may fulfill one's threat simply as a matter of keeping one's word or because the sanction deserves to be carried out.

Gauthier has argued recently that it can be rational to commit oneself to carrying out a threat, which apart from the context of strategic interaction would be irrational.[12] This view, which seems paradoxical to many, ought not to be. Schelling gives the example of the country which by making it clear that it intends to fight to the death makes it less likely that it will have to. And on a more mundane level any bargaining scenario demonstrates the same phenomenon in small scale. If I have something which I am willing to sell to you for $100 or more, and you are willing to pay $150 or less, there is room for mutual gain from trade. If these values are known to both of us, then if you offer me $110 I may still commit myself to not selling for less than $125 in the hopes that you will change your offer. If you do not, this may result in a situation in which, at that point, what is in my interest is to change my mind and accept your offer of $110. But my best chance for getting the $125 may be irrevocably to commit myself to not accepting your first offer.

It will not do to say that, when the stakes are so different, as in the nuclear context, the analogy cannot hold. For the difference in stakes only implies that it will be much more unlikely that the expected gains will outweigh the possible costs. But if they do, the same principles of rationality should apply.

What about the possibility of changing one's mind? Does this view imply that one cannot come to the conclusion that one has made a mistake? Of course not. But one must be careful about what one changes one's mind about. It is possible that one comes to the conclusion that one ought not to have formed the conditional intention in the first place, that it was not rational to be prepared to risk those costs for these benefits. But note that it cannot be the mere failure of one's strategy that one relies on to make this recalculation. For there was always the possibility of failure.

12. Gauthier.

Or, again, there is the possibility that, while then it was rational, given one's beliefs and values, to have made the commitment, one's values and beliefs have changed so that now one would not make the commitment.

Note also that one's opponent is entitled to take into account the likelihood of that kind of reassessment in calculating how likely it is that you will fulfill your commitment. He is also going to take into account how likely some form of nonrational backsliding is.

It also may be the case that one is not strong willed enough to be confident that one will carry out the threat in the knowledge that, at that point, there is no independent reason to carry it out. One then may seek to provide oneself with independent reasons (side bets) or to set up institutional mechanisms which insure the carrying out of the threat. But it seems to me an empirical question whether for a particular individual the existence of a good argument is by itself sufficient to provide him with enough motivation to carry out his intention or whether he needs external aids.

Gauthier goes on to argue the more controversial point not only that it is rational to form the conditional intention but also that the rationality of forming the intention shows that it is rational to carry out the threat if deterrence fails. For Gauthier there is no separate question that needs to be raised about the rationality of carrying out the intention since the rationality of the act is assessed as part of the policy of forming the intention ab initio.

I think it preferable to hold, as Kavka and Lewis argue, that, while the agent may not be irrational to carry out the threat since it stems from a commitment that it was rational to form, the act itself is irrational. By assumption it is an act which the agent has no independent reason to perform and reason not to perform. It is true that individuals who are able to make such commitments will achieve gains in utility that those who cannot must forfeit. But if the question arises whether one has reason to do what one threatened to do, given the failure of deterrence, the answer must be negative.

But the question I want to explore is whether the analogue for morality holds. Can it be moral to commit oneself to actions which, independent of the policy in which they are imbedded, are immoral?

In the case of deterrent intentions it is not enough to show that utility is maximized by the formation of such intentions, for that merely shows that it is rational to do so if one wants to maximize satisfaction of preferences. Nor is it enough to show that some important values, freedom or national security, are most efficiently secured by such intentions, for that merely shows that there is a moral reason in favor of such actions. But one function of morality is to put limits or constraints on what one may do to maximize satisfaction or to achieve important values.

If one takes as a heuristic notion here the idea of being able to justify one's actions to those whose interests are adversely affected by them, the question becomes, Can one justify to those affected being prepared to take a risk of doing something the actual doing of which cannot be, independently, justified to them?

The central examples used by philosophers have been deterrent threats. The essential elements are that the coming about of C is up to those who are put at risk, they would be at fault if they brought about C, some important good is achieved by preventing C from being performed, and it is believed that the threat of x may prevent those put at risk from bringing about C. But there may be other kinds of cases which do not rely on deterrent aims.

Think, for example, of those who risk causing accidents by driving when drunk. Suppose we announce that such drivers will have to pay fines into a fund which goes toward the medical expenses of those who are injured in automobile accidents. We do this, not because this may have a deterrent effect (although it may), but in order to raise a fund to compensate accident victims. Since there is no causal connection between the behavior of those fined and any accident victim we are not entitled (in the absence of formulating and announcing such a policy) simply to confiscate property from such drivers on the normal tort grounds of making people bear the costs of their faulty conduct. But the charge of being used for a useful social purpose is, plausibly, defeated by the claim that it is not unfair to make those who voluntarily engage in faulty conduct pay the costs of those who are put at risk by their faulty conduct.

The crucial elements here are the fact that the carrying out of the intention is avoidable by the person put at risk, the fact that the condition which brings about the carrying out of the intention is not one which the person put at risk is entitled to bring about, and the fact that the person put at risk has been informed of the conditional intent.

A second case in which this kind of reasoning seems plausible is one in which one can address a justification to those whose interests are put at risk in terms of their interests having the best chance of being promoted by such measures. Suppose A is being threatened by B to stop conduct which is completely within A's rights. A is stubborn, will refuse to desist, and will suffer great harm from B. To avoid this I pretend to be so offended by the conduct that I threaten (sincerely) to punish A for the conduct in question. I believe he will refrain, not out of fear of my carrying out the threat (which I would carry out), but because he believes I am offended by the conduct and wishes to avoid hurting me. If, in fact, I am forced to carry out the threat (my policy fails), could I not justify this (otherwise immoral) action on the grounds that the policy of which it was a part provided the best chance to avoid harm to A?

These are essentially paternalistic cases where we impose a risk of bringing about (otherwise impermissible) harm as the best chance of avoiding worse harm.

The point in all these cases is that we start with a situation in which we are not entitled to do certain things to people. However, in these situations we are entitled to threaten or warn that we will do these things unless those threatened or warned refrain from certain actions. The justification for the initial intention then carries over to the carrying out of the intention. We do not need additional moral reasons for being justified in carrying out the intention, although we may need practical reasons for being motivated to do so. Being entitled to perform some action does not necessarily give one a reason to do it. In the case we have been considering, the direction of moral justification is from the conditional intention to the carrying out of the intention. What needs to be established morally is that we are entitled to threaten or warn these agents in these situations.

It would seem then that there is the following parallel between rationality and morality. In both cases it can be justified to form a conditional intention, or to change one's dispositions, so that one is prepared to do what would otherwise be unjustifiable. Of course, in both cases there must be an argument to show that one is entitled to form the conditional intention in the first place. I turn now to the issue of deterrent intentions.

VIII

Since the intention in question is to inflict, under certain conditions, severe harm on other moral agents, there must be a justification which can be addressed to those agents as to why we are prepared to risk their harm. In the case where the person being threatened with harm is the person whose aggression against us we are trying to deter, the justification is obvious. Just as we would be entitled to use force in self-defense if we were in the process of being attacked, so we are entitled to threaten in advance in order to deter that attack. Whether the correct theoretical account of why we are entitled to use force in self-defense, and the derived entitlement to threaten to use force, is one in terms of the aggressor forfeiting his right not to be the object of force or the threat of force, or a notion of fault forfeits first, or the idea that we all stand to gain from an agreement permitting such force, is something I shall not attempt to settle here.[13]

It is also the case that there are certain limits which must be established on the amount of harm that potential aggressors may be threatened with. Again, I believe that these limits are established not by what we are entitled to do after the aggression but rather by what we would be entitled to do in the course of stopping the aggression, so that the justification for the threat explains the legitimacy of carrying out the threat rather than conversely. It is because it is impermissible to threaten noncombatants (on grounds of self-defense) that it is impermissible to bomb them, and not the other way round.

What about the other possible exception? Can we address to those

13. For some thoughts on this subject, see T. Hurka, "Rights and Capital Punishment," *Dialogue* 21 (1982): 647–60.

noncombatants who neither use force against us nor aid those who use such force, and whose welfare we risk by our deterrent intentions, an argument to the effect that they could have expected to gain from our policy of deterrence? The possibility of such an argument seems dubious both on empirical and on moral grounds. On empirical grounds we would have to establish that the expected gains to Soviet citizens (and citizens of other nations at risk of nuclear winter) from our policy of deterrence outweigh the expected risks to them. These gains cannot include a reduced risk of being exposed to our nuclear weapons, for a policy of unilateral nuclear disarmament assures them that that cannot happen. If it is argued that they have a reduced risk of being exposed to the nuclear weapons of other countries, for example, China, that assumes that we are prepared to threaten China with nuclear attack if they attack the Soviet Union. A policy which, as far as I know, we do not have.

The best argument along these lines is that the presence of nuclear weapons produces a greatly reduced risk of conventional war because of the fear of nuclear escalation. Since it doesn't matter a great deal to the average Soviet citizen whether he dies from a bullet or from a missile, if, in fact, the chances of being killed unjustly in conventional warfare (absent nuclear deterrence) were much greater than the chances of being killed unjustly in a nuclear war (with nuclear deterrence), there would be an argument along the lines I have suggested. I have no idea as to what the evidence for this assertion would be, nor do I think anybody else does.

But even if the facts were as indicated, it seems to me that there are a number of important moral objections to this argument. First, the facts are as they are only because it is assumed that we are willing to act immorally in the first place, that is, not to take much greater precautions than we do now to reduce the risks to noncombatants in conventional warfare. Second, such an argument only seems to me reasonable when it is addressed to members of one's own moral community. The argument is essentially paternalistic in form—we're doing this against your expressed will for your own (expected) good—and such an argument requires an ability to control, limit, and direct such powers by those whose liberty is being infringed.

Finally, and this brings us back to intentions once more, there is a special wrong where the risk is one of being the target of intentional harm. It is sometimes argued that as drivers we impose risks on pedestrians which are ultimately justified by the benefits that pedestrians gain by allowing the driving of automobiles. But I do not believe that we would accept an institution which imposed the same risks of injury and death that accidents cause, but risks brought about by actions aimed at the injury or death. Unlike an Aztec ritual of sacrifice or Shirley Jackson's lottery, we do not aim at the death of particular persons as the means of securing whatever benefits are at stake. In the case of deterrent intentions that is precisely what we do.

Morality and Deterrence

Robert W. Tucker

I

We live in the age of deterrence. It is deterrence that constitutes the
limiting condition of all our lives. And it is deterrence that forms the
object of the faith by which we have come to live. For we are nearly all
believers in deterrence, though we may express a common faith in different
ways. We are nearly all believers in deterrence if only for the reason that
once we seriously admit nuclear war as a distinct historical possibility,
we conjure up not only a very dark landscape but also one in which our
accepted categories of political and moral thought no longer seem relevant.
In the still alien world of nuclear weapons, it is only a faith in deterrence
that preserves continuity with a familiar past. Without this faith, we could
not entertain familiar convictions about nuclear weapons and nuclear
war that are otherwise quite irreconcilable.

At the same time, there have always been those unhappy with this
faith. Their unhappiness is not to be equated with disbelief, though a
number of them have recently experienced a decline in faith. Instead,
their distress may be attributed to the conviction that morally deterrence
represents a fall from grace and that it constitutes a kind of moral purgatory,
a state of near sin from which we should do our utmost to escape. Yet
with the exception of a few determined optimists, the prospects for escape
appear to be virtually nonexistent. Hence the unhappiness with what
seems to be a near permanent state of things.

Deterrence not only forms a common object of faith, it is also the
contemporary embodiment of what an enlightened age was supposed to
exorcize: reason of state. Indeed, deterrence forms what may be considered
the perfect—certainly the extreme—expression of reason of state. It is
the ultimate manifestation of the necessity that is ostensibly imposed on
the statesman and that is justified in terms of the security and independence
of the state and of those values the state protects. Deterrence lays bare
the nature of reason of state as it has never before been laid bare and
points to the depressing fact that even a democratic version of reason
of state need admit of no limits to the measures that may be taken to
preserve the political community's independence and continuity. The
necessity of democratic states may reach out to take and to justify the
same extreme measures as the necessity of nondemocratic states.

Are there, in either case, any limits to the measures that may be taken to preserve the state's independence and continuity? This is the crucial question reason of state has always raised. The answer has regularly been that there are no limits. Thus it is not the abuse to which the argument of necessity so readily lends itself that is its profoundly disturbing feature but the refusal to acknowledge any restraints on the measures that may be taken on behalf of the state. The argument of necessity does not leave the critical issue of means unresolved. On the contrary, it is precisely in the manner by which this issue is in principle resolved that the distinctive character of "necessity of state" must be found.

II

Any serious critique of necessity must be directed to the critical issue of means. While not simply abandoning statecraft and its distinctive means, this critique must seek to impose limits on the alleged necessities of the state. It must seek to limit the distinctive means of statecraft, not to abandon these means. The issue of means may of course be resolved simply by abandoning the ultima ratio of statecraft. Pacifism has always formed one response to necessities of state and continues to do so today. But it does so by renouncing altogether the threat or use of force. Pacifism has often been defended as another kind, a different and higher kind, of policy. In fact, it is the abandonment of policy, for it is the abandonment of the means distinctive to statecraft. In refusing to threaten a potential aggressor with retributive measures, more generally, in refusing to confront an adversary with the prospect of returning like for like, pacifism disavows the principle of reciprocity so vital to the conduct of statecraft.

In contrast to pacifism, the doctrine and tradition of *bellum justum* does set itself the goal of imposing limits on the means permitted to the statesman. Without abandoning the distinctive means of statecraft, while acknowledging that the state does have its necessities and that they must be viewed as legitimate, the doctrine of *bellum justum* nevertheless insists that these necessities are circumscribed and that even when acting in defense of the state's independence and survival there are certain restraints that a government is never justified in exceeding.

In the American Catholic bishops' pastoral letter on war and peace in the nuclear age we have a recent and impressive effort in a tradition that has been in Western thought perhaps the principal alternative to the plea of reason of state.[1] The bishops observe that the source of their doctrine is independent of and superior to the state and its necessities. At the same time, they both acknowledge and emphasize those necessities

---

1. National Conference of Catholic Bishops, "The Challenge of Peace: God's Promise and Our Response" (The pastoral letter of the U.S. bishops on war and peace), *Origins* 13 (May 19, 1983): 1–32; hereafter cited as "The Challenge of Peace," with page number and column reference.

for the preservation of key values. Still, they are insistent that even for the preservation of these values certain measures may never be justified.

The doctrine of *bellum justum* is addressed to both the justification for resorting to force and to the permitted methods of employing force. There is little that needs to be said here about the justification for resorting to force. Whatever the earlier position taken toward the *jus ad bello,* in the twentieth-century reconstruction of *bellum justum,* war is no longer a means generally permitted to states for the redress of rights that have been violated. Still less is war considered a legitimate means for changing the status quo. Armed force remains a means permitted to states only as a measure of self-defense against a prior and unjust attack. This is also the position taken in the bishops' letter, and it echoes the earlier position taken in 1964 by the Second Vatican Council. The Council declared: "As long as the danger of war persists and there is no international authority with the necessary competence and power, governments cannot be denied the right of lawful self-defense, once all peace efforts have failed."[2]

It is not primarily here that *bellum justum* today confronts reason of state but, rather, in the restraints placed on the means or conduct of war. The general nature of that conflict is clear enough. Whereas reason of state must reject the claim that there are any inherent limits on the means that may be threatened or employed on behalf of the state, *bellum justum* must insist that there are such limits and that they may never be transgressed, whatever the circumstances. The argument of necessity must reject the claim of inherent limits on the means of war, not because it is informed by an "ethic of responsibility" requiring the statesman to calculate and to weigh the possible consequences of alternative courses of action, but because it presupposes as an ultimate end the preservation and continuity of the state. *Bellum justum* evidently cannot share this presupposition, else it could not insist that there are means that may never be employed. There is no denial here of the need to calculate and to weigh but simply the insistence that whatever the results of calculation, certain limits must be imposed on the means permitted the statesman, limits that may never be transgressed. *Bellum justum* has a distinctive quality in that it is an "ethic of ultimate means."[3]

2. Second Vatican Council, *Pastoral Constitution on the Church in the Modern World,* December 7, 1965 (National Catholic Welfare Conference, 1966). The statement on war appears in pt. 2, chap. 5.

3. The term "ethic of responsibility" is taken from Max Weber's classic essay, "Politics as a Vocation," in *Max Weber: Essays in Sociology,* ed. H. H. Gerth and C. Wright Mills (New York: Oxford University Press, 1958), pp. 77ff. Weber contrasts an "ethic of responsibility" with an "ethic of ultimate ends," the former being identified with the statesman and the latter with the Christian. One might just as reasonably, though, identify his ethic of responsibility with an ethic of ultimate ends, and his ethic of ultimate ends with an ethic of ultimate means. That, at any rate, is the position taken here for reasons elaborated in the text.

What are the restraints on means that may never be transgressed? In the conduct of war there is only one, but it is all important. It is the principle forbidding the direct and intentional attack on noncombatants. The distinction between those who may be made the object of attack and those who may not be so made is held in *bellum justum* to define the essential difference between war and murder—between the permitted and the forbidden taking of human life. It is the deliberate killing of the innocent that is always to be avoided, that may never be justified even as a measure of reprisal taken in response to similar measures of an adversary. This is, in substance, the evil that may never be done or threatened, whatever the good that may be thought to come. In Vatican Council II indiscriminate warfare is condemned in these terms (terms that are repeated in the bishops' letter): "Any act of war aimed indiscriminately at the destruction of entire cities or of extensive areas along with their population is a crime against God and man himself. It merits unequivocal and unhesitating condemnation."[4]

This condemnation of indiscriminate warfare is, in effect, the condemnation of total war. Almost by definition, total war must prove indiscriminate in its conduct. Total war is also very likely to violate the other general principle regulating the conduct of war, the principle of proportionality. The norm requiring that the values preserved through force must be proportionate to the values sacrificed through force is no more than a counsel of prudence. It expresses the common sense of the matter. When war becomes disproportionately destructive to the good it serves, it must be condemned. The judgments of proportionality, and its converse, are necessarily rough and subject to uncertainty and controversy. Still, they are indispensable to make if war is to be (anything close to) a rational and moral activity.

The principles of discrimination and proportionality determine, by and large, the justice of warfare. We have here, it needs hardly be said, a rough and minimal justice, a *Grenzmoral,* as John Courtney Murray once observed. Still, these principles are critical if war is to be even a barely tolerable activity. Of the two, it is the principle of discrimination that is the more significant in the sense that it poses the clearer obstacle to, and stands in more apparent conflict with, the state and its necessities. It is of course the case that difficulty and uncertainty also attend application of the principle of discrimination. In forbidding the deliberate attack on the innocent (civilian) population, we must still determine who are the innocent and what constitutes a deliberate attack on them. The latter determination, particularly, has often been attended by considerable difficulties. These difficulties continue to lend themselves today, as they have lent themselves in the past, to manipulation by the state. Even so, if the principle of discrimination is not to be all but abandoned in practice, there is a point beyond which the line must be fairly clearly drawn

4. "The Challenge of Peace," p. 15, col. 1.

between the demands of that principle and the necessities of the state. If conventional warfare in this century has already made increasingly imperative the drawing of this line, the prospect of nuclear warfare must make it manyfold more urgent.

III

Do nuclear weapons and the prospects held out by nuclear war invalidate reason of state? If the answer is that they do, there is no need to go beyond this question and to ask whether the use of nuclear weapons may be reconciled with the requirements of *bellum justum*. If the use of nuclear weapons holds out the likely prospect of destroying the state along with those values the state is supposed to protect, nuclear war represents the very antithesis to the idea of the state's *ratio*. This ancient justification of force is now at last turned against itself, as it were, by weapons which represent the hypertrophy of power. This being so, the question of fulfilling the requirements of *bellum justum* can be no more than rhetorical.

Of course, whether the prospects held out by nuclear war—virtually any nuclear war—do invalidate reason of state and are irreconcilable with even the barest requirements of a just war depends on the character of such a conflict. But we are almost as much in the dark today about this as we have always been. After more than a generation of speculation and debate we cannot say with assurance what a nuclear war would be like and, above all, whether it might be subject to meaningful limitation. We do not know and cannot know short of the event itself whether a "central" war between the United States and the USSR might be limited in any meaningful way. Nor do we or can we know short of the event itself whether the theater use of nuclear weapons in the central front in Europe might be kept from spreading to much of the rest of the continent and, eventually, engulfing the homelands of the nuclear superpowers.

Our persisting ignorance in these matters must be asserted despite those who seem to know what a nuclear war, any and all nuclear war, would be like. No one knows or can know what remains and, it is hoped, will continue to remain unknowable. What we do know is that nuclear weapons are terribly destructive and that their rate of destructiveness leaves almost no time for second thoughts. We also know that our ability to cope with the demands imposed by nuclear war will be put, under the best of circumstances, to the most severe strain. Thus we have strong reason for believing, even if we cannot quite know, that virtually any war fought with the nuclear weapons we now have would prove very difficult to control and would involve, at the very least, casualties in the several millions on each side.[5] This is a very modest statement. Many would find it modest to the point of being quite misleading. Even so, on a matter

---

5. The emphasis on weapons "we now have" is to distinguish them from weapons of great accuracy we may well have in the years ahead. Compare Sec. V below.

that has invited and continues to invite almost unparalleled hyperbole, a little understatement can do no great harm.

It is not necessary to postulate the end of humanity in order to conclude that the use of nuclear weapons invalidates reason of state and is irreconcilable with the requirements of *bellum justum* or any reasonable variation of that doctrine. Nor, for that matter, is it necessary to postulate a nuclear war resulting in hundreds of millions of casualties in order to reach these conclusions. Often in thinking about nuclear war our political and moral calculus has simply run amok. It has been inflated to the point of absurdity. The political and moral justification of nuclear war fails by applying far more modest standards than these. If it can be shown that a nuclear war is likely to destroy the end(s) for which it is waged, it can have neither political nor moral justification. If a nuclear war, though limited to Western Europe, is likely to result in the destruction of the countries in which it is waged, it is difficult to find its political or moral justification. If a nuclear war, involving the territories of the two super-powers, results in the kind of devastation that makes impossible the retention of democratic processes and values, the war can have neither political nor moral justification. This may be said quite apart from any direct consideration of the manner in which the war is conducted, though the consequences of the war would themselves strongly suggest that the means of conducting it afford an independent ground for moral condemnation.

May one make the very uncertainty—the persisting uncertainty— attending the conduct and consequences of nuclear war a principal reason for denying moral justification to the use of nuclear weapons? Recently a notable effort has been made to do so. In the American bishops' letter, the uncertainties attending the use—any use—of nuclear weapons is given great emphasis. The bishops repeatedly express their "extreme skepticism" over whether a nuclear conflict could be controlled, however limited a manner in which it might begin. This skepticism over the prospects of limiting nuclear conflict in a way that would satisfy the requirements of political and moral rationality leads them to support a no-first-use position. Perhaps even more significant, it leads them to come very close to denying even the legitimacy of the retaliatory use of nuclear weapons in a limited exchange.

Moreover, the result of placing the emphasis the bishops do on the issue of control is to come very close to condemning any and all use of nuclear weapons. The bishops do not directly and expressly support this conclusion. They do not say that the use of nuclear weapons is intrinsically evil. But this is surely the central thrust of their message, and it would be disingenuous to contend otherwise. Nuclear weapons may not quite represent an intrinsic evil. Still, they are seen as something very near to that. It is for this reason, the bishops conclude, that "to cross the nuclear threshold is to enter a world where we have no experience of control, much testimony against its possibility, and therefore no moral justification for submitting the human community to this risk."[6]

Even if we do not consider this argument conclusive, it is still a very persuasive one. There is no morality in statecraft without prudence. But how is one to be prudent in the use of nuclear weapons? At the very least, prudence would seem to require an experience and knowledge about the use of nuclear weapons that we do not have. In this respect, it is useful to contrast the use of nuclear weapons with the threat to use them. We do have an experience, an ever-growing experience, with deterrence. Here, there is reason to expect that prudent behavior can be maintained by both sides. For both sides have already behaved quite prudently for nearly three decades. This is no guarantee of the future, as critics of deterrence insistently point out. But it is at least a substantial reason for believing that deterrence may be a manageable arrangement for an indefinite period ahead. Nuclear deterrence, it may then be argued, is compatible with prudence. By contrast, nuclear war may well put prudence to an unbearable test.

IV

It is deterrence rather than nuclear war that expresses today the spirit of reason of state, just as it is deterrence rather than nuclear war that raises the more significant—certainly the more immediate—moral issues. Nuclear war is a recurrent nightmare that we hope will never materialize. Deterrence is part of our daily existence, even if it is an unseen part. The same air of unreality that attaches to speculation over how a nuclear war might arise and the character it would have, also attaches to the moral considerations attending the use of nuclear weapons. Do the moral judgments we may make on nuclear war really matter, however, save to moralists and a few kindred souls? More pointedly, perhaps, do these judgments really matter much save as they bear on what undoubtedly does matter—deterrence?

The first and, indeed, the last thing that needs to be said in any moral assessment of deterrence is that it should not be regarded as a temporary arrangement. Deterrence should not be seen as a mere way station on the road, even if a long road, to a world without nuclear weapons. In retrospect, deterrence may one day be seen as just that. But its justification now cannot be made to turn on a prospect that from the vantage point of the present must appear as near utopian. It is true that the alternative to this proposition seems grim, since a world that is condemned to rely indefinitely on deterrence is a world that seems to have a permanent sentence of death hanging over it. Deterrence is merely a social contrivance, and as such it is fallible. This being so, time must appear as the great nemesis, as we are constantly reminded. Over time,

6. "The Challenge of Peace," p. 16, col. 1.

the familiar argument runs, the odds lengthen that deterrence will break down.

There is no satisfactory response that may be made to this argument. The American bishops echo a rather general sentiment when, in giving their "strictly conditioned moral acceptance" to deterrence, they urge that deterrence "should be used as a step on the way toward progressive disarmament."[7] An arrangement that is only barely sanctioned morally must be marked by this corrective or redeeming process (progressive disarmament) if it is to be given continued approval. But the more specific measures the bishops propose in support of progressive disarmament would not achieve a nuclear-free world even if they were carried out. At best what they would do is freeze the nuclear strategic status quo and make it marginally safer. To do that would not be an insignificant achievement. At the same time, it would not alter in any fundamental way the present structure of deterrence.

Nuclear weapons present us with a danger for which there simply is at present no apparently feasible way out. There are, of course, ways out if one is willing to pay the price and brave the consequences of these ways. Pacifism is one way—not "nuclear pacifism" which is, in effect, a misnomer, but pacifism. Once having submitted militarily to the adversary, the structure of deterrence maintained by the submitting side would become pointless. A far smaller price than that entailed in all likelihood by pacifism, would be the price attending an American withdrawal to this hemisphere. Such withdrawal would leave intact the structure of deterrence, but it would alter radically the meaning and risks of deterrence. If the interests in defense of which we were prepared to risk not only nuclear war but any war did not extend beyond the North American continent, the prospect of our future involvement in a nuclear conflict would sharply decline. For deterrence would then become synonymous with the prevention of a direct attack by the Soviet Union on the United States. In a world where we no longer contested the Soviets, what incentive would they have to run the terrible risk of attacking us?

Apart from submission or withdrawal, however, there are no apparently feasible ways out of the dangers imposed by deterrence. These dangers may be moderated by technology (precision-guided munitions; missile defense systems, etc.), just as they may be moderated by politics (détente). Nevertheless, any basic change in the deterrence relationship is unlikely to result from these developments. Deterrence, it appears, will remain a part of our "condition" for as far as we can presently see.

V

The principal moral issue deterrence raises is whether one may threaten what would be evil to do. This is of course not the only issue raised by

7. Ibid., p. 18, cols. 2, 3. In this the bishops follow previous utterances of the Catholic hierarchy that go back to the 1960s.

deterrence. Even if the moralist concludes that in this instance the threat to do evil is morally tolerable, he may also be expected to conclude that deterrence represents an extreme, or limiting, case. As such, it is a condition that must be made as effective as possible. Still, the prospect that the condition of deterrence may fail is one that cannot be excluded. This being so there is a duty to limit the evil wrought by nuclear war, as far as this is possible. These imperatives, as we know, are not easy to give meaning to in practice. They have provoked bitter and continuing controversy. Among many, perhaps most, the view persists that the two imperatives are and must remain mutually incompatible, that the effectiveness of deterrence rests largely on the conviction—and reality—of the impossibility of limiting the evil of nuclear war. It is particularly among those holding this view that there is an emphasis amounting to an obsession, on the imperative to transcend the condition of deterrence, although the prospects for effecting such transcendence are, as already noted, negligible.

In asking whether one may threaten what would be evil to do, it is evidently assumed that the ends of action are good. Were this not the case, no moral quandary would arise. One does arise only because of situations or circumstances in which there seems no alternative to threatening evil, and intending to do evil, that good may come. In the case of deterrence, what is the threat that it would be evil to carry out?

The answer will be apparent from the earlier discussion. Given the perspective of *bellum justum*, it is wicked to wage indiscriminate warfare, even in retaliation for acts of indiscriminate warfare. Equally from this perspective, a war that either destroys or does irreparable damage to the values in defense of which it is undertaken must be condemned. Years ago, Paul Tillich declared that nuclear war would be evil if it could not serve the principle of "creative justice." A war, Tillich wrote, that does not hold out "the possibility of a creative new beginning" because it "annihilates what it is supposed to defend" must be condemned.[8]

If discrimination and proportionality are accepted as the principal moral criteria by which justice in war is determined, what kind of nuclear deterrent, if any, would permit the solid prospect, if ever put to active use, of not doing evil? Evidently a deterrent that could be quite closely controlled, one that would permit us, in Albert Wohlstetter's words, "to hit what we aim at and only what we aim at."[9] The development of ever

8. Paul Tillich, "The Nuclear Dilemma—a Discussion," *Christianity and Crisis* (November 13, 1961), p. 204. Tillich nevertheless justified deterrence, however destructive. His qualms were overcome by faith in deterrence—indeed, "existential" deterrence. "Practically," he wrote, "the very existence of atomic weapons on both sides is probably a sufficient deterrent."
9. Albert Wohlstetter, "Bishops, Statesmen and Other Strategists on the Bombing of Innocents," *Commentary* 75 (June 1983): 15–35. Wohlstetter writes that the revolution in precision is "in some ways more revolutionary than the transition from conventional to fusion weapons." The reason is that an improvement in accuracy "by a factor of 100 improves blast effectiveness against a small hard military target about as much as multiplying the energy released a million times."

more accurate weapons opens up the prospect of a deterrent, nuclear and even conventional, that might be employed with considerable discrimination and within the broad limits of the principle of proportionality. The new technology of smart weapons promises a radical decrease in collateral damage by permitting conventional weapons to replace nuclear weapons in many tasks, by dramatically raising the nuclear threshold, and by diminishing the prospects of escalation.

The precision-guided munitions do not and cannot free us from the great danger created by nuclear weapons. May they not, however, mitigate this danger by affording a greater opportunity to act in a more restrained and discriminate manner? Against the belief of some that they would have this effect, there is the conviction of others that they will be used to rehabilitate nuclear war. The new technology presumably will give rise to the illusion that nuclear weapons have at last been domesticated and are now virtually as usable as conventional weapons. Once they are employed, however, the danger of escalation will inevitably arise. It is for these reasons that the American Catholic bishops take a dim view of the promise of the new technology. "The problem," the bishops declare, "is not simply one of producing highly accurate weapons that might minimize civilian casualties in any single explosion but one of increasing the likelihood of escalation at a level where many, even 'discriminating' weapons, would cumulatively kill large numbers of civilians."[10]

The bishops are right in insisting that, while highly accurate weapons do not resolve the critical issue of limits, they may well prompt the illusion that this issue has now been resolved. Men have not been indiscriminate in war simply because they lacked the means to be discriminate. Discriminate means may be used in pursuit of immoderate ends. When they are, the means are very likely to be used indiscriminately. At the same time, this is an argument that may be employed against virtually any weapon. Indeed, in the end it is an argument against war itself, and certainly against war—whether nuclear or conventional—in the late twentieth century.

The precision-guided weapons raise to a new level the persisting issue of the nuclear age between those who would seek safety in refusing to countenance almost any development that might have the effect of making nuclear war—or, for that matter, any war between the superpowers—more thinkable and those who are prepared to accept an incrementally greater risk of nuclear war in order to make its conduct less than apocalyptic. As a moral choice, it is difficult to see how this issue can be settled by an appeal to experience, although each side is constantly invoking history in support of its position. But history, as far as I can read it, does not seem to vindicate either position.

At any rate, the moral problem we presently face is not one of determining what kind of deterrent might be actively employed with the

10. "The Challenge of Peace," p. 18, col. 1.

substantial prospect of not doing evil. Instead, it is one of deciding whether the deterrent we have today and are likely to have for some years allows the reasonable possibility of not doing evil. No one can answer this question with assurance. Still, to the extent we can answer it at all—and the effort must be made to do so—this answer appears to be negative.

It is, of course, possible to imagine a nuclear war in which this conclusion would not hold. But we must address the moral problem of deterrence not in terms of imaginable nuclear war but in terms of likely nuclear war. In this context, what matters is the kind of nuclear war the great nuclear powers are capable of waging and, so far as we know, have made plans to wage. If these plans include the attack and destruction of most major military targets in the adversary's homeland—and all indications are that this is the case—then the distinction that so much has been made of, between counterforce and countervalue targeting strategies, is of limited significance. The targeting plans of both sides are such that the resulting destruction will seem, by any reasonable application of established principles, both indiscriminate and disproportionate.

To this extent, it makes very little difference that the United States government declares its intention not to target civilian centers as such (or without "as such"). In the bishops' letter, government officials are cited as stating "that it is not U.S. strategic policy to target the Soviet civilian population as such or to use nuclear weapons deliberately for the purpose of destroying population centers."[11] Although the bishops were apparently satisfied that these statements met one moral criterion for assessing deterrence policy, the immunity of noncombatants from direct attack, they were anything but satisfied that the government's declared position responded to another moral problem, "namely, that an attack on military targets or militarily significant industrial targets could involve 'indirect' (i.e., unintended) but massive civilian casualties."[12] In turn, administration officials did little to assuage the bishops' doubts. On the contrary, they are cited in the letter as "hoping" any nuclear war could be kept limited but "prepared" to retaliate in a "massive way if necessary." They also agreed that in a substantial exchange civilian casualty levels "would quickly become truly catastrophic" and that even if attacks were limited to military targets the resulting number of deaths "would be almost indistinguishable from what might occur if civilian centers had been deliberately and directly struck."[13]

The bishops conclude from these statements of the administration and from what is known of targeting plans that it is not enough to assert and even to have an intention not to strike civilians directly. However sincere that intention and however honest the efforts made to implement it, a nuclear war is still likely to be "morally disproportionate, even though

11. Ibid., p. 17, col. 3; and administration sources cited in n. 81.
12. Ibid., p. 17, col. 3.
13. Ibid.

not intentionally indiscriminate."[14] In this conclusion, one might almost suspect the bishops of a fine irony. Either that or they must be considered as seriously subscribing to the notion of the "intentless" destruction of entire societies. In truth, the prospect held out by nuclear war threatens to make of the issue of intent a grotesque parody.

If we are instead to preserve a sense of realism in these matters, we must acknowledge that the significance of intention decreases roughly as the destructiveness of war increases. There is no mystery in why this is so. As war becomes more and more destructive, the principle of proportionality must take on ever greater significance. At some extreme point, we must assume that principle is clearly breached, and this quite apart from the interests at stake in the conflict. Nuclear war, we have strong reason to believe, represents that extreme point. It does so even if we continue to insist on an intentionality that seems at complete odds with events in the objective order.

VI

The threat on which deterrence rests today is a threat to do evil despite a strategic policy that does not target the Soviet civilian population—or, at any rate, that does not directly target the Soviet civilian population. It is a threat to do evil whether or not it is regarded as intentionally indiscriminate. For the consequences of a nuclear war that goes beyond the most limited exchange are not only expected to go beyond any reasonable application of the principle of proportionality; they are also expected to be indistinguishable from a war in which the civilian population has been made the direct object of attack. Moreover, we must remind ourselves that this nation's strategic policy remains based today, as it has been based in the past, on the threat of retaliating in kind to any one of several types of attack by the Soviet Union. This threat of retaliation is evidently a conditional threat to do evil if driven to it. The threat of retaliation that constitutes the foundation of deterrence, and has done so from the outset, also expresses with a clarity that is as striking as it is depressing the conflict between the requirements of *bellum justum* and the requirements of reason of state.

Nevertheless, efforts to effect a reconciliation of the two continue today, though they are no more successful than they were a generation ago. Almost invariably, these efforts have taken the form of drawing ingenuous distinctions in the case of deterrence between threat and intent as well as between different types of intent. Thus it has been argued that even if deterrent strategies rely on the threat to do evil, that threat still does not necessarily imply an actual intent to do evil. If what is evil to do must also be evil to intend to do, however small the chance that this intent will have to be carried out, it does not follow that what is evil to intend to do must also be evil to threaten to do. Deterrence structures

14. Ibid.

may rest on a threat to do evil that still need not betray an intent to do evil. The moralist may question the justification of threatening to do evil, though not intending to do evil. Even so, there is a difference between a threat that carries no intent to act in the manner threatened and a threat that does so.

But all this argument succeeds in doing is to establish that a threat to act may be distinguished from an intent to act. It does not indicate how the threat on which deterrence is based can be effectively maintained without also maintaining the intent to carry out the threat if necessary. Nor does it indicate how, in practice, an intentless threat may be distinguished from an intentful threat without putting the threat to the one and only reliable test. In the absence of this test, it is true, the argument cannot be disproved. Still, it seems reasonable to assume that, in the absence of persuasive evidence to the contrary, a deterrent threat to do evil also implies an intent to do evil.

Deterrence rests on the threat, and the intent, to do evil. Must it for this reason be condemned? Among Catholic moralists, at least, one might expect the condemnation of deterrence, since there is no apparent way that one can reconcile deterrent structures with the injunction against doing or intending to do evil that good may come. Yet with few exceptions, Catholic moralists have refrained from condemning deterrence. In this they have but followed the most authoritative voices of the Church.

Thus, although the Second Vatican Council in 1965 condemned indiscriminate warfare, it did not condemn structures of deterrence that rested, in the last resort, on the threat of indiscriminate warfare. On the contrary, the most reasonable interpretation of the council's position on the morality of deterrence is that the means that may never be employed and the evil that may never be done may nevertheless be threatened. While warning that the "method of deterrence" was "not a safe way to preserve a steady peace," the council nevertheless approved of deterrence in stating: "Many regard this as the most effective way by which peace of a sort can be maintained between nations at the present time."[15]

The subsequent declarations of church authorities have been less acquiescent of deterrence. Still, they have stopped short of condemnation. In 1976, the American bishops stated that "not only is it wrong to attack civilian populations but it is also wrong to threaten to attack them as part of a strategy of deterrence."[16] Beginning with this statement, there is an injunction in all such declarations that the attitude of the church toward deterrence will be heavily, perhaps even decisively, influenced by the efforts of government to reduce, and ultimately to remove altogether, nuclear weapons. In 1979, Cardinal John Krol expressed a willingness "to tolerate the possession of nuclear weapons for deterrence as the lesser

15. Second Vatican Council, p. 87.
16. National Conference of Catholic Bishops, *To Live in Christ Jesus* (Washington, D.C.: U.S. Catholic Conference, 1976), p. 34; cited in "The Challenge of Peace," p. 17, col. 1.

of two evils" but only so long as there is hope of "phasing out altogether of nuclear deterrence." Barring that hope, Cardinal Krol warned, "the moral attitude of the Catholic Church would certainly have to shift to one of uncompromising condemnation of both use and possession of such weapons."[17] A less emphatic but essentially similar position toward deterrence was expressed by Pope John Paul II in 1982.[18]

It is the position taken by the American bishops in their 1983 letter, however, that has attracted a degree of attention and provoked an amount of comment and controversy that is virtually without precedent in these matters. What did the bishops have to say about nuclear war and particularly about deterrence that is so startling as to merit the attention it has thus far received?

In part, the answer is that the attention given the pastoral letter must be accounted for simply by the unusual circumstances in which it appeared—that is, the circumstances of an antinuclear weapons movement of unprecedented size and momentum. In part, however, the letter has attracted widespread attention because it has carried the efforts of predecessors a large step further. In so doing, it has come very close to condemning any and all use of nuclear weapons. The use of these weapons is rejected whether they are employed against military targets or against civilian centers of population, whether in a first strike or a retaliatory second strike, whether in a strategic or theater nuclear war. The condemnation of nuclear war is very nearly complete. Although the barest trace of ambiguity remains in the bishops' discussion of limited nuclear war, that is all that remains.

This near absolute condemnation of nuclear war cannot but have a bearing on the moral assessment of deterrence. If nuclear weapons are by their very nature illegitimate because their use cannot be controlled or their effects limited, must not deterrence structures that rest on the threat to use these weapons also be in principle illegitimate? So it would seem. But the rejection of nuclear war is one thing and the rejection of deterrence quite another. As the supreme expression of reason of state today, the rejection of deterrence is—or would be—a momentous step.

The bishops do not take this step. Instead, they are led "to a strictly conditioned moral acceptance of nuclear deterrence." But what this conditionality amounts to is not altogether apparent in the light of the bishops' statement. Opposed to both "counter value" and "counter force" targeting, the bishops do not indicate what targeting plan in support of a deterrent strategy they would approve. What they do indicate is that the kind of deterrent sufficient to elicit their "conditioned" acceptance is one designed "only to prevent the use of nuclear weapons by others."

---

17. Cardinal John Krol, "Testimony on Salt II," *Origins* 8 (1979): 197. Cited in "The Challenge of Peace," p. 17, col. 1.

18. John Paul II, "Message," U.N. Special Session, 1982:3; cited in "The Challenge of Peace," p. 17, cols. 1, 2.

Any proposals to go beyond this, they declare, "to planning for prolonged periods of repeated nuclear strikes and counterstrikes, or 'prevailing' in nuclear war, are not acceptable." It is, to use a familiar dichotomy, a purely war-deterring and not a war-fighting strategy that they find acceptable. For this reason as well, we read, "'sufficiency' to deter is an adequate strategy; the quest for nuclear superiority must be rejected."[19]

What the bishops have done is to tie a moral theory to a particular view of deterrence. The principles governing the just conduct of war have been linked to a strategic doctrine. As between those who believe that deterrence follows very largely from the existence of nuclear weapons and those who believe a credible theory of use must be developed if deterrence is to be assured, the bishops have plainly decided for the first. Having done so, they have also endowed their chosen view with minimal moral acceptability while judging as morally unacceptable the alternative view.

Although asserting that only one view of deterrence is morally acceptable, they have not persuasively demonstrated why this is so. Indeed, they often seem quite unaware that what they reject as morally unacceptable is also primarily a strategy for deterring nuclear war and not one for waging such a war. Moreover, the manner of deterrent to which the bishops do give their moral sanction is not at all clear from their "criteria." It is, for example, not enough to declare that "deterrence exists only to prevent the use of nuclear weapons by others." This only begs the question of adequacy; it does not answer it. For the great question is, What kind of deterrent is most effective in preventing the use of nuclear weapons by others? The bishops apparently think they have answered this question by the term "sufficiency." In fact, they have only found another way of phrasing the question.

Have the bishops in their "strictly conditioned moral acceptance" of deterrence nevertheless managed to eviscerate it? A number of critics so argue. "You may keep the weapons," Charles Krauthammer interprets the bishops as saying, "but you may not use them. In sum, the only moral nuclear policy is nuclear bluff." But deterrence, Krauthammer argues, "is not inherent in the weapons. It results from a combination of possession and the will to use them. If one side renounces, for moral or other reasons, the intent of ever actually using nuclear weapons, deterrence ceases to exist."[20]

This view goes too far in its rejection of "existential" deterrence. In some measure, deterrence *is* inherent in nuclear weapons and the fact of possessing them. There is, after all, some merit in doctrines of existential deterrence. Admittedly, the bishops have put existential deterrence to an exacting test by virtually renouncing any use of nuclear weapons while retaining possession of them. But it was only in this manner that the

---

19. "The Challenge of Peace," p. 18, cols. 1, 2.
20. Charles Krauthammer, "On Nuclear Morality," *Commentary* 76 (1983): 49.

bishops could apparently effect a compromise between the demands of moral principle and the necessities of state.

It is another matter to ask whether this compromise may not have been made at the expense of both moral principle and necessity of state and that in trying to be as wise as serpents while as innocent as doves the bishops were neither.[21] One may sympathize entirely with the bishops' dilemma in trying to come to terms with deterrence and yet conclude that their almost heroic effort may not, in the end, serve either moral principle or state necessity. Surely, the effect of the bishops' efforts, and of similar efforts, must be, if persisted in, to weaken the credibility of the deterrent. For the renunciation of use they advocate does have consequences in a democratic society, and it is an illusion to believe otherwise. The bishops' effort must therefore increase the risk, however small the increase may be, of Soviet behavior that leads to the nuclear precipice. Is this increased risk the price of adhering to moral principle? One must doubt that it is. The bishops may not intend using nuclear weapons, but they do obviously intend that the Soviets remain uncertain about whether the weapons may not after all be used despite our firm renunciation of their use. Is this not, however, a case of entertaining a wrongful intent, only at one remove? If nuclear war and particularly deterrence raise novel and difficult moral issues, as the bishops insist, is it plausible to credit the solution of these issues by clever devices?

VII

The principal moral issue deterrence has raised from the outset seems no nearer resolution today. Why should this continue to trouble some? Why should it matter that the peace of deterrence ultimately rests on the threat and the intent to do evil? If the ends sought by deterrence are good, why should it not serve as the means to achieve that good, whatever the quality of the intention that may inform it?

One answer to these questions is simply that the intent to do evil is the precondition for doing evil. If one has an intent to do evil, the day may well come and likely will come, when evil will be done. And even if it is not done, the entertaining of an intent to do evil must have an effect on the character of those who harbor such intent. The price of holding an evil intent is the moral deformation of the holder, a deformation that will eventually manifest itself in other and perhaps quite unexpected ways.[22]

21. Compare Francis X. Winters, S.J., "The American Bishops on Deterrence—'Wise as Serpents: Innocent as Doves,'" *Science, Technology and Human Values* 8 (Summer 1983): 23–29, for the argument that the bishops successfully combined moral purity and political relevance.

22. We are also told that unless there are absolute limits on the means permitted the statesman, the door is opened to any and every evil. Why this must be so has never been quite clear. Even if there are no absolute limits on means, there are still means and means just as there is still evil and evil. If the issue that must be faced and somehow resolved is not whether one may do evil that good may come but, rather, how much evil one may do

In the case of deterrence, these considerations are invoked today as they were invoked a generation and more ago. Deterrence it was said then, as it is said now, cannot go on indefinitely. Eventually, it must break down and this probably sooner rather than later. In the early 1960s, as in the early 1980s, prophetic voices were heard to the effect that deterrence would not last out the decade. Yet the relationship of mutual deterrence between the Soviet Union and the United States is now well into its third decade. With one exception, the Cuban missile crisis, this relationship has not come close to the breaking point, and even with respect to the Cuban missile crisis it remains a matter of controversy how close the great nuclear powers came to the precipice.

The historical record of deterrence, such as it is, is not invoked to suggest that the future must prove to be as benign as the past. It may not be. Besides, everyone knows that the distinctive problem of the deterrence relationship is that one failure may prove quite fatal to the parties. But if the historical record cannot be viewed as a source of great comfort and reassurance, it also cannot be viewed as a source of despair. The deterrence relationship has been a learning experience on both sides. The degree of sophistication and—yes—wisdom in regard to deterrent structures is considerably greater in the 1980s than it was in the 1960s. Although deterrence rests today, as it rested yesterday, on the threat and intent to do evil, the prospects that evil will one day be done have not increased. If anything they appear to have modestly diminished.

Nor, after a generation, is the evidence of moral deformation very impressive. In the earlier years of the age of deterrence, one moralist plaintively asked: "How can a nation live with its conscience and know that it is preparing to kill twenty million children in another nation if the worst should come to the worst?"[23] The same kind of question is still asked today, though now it should be quite apparent that a nation can without difficulty live with its conscience even though its security is ultimately based on the threat to annihilate another nation. It can do so because the conscience of a nation is not as susceptible to moral deformation as is the conscience of individuals. What leads to the moral deformation of individuals need not do so in the case of nations. The cynic will tell us that the reason for this is that the moral sense of nations is congenitally deformed. Even if the cynic goes too far, there is little reason to question the considerable difference between the moral sensitivity of individuals and of nations.

---

that any good may come, it is not for this reason without significance. The assumption that once we accept that evil must be done in war any behavior is sanctioned is no more compelling than the assumption that if we only believe evil may never be done our behavior will thereby be restrained. Instead of restraining our behavior, the belief that evil may never be done may only strain our ingenuity. In the several attempts that have been made in the past generation to reconcile the requirements of a just war with the conduct of nuclear war we may find ample evidence of this.

23. John C. Bennett, "Moral Urgencies in the Nuclear Context," in *Nuclear Weapons and the Conflict of Conscience*, ed. John C. Bennett (New York: Charles Scribner's Sons, 1962), p. 101.

Then, too, the relatively limited effect of deterrence on the collective psyche must be attributed in part to the nature of deterrent structures and the manner in which the deterrence relationship and the threat that sustains it are generally perceived. It has long been noted that by comparison with an earlier age the establishment required by deterrent structures is relatively unobtrusive in its physical presence. This quality of relative unobtrusiveness in the daily life of society, when coupled with the almost incalculable effects of employing nuclear weapons, conferred an esoteric character on deterrence from the outset. It is this character that in large part accounts for the moral indifference attending the implications of deterrent strategies. It is the same character that also largely explains the marginal effects deterrent strategies appear to have had on the societies supporting them.

These considerations may be pushed too far. Clearly, in some sense it is the case that even for collectives the intent to do evil is the precondition for doing evil and that the price for holding an evil intent is the moral deformation of the holder. But the questions persist: In what sense is this the case? And what is the alternative to deterrence, with its threat to do evil? Surely it makes a difference for moral judgment if one assesses the prospects for deterrence breaking down as something close to infinitesimal and the debilitating effects of the deterrent threat as no more than marginal. In this case we are left with the argument that an act which would be unjust to commit ought never to be threatened, however remote the contingency that the act will ever be committed and whatever the consequences that may follow if the threat is abandoned (and, in contrast to the position taken by the bishops, the abandonment of the deterrent threat is persuasively conveyed to the adversary through measures of unilateral disarmament). When reduced to this pure form, the argument seems singularly unpersuasive. One may question whether the moralists themselves are consistently prepared to accept it.

Even if the prospect that deterrence might fail is acknowledged as a not too finite possibility, there remains the question, What is the alternative to deterrence with its threat to do evil? Obviously, the one clear alternative, in principle, is the abandonment of the means heretofore distinctive to a strategy of nuclear deterrence in particular *and* to statecraft in general. It is not unilateral nuclear abnegation that constitutes a viable alternative but pacifism as it is traditionally understood. To confront an adversary who remains in possession of nuclear weapons with conventional weapons is only to insure the prospect of eventual annihilation. George Kennan may now believe that nuclear weapons are useful only for frightening people with weak nerves. But the answer to Kennan is that the world is, and has always been, full of people with weak nerves. Besides, it scarcely requires weak nerves to fear nuclear weapons when they are possessed only by an adversary. All that is required is a sane respect for the most destructive force man has yet been able to extract from nature.

A JUST WAR ANALYSIS OF TWO TYPES OF DETERRENCE

Theodore Roszak

FOR some months the Kennedy Administration has been involved in an intensive reappraisal of American defense policy. As is usual in such matters, the discussion has been undertaken in great secrecy and the decisions to which it has led have been communicated to the public in obscure and subtle ways. Thanks to the efforts of two or three competent students of military affairs, the substance of the discussion has now been pieced together for the general public, mainly from the fragmentary information and scattered hints contained in congressional testimonies, presidential press conferences, the speeches of high-ranking officials, military procurements contracts, and budgetary allocations.[1]

The top-level discussion, which will have, or indeed *is* having, far-reaching effects on American foreign policy, has as its subject two military strategies: minimum deterrence and counterforce deterrence. The problem has not been that of making a choice between these two types of deterrence, but rather of deciding whether counterforce should be developed *in addition to* minimum deterrence. To all appearances, the decision has been affirmative. What follows is an analysis of these two types of deterrence from the point of view of the traditional Judeo-Christian doctrine of the Just War, some form of which, I should imagine, is accepted by all but the pacifists and chauvinists among us. We will try below to arrive at a somewhat stricter definition of the Just War.

At this point, suffice it to say that the doctrine treats war as a morally neutral political instrument, capable of being wielded in pursuit of a good cause as well as a wicked one—provided the act of violence meets certain limitations of means. In the words of St. Augustine:

What is blamed in war? . . . The desire of harming, the cruelty of avenging, an unruly and implacable animosity, the rage of rebellion, the lust of domination and the like—these are the things which are to be blamed in war: and often to punish these things wars are waged justly by the good against those who resist with violence.[2]

Hopefully this analysis will contribute to the discussion of Just War doctrine that Paul Ramsey develops in his recent book, *War and the Christian Conscience*.[3] In that study, which is among the most important contributions to Just War analysis to appear in recent years, Ramsey urges, on the basis of a closely reasoned ethical argument, that the United States cultivate its capacity for counterforces warfare. What I wish to suggest in this essay are some of the complications moral theology is confronted with by modern warfare, complications that even as astute a moralist as Ramsey overlooks. Perhaps these observations will lead to a more refined ethical calculus for dealing with the awful dilemmas of thermonuclear war than we presently possess.

The two types of deterrence can be, for the purposes of this discussion, briefly described. Minimum deterrence is a strictly retaliatory weapons sys-

Reprinted from *Ethics* 73 (January 1963): 100–109.

tem. It is designed to discourage a direct attack upon the United States, or some form of "extreme provocation"—say, Russian aggression against western Europe. The weapons of minimum deterrence may be relatively few in number and "small"—as hydrogen weapons go—in destructive capacity.[4] Above all, they must be invulnerable, either due to their mobility (as in the case of the Polaris submarine) or due to the "hardness" of the base in which they are located (as in the case of the Minuteman ICBM that is buried in a thick concrete silo). The object is to guarantee the survival of a large number of weapons after the United States has been bombarded by the enemy. This "strikeback" capacity is, of course, aimed mainly at the enemy's civilian population, for it will presumably not be fired until the enemy's weapons have been used and thus his bases are no longer important as targets.

The purpose of such retaliation would be "to eliminate the Soviet Union as a functioning political entity . . . to inflict as much damage on the Soviet Union as we could, in order to create a severe reconstruction problem for them."[5]

One might ask how much damage a "minimum" deterrent must be able to inflict in order to dissuade the enemy from attacking the United States. One strategist concludes that we must make the minimum quite high in order to play it safe.

Although we thought the prospect of losing 30 cities, for example, would deter any rational Soviet leadership, we might want to double this prospect, or even triple it, to make sure it was sufficient to deter a leader who was subject to certain moderate forms of irrationality such as fits of temper, . . . or just plain inability to comprehend the consequences of war.[6]

Counterforce deterrence, on the other hand, is based on a "first-strike" capacity aimed at the enemy's military bases, not his civilian population. The object is to cripple the enemy's capacity to make war in the event he should attack, or prepare to attack, an area vital to American interests, but not the United States directly. The weapons this strategy requires, such as the Titan ICBM and the Thor IRBM, can be housed in vulnerable quarters, because they are meant to initiate an attack, not absorb one. They must also exist in quantities sufficient to match enemy missiles in a ratio of two or three to one; for we cannot assume that every American missile will be accurate enough to destroy the Russian missile it has as its target. Counterforces weapons must also be extremely powerful, perhaps ten to thirty times as powerful as a Polaris or Minuteman missile, for they may be aimed at hardened enemy bases that are supposed to be invulnerable.

A counterforces first strike could not, of course, be expected to destroy all enemy weapons; some would be bound to get off the ground in time to retaliate for our attack. Therefore the threat of initiating such an attack would not be credible to the enemy, if he could be sure of striking back at us with intolerable destructiveness. For this reason, a well-developed civil defense program is essential to counterforce. So also would be an effective antimissile system. Both may appear to be purely defensive, but by the peculiar logic of deterrence they emerge as adjuncts of a first-strike capability. For by obstructing the enemy's ability to devastate our society, they would convince him that the initiation of thermonuclear war was a live option for us. Because counterforce seems to make even large-scale war a feasible alternative for us, one we could "afford," its supporters feel it would permit us to control "nibbling" aggression by threatening the guilty enemy with the very worst.

To be sure, counterforce is not always identified publicly as a first-strike strategy. Thus, Secretary of Defense McNamara has suggested that a counterforce capability might be used to "limit damage done to ourselves and our allies by knocking out the enemy's bases before he has had time to launch his *second* salvos."[7] (Not his *first* salvo, that is.) This is, of course, one way in which counterforce might be used, and would *have* to be used, if the United States suffered a surprise nuclear attack. Implicit in the system, however, is a first-strike capability and that would clearly be the most efficient way to use the weapons.

Each of these strategies has strong and influential supporters in American politics. Their advocates can muster many arguments that are superficially appealing to one's ethical sensitivities. But how well do their arguments meet the requirements of Just War limitations?

Here we must pause a moment, for there is bound to be disagreement among moralists as to the proper formulation of the Just War doctrine. Various thinkers produce more or fewer criteria any war must meet to be justified. E. I. Watkin, for example, lists seven provisions,[8] Ernest Lefever, three.[9] Paul Ramsey holds that the essential doctrine is expressed in the single provision of civilian immunity from *direct* attack. I think we can make do here with Ramsey's abbreviated version of the traditional doctrine, which forbids only those "acts of war which *directly* intend and

directly effect the death of non-combatants." These acts, Ramsey insists, "are to be classed morally with murder, and are never excusable." On the other hand, his restriction does not condemn actions that result in *incidental* damage to the innocent *"on however colossal a scale,* if there is proportionate grave reason for doing this."[10]

This does not strike me as an overly scrupulous interpretation of the doctrine. I suspect that those who are willing to dispense with noncombatant immunity have in reality rejected the moral analysis of war completely. They need read no further.

One more point. Note that we are assuming—let us say for the sake of the argument—that the justice of the *casus belli* lies wholly on the side of the United States, an assumption that ought to satisfy even the most patriotic. In other words, we are dealing with the entire problem as one of the morality of means. Let us do this in order to focus all our attention on only one provision of the doctrine.[11]

Working then with this one, seemingly irreducible, moral restriction, let us see how the two types of deterrence I have described affect noncombatant populations.

It is obvious that minimum deterrence fails wholly to qualify as a form of justified warfare. The threat it makes is made directly against civilian populations. It has nothing else to shoot at. In the words of Paul Ramsey:

> The readiness and preparation to kill the "innocent" partakes of the crime of actually doing so. . . . No ethics—least of all Christian ethics—gives [us] leave . . . to kill another man's children directly as a means of weakening that man's murderous intent or act.[12]

We can perhaps even strengthen Ramsey's protest to the extent of removing his quotation marks from the word "innocent." By common admission in the United States, the Russian people are without control over the foreign policy of their society. Their subjugation is exactly the crime we hold against the commissars of the Soviet Union. Should their leaders secretly decide upon and rapidly initiate war, the Russian people could not be more innocent of the crime. Yet they would be the intended victims of our anger. Worse still, that "anger" would be the cold, mechanical vengeance of a weapons system, an action inhuman and futile. A dead society would be retaliating from the grave, uselessly, and against millions of innocents.

At this point, the advocates of minimum deterrence might seek to complicate our analysis by holding out to us some rather tempting political advantages. For one thing, their strategy offers, by its threat of maximum destructiveness, the strongest imaginable guaranty that all-out war will not occur. And, if by some mistake or unaccountable act of madness, it should occur, it would not be the United States that started it. Though we do not agree to turn the other cheek, we do agree to accept the first blow before striking back. Furthermore, the system is stable. That is, there is very little chance of the deterrent weapons being fired by accident or miscalculation. This is because the delivery systems involved possess no hair-triggers. They need not fire on short order, in response to ambiguous radar signals. Instead, we can wait and see whether we are dealing with a false alarm or the real thing, knowing our weapons are invulnerable and will still be capable of striking back.

These are, at first sight, three very real advantages. But they become less

real once we realize that it is really only *thermo*nuclear war we are deterring with any effectiveness or agreeing never to initiate. Because the threatened destruction of minimum deterrence is hideously vast for both sides, it would not be credible to make that threat if the enemy were guilty only of "nibbling" or marginal aggression. Therefore, minimum deterrence must be supplemented by other, more plausible forms of warfare—perhaps even "tactical" atomic warfare. And "tactical" atomic weapons, it should be remembered, now include devices up to four times as destructive as the Hiroshima bomb.[13] Under minimum deterrence, engagement in, and even the initiation by the United States of, all forms of subthermonuclear war remain live options. And there is a real danger that any such war, especially one involving tactical atomic weapons, will escalate into all-out war.

Nonetheless, as deterrence strategies go, minimum deterrence does offer relatively more stability—to the point of being accepted by many strategists as a form of arms control and even a step toward disarmament. On this point there is widespread agreement among experts.[14] But the price of this stability comes, as we have seen, by way of a direct violation of civilian immunity. And Ramsey, for one, has flatly rejected this holding of enemy civilians hostage: "it would be immoral," Ramsey objects, "to 'stabilize' the deterrent and 'prevent' war by such means . . . *even if this succeeded.*"[15]

Such are the ethical objections the advocates of counterforce can raise against minimum deterrence, though, as we shall see, many of them are ready enough to accept the strategy as a supplement to their own.

Counterforce enjoys the obvious advantage of permitting us to claim that we plan not to attack civilian populations. Thus in a recent address (an address which makes it clear that our government has officially adopted this strategy) Secretary McNamara informs us that

the United States has come to the conclusion that to the extent feasible, basic military strategy in a possible general nuclear war should be approached in much the same way that more conventional military operations have been regarded in the past. That is to say, principal military objectives, in the event of a nuclear war stemming from a major attack on the alliance, should be the destruction of the enemy's military forces, not of his civilian population.[16]

Since the destruction of Russian missiles and bombers could only be made possible by striking first, this strategy does not permit us to promise we will never initiate thermonuclear war. Presumably, however, it does offer us the humanitarian consolation of exempting enemy civilians from attack, and no doubt this will appeal strongly to many moralists.

But let us look more closely at this strategy, for there is more here than is immediately apparent. To begin with, one should note the assumption that "military forces" and "civilian populations" can be meaningfully segregated from one another for destruction. Yet it is quite clear that this is impossible, since the Russians, as well as ourselves, have located many of their bomber and missile bases close to cities—this is especially true of anti-aircraft missile installations, such as the American Nike bases, which would be prime counterforce targets. Michael Brower quotes recent testimony to this effect by Admiral Burke:

Many of these missile bases are right close to our cities, right close. . . . So an attack on our major bases would necessarily destroy a great many cities and a great many of our people. When those missiles start coming over you do not know whether the intent of the enemy was to hit or not to hit a city if he hits it. The same thing is true with the Russian military installations.[17]

Moreover, as we have seen, the megatonnage of a counterforce attack is apt to be immensely higher than that of a minimum deterrence attack. Atlas and Titan missiles, for example, can carry several megatons of thermonuclear explosives, each megaton equaling fifty Hiroshima bombs. This means that the fallout from the exploded weapons is very much greater and thus the worldwide damage to civilians is bound to be immense.

All of which is another way of saying that, if not by intention, certainly by consequence, the new "no civilians" policy *is* quite as much an anticivilians policy as minimum deterrence. In terms of human suffering, the two strategies are equivalent. This should be clearly understood by all those who support counterforce warfare. The moral satisfaction to be taken in this strategy is not that it will spare civilian lives, but rather that the colossal human carnage the strategy may produce is "incidental" or "indirect." I can find no satisfaction in this myself.

Moreover, if I may digress for a moment, I am convinced that if a second provision of the traditional doctrine were introduced here, that of "proportion," counterforce warfare would be found sadly wanting. The rule of proportion simply states that no act of war is justified if the total moral and physical damage it produces is greater than would be incurred if the war were not fought.

Thus, one must ask if the "defense" of West Berlin or Formosa would be worth the world-wide devastation and suffering of the thermonuclear war to which either might now lead. It is legitimate, of course, to protest that our failure to meet such aggression might encourage further aggression. But this dilemma has another horn, not to be ignored: the weapons we intend to use in making war are apt to destroy far more than we salvage by large-scale resistance. And this is, of course, not an act of heroism at all. It is a pitiable example of the way in which modern Western man is stupidly victimized at the hands of his own uncontrolled lust for technological "progress."

We have agreed, however, to restrict ourselves to the single proviso that just warfare must spare the innocent only from *direct* attack. Seemingly, on the basis of this purely formal requirement, and eliminating any calculative ethical considerations, counterforce measures up to a Just War analysis.

Or does it? Let us go a little further. In his June 7 address, Secretary McNamara stated that in adopting our new strategy, "we are giving a possible opponent the strongest imaginable incentive to refrain from striking our own cities." And in an earlier address on February 17, he suggested that a counterforce strategy would permit us to "seek to terminate a war on favorable terms by using our forces as a bargaining weapon—by threatening further attack."

Such presentations of the strategy are bound to be appealing to many. They promise limited civilian losses and even the possibility of a favorable settlement of the war. Along these lines, General Frederic Smith, Air Force Vice Chief of Staff, has described counterforce as "an

effective capability to prosecute successfully a general war . . . a war-winning strategy."[18]

But how are these desirable ends to be achieved? The answer is not a pretty one, for what Secretary McNamara and General Smith are talking about is "nuclear blackmail" (as Herman Kahn calls it)—a particularly gruesome form of extortion. They are saying that once we have lamed the enemy's war-making capacity by initiating a large-scale attack on his military bases, we will be in a position to strike a bargain with him by threatening to use our preponderant nuclear power against his cities. By menacing Russian civilians in this way, we will at least ward off attack upon our cities by the prospect of retaliation; and at most, we may force the Russians to relinquish their conquests. As Glenn Snyder puts it:

The United States must be able to hold back sufficient strategic forces from the first-strike to threaten the Soviets with enough countercity damage on later strikes to persuade them to restore the territorial *status quo*.

Snyder is quite sanguine with respect to how much might be achieved by such forced bargaining. He suggests that our war aims might "include the toppling of the Soviet regime itself, and the establishment of democratic institutions in Russia and the Eastern European satellites."[19]

In short, *after its first strike, counterforce becomes morally identical with minimum deterrence*: it poses a direct and unambiguous threat to whatever remains of the enemy's civilian population. Moreover, it poses this threat not only for the sake of defending American civilians but for the purpose of prosecuting the war to a "successful" conclusion. In order to achieve "success," the strategy involves not only murdering enemy civilians, but deliberately sacrificing American civilians. To quote Snyder once again:

> The contemplation of the possibility of this positive gain, as well as the reduction of the Russian threat to the future security of the United States, might make the United States willing to suffer much greater losses in all-out war than if the only object of the fighting were to save Europe and Asia from Communist control.[20]

Thus, what is called counterforce warfare turns out to be war *directly* involving civilians, our own, as well as the enemy's. The strategy assumes that the United States can fight a thermonuclear war and win it ("prevail" is the word usually used). It accepts such war as a rational instrument of policy, perhaps capable even of achieving an unconditional victory. Those who support this strategy are apt to keep this aspect of the policy well masked. However, I know of no developed counterforce strategy that does not include "nuclear blackmail" as an essential element, and indeed as the instrument that supposedly makes "prevailance" possible.

There have been serious doubts raised as to whether counterforce can really achieve what it promises in the way of inhibiting enemy retaliation against our cities. We need not go into them here, except to note that whatever ethical strength the strategy seems to gain from its prospective protection of "one hundred million civilian lives" (Richard Fryklund's estimate) has been called quite cogently into question by competent critics.[21]

There are, however, two further objections to counterforce that should be presented. The first of these has to do with the instability of the system. Since, unlike minimum deterrence, counter-forces warfare is based on a vulnerable, first-strike capability, it requires a fine hair-trigger. If first-strike weapons are to do their job, they may have to be fired on the assumption that an enemy attack on the United States is imminent and inevitable. But what kind of evidence and how much evidence is necessary to prove that assumption? Realizing that World War III may follow from an ambiguous reading of electronic information or a mistaken interpretation of Russian intentions, to whom shall we intrust the decision that the evidence is sufficient? One should remember too that, from the enemy's point of view, a first-strike capability will look extremely menacing and hence provocative. In a tense moment he may be expected to consider a pre-emptive nuclear strike, thereby producing exactly the disaster we hope to deter.

The final objection to counterforce has to do with its adverse effect upon prospects for arms control and/or disarmament. Counterforce is an unstable system in design and in action a genocidal one. But to round things out, it makes impossible the very measures that might permit us to escape the dilemmas of thermonuclear war; in fact, it leads us in exactly the opposite direction. Counterforce commits us to an endless arms race in which we must outbuild the enemy two or three missiles to one. In addition, we must invent new surveillance systems to hunt out enemy installations, develop countersubmarine and antimissile defenses and in turn new means of penetrating enemy antimissile defenses, and finally, invest massively in civil defense.[22] All of this can only lead to a further deterioration of our strained relations with the Russians.

These last two points are important for the purposes of this analysis because they suggest that counterforce is very likely to generate war. The threat it makes is much more apt to be actualized than the more obviously immoral threat of minimum deterrence. Indeed, this is why its proponents are exactly those who ask us to think seriously about the entire course and consequences of thermonuclear war. Their literature abounds with phrases like "should deterrence fail," "in the event deterrence fails," "we can never have absolute confidence in deterrence," etc. They know how very probable the hideously possible is made by their strategy.[23]

Hopefully, the points raised here will contribute to a keener over-all ethical assessment of these two strategies. It is important to weigh each strategy with respect to its short- and long-range ethical advantages or disadvantages and to discriminate carefully between the theoretical and practical implications of each. Below I offer a brief chart which summarizes most of the ethical-political pros and cons of the two types of deterrence (Table 1).

It is my own conclusion that *neither* of the strategies meets the single, basic requirement of the Just War I have used in this analysis. Both are, either by explicit or implicit threat, in theory or in practice, civilian-killing forms of warfare. Should war break out, both strategies would be bound to threaten and to attack noncombatants *by direct intention;* both would slaughter them in genocidal proportions. While peace exists, both require us to live with that wicked intention in our hearts and to steel ourselves to it. If one were to introduce further criteria for gauging the justness of wars, the absolute im-

morality of these strategies would be even more apparent.

Now one final word. Throughout this analysis, I have dealt with the two types of deterrence pretty much as if one had to choose between them. But this is not so—or at least our govern-

TABLE 1

A JUST WAR ANALYSIS OF TWO
TYPES OF DETERRENCE

	Minimum Deterrence	Counterforce
1. Implied threat to civilians............	Basic	Secondary, but real (via nuclear blackmail)
2. Potential damage to civilians from heat and blast:		
Theory..........	Vast	Marginal
Practice..........	Vast	Very great
3. Potential damage to civilians from fallout	Great	Vast
4. Proneness to accident or miscalculation (instability)............	Low	High
5. Capacity to control (dampen) thermonuclear war:		
Theory..........	None	Very great
Practice..........	None	Highly questionable
6. Conduciveness to disarmament..........	Hopeful	None
7. Conduciveness to arms race..........	Slight	Complete

ment does not believe it is so. As I indicated earlier, the recent high-level reappraisal of our defense policy has led to the *inclusion* of counterforce in our national strategic planning, which had long ago embraced minimum deterrence. Those who officially advocate counterforce implicitly accept the continued existence and implications of minimum deterrence. In short, we are about to commit ourselves to *both* types of deterrence at once. This is what is called in official circles "the mix."[24]

For the purposes of ethical analysis one fact is paramount about mixed deterrence. By combining the two types of deterrence and confronting the enemy with one multipurpose, ill-defined, and thoroughly ambiguous weapons system, one loses whatever moral advantages either strategy offers by itself. That is, *the ethically negative aspects of one strategy will cancel out the possibly positive aspects of the other*. The "mix" will not be twice as good; it will be twice as bad. I think I have offered enough details about the two strategies

to permit the reader to convince himself that this is so.[25]

Thus, although many may disagree with the conclusion of this article, feeling that one or the other of the two strategies does meet the requirements of the Just War, it is difficult to see how anyone concerned with the moral analysis of war can support the present defense policy of our government. It would be interesting to know from those moralists—and from morally sensitive people in general—who see fit to withhold any criticism of that policy, what justification they feel exists for their continued silence.

STANFORD UNIVERSITY

NOTES

1. See esp. Michael Brower, "President Kennedy's Choice of a Nuclear Strategy," *Council for Correspondence Newsletter* (Supplement), June, 1962; Arthur Waskow, *The Limits of Strategy* (Garden City, N.Y.: Doubleday & Co., 1962); and Richard Fryklund, *100 Million Lives* (New York: Macmillan Co., 1962).

2. *Contra Faustum*, Book XII, chap. lxxiv.

3. Durham, N.C.: Duke University Press, 1961. For other recent contributions to the Just War doctrine see William Nagle (ed.), *Morality and Modern Warfare* (Baltimore: Helicon Press, 1960), and Robert Tucker, *The Just War* (Baltimore: Johns Hopkins Press, 1960).

4. The Polaris and Minuteman missiles, which are the staples of minimum deterrence, carry one-half megaton warheads; that is, an explosive power twenty-five times greater than the Hiroshima bomb.

5. Glenn Snyder, *Deterrence and Defense* (Princeton University Press, 1961), p. 69.

6. *Ibid.,* pp. 61–62.

7. Quoted in Brower, *op. cit.,* p. 12. (My italics.)

8. E. I. Watkin, "Unjustifiable War" in C. S. Thompson (ed.), *Morals and Missiles* (London: James Clarke & Co., 1959).

9. E. W. Lefever, "The Just War Doctrine," *Worldview*, October, 1961.

10. "The Case for Making 'Just War' Possible," in J. C. Bennett (ed.), *Nuclear Weapons and the Conflict of Conscience* (New York: Charles Scribner's Sons, 1962), pp. 148–49.

11. For a brief discussion of the manifold prob-

lems of defining the just cause in war see my "Dilemma of the Just War," *The Nation,* April 14, 1962.

12. *War and the Christian Conscience,* p. 310.

13. P. Noel-Baker, *The Arms Race* (New York: Oceana Publications, 1958), p. 147.

14. See, e.g., Arthur Hadley, *The Nation's Safety and Arms Control* (New York: Viking Press, 1961); see also S. R. Rivkin, "The Hobbled Weapon," *Bulletin of the Atomic Scientists,* May, 1962.

15. In Bennett (ed.), *op. cit.,* p. 163. But as we shall see, Ramsey's counterforce strategy makes impossible the arms control he also desires.

16. Address at the University of Michigan, reported in the *New York Times,* June 17, 1962.

17. *Op. cit.,* p. 17. In the United States, e.g., the government is building some 150 missile bases in the New England area alone.

18. The quotes from McNamara and Smith appear in *ibid.,* p. 20.

19. *Op. cit.,* p. 80.

20. *Ibid.* The second "United States" in this quote is not defined by Snyder. But in the mid-war situation he is describing, we can be sure he is not referring to the people of the United States generally or in Congress asembled. Who is then "willing" to do the greater suffering he speaks of? We are left to wonder.

21. See Waskow, *op. cit.,* pp. 22–30.

22. Glenn Snyder as much as admits that the quest for a first-strike capability, as tension-producing as it will be, will fail (see *op. cit.,* pp. 82–84).

23. The foremost proponent of counterforce is, of course, the former Air Force strategist, Herman Kahn, author of *On Thermonuclear War* (Princeton, N.J.: Princeton University Press, 1961). His most recent book is *Thinking about the Unthinkable* (New York: Horizon Press, 1962).

24. For an interesting account of the way in which military policies are formulated in all their dizzying confusion, see Eric Larrabee, "The Politics of Strategy," *Bulletin of the Atomic Scientists*, March, 1962; see also Brower's analysis of "why minimum deterrence [alone] wasn't adopted" (*op. cit.*, p. 32).

25. If the reader needs help in working out this little exercise, I refer him to Waskow, *op. cit.*, pp. 45–55.

A Contractarian Defense of Nuclear Deterrence*

Christopher W. Morris

It is widely believed that killing the innocent is morally wrong. A widely accepted moral principle is, It is wrong to kill the innocent. Yet this is precisely what we threaten to do in the event of an enemy nuclear attack. This is an essential part of nuclear deterrence. Is nuclear deterrence then immoral? Many in the peace movement—as well as some in the Reagan administration—appear to think so.

The principle prohibiting killing the innocent as stated above is implausible, as it does not make allowances for accidental and unintended killings. Thus many moral philosophers distinguish between "direct" and "indirect" killings and argue that indirect killings are not always wrong. One very influential way of drawing the relevant distinctions is the traditional "doctrine of double effect." According to this doctrine, only acts of direct killing are morally prohibited; acts of indirect killing are morally permissible. According to the doctrine, an act of killing is indirect and morally permissible if and only if

1) the act in itself is not impermissible,
2) the bad effect of the act is not the means to the good effect,
3) the good but not the bad effect is intended, and
4) the good effect is proportional to (i.e., not outweighed by) the bad effect.[1]

* Earlier versions of this essay were presented at California State University, Los Angeles, at the Colloquium on Philosophy, Morality, and Nuclear Public Policy at the University of Dayton, at the meeting of the American Philosophical Association, Pacific Division, March 22–24, 1984, Long Beach, California, and at the Aspen Conference on the Ethics of Nuclear Deterrence and Disarmament, sponsored by the Ford Foundation and the Exxon Educational Foundation; I am grateful to discussants for helpful comments and criticisms. I am especially indebted to Peter Danielson, Gerald Dworkin, David Gauthier, Robert Goodin, David Gordon, Gregory Kavka, Donald C. Lee, Steven Miller, Howard Sobel, Wayne Sumner, Manuel Velasquez, Alan Vick, and Richard Werner for comments on various drafts. A shortened and less technical version of this article will appear as "The Ethics of Nuclear Deterrence: A Contractarian Account," in *Ethics, Theory and Practice*, ed. Manuel Velasquez and Cynthia C. Rostankowski (Englewood Cliffs, N.J.: Prentice-Hall, Inc., 1985), pp. 203–13.

1. See G. E. M. Anscombe, "War and Murder," in *Collected Philosophical Papers* (Minneapolis: University of Minnesota Press, 1981), vol. 3, pp. 51–61; Philippa Foot, "The Problem of Abortion and the Doctrine of Double Effect," in *Virtues and Vices* (Berkeley and

Killing some civilians while bombing an enemy military installation might
thus be permissible if the bad effect (killing the civilians) is neither intended
nor the means to the good effect (destroying the installation) and if, say,
the number of lives saved by the bombings is greater than the number
of civilian casualties. The doctrine would thus justify killings where the
deaths are unintended side effects of permissible acts.

Appeal to the doctrine of double effect may not, however, help the
defender of nuclear deterrence. For the innocent slaughtered by nuclear
retaliation surely would not be killed indirectly in the relevant sense.
Consider "countervalue" retaliation, the nuclear targeting of enemy centers
of population. Such bombings clearly would involve acts of direct killing.
For conditions 2 and 3 would not be satisfied: the bad effect (killing
massive numbers of innocent civilians) would be both intended and a
means to the good effect (making good on a threat, "punishing" enemy
aggression, deterring future aggression, or whatever).

Some therefore counsel that we use only "counterforce" strategies,
aiming our missiles at military targets. However, given the huge numbers
of Soviet casualties to be expected at present from counterforce retaliatory
strikes,[2] condition 4 surely is not satisfied: counting lives equally, the
good effect surely is outweighed by the bad.

Lest anyone believe that counterforce strategies are nonetheless more
appealing morally, let us note how destabilizing they are, especially given
recent developments in weapons technology and the current climate of
distrust. Accurate missiles aimed at enemy missiles for purposes of defense
may be used for offensive first strikes as well as for retaliatory second
strikes. Part of the instability of our current situation might be attributed
to the claims of each party that the other possesses or is acquiring offensive
weapons. The present U.S. administration, for instance, accuses the Soviet
Union of seeking to build up what is called a "first strike capacity," that
is, the capacity to destroy much of the adversary's (land-based) nuclear
force in a swift blow. The Soviet leaders point out that the United States
(and NATO) refuse to renounce first strikes. A counterforce strategy,
then, even if intended for retaliatory use only, may appear offensive to
a suspicious (but rational) adversary.

Countervalue strategies (with limited counterforce capacities), by
contrast, when bilaterally adopted, render first strikes extremely improbable. Should one side attack, the other's nuclear forces would be
able to retaliate. Such strategies, when bilateral, are inherently stabilizing.
Further, they greatly decrease the chances of an "accidental" nuclear

Los Angeles: University of California Press, 1978), pp. 19–32; L. W. Sumner, *Abortion and
Moral Theory* (Princeton, N.J.: Princeton University Press, 1981), pp. 115ff.; Michael Walzer,
Just and Unjust Wars (New York: Basic Books, 1977), pp. 152ff. See also Alan Donagan,
The Theory of Morality (Chicago: University of Chicago Press, 1977), pp. 157ff.
    2. Ground Zero, *Nuclear War: What's in It for You?* (New York: Pocket Books, 1982),
pp. 126ff.; Albert Carnesale et al., *Living with Nuclear Weapons* (New York: Bantam Books,
1983), pp. 117–18.

conflict since a retaliatory strike, in the unlikely case one would be provoked, would not have to be "launched on warning," as would a response to a counterforce attack. So countervalue strategies (with limited counterforce capacities) may be preferable to counterforce strategies insofar as we are concerned with reducing the likelihood of nuclear conflict.[3]

In any case, both deterrent strategies, as well as mixed strategies, involve threatening to kill directly massive numbers of innocents. Such acts of killing could not be justified by the doctrine of double effect.

Threatening to kill, however, is not the same as actually killing. Perhaps we are justified in threatening nuclear retaliation, as long as we do not intend to carry out our threat (and as long as we do not in fact carry it out). That is, perhaps the morally appropriate deterrent strategy is bluffing. Let us say that a "sincere threat" to do x (if C) carries with it an intention to do x (if C) and that an "insincere threat" lacks such an intention. Then sincerely threatening nuclear retaliation would not be justified but insincerely threatening might be. Naturally, we should not expect a threat of the latter sort to be credible once our moral reluctance became known to our adversaries. The effectiveness of such a bluff depends on our adversaries' belief that we would (or might) launch a retaliatory second strike in the event of nuclear attack. Such a policy depends on deception or at least dissimulation for its effectiveness, and this may be impossible to achieve in an open society. Moreover, it should be noted that such a policy is inconsistent with the values of such a society. Finally,

---

3. For a recent defense of Mutual Assured Destruction (MAD), see Robert J. Art, "Nuclear Strategy: The Search for the Middle Road," in this volume. I have relied on Thomas Schelling's writings for much of my understanding of classical notions of nuclear deterrence (see his *Strategy of Conflict* [New York: Oxford University Press, 1960]). For a historical account of deterrence, see Lawrence Freedman, *The Evolution of Nuclear Strategy* (New York: St. Martin's Press, 1983); and for a game-theoretical account, see Alan Vick, "Some Thoughts on Deterrence," Rand Paper P-6916 (Rand Corp., Santa Monica, Calif., October 1983). The stability of MAD, however, requires that both superpowers possess invulnerable retaliatory systems. Recent developments in weapons technology may make that a thing of the past. For an accessible account of some of these developments, see James Meacham, "Another Age? The Technology of Nuclear Weapons: A Survey," *Economist* (September 1, 1984). For a discussion of the moral implications of these developments, see Albert Wohlstetter, "Bishops, Statesmen, and Other Strategists on the Bombing of the Innocent," *Commentary* 75 (1983): 15–35. In addition to preventing a nuclear conflict between the superpowers, there are other concerns that we might have, for instance, forestalling a Soviet attack on Western Europe. "Extended deterrence" may require limited counterforce capabilities (including some sort of "flexible response"), as a MAD threat may not have sufficient credibility during a crisis as Warsaw bloc tanks prepare to roll into West Germany. The general problem here is that we seek (1) to reduce the likelihood of (*a*) nuclear and (*b*) nonnuclear war as well as (2) to reduce the costs (human and other) should war occur. (Also, we seek [3] to reduce the peacetime costs of defense.) But striving toward 2—e.g., by developing our capacity for "war fighting"—may lead us further from 1. Thus the cycles in strategic debates. These issues are complicated, and I shall leave them to military strategists and defense planners. My concern is to provide a general defense of nuclear deterrence, including MAD. Should some counterforce strategy prove more effective at forestalling nuclear as well as conventional conflict between the superpowers, my argument should not be affected.

it seems incredible that the most effective means of national defense should depend on deception. So I do not think that this approach will salvage our deterrence practices.[4]

A variant on this suggestion is the idea that we should retain some nuclear weapons while refraining from threatening, sincerely or insincerely, to use them. It might be argued that our mere possession of them would suffice to deter Soviet nuclear attack even if we did not explicitly threaten to retaliate.[5] For instance, Israel (it is widely believed) possesses some nuclear weapons. It need not explicitly threaten its adversaries; mere possession of such weapons may be sufficient deterrent against a repetition of 1973.

Note that this suggestion depends for its effectiveness on the Soviets' belief that we might retaliate in the event of attack. By retaining these weapons would we not intend that the Soviets come to believe this? Further, this approach, like the last, requires deception and is thus vulnerable to some of the objections made above. It is possible that this strategy might be even less workable than the last. How is it to be implemented? Are soldiers to be trained to maintain and fire the weapons? That would blur the distinction between the mere possession of and the insincere threat to use nuclear weapons. Are the weapons merely to be stored in strategic depots, without trained personnel to maintain them for use? It is hardly credible that this would amount to much of a deterrent.[6]

Faced with the conclusion that threatening to use nuclear weapons is morally unjustifiable, some moral theorists counsel unilateral nuclear disarmament. I cannot argue here against this alternative. However, I should note that I find it unacceptable for a number of reasons. The claims of some proponents of unilateral nuclear disarmament, that the dangers of Soviet domination or Soviet nuclear blackmail are small, simply lack credibility. And many cases for unilateral nuclear disarmament depend on such a claim. To disarm unilaterally would be to make ourselves vulnerable to domination and exploitation. Note that to date nuclear weapons have only been used against a nation that did not possess any. It is not to attribute especially malevolent motives to Soviet leaders to

4. "Deterrence is not, and cannot be, bluff," according to the Scowcroft Commission (see *Report of the President's Commission on Strategic Forces* [Washington, D.C.: Government Printing Office, April 1983], pp. 2–3). Some critics have argued that many failures of American foreign policy are due to the propensity of our adversaries to call our bluff (see Harry G. Summers, Jr., "Critics Say Pentagon Is Dovish," *Los Angeles Times* [May 6, 1984]). In any case, it may simply not be possible to set up institutions none of the members of which possessed the relevant intention (see Jeff McMahan, "Deterrence and Deontology," in this volume).

5. See Paul Ramsey, *The Just War* (New York: Charles Scribner's Sons, 1968), pp. 253–58. I also owe this suggestion to Gerald Dworkin.

6. Adapting a remark Thomas Schelling makes about impetuosity, irrationality, and nuclear retaliation, we might say that we ought to get something a little less idiosyncratic for three hundred billion dollars a year of defense expenditure (see *Arms and Influence* [New Haven, Conn.: Yale University Press, 1966], pp. 39–40).

believe that they would be willing to do as we did in Hiroshima and Nagasaki.[7]

Suppose then that unilateral nuclear disarmament is unacceptable; how is it possible to justify nuclear deterrence? Nuclear deterrence involves threatening to kill directly massive numbers of innocents in the event of an enemy nuclear attack, an act not justified by the traditional doctrine of double effect. Is nuclear deterrence then morally impermissible? I shall argue that it is not impermissible.

Let us now state clearly the moral principle and notions involved in this issue. Nuclear deterrence involves threatening to kill directly massive numbers of innocents. Directly killing the innocent is thought to be morally wrong. The relevant moral principle would thus seem to be:

It is wrong directly to kill innocent human persons,

where the technical terms should be understood as follows. An act of "direct" killing is one that is not an act of indirect killing as defined by the doctrine of double effect. A "person" is any creature that possesses moral standing; any creature that is owed (some) moral consideration has (some) moral standing. An "innocent" person is someone who is not threatening another.[8] This principle—let us call it P—prohibits the killing of nonthreatening human persons except in those cases of indirect or unintentional killing justified by the doctrine of double effect.

According to the natural law tradition, killing the innocent directly is absolutely wrong, that is, impermissible whatever the consequences.[9] But I reject the interpretation of P as absolute. Unless we engage in what

7. See Douglas Lackey, "Missiles and Morals: A Utilitarian Look at Nuclear Deterrence," *Philosophy & Public Affairs* 11 (1982): 189–231; Russell Hardin, "Unilateral versus Mutual Disarmament," Gregory S. Kavka, "Doubts about Unilateral Nuclear Disarmament," and Douglas Lackey, "Disarmament Revisited: A Reply to Kavka and Hardin," *Philosophy & Public Affairs* 12 (1983): 236–54, 255–60, 261–65. See also Jeff McMahan, "Nuclear Blackmail," in *Dangers of Nuclear Deterrence*, ed. N. Blake and K. Pole (London: Routledge & Kegan Paul, 1983), pp. 94–111. Many defenses of unilateral nuclear disarmament are conditional on a simultaneous buildup of conventional military forces to deter conventional (and nuclear) attack. But citizens of the Western alliance are notoriously unwilling to shoulder the costs of such a rearmament program, especially were it to include military conscription. It is often forgotten that nuclear weapons are inexpensive by comparison to conventional weapons and forces.

8. Sometimes this is called the "causal" sense of innocence, to be contrasted with the "moral" or "juridical" sense, according to which innocence is equivalent to absence of guilt. See Anscombe, p. 53; Sumner, pp. 109–11; Jeffrie G. Murphy, "The Killing of the Innocent," *Monist* 57 (1983): 527–36. See also George I. Mavrodes, "Conventions and the Morality of War," *Philosophy & Public Affairs* 4 (1975): 117–31; and Robert K. Fullinwider, "War and Innocence," *Philosophy & Public Affairs* 5 (1975): 90–97. Judith Thomson's well-known argument in "In Defense of Abortion," *Philosophy & Public Affairs* 1 (1971): 47–66, can be restated using the causal sense of "innocence."

9. See G. E. M. Anscombe, "Modern Moral Philosophy," in *Collected Philosophical Papers*, vol. 3, pp. 26–42; Alan Gewirth, "Are There Any Absolute Rights?" in *Human Rights* (Chicago: University of Chicago Press, 1982), pp. 218–33. See also Murphy; and Donagan; as well as Anscombe, "War and Murder."

Elizabeth Anscombe has called "double-thinking about double effect,"[10] interpreting P as absolute commits us to refrain from using (or threatening to use) nuclear weapons. Given what I have said above, so interpreting the principle would commit us to bluffing or, more likely, to unilateral nuclear disarmament, and that, I am assuming, is unacceptable in the present circumstances.[11]

Further, insofar as the practice of nuclear deterrence actually reduces the chance of nuclear domination and conflict, absolutist interpretations of P do not enable us to take advantage of these means of averting nuclear war. Any ethical tradition that does base the moral worth of actions largely (though not exclusively) on their consequences will find such implications of absolutist interpretations of P grounds for rejecting these traditions. Given that some deterrent strategies reduce considerably the likelihood of nuclear conflict[12] and that absolutist interpretations of P commit us to rejecting such strategies, then surely that is a (partial) reason for rejecting such traditions.[13]

I reject, then, the absolutist interpretation of P. Insofar as such an interpretation of P commits one to unilateral disarmament or a total abandonment of nuclear deterrence, it is unacceptable. Natural law (and natural rights) moral theories often interpret P as absolute, so my rejection of this interpretation of the principle commits me to rejecting (most) such theories.

Let us note the nature of my rejection of absolutist natural law (and natural rights) ethics. Natural law (and natural rights) theories, as I understand them, suppose that we have certain basic natural duties (and natural rights) from which our moral obligations flow. Such moral theories generally evaluate agents not by (exclusive) attention to the consequences

10. The phrase is from Anscombe, "War and Murder," p. 58.

11. The American Catholic bishops would appear to disagree, given their conditional justification of some forms of deterrence. However, I cannot find in their text any argument in support of this claim—which is not surprising, given their natural law premises. (See National Conference of Catholic Bishops, *The Challenge of Peace* [Washington, D.C.: United States Catholic Conference, 1983], esp. pp. 44–62.) William Shaw has recently argued that "deontologists" can justify nuclear deterrence with the use of a threat principle which he constructs. He argues that the threat to retaliate need not be immoral while assuming that the act of retaliation would be. The deterrent threat he thus justifies, however, should have the same efficacy as a bluff. (See "Nuclear Deterrence and Deontology," *Ethics* 94 [1984]: 248–60.)

12. *Contra* Lackey, "Missiles and Morals." See Gregory S. Kavka, "Deterrence, Utility, and Rational Choice," *Theory & Decision* 12 (1980): 41–60, or just about any of the essays in this volume written by political scientists or defense planners.

13. William Shaw notes, "Many will simply see the endorsement of unilateral disarmament as a *reductio* of the absolutist position" (p. 259). Note that, if it is thought that the doctrine of double effect does not rule out counterforce retaliation, then the absolutist interpretation of P may commit us to deploying increasingly accurate and sophisticated nuclear weapons and to adopting counterforce deterrent strategies (see Wohlstetter). Defenders of the absolutist interpretation of P might also welcome President Reagan's "Strategic Defense Initiative" (or "Star Wars" proposal) (see Colin S. Gray, "Strategic Defenses, Deterrence, and the Prospects for Peace," in this volume; and Gregory S. Kavka, "Space War Ethics," in this volume).

of their actions but by their degree of moral responsibility for these actions. Should our acts lead to the death of innocent people, we are morally culpable, according to these traditions, only to the degree that we are morally responsible for the consequences, such responsibility being determined by reference to our basic moral duties (and the rights of others). That nuclear conflict or nuclear blackmail are made more likely by holding P to be absolute would not in itself make us morally responsible, in this view, for the harm unless we also violate some basic duty (or right). Thus my criticisms of these traditions are external.

Does my rejection of "absolutism," the position that P is absolute, commit me to interpreting P as defeasible? A moral principle is defeasible when it may be overridden in certain circumstances by certain other moral considerations. Thus we might say that P is defeasible and may be overridden in contexts of nuclear war.

Utilitarian interpretations of P are likely to suggest themselves to contemporary readers at this point. Utilitarianism is the moral theory that supposes that all our duties are derived from the principle, Maximize the total quantity of the good, where the good is identified with happiness, well-being, or utility. According to such a view, all our duties are defeasible since whatever may maximize aggregate happiness in one situation may very well not do so in another. This and other features of the theory are, of course, familiar to students of contemporary ethical theory.

Utilitarian interpretations of P are but one way of rendering the principle defeasible; other moral theories may do this as well. But understanding the inappropriateness of utilitarian accounts helps to set the stage for the interpretation of P that I wish to defend.

Utilitarianism would have us consider in our moral deliberations the welfare of all individuals that could be affected by our actions. Further, not only are we to do this, but we are also to count their well-being equally with ours ("each to count as one"). Utilitarianism has often been criticized as too "flexible" a moral theory; depending on the circumstances, it justifies too much that we think wrong. It is not always clear that such criticisms are correct, but they seem beside the point here. What is striking about utilitarianism applied to matters of conflict and war is not how flexible but how demanding a theory it is. It requires us to count our adversary's welfare equally with our own.

Sharing and extraordinary self-sacrifice are often to be found among family and friends or in small communities. Utilitarianism would have us guide our conduct toward all people (and sentient creatures) by such ideals. Countless critics have remarked on the inappropriateness of founding justice on such values, the social virtue of individuals who do not necessarily, to use Rawls's phrase, take an interest in each other's interests. This much is true. What needs to be emphasized is the irrationality of utilitarianism in contexts of major or total conflict, such as nuclear war. While most wars are not zero sum—that is, both sides have some interests in common—it is doubtful that any argument could be given for the rationality of accepting the principle of utility in such situations, at least if we understand rationality in the usual way, as (allowing but) not requiring total self-sacrifice.[14] The interests in conflict in war may be too important to be constrained or abandoned in the manner required by utilitarianism. It is one thing to commit oneself to the principle of utility when one anticipates that others will do so and that the result will be mutually beneficial. It is completely different to commit oneself to the principle of utility in contexts of war.

There is another criticism that may be made of the utilitarian as well as of other defeasible interpretations of P, which leads us naturally to a contractarian account of P. It might be argued that those extreme circumstances in which P might justifiably be overridden, according to utilitarianism (or some other theory), would be circumstances in which one would be tempted to say that all principles of justice had been suspended. Thus in such circumstances P would not be defeasible; it (and other principles of justice) would simply cease to be requirements of morality.

Normally, in moral theory, it is thought that 'absolute' and 'defeasible' are contradictories; that is, it is assumed that a principle is absolute if and only if it is not defeasible. However, 'defeasible' and 'absolute' may merely be contraries. I shall argue that, even though P is not absolute, it is not defeasible, for there may not be any moral considerations that could override P.

I wish to defend the position that, contrary to the views criticized above, P is neither absolute nor defeasible. I shall argue that, in certain circumstances where respecting P would be irrational, P (and other principles of justice)[15] no longer is (are) rationally binding. Thus in such circumstances directly killing the innocent would not be unjust because nothing would be unjust.[16] Such circumstances, which I shall call "Hobbesian states of nature," are, I believe, exceedingly rare in the modern world, the behavior of nation-states to the contrary. However, an enemy nuclear

---

14. The notion of rationality I am using here is basically that widely used in the social sciences, especially in economics and game theory, where (roughly) a person is rational insofar as she maximizes the satisfaction of her preferences. I would want, however, to amend this conception in the manner suggested by David Gauthier, "Reason and Maximization," *Canadian Journal of Philosophy* 4 (1975): 411–33, so as to handle certain types of problems of strategic interaction (namely, Prisoner's Dilemmas, for readers familiar with these issues). See David Gauthier, "Deterrence, Maximization, and Rationality," in this volume; and Peter Danielson, "Rationality and Ultimate Commitment" (York University, 1984, typescript), for amendments necessary for the rationality of deterrence. (Game theorists unfamiliar with moral philosophy might find it useful to think of the contractarian account of justice developed in this essay as a rational choice theory of ethics.)

15. My concern in this essay is with justice. I am assuming that what is true of justice need not be true of the other virtues. For instance, the virtue of benevolence may compel in situations where justice no longer binds. On the differences between justice and some other virtues, see Foot, *Virtues and Vices;* and John Rawls, *A Theory of Justice* (Cambridge, Mass.: Harvard University Press, 1971), esp. pp. 3–17.

16. The 'nothing' will be qualified later, with regard to uninvolved third parties; see also n. 39 below.

attack would bring about such circumstances, or I so shall argue. Therefore massive nuclear retaliation would not, in those circumstances, be unjust. P, on this account, would not be absolute, for it would not be the case that it would be wrong to do what P prohibits, regardless of the consequences. But neither would P be defeasible, I shall claim, for there would be no moral considerations that could override the principle.

Principle P is a "basic" moral principle, I will assume. A moral principle is basic in some theory if it is not derivable from any other moral principle in that theory. A moral principle grounded only on nonmoral principles or propositions would be basic. For instance, moral principles such as, One ought to keep one's promises, or, It is wrong to steal, are not usually considered basic, as they are, in most moral theories, derived from some prior moral principle and hence defeasible. Natural duty and natural rights theories, respectively, take certain duties and rights to be basic. For such theories all other moral notions and principles are derived from the basic duties and rights. This does not entail that such duties and rights are absolute, though many such theories claim this as well. It does entail that a defeasible but basic duty or right (or principle) is not overrideable except by another basic duty or right (or principle), for the overriding considerations cannot have their source in a less basic duty or right. Thus I shall say that P is basic and derived from no other moral principle.

Principle P is not absolute. We have rejected natural law and natural rights interpretations. However, this does not entail that P is defeasible in the usual sense, for P may not be justifiably overridden by other moral considerations. If P is basic, it is likely that there are no overriding moral considerations since we would expect that these would themselves be derived from basic principles.[17] What I shall argue is that some of the circumstances in which utilitarians are likely to say that P is justifiably overridden are circumstances in which justice has been dissolved.

Faced with the apparent choice between interpreting P as absolute (as recommended by many natural law and natural rights theories) and the demand to accord equal weight to the welfare of the enemy (as recommended by utilitarianism), some counsel retreat into moral nihilism: in war, anything goes, nothing is prohibited. In the social sciences and in politics, such a position often goes under the name "realism."[18]

Such talk is dubious as well as dangerous. For one, it contradicts seemingly entrenched patterns of ordinary discourse.[19] In war, as well as other times, most people attempt to justify their actions by reference to moral standards. It is extremely difficult to talk about war without

17. The discussion of basic principles and of overriding moral considerations given here is, needless to say, a mere sketch.

18. For some recent accounts and criticisms, see Walzer; and Charles R. Beitz, *Political Theory and International Relations* (Princeton, N.J.: Princeton University Press, 1979). Different species of "realism" are represented by some of the political scientists' essays in this volume.

19. Essentially this is Walzer's argument.

using moral language. Even appeals to "tough-minded" slogans such as "war is hell" do not usually allow us to dispense with moral categories.[20]

Equally important, however, is the danger of destabilization that comes from nihilism in these contexts. Nihilism may reinforce mutual suspicion. Recall my account of our current situation. The United States and the Soviet Union greatly distrust each other, and each appears to believe that the other is acquiring or already possesses offensive nuclear weapons. Should either party come to believe, or be reinforced in its belief, that the other thinks that nothing is forbidden, then that party could with difficulty trust the other to refrain from seeking to acquire first strike advantage. Assurance that the other is capable and willing to impose constraints on his or her behavior is crucial to stabilization. Since abstention from first strike advantage is stabilizing, retreat to nihilism may have a significant destabilizing effect. Suspicion that the other seeks to use allegedly defensive weapons for offensive, first strike ends can only be enhanced by skepticism.

Nonetheless, the retreat to nihilism has an important grain of truth to it. And this is the truth expressed in Thomas Hobbes's account of the relations between nations. According to Hobbes, nations find themselves in a state of nature in which there are no binding moral obligations. Relations between nations thus are relations of power, unconstrained by moral rules. Relations between individuals in a state of nature are also mere relations of power, unconstrained by moral considerations. The difference for Hobbes is that individuals have the possibility of establishing an enforcer or sovereign and thus of escaping from their plight. No such escape from the world of nations seemed possible to Hobbes.[21]

Now Hobbes's account here may be defective. It may be possible to accept his analysis of the problem facing rational individuals in such a state of nature without accepting his solution of absolute and unconstrained sovereignty, that is, without accepting his view that only the establishment of an all-powerful and indivisible ruler can end the state of nature. These issues cannot be explored here, but they are familiar to students of Hobbesian thought.[22]

Further, it is not clear that Hobbes's application of his basic analysis of international relations must be accepted.[23] I shall not pronounce on the accuracy of his account of the relations between nations in the seventeenth century. Nations today, however, are interdependent in ways which relevantly transform their situations.[24]

20. On the uses of General Sherman's phrase by some of the defenses of the atomic bombings of Hiroshima and Nagasaki, see Walzer, p. 265.
21. See Thomas Hobbes, *Leviathan* (1651), ed. C. B. Macpherson (Harmondsworth: Penguin Books, 1968), esp. chap. 13.
22. See, e.g., David Gauthier, *The Logic of Leviathan* (Oxford: Oxford University Press, 1969), esp. chap. 4, sec. 4.
23. See H. L. A. Hart, *The Concept of Law* (Oxford: Oxford University Press, 1961), pp. 208–31.
24. See Beitz, although I do not endorse his entire account.

According to contractarian ethicists, relations of justice obtain only between parties that find themselves in certain situations. Following John Rawls, we may call these the "circumstances of justice."[25] According to this tradition, relations of justice obtain only between parties that are interdependent in certain ways. Individuals in the circumstances of justice are roughly equal in physical and mental powers and thus unable to dominate one another and vulnerable to attack; resources are moderately scarce (relative to needs and wants); needs and wants, although in conflict to some degree, are such as to allow for mutually beneficial interaction. The most important condition here for our purposes is that of mutual advantage: individuals find themselves in the circumstances of justice only if there exists the possibility of mutually beneficial interaction. In the absence of possible mutual advantage, in this view, there is no place for justice as individuals have no (nonmoral) reason to constrain their self-interested activity.

"Cooperative interaction," I shall say, is mutually beneficial interaction made possible by constraints on self-interested behavior. Between interdependent nations today there appears to be room for (at least some) mutually advantageous interaction. Thus, we have one of the most important conditions for cooperative interaction. In such a situation, assuming the remaining circumstances of justice to obtain, norms of cooperation such as Hobbes's first few "laws of nature" are rationally binding.[26] If we do not follow Hobbes in requiring an absolute (international) sovereign but instead require only some weaker system of enforcement (see the next paragraph below), then it would seem that certain norms of cooperation, for example, "seek Peace, and follow it," are morally binding on nations in situations of interdependence.[27]

Such norms, exemplified by Hobbes's laws of nature, morally bind only insofar as others are willing to abide by them.[28] The problem in international contexts, of course, is to obtain assurances that others are willing to abide by norms of cooperation. Between nations there is no Leviathan or absolute sovereign capable of impartial enforcement of agreements. Some system of enforcement, however, is necessary if cooperation in international contexts is to be rational.

25. See David Hume, *Enquiry Concerning the Principles of Morals* (1777), in *Enquiries*, 3d ed., rev. by P. H. Niddich (Oxford: Oxford University Press, 1977), sec. 3; and Rawls, pp. 126ff.

26. The first few laws require that one pursue peace, be willing to give up an equal amount of natural liberty on the condition others do so as well, and keep agreements. Hobbes believed that the laws of nature are summarized in the counsel, "Do not that to another, which thou wouldest not have done to thy selfe" (chap. 15, p. 214; see generally chaps. 14, 15).

27. Hobbes, chap. 14, p. 190.

28. " . . . be willing when others are too . . ." (Hobbes, chap. 14, p. 190). (Supposing the Hobbesian state of nature to be an n-person Prisoner's Dilemma, then acceptance of the laws of nature might be thought to transform the situation into an Assurance Game. The sovereign is then required to stabilize the latter.)

It may be a mistake to think that the requisite enforcement mechanism in international contexts is a supranational state, as "realists" generally suppose. In many relations between individuals, where police protection is unavailable, norms of cooperation are often adequately enforced by the parties themselves. The threat to retaliate can, in many situations, provide adequate enforcement. So with international contexts, we may suppose that threats to retaliate can provide the requisite enforcement mechanism. If such threats are morally permissible, then we need not search for an international sovereign to ensure international cooperation.

We want, I am assuming, to make nuclear as well as nonnuclear conflict between the superpowers extremely unlikely (extended deterrence). What strategies might enable us to do this? Following a recent popular defense of deterrence, let us suppose that "in the long run, insofar as nuclear weapons are concerned, what each superpower needs for the deterrence of nuclear and conventional attacks on itself and its main allies is the capacity for assured destruction . . . and a *limited* capacity for actual warfare. A complete counter-force capability would be disastrous for crisis stability if it consisted of vulnerable forces; and even a complete invulnerable counter-force capability might incite the opponent to strike first in order to use his vulnerable weapons."[29]

However, a threat to retaliate with massive strikes is a morally acceptable means of deterrence only if not morally impermissible. For the purposes of my argument let me invoke a weak principle concerning the justification of threats. We are justified in (sincerely) threatening to do x under certain conditions if we are not wrong in doing x under those conditions. More precisely:

> *Weak Threat Principle.*—A (sincere) threat to do x in circumstances C is morally permissible if doing x in C is not morally impermissible.[30]

29. Carnesale et al., p. 250. We need not suppose that the United States should adopt a policy of "no first strike," although bilateral adoption of the recommendations quoted above—maintaining the capacity for assured destruction—might assure each party that the other renounces striking first (see McGeorge Bundy et al., "Nuclear Weapons and the Atlantic Alliance," *Foreign Affairs* 60 [1982]: 753–68; and Josef Joffe, "Nuclear Weapons, No First Use, and European Order," in this volume).

30. A "sincere" threat is a threat that one intends to carry out. I am assuming that, if an act is not impermissible, then neither is threatening that act. This is the Weak Threat Principle. It may be the case that sincerely threatening an act is not impermissible if and only if the act itself is not impermissible. Call this the "Strong Threat Principle." The latter is much more controversial, and my argument in this essay does not require it. On this issue, see Gregory S. Kavka, "Some Paradoxes of Deterrence," *Journal of Philosophy* 75 (1978): 285–302; Gauthier, "Deterrence, Maximization, and Rationality"; and Gregory S. Kavka, "Deterrent Intentions and Retaliatory Actions," in *The Security Gamble*, ed. D. MacLean (Totowa, N.J.: Rowman & Littlefield, 1984), pp. 155–59. See also Warren Quinn, "The Right to Threaten and the Right to Punish" (University of California, Los Angeles, 1984, typescript), for a discussion of these issues in the context of punishment. The Weak Threat Principle is not adequately stated. Threats may have consequences or meaning independent of their relation to the action threatened. Thus, there may be circumstances in which it is wrong to threaten something that is permissible. I am not yet sure how to qualify the

Since P is, I have assumed, basic and not overrideable by other moral considerations, a (countervalue) nuclear strike is not prohibited only if norms of justice no longer bind, that is, if cooperation between the two parties no longer is possible. In the event of any enemy attack, cooperative relations have in fact ended. Effectively, in such an event, the parties are back in a Hobbesian state of nature. Thus, in such a state, a (countervalue) nuclear strike would not be morally impermissible; thus threatening to retaliate with such a strike in a state of nature is morally permissible.

In the event of an enemy nuclear attack (or a massive attack on NATO forces), not only have cooperative relations in fact ended, but cooperative relations are also no longer possible on terms acceptable to rational agents. This latter point is controversial and is not a feature of Hobbes's contractarian theory. Cooperative relations presuppose a baseline for determining terms of cooperation. I suppose, *contra* Hobbes, that such a baseline precludes worsening the position of the other prior to negotiating a cooperative agreement.[31] Should another first worsen one's position before endeavoring to cooperate, then cooperation is no longer possible on terms acceptable to rational agents. Cooperation is rational only from a baseline of noncoercion.

Let me expand here. Contractarian moralists suppose that principles of justice are rationally acceptable only if it is advantageous to live in a world where individuals thus constrain their self-interested behavior. Thus to be acceptable to all members of a society, such principles must be mutually beneficial. Advantage in this tradition is to be determined by reference to some nonmoral state; otherwise no claim could be made about the (nonmoral) rationality of moral practices that was not question begging.

Hobbes supposes that the baseline from which contractarian moralities are determined is one in which individuals interact noncooperatively. Thus, if one party, holding a pistol to another's head, secures the latter's "consent" to enslavement, genuine moral obligations are created; the deal is mutually advantageous. Now we need not follow Hobbes here; we need not suppose that such a baseline is the proper starting point for the conventionalist's construction of morality. For would it be rational for someone to comply with an "agreement" that had been secured by coercion? Clearly not, once the means of coercion had been withdrawn.[32]

Thus we shall say that the proper baseline for adoption of principles of justice is one of noninteraction. Such a standpoint precludes one party worsening the position of another immediately prior to agreement. I

principle so as to handle such cases. I am indebted to David Gordon, Martin Hahn, and Thomas Hill for useful discussions about this principle.

31. This account is developed in David Gauthier, *Morals by Agreement* (Oxford: Oxford University Press, 1985), chap. 7. See also Robert Nozick, *Anarchy, State, and Utopia* (New York: Basic Books, 1974), chaps. 2, 3, 7, for a noncontractarian account of such a condition on cooperation.

32. See Gauthier, *Morals by Agreement*, chaps. 6, 7.

shall suppose, then, that the baseline of contractarian cooperation precludes coercion.

In the event of an enemy nuclear attack (or of an enemy attack on important allies), the parties are back in a Hobbesian state of nature. In such a state of nature, the prohibition on the direct killing of the innocent, like all other principles of justice, becomes a mere counsel of (nonmoral) prudence. Threatening an adversary with (countervalue) retaliation in the event of a nuclear attack is permissible because, in the circumstance in which such a threat would rationally be carried out, it would not be impermissible to do so. The important assumption here is the Weak Threat Principle: a threat to do *x* in circumstances C is morally permissible if doing *x* in those circumstances is not morally impermissible.[33]

The prohibition against killing the innocent directly is, I assume, to be found in an acceptable contractarian morality. Rational agents, in a contractarian choice situation, would find such a prohibition mutually advantageous. Further, I suppose that it is a basic principle and that it binds as long as that morality is "in force." A morality is in force, I shall say, when rational agents are in the circumstances of justice and are not forced back into a state of nature; in those situations, such a morality is binding on rational agents.

Principle P, then, morally binds rational agents up until the point they are forced back to a state of nature. It is never morally permissible, I shall assume, to return unilaterally to a state of nature. This would violate Hobbes's first law of nature, which is to seek peace and to follow it. But should another unilaterally return to a state of nature, for example, by launching a nuclear attack, then P and all other principles of justice become mere counsels of (nonmoral) prudence. Thus massive retaliation is not, under such circumstances, morally impermissible. Thus a threat to retaliate massively is morally permissible.[34]

---

33. Note the analogy with punishment: one may legitimately threaten another some specified harm should this person commit some action if so harming her would not be impermissible in the event that she commits the specified action. See Quinn for the view that we are morally justified in punishing someone if we are morally justified in threatening her.

34. The account of the state of nature that I have sketched here is Hobbesian primarily in inspiration; in practice it departs from many features of his account. A pure Hobbesian state of nature is one with no moral obligation or rights (in the sense of Hohfeldian claim rights). In such a world nothing is morally impermissible. This corresponds to stage 1 of the state of nature in my account. At this stage, as with Hobbes, nothing is unjust (or just). I follow Gauthier, who argues that rational individuals will at this stage impose certain constraints on themselves in order to be able to negotiate (tacitly or explicitly) principles that will enable them to leave the state of nature (*Morals by Agreement*, chap. 7). Acceptance of such constraints as the appropriate baseline for determining binding principles of conduct constitutes stage 2 of the state of nature. *Contra* Hobbes, there are some moral constraints in the (second stage of the) state of nature. But *contra* Locke, these constraints are not derived from a law of nature but are conventional. A nuclear first strike or an unprovoked invasion of Western Europe by the Soviet Union would return us to stage 1 of the state of nature, as it would demonstrate that the Soviets are unwilling to impose on themselves

Such an account of P does not make it permissible to kill the innocent in any situation of conflict. The account that I have developed shows how P is suspended in certain situations, namely, when an adversary unilaterally returns to a Hobbesian state of nature. In the event, say, of an enemy nuclear attack (or of a massive strike against NATO forces), the United States (or, mutatis mutandis, the Soviet Union) would no longer be bound by P. This does not entail that P is suspended in all conflicts. For surely not all wars involve the complete return to a pure Hobbesian state of nature. In most wars there is an important residue of mutual interest, enough to generate binding rules of conduct—for instance, rules prohibiting certain weapons, protecting noncombatants, governing the treatment of prisoners, et cetera.[35] Thus this argument is not, for instance, a justification of obliteration bombing or terrorism. For instance, it is doubtful that the Allies during the latter years of World War II were in a situation in which P was suspended.[36] Certainly the bombings of Dresden and Tokyo, of Hiroshima and Nagasaki, could not be justified by the account I offer here; nothing has been said about suspending P in the pursuit of the unconditional surrender of an enemy state. Mere expediency in the conduct of war would not, in my account, warrant the suspension of P.

An important objection to my account deserves to be considered. In the event of an enemy attack, massive nuclear retaliation is not prohibited, I have argued, because P (and other principles of justice) no longer would be in force. Thus killing the innocent would not be wrong (or right). Now someone might grant that we would be in a state of nature relation with regard to the Soviet leaders and other officials involved in the decision to attack but demur at the idea that (causally) innocent Soviet citizens would be in a similar position. After all, inhabitants of uninvolved third countries would not be placed in a state of nature by Soviet aggression against us. We would not thereby be relieved of the prohibition on attacking them. Why should, for instance, Soviet children be different?

Such an objection to my argument is difficult to meet. For I do not wish to argue that all persons are plunged back into a state of nature by enemy aggression and that we would not be acting wrongly were we to

---

the minimal constraints (of stage 2) that are necessary in order to determine the principles of interaction that would enable all parties to leave the state of nature. The nation attacked is not morally prohibited from nuclear retaliation since the aggressor has unilaterally returned to stage 1 and thus no longer avails itself of the protection of either the strong constraints of justice or the weak constraints of stage 2.

35. Richard Brandt, "Utilitarianism and the Rules of War," *Philosophy & Public Affairs* 1 (1971): 145–65. With regard to World War II, I might argue that some of the war conventions (e.g., those governing gas) were requirements more of prudence than of morality.

36. Although it is possible that the British were in precisely such a situation in the early years of World War II and that they were (only) then justified in suspending P and initiating the bombing of German cities. See Walzer's interesting account of "supreme emergencies" (pp. 255ff.).

use the occasion to drop bombs on other peoples. Yet I do want to hold that we would not be acting wrongly to retaliate against innocent Soviet citizens in the event of a Soviet attack.

May we deter, for instance, an enemy nuclear attack by threatening some third party about which enemy leaders happen to care? Would the inhabitants of this (otherwise) uninvolved nation also be in a state of nature with respect to us in the event of an enemy nuclear attack? If innocent Soviets may be held hostage,[37] then may we also threaten innocent third parties?

In my account, members of society A are not prohibited from deterring a nuclear attack by B by threatening to kill innocent members of B. Is A, however, not prohibited from deterring B by threatening to kill members of C, where C is an uninvolved third country? Should I agree, then am I not supposing that members of B are in some way collectively responsible for the aggressive acts of their leaders? It is hard to conceive of a plausible account of collective responsibility that could hold Soviet children responsible for the aggressive acts of Kremlin officials. Yet I must be able to distinguish between innocent Soviets and innocent third parties since I wish to hold that the latter are not placed in a state of nature by the aggressive actions of Soviet leaders. A reply to this objection requires further analysis of the nature of contractarian moral relations between individuals and groups.

Two individuals who are in the contractarian circumstances of justice and who directly interact with one another are bound to one another by obligations of justice. This much is granted by all contractarian moral theories. What if the individuals are in the circumstances of justice yet do not directly interact with one another? Suppose two individuals, Ann and Boris, stand to benefit mutually from cooperative interaction yet do not interact directly because they live very far apart, Ann in Los Angeles, Boris in Leningrad. Yet the two are in the circumstances of justice. While Ann and Boris do not stand to benefit mutually from direct cooperative interaction (until they directly interact), they do stand to benefit from indirect cooperative interaction as members of different societies.

Cooperative relations can be direct or indirect. Obligations of justice can thus bind individuals directly, as natural individuals, or indirectly, as members of a group. Ann and Boris each have obligations of the first sort to the individuals with whom they directly interact, perhaps most members of their respective societies. But Ann and Boris have only obligations of the second sort to one another. Their obligations to one

37. Nuclear deterrence as an exchange of hostages was noted long ago by Thomas Schelling: "'The balance of terror,' if it is stable, is simply a massive and modern version of an ancient institution: the exchange of hostages. . . . As long as each side has the manifest power to destroy a nation and its population in response to an attack by the other, the 'balance of terror' amounts to a tacit understanding backed by a total exchange of all conceivable hostages" (*Strategy of Conflict*, p. 239). See also Steven Lee, "Nuclear Deterrence: Hostage Holding and Consequences," in this volume.

another they have by virtue of their membership in societies that stand to benefit from cooperative interaction. Obligations of international justice thus bind individuals only qua members of a society; obligations of individual justice bind natural individuals.

Suppose that cooperative relations between two countries break down due to a nuclear attack of one on the other. Then Ann and Boris would find themselves in a Hobbesian state of nature with respect to one another. While it is possible that they would be able to return to civil society with greater ease than their aggressive leaders would, nonetheless relations of justice no longer obtain between the two.

Note, however, that, were Boris visiting Los Angeles when his leaders launch an attack, then each would be bound by justice to one another as natural individuals, even though neither would be bound to one another qua members of different societies. Ann, or any other American, would be bound by justice not to kill Boris (assuming his innocence in the relevant sense).

What distinguishes Soviet citizens from third parties is that we remain bound by justice to the latter even when our obligations to the former are dissolved. In the absence of aggressive behavior on their part, relations of justice continue between the United States and third party nations, thus rendering nuclear strikes against them morally impermissible.[38]

It is important to note that my account does not have the consequence that there are no moral constraints on nuclear retaliatory strikes. If we remain bound by justice to uninvolved third parties, then the doctrine of double effect (which I accept in some form) obligates us to minimize the adverse side effects of nuclear retaliation on third parties. Were massive nuclear retaliation against the Soviet Union to destroy human life on the planet, then the fourth condition of the doctrine of double effect would prohibit it. Note, though, that our obligations, in my account, would be to the third parties and not to Soviet citizens. My argument thus places some moral restrictions on the nature of a permissible retaliatory strike against an enemy nuclear attack. Such retaliation could not directly kill innocent third parties. If it is true that a single massive nuclear strike would destroy the planet in a "nuclear winter," then the fourth condition of the doctrine of double effect would make such a strike morally wrong. My argument could only show that a less massive strike was permissible.[39]

38. I am grateful to Dan Farrell for conversations which helped me to clarify the position I am developing here.

39. A nuclear strike that would bring about a nuclear winter would not be rational. *Contra* many defense theorists, my defense of deterrence is restricted to rational deterrent policies. By such a policy I mean a nuclear strategy with greater expected benefits (to the nation in question) than possible nonnuclear deterrent strategies would have. (It is crucial that the expected costs of carrying through on one's threat should deterrence fail be counted in the expected-benefit analysis. Thus the expected benefits of a policy should include the expected costs of compliance with that policy should deterrence fail. I assume that this would rule out threats to bring about nuclear winters.) This rationality constraint on deterrent strategies may be quite strong.

The distinction I made (in n. 34 above) between the two stages of the state of nature enables me to generate further constraints on nuclear retaliatory strikes. Suppose that we have a choice of two retaliatory strategies, one promising n enemy casualties, the other n plus a nonnegligible number of further casualties, most of which would be innocent. Supposing the deterrent effect of each is equal, should we not, other things being equal, adopt the first strategy? I have argued that in the event of a Soviet nuclear attack we would be freed of moral obligations toward members of that society; thus it would seem difficult for me now to argue that we would be committed to the first of the above strategies.

Our relation to all Soviet citizens may not, however, be the same. With regard to some (e.g., those in some way responsible for a nuclear attack), we would be in a pure Hobbesian state of nature. With regard to others (e.g., those in no way responsible for an attack), we could be in a stage 2 state of nature since cooperation with them might at a later date be possible. Thus were we able to constrain our behavior toward the latter without risking annihilation by others, we should do so. Should our choice of deterrent strategies be like that described above, we should adopt the first strategy. Thus our choice of strategies may be subject to some weak moral constraints binding in a (stage 2) state of nature.

I have sketched a contractarian account of the moral prohibition on the killing of the innocent. If my account should prove to be sound, then we shall have provided reason to believe that threatening massive slaughter of the innocent is not a morally prohibited response to enemy nuclear threat. Nuclear deterrence, as it has been traditionally understood, is under attack both on the left and on the right; defenders of unilateral nuclear disarmament and supporters of the current administration alike condemn it as immoral.[40] If one believes, as I do, that nuclear deterrence is a more promising means of avoiding nuclear (and nonnuclear) conflict between the superpowers than present alternatives are, then the argument of this essay may prove to be a useful contribution to current debates.

40. For the latter, see Wohlstetter. It is not clear, however, that these defenders of the current administration would be so enthusiastic in their moral condemnation of MAD and similar strategies were they not to believe that we have other alternatives, all of which are far preferable to unilateral nuclear disarmament.

Deterrence, Maximization, and Rationality*

David Gauthier

I

Is deterrence a fully rational policy? In our world deterrence works—
sometimes. But in a more perfect world, in which actors rationally related
their choices to their beliefs and preferences, and in which those beliefs
and preferences were matters of common knowledge, could deterrence
work? Some say no.[1] Others hold a conception of rationality that would
commit them to saying no, were they to consider the issue.[2] I say yes.
Deterrence can be part of a fully rational policy. I propose to demonstrate
this.

At the heart of a deterrent policy is the expression of a conditional
intention. An actor A expresses the intention to perform an action x
should another actor B perform an action y. If B would do y did A not
express her intention, then we may say that A's expression of intention
deters B from doing y. In expressing her intention as part of a deterrent
policy, A seeks to decrease the probability of B's doing y by increasing
his estimate of her conditional probability of doing x should he do y.

We need better labels than x and y if our talk about deterrence is to
be perspicuous. In at least some situations, A's deterrent intention is
retaliatory; A expresses the intention to retaliate should B do y. So let us
call x *retal*. And what A seeks to deter is an action that would advantage
B in relation to A; let us then call y *advant*. We shall then say that an
actor A expresses the intention to *retal* should another actor B *advant*.

A seeks to affect B's estimate of her conditional probability of *retal*
should he *advant*. Why does she expect her expression of conditional
intention to have this effect? Let us suppose that A and B are rational;
on the received view of rationality, an actor seeks to maximize expected

---

* This paper was prepared for delivery at a conference on "Nuclear Deterrence: Moral
and Political Issues," sponsored by the Center for Philosophy and Public Policy, University
of Maryland at College Park. It will appear in *The Security Gamble: Deterrence Dilemmas in
the Nuclear Age*, edited by Douglas MacLean, Maryland Studies in Public Philosophy (Totowa,
N.J.: Rowman & Allanheld, in press).
    1. One who says no is Jonathan Schell, *The Fate of the Earth* (New York: Alfred A.
Knopf, Inc., 1982), pp. 201–4.
    2. Among these others are game theorists who insist that strategic rationality demands
perfect equilibria.

Reprinted from *Ethics* 94 (April 1984): 474–495.

utility, the fulfillment of her preferences given her beliefs. If A expects to affect B's estimate of what she will do, then she must expect to affect his beliefs about her preferences and/or beliefs. Or so it seems.

A wants to deter B from *advant*. She believes that B is less likely to *advant* if he expects her response to be *retal* than if he expects a different response, *nonretal*. She therefore expresses the intention to *retal* should he *advant*. For this to affect B, it would seem that he must take her expression of intention to indicate her preference for *retal* over *nonretal*, given *advant*. Perhaps A does have this preference and so seeks to inform B that she prefers *retal*. Perhaps A does not have this preference but seeks to deceive B into supposing that she prefers *retal*. But in either case the deterrent effect of her expression of intention would seem to require that B be initially uninformed, or at least uncertain, about her preference. Were he informed of her preference, then his estimate of her conditional probability of choosing *retal* should he *advant* would be unaffected by any claim she might make about her intention.

But is this so? Must the actor to be deterred be initially uncertain about the preferences of the would-be deterrer? Let us consider the matter more closely. We suppose that B knows A's preferences between *retal* and *nonretal*, given *advant*. If she prefers *retal*, then his knowledge should suffice to deter him from *advant*, supposing that his preferences are such that he can be deterred at all. A needs no deterrent policy. If she prefers *nonretal*, then how can her expression of the conditional intention to *retal* should he *advant* be credible? How can it affect his estimate of what she will do?

First we might suppose that, although A prefers *nonretal* to *retal* ceteris paribus, yet she also prefers being a woman of her word. She may value sincerity directly, or she may find it instrumentally useful to her. In expressing her intention to *retal* should B *advant*, she stakes her reputation for being a woman of her word, and B, knowing or believing this, realizes that by expressing her intention she has transformed the situation. She prefers *nonretal* to *retal*, but she also prefers honoring a commitment leading to *retal* to dishonoring a commitment even if it brings about *nonretal*. Her expression of conditional intention does not affect her preferences but brings a different set into play and so affects B's estimate of the utilities of the courses of action open to her should he *advant*.

Second, A may be imperfectly rational, unable fully to control her behavior in terms of her considered preferences. If B *advant*s, then her cool preference for *nonretal* may be overcome by anger, or rage, or panic, so that she may *retal*. In this case we should no doubt say, not that A expresses a conditional intention to *retal*, but rather that she expresses a warning that she will, or may, find herself choosing *retal* should he *advant*. Fortunately for A, her inability to control her behavior stands her in good stead, enabling her to deter, or at least to seek to deter, B from *advant* by warning him of her probable folly should he do it. Such an inability may seem suspect, as altogether too convenient, making us hesitant to accept this apparent mode of deterrence at face value.

Third, A's expression of intention may not stand alone but may activate forces themselves beyond her control, which may make *nonretal* less desirable, or *retal* more desirable, than would otherwise have been the case. Perhaps A has made a side bet which she loses should she fail to abide by her stated intention, or perhaps she has insured herself against the costs of having to carry out what otherwise would be an unprofitable course of action. And fourth, in expressing her intention, A may also delegate her power to choose; some other person, or some preprogrammed device, capable of ignoring her preferences, will ensure that if B *advants*, *retal* will ensue. These complicating cases will play no part in our discussion. My interest in this paper is in deterrent policies that do not call into play external factors no longer within the actor's control.

My interest is also in genuine expressions of intention, and not in warnings. No doubt we are not always in such control of our actions that our cool, long-term, considered preferences prevail. But as I have noted, there is something suspect about arranging to gain from this lack of control, about extracting rational advantage from seeming irrationality. I shall consider would-be deterrers who are able to carry out what they intend and who form their intentions on a rational, utility-maximizing basis. A then does not warn B but coolly informs him that she will deliberately *retal* should he *advant*.

And lastly, my interest is not in the provision of deterrent information about preferences. Rather we shall examine situations in which there is no doubt, in the minds of those concerned, that, at least if other things are equal, the would-be deterrer A disprefers *retal* to *nonretal*, should B *advant*.

It would therefore seem that we are left with but one possibility for a deterrent policy among rational persons informed of each other's preferences and beliefs. We must suppose that the would-be deterrer prefers to be a person of her word. A, in expressing her conditional intention, must transform the situation, preferring to abide by her commitment even though, ceteris paribus, she would prefer the outcome of ignoring the commitment. She prefers *nonretal* to *retal*, but having expressed the intention to *retal* given *advant*, she prefers to carry out her intention to ignoring it, should her attempt to deter fail.

Although some deterrent policies may seem to invite this characterization, there are, in my view, insuperable difficulties with it, if we insist firmly on the full rationality of the actors. Of course, since we impose no a priori constraints on the content of preferences, an actor may simply take satisfaction in making commitments which she then carries out. But why would a rational actor choose to make commitments to dispreferred courses of action? Perhaps she finds masochistic satisfaction in making and carrying out such commitments. But if deterrent policies

102   David Gauthier

are rational only for a peculiar variety of masochist, then most real-world examples of such policies survive only because of irrationality. Let us not be so hasty to judge them. I shall suppose that in general, the actor's concern is with the instrumental and not the intrinsic benefits of adhering to an expressed intention. What are these benefits? What does A gain if she actually responds to *advant* by *retal*, having expressed the intention so to respond?

If B *advant*s, then A's attempt to deter him has failed. Any gain that would compensate for the cost of *retal* must then derive from further, future consequences of choosing *retal* that extend beyond the particular deterrent situation. Presumably these consequences are the effects of carrying out her expressed intention, on the deterrent value of expressing similar intentions in other situations. If A *retal*s, showing that her expression of intention was seriously meant, then future, similar expressions of intention should have a greater effect on others' expectations of what she will do than if she fails to *retal*.

But among fully rational persons is this effect possible? If A is rational, then B rationally expects her to do what she believes will maximize her expected utility. What she has done in the past may provide information about her preferences and beliefs, but we are supposing these to be common knowledge. How then can what A has done affect B's expectation of what she will do in the future? He expects her to maximize her expected utility; how can what she has done affect her expected utility? We are not concerned with behavior that alters the payoffs or outcomes possible for A. If in choosing *retal* A neither informs B about her preferences nor alters the possible outcomes of her future choices, then B has no reason to take what she has done into account in forming his expectations about what she will do in the future. A rational observer, informed of A's preferences, could only interpret her choice of *retal* as a lapse from rationality, in no way affecting expectations about her future choices on the supposition that they will be made rationally.

The only expectation one can rationally form about rational utility-maximizers is that they will seek to maximize expected utility. The only reputation they can rationally gain is the reputation for maximizing expected utility. If carrying out an expressed intention is not itself utility maximizing, then it can have no effect on the expectations of rational and informed persons that would suffice to make it utility maximizing.

To suppose otherwise is to fail to think through the forward-looking implications of maximizing rationality. A utilitarian, dedicated to collective maximization, cannot have reason to keep his promises in order to gain a reputation as a promise keeper among a community of utilitarians, although he may have reason so to act among us nonutilitarians. Similarly, an individual utility maximizer can have no reason to carry out her intentions, in order to gain a reputation as a woman of her word, among a community of informed individual utility maximizers, although she may have reason so to act among less rational persons. We seem then to have exposed a deep irrationality at the core of deterrent policies. Leaving aside the provision of information about one's preferences, or the issuance of a warning about one's irrationality, or the invocation of factors beyond one's control that would determine one's response, we seem forced to conclude that A cannot expect B to alter his estimate of her conditional probability to *retal* should he *advant*, on the basis of her expressed intention to *retal*, if ceteris paribus she would prefer *nonretal*. And so A cannot expect to decrease the probability of B choosing *advant* by her expression of conditional intention; she is not able to deter, or rationally to attempt to deter, B from *advant*.

II

Or so it would seem. I shall show that things are not what they seem and that it may be rational to adopt a deterrent policy committing one to the performance of a disadvantageous, non-utility-maximizing action should deterrence fail. But before turning to this demonstration, let us pause to entertain the possibility that my argument has been mistaken and that A might have reason to carry out an otherwise disadvantageous expressed intention because of its effect on expectations about her future behavior. It is clear that this can be relevant to the rationality of a deterrent policy only if A is concerned about future deterrence.

Although our analysis of deterrence is intended to apply generally, yet I am particularly concerned with the rationality of deterrent policies in the context of relations among those nations possessing nuclear weapons. More precisely, I am concerned with a policy which has as its core the expressed intention to respond to a nuclear strike with a counterstrike. I shall call this the policy of "nuclear retaliation."

To exemplify this policy and set it in the context of deterrence, let us suppose that one nation—call it the SU—is perceived by another nation—call it the US—to constitute a nuclear threat. The US fears that the SU will launch a nuclear strike, or, perhaps more plausibly, will credibly threaten to launch such a strike should the US refuse some demand or resist some initiative, or, perhaps more plausibly still, will act in some way inimical to the interests of the US that could be effectively countered only by markedly increasing the probability that the SU will launch a nuclear strike. The US seeks to deter the SU from a policy that would or might lead to a nuclear strike, whether unconditionally or as a result of US refusal to acquiesce in or endeavor to counter some SU initiative. To do this, the US announces the intention to resist any SU initiative even if resistance invites a nuclear strike and, should a strike occur, to retaliate even if this provokes full-scale nuclear combat. In talking about the "strike policy" of the SU, and the "retaliatory policy" of the US, I shall intend the policies just sketched. In particular, a strike policy may center on the threat to strike should some demand not be met, and a retaliatory policy may center on the refusal to submit to such a demand even though a nuclear exchange may result.

Now it is possible that the US prefers suffering a nuclear strike to submitting to a demand by the SU. And it is possible that the US prefers retaliating against a nuclear strike, with the prospect then of fighting a nuclear war, to accepting passively a single strike and so, effectively, cutting its nuclear losses by capitulating. But suppose, plausibly, that the consequences of nuclear warfare are such that the US would always prefer less nuclear devastation to more; nevertheless it seeks to deter the SU from a strike policy by expressing the intention to choose its less preferred retaliatory response. It is then engaged in just the type of deterrent policy that we have put rationally in question. And it seems clear that an appeal to future expectations would not here provide ground for altering US preferences in order to defend deterrence in terms of future effects. For the US to claim that, despite its preference for minimizing nuclear devastation, retaliation would be advantageous in the long run because it would make the future use of a retaliatory policy credible and so effective would be to overlook the probable lack of a relevant long run. After a nuclear exchange, future expectations, if any, would likely have very little basis in the policies of the nations prior to the exchange. Thus, even if in some cases a deterrent policy could be rationalized by an appeal to future expectations, nuclear retaliation lacks such a rationale.

Retaliation would therefore seem to be an irrational policy. If submission is preferred to retaliation, as minimizing the expected nuclear devastation one suffers, then the expression of the conditional intention to retaliate would lack credibility. The US could not expect to affect the SU's expectations about US behavior by expressing such an intention, and so the US could not decrease the probability of the SU's pursuing a strike policy by announcing its own policy of nuclear retaliation. Among sufficiently rational and informed nations, nuclear deterrence must fail. If it succeeds in the real world, then the expressed intention not to submit and to retaliate must serve, it seems, to inform the potential attacker of the would-be deterrer's real preferences, or to deceive the attacker about those preferences, or to warn the attacker to expect an irrational response to a strike policy.

But this conclusion is mistaken. We have reached it by focusing entirely on the benefits and costs of actually carrying out the conditional intention that is the core of a deterrent policy. We have failed to consider the benefits and costs of forming or adopting such a conditional intention. The argument against the rationality of nuclear retaliation, or more generally against a deterrent policy, has this structure: it is not utility maximizing to carry out the nonsubmissive, retaliatory intention; therefore it is not rational so to act; therefore it is not rational to form the intention; therefore a rational person cannot sincerely express the intention; therefore another rational and informed person cannot be deterred by the expression of the intention. The structure of the argument that I shall present and defend is: it may be utility maximizing to form the nonsubmissive, retaliatory intention; therefore it may be rational to form such an intention;

if it is rational to form the intention it is rational to act on the intention; therefore a rational person can sincerely express the intention; therefore another rational and informed person can be deterred by the expression of the intention. We shall of course have to consider why this argument succeeds and the former argument fails.

I shall therefore defend the rationality of deterrent policies and, more particularly, of nuclear retaliation. But my defense is a limited one. Indeed, among rational and informed actors, a policy of pure and simple deterrence is not rational, although it may be rational as part of a larger policy directed, among other things, at the obsolescence of deterrence. Putting my position into a historical context, I shall defend Hobbes's formulation of the first law of nature: "That every man, ought to endeavour Peace, as farre as he has hope of obtaining it; and when he cannot obtain it, that he may seek, and use, all helps, and advantages of Warre."[3] Deterrence is both an advantage of war and, among rational actors, a means to peace. Or rather, some deterrent policies may have these features. But as a means to peace, a deterrent policy looks to its own supercession. For recognition of the rationality of deterrence is inseparable from recognition of the rationality of moving, not unilaterally but mutually, beyond deterrence.

III

To give precision to our analysis of deterrence, I shall focus on situations with a very simple structure. An actor who, consistently with our previous usage, we call B, has a choice between two alternatives, y and y', where y corresponds to *advant*. If he chooses y, then another actor, A, knowing B's choice, has a choice between two alternatives, x and x', where x corresponds to *retal* and x' to *nonretal*. If B chooses y', then A may or may not have a choice between x and x' or other alternatives; initially we need suppose only that some outcome is expected. There are, then, three possible outcomes relevant to our analysis: yx, or *advant* followed by *retal*; yx', or *advant* followed by *nonretal*; and y'—, or B's choice of his alternative to *advant* followed by a possible but unspecified choice by A. Each actor orders these possible outcomes; for simplicity we assume that neither is indifferent between any two. There are then six possible orderings for each actor, and so thirty-six different possible pairs of orderings.

Only one of these thirty-six pairs determines a deterrent situation. Consider first A's orderings. Since she seeks to deter B from *advant*, she must prefer y'—, the expected outcome if B chooses his alternative action, to both yx and yx'. And since she seeks to deter B from *advant* by expressing a conditional intention to *retal* contrary to her known preferences, she must prefer yx' to yx. Now consider B's orderings. Since A seeks to deter him from *advant* by expressing her conditional intention to *retal*, he must prefer yx' to yx. If A has any need to seek to deter B from *advant*, then

3. Thomas Hobbes, *Leviathan* (London, 1651), chap. 14.

he must prefer yx' to y'—, and if she is to have any hope of deterring him, then he must prefer y'— to yx. A's ordering is: y'— $> yx' > yx$; B's ordering is: $yx' > y'$— $> yx$.

Let us take a brief, closer look at the outcome if B chooses y'. I shall not pursue the implications of this discussion in the present paper, although it raises issues of some interest and importance. If deterrence is to be possible, then, should B choose y', A must have a choice w (where this includes the limiting case in which she has no alternative to w) such that she prefers $y'w$ to yx' and he prefers $y'w$ to yx. If for every alternative w' such that A prefers $y'w'$ to yx', B prefers yx to $y'w'$, then, much as A might wish to deter B from choosing y she has no conditional intention sufficient. If for every alternative w'' such that B prefers $y'w''$ to yx, A prefers yx' to $y'w''$, then even though A may have a conditional intention sufficient to deter B she has no interest in using it.

Suppose then that A prefers $y'w$ to yx', and B prefers $y'w$ to yx. If B also prefers yx' to $y'w$, then A will seek to deter B from choosing y. But the expression of a conditional intention to choose x in response to y, even if fully credible, may be insufficient to deter B. For A may have an alternative w' to w such that A prefers $y'w'$ to $y'w$, but also such that B prefers yx to $y'w'$. Were B to choose y' in response to A's conditional intention to respond to y with x, then he would expect A to choose w' rather than w, so that he would be worse off than if he had ignored A's attempt to deter. However, were A to combine her expression of conditional intention to choose x in response to y with the credible expression of a conditional intention to choose w in response to y', then B, preferring $y'w$ to yx, would choose y'. In this case A is able to deter B only if she is able to combine her threat with an offer—an offer to refrain from her utility-maximizing choice in order to leave B open to her threat. Note that, although A's offer requires her not to choose her utility-maximizing response to B's choice of y', by making it she may expect an outcome $y'w$ which affords her greater utility than the outcome yx' which she would otherwise expect. Note also that B would prefer A not to be in a position to make such an offer.

It will be evident that A's conditional intention to choose a non-maximizing w in response to y' raises precisely the same problem of rationality as her conditional intention to choose a nonmaximizing x in response to y—*retal* in response to *advant*. In both cases she must form an intention to choose a course of action in itself nonmaximizing, as part of a policy intended to maximize her expected utility. I shall not address the problem of nonmaximizing offers in this paper, but an argument for the rationality of deterrent threats can easily be applied to the offers as well.

Before proceeding to that argument let us relate our abstract treatment of deterrence to the particular issue of nuclear retaliation. In the terms in which we have posed that problem, the US corresponds to actor A, the SU to actor B. The policy of nuclear retaliation by the US corresponds to x or *retal;* the strike policy for actor A corresponds to y or *advant.* Recall that "strike" and "retaliation" are shorthand for more complex policies; the core of a strike policy may be the threat to launch a nuclear strike should some initiative be resisted; the core of a retaliatory policy may be the refusal to acquiesce in such a threat—with, of course, the intention to retaliate should such refusal lead to a strike.

I suppose then that the US orders the possibilities: no strike > strike and no retaliation > strike and retaliation. The first preference is evident; the second preference follows from the assumption that the US wishes to minimize nuclear devastation, given that retaliation, as we have characterized it, increases its expectation of suffering such devastation. And I suppose that the SU orders the possibilities: strike and no retaliation > no strike > strike and retaliation. As I noted in the preceding paragraph, a strike policy may center on a threat; the SU's first preference need not indicate a passion for blood but only a desire to get its way by resorting to whatever threat may be needed. The SU's second preference follows from the assumption that it too wishes to minimize being the victim of nuclear devastation.

These preference orderings satisfy the requirements for a deterrent situation. I suppose that they are a plausible schematic representation of the preferences of possible real-world counterparts of the US and the SU. Thus our argument for the rationality of deterrent threats is not intended to be an enquiry into merely possible worlds. However, some of the points raised abstractly in this section should be borne in mind in any attempt to apply our argument. In particular, it is worth noting that the SU may suppose that the US has several possible responses to its no-strike policy, some of which, such as a unilateral US strike, might indeed be worse from its perspective than a strike policy coupled with US retaliation. Effective deterrence by the US may then require an offer sufficient to allay SU fears of possible unilateral US action in response to a no-strike policy. I shall not pursue this matter here, but it is essential to be aware that the components of an effective policy of nuclear deterrence are matters that require the most careful evaluation.

IV

The key to understanding deterrence, or, for that matter, the key to understanding all forms of interaction, such as agreement, that require constraints on directly maximizing behavior, is that in interaction, the probability that an individual will be in a given situation or type of situation may be affected by the beliefs of others about what that individual would do in the situation. B's willingness to put A in a situation, to face A with a choice, will be affected by his belief about how she will act in that situation, how she will choose. His belief about how she will act will be affected by his assessment of her intentions. In particular, if he knows that she is fully in control of what she does, he will, ceteris paribus, expect her to do what she conditionally intends to do should she be in that situation. Hence the probability of A being in a given situation, insofar as her being in that situation is determined by the actions of B, is affected by A's prior intentions about what she will do in that situation.

It is of course true that, if A is rational, then her intentions must be those that it is rational for her to hold. But neither A nor B can ascertain the rationality of her intentions merely by considering the actions to which various possible intentions might commit her, and their payoffs. If B's beliefs about A's intentions partially determine what situations she will be in, then A, in forming her intentions, must consider the situations she may expect to face given the possible intentions she might form, and the payoffs from those situations. It may be tempting to suppose that it is rational to form an intention if and only if it would be utility maximizing to execute the intention. Instead we argue that it is rational to execute an intention if and only if it is utility maximizing to form it.

Let us then examine the calculations of a rational actor choosing among possible intentions. I shall restrict our analysis to the simplest case, corresponding to our analysis of deterrent situations in the preceding section. Suppose then that A must decide whether to adopt the intention to do x in a situation characterized by the performance of some action y by another actor B. Let $u(yx)$ be the utility she would expect were she to do x given y. Let x' be the alternative intention to x so that $u(yx')$ is the utility she would expect were she to act on x' given y. Let $u(y')$ be the utility she would expect were B not to do y. And let p_x be the probability that B will do y should A adopt the intention to do x given y, and $p_{x'}$ the probability that B will do y should A adopt the intention to do x' given y.

Then A's expected utility should she intend x is:

$$p_x u(yx) + (1 - p_x)u(y') .$$

And her expected utility should she intend x' is:

$$p_{x'}u(yx') + (1 - p_{x'})u(y') .$$

Our concern is with the rationality of a deterrent policy. Hence we suppose that A does not want to be faced with y, which corresponds to *advant*, so that her utility $u(y')$ is greater than both $u(yx)$ and $u(yx')$. Furthermore, we suppose that doing x, which corresponds to *retal*, is not utility maximizing for A, so that $u(yx')$ is greater than $u(yx)$. And finally, A must suppose that intending x should B do y reduces the probability of his doing y, so that $p_{x'}$ is greater than p_x.

Since A prefers facing y' to doing x' given y, and doing x' given y to doing x given y, there must be some lottery over facing y' and facing y with the intention of doing x, that A considers indifferent to the certainty of facing y with the intention of doing x'. Let p be the probability of facing y' in that lottery. Then we may express the utility of facing y with the intention of doing x', $u(yx')$, in terms of the utilities of facing y', $u(y')$, and of facing y with the intention of doing x, $u(yx)$:

$$u(yx') = pu(y') + (1 - p)u(yx) .$$

Without loss of generality for our argument we may set $u(y') = 1$, and $u(yx) = 0$. Then:

$$u(yx') = p .$$

And so A's expected utility if she intends x given y is:

$$1 - p_x .$$

And her expected utility if she intends x' given y is:

$$p_{x'}p + (1 - p_{x'}) .$$

Suppose that A maximizes her expected utility by forming the intention to do x should B do y, that is, by forming the intention to *retal* should B *advant*. Then it must be the case that:

$$(1 - p_x) > [p_{x'}p + (1 - p_{x'})] .$$

Or equivalently:

$$[(p_{x'} - p_x)/p_{x'}] > p .$$

To interpret this condition, we note that avoiding y constitutes "deterrent success," whereas facing y and doing x constitutes "deterrent failure." Facing y and doing x' we may identify with nondeterrence. Then p is that probability of deterrent success, where the alternative is deterrent failure, that makes a deterrent policy indifferent to nondeterrence from the standpoint of the prospective deterrer. We may therefore call p the "minimum required probability" for deterrent success; it reflects the value of nondeterrence relative to deterrent success and failure. The expression $[(p_{x'} - p_x)/p_{x'}]$ is the "proportionate decrease" in the probability of being in the situation that the prospective deterrer would avoid, that is achieved by her policy of deterrence. Thus the condition states that, for a deterrent policy to be rational, the proportionate decrease that it effects in the probability of facing the undesired action, *advant*, must be greater than the minimum required probability for deterrent success.

Consider a simple example. B, a university professor in Boston, is offered a position in Dallas. His wife, A, wishes to deter him from accepting the appointment, and so tells him that, if he accepts it, she will leave him and remain in Boston, even though she would prefer to accompany him to Dallas. Then if A is indifferent between a lottery that would offer a 70 percent chance that B would stay in Boston and a 30 percent chance that he would go alone to Dallas, and the certainty that both would go to Dallas, .7 is a minimum required probability for deterrent success. If A supposes that there is a 50 percent chance that B will accept the appointment in Dallas if she will accompany him, but only a 10 percent chance that he will accept it if she won't, then the proportionate decrease effected by deterrence in the probability that he will accept the appointment is $(.5 - .1)/.5$, or .8. Since .8 is greater than .7, A indeed maximizes her expected utility by her adoption of a deterrent policy, requiring her to form the conditional intention not to accompany B should he accept an appointment in Dallas.

Consider now the application of our analysis to the policy of nuclear retaliation. Deterrent success for the US lies in not facing a strike policy by the SU—a policy that intends directly, or threatens and so intends conditionally, a nuclear strike. Deterrent failure lies in being faced with such a policy and being committed to a retaliatory response—to ignoring any threat by the SU and to responding to a nuclear strike by a counterstrike. Nondeterrence lies in facing a strike policy by the SU without being committed to a retaliatory response, and so it involves acceptance of the lesser evil between acquiescing in whatever initiative the SU takes and engaging in retaliation. Given these alternatives, we may suppose that, although deterrent success is of course preferred to nondeterrence, both are strongly preferred to deterrent failure. It may indeed be better to let the Reds have their way than to be among the nuclear dead. Thus a substantial decrease in the probability of facing a strike policy by the SU is required if the deterrent policy of nuclear retaliation is to maximize the expected utility of the US and so be rational to adopt.

I shall not try to estimate the extent of this decrease or, equivalently, the minimum required probability for deterrent success. This is a difficult empirical question. What is clear is that a merely ordinal ranking of preferences over possible outcomes does not afford sufficient information to assess the rationality of a deterrent policy, either in general or in the specific case of nuclear retaliation. An actor might prefer, and strongly prefer, to avoid facing a situation brought about by some other actor doing *y*, but the proportionate reduction in the probability of facing *y* that could be effected by a deterrent policy might not be worth the expected cost of facing it with the deterrent intention. The benefits of deterrent success must always be balanced against the costs of deterrent failure, and only the relevant probabilities of being in the undesirable situation, both with and without a policy of deterrence, together with an interval measure of utility in terms of which we may calculate the minimum required probability for deterrent success, enables us to calculate the balance of benefits and costs. If our argument shows that deterrent policies in general, and nuclear retaliation in particular, may be utility maximizing, it also shows that such policies may *not* be utility maximizing, and it may be extraordinarily difficult to determine, in a particular case, whether deterrence or nondeterrence is less disadvantageous.

But while I want to emphasize this cautionary note, I do want to insist that my argument refutes the claim that deterrence is necessarily an irrational policy because carrying out the deterrent intention is not utility maximizing. The argument for the irrationality of deterrence looks only to the costs of deterrent failure. Because there are such costs, it rejects the policy. My argument, on the other hand, relates the probability-weighted costs of deterrent failure to the probability-weighted benefits of deterrent success, in order to assess the rationality of forming the conditional, nonmaximizing intention which is the core of a deterrent policy. I claim that if it is rational to form this conditional, deterrent intention, then, should deterrence fail and the condition be realized, it is rational to act on it. The utility cost of acting on the deterrent intention enters, with appropriate probability weighting, into determining whether it is rational to form the intention. But once this is decided, the cost of acting on the intention does not enter again into determining whether, if deterrence fails, it is rational to act on it. Acting on it is part of a deterrent policy, and if expected utility is maximized by forming the conditional, deterrent intention, then deterrence is a rational policy.

V

Let us turn to some possible objections to this argument. We may forestall one counterargument by noting that, of course, if one is able to achieve the same deterrent effect by pretending to form a conditional, nonmaximizing intention as by actually forming it, then such pretense would be rational. Even if pretense offers a lesser deterrent effect, its lesser possible costs may make it rational. But there is no reason to suppose that pretense must always have as great a net benefit as the actual formation of an intention. It must be judged on the same, utility-maximizing basis as the real thing.

An objector may insist that pretense can be rational because it does not commit one to nonmaximizing behavior, but that a genuine commitment to nonmaximization cannot be rational. If it is rational to form an intention that commits one to what, ceteris paribus, would not maximize one's utility, then the utility of forming the intention must affect the utility of carrying it out, increasing it so that execution is utility maximizing. The US would, in the abstract, prefer not to engage in a nuclear exchange with the SU. Our objector admits this but urges that, if a nuclear exchange arises from a rational policy of deterrence, then the US would prefer to maintain that policy and so prefer to engage in the exchange. On his view, preference for forming a conditional intention entails preference for executing it should the condition be met.

But what reason has he for claiming this, other than his insistence on a simple, and in my view simpleminded, account of the connection between utility maximization and rationality?[4] I have shown that the adoption of an intention can be utility maximizing even though acting on it would not be, at least considered in itself. Why then should we suppose that, because adoption is utility maximizing, implementation magically becomes utility maximizing? Why should we suppose that a preference for adopting or forming an intention must carry with it a preference for implementing or executing the intention? The two preferences are logically and actually quite distinct. We may grant that in most situations one prefers to adopt an intention because one would prefer to execute it. But my argument is intended to show that this connection does not hold between conditional intentions and their implementation in deterrent situations. I have shown why the connection does not hold—because adoption of the intention affects one's expected utilities by affecting the probability that the condition for implementation will be realized.

Our objector must surely take another and stronger tack. If he allows our argument about the rationality of adopting a nonmaximizing intention, then he must claim that it may be rational to adopt an intention even though it would be, and one knows that it would be, irrational to act on it should the condition for implementing it be realized. If our objector takes this tack, then he acknowledges the rationality of some deterrent policies, but nevertheless insists that these policies, although fully rational, involve the performance of irrational actions if certain conditions are satisfied. How then does his position differ from mine, in which I claim that deterrent policies may be rational, and if rational, involve the performance of actions which, in themselves and apart from the context of deterrence, would be irrational, but which, in that context, result from rational intentions and so are rational?[5] Surely he grants the substance of my argument but expresses his agreement in a misleading and even paradoxical way, insisting that actions necessary to a rational policy may themselves be irrational. To assess an action as irrational is, in my view, to claim that it should not be, or have been, performed. If our objector accepts deterrent policies, then he cannot consistently reject the actions they require and so cannot claim that such actions should not be performed.

Suppose, then, that our objector confronts my position head on and rejects the rationality of deterrent policies. He insists that the execution of an intention must take precedence, rationally, over its adoption. He

4. If preference is necessarily revealed in behavior, then choosing a nuclear exchange shows that one prefers it to one's alternatives. Conceptually, we can (and many economists and game theorists do) fit preference and choice so tightly together that nothing could count as non-utility-maximizing behavior. But this mode of conceptualization is a Procrustean bed for the treatment of such issues as the rationality of deterrence.

5. How his position may differ is made clear by David Lewis, "Devil's Bargains and the Real World," in *The Security Gamble: Deterrence Dilemmas in the Nuclear Age*, ed. Douglas MacLean (Totowa, N.J.: Rowman & Allanheld, in press). I begin a rejoinder to Lewis in "Response to the Paradox of Deterrence," in MacLean, ed.

must insist that it is rational to form an intention if and only if one maximizes one's expected utility both in forming it and in executing it. If either condition fails, then formation of the intention is not rational.

This objector insists that the rationality of an action is always to be assessed *from now*, in the words of Bernard Williams.[6] The rationality of an action is to be assessed from the point at which the question, not of intending it, but of performing it, arises. And this is, I think, the heart of the matter. In taking this position the objector applies the utility-maximizing standard of rationality in the way generally approved by economists, decision theorists, and game theorists. But he, and they, are mistaken. The fully rational actor is not the one who assesses her actions from now but, rather, the one who subjects the largest, rather than the smallest, segments of her activity to primary rational scrutiny, proceeding from policies to performances, letting assessment of the latter be ruled by assessment of the former.

A utility-maximizing policy may include non-utility-maximizing performance. Deterrence exemplifies this. The expected utility of a policy is the sum of the probability-weighted expected utilities of the performances it allows or requires. The apparent paradox, that a utility-maximizing policy may contain non-utility-maximizing performances, is resolved in the realization that altering the performances need not be independent of altering their probabilities. An assessment that begins and remains at the level of the performances neglects this crucial fact. And so the actor who assesses the rationality of his actions only from now, from the point at which the question of performance arises, may expect a lesser overall utility than the actor who assesses the rationality of her actions in the context of policies, who adjusts performances so that the probability-weighted sum of their utilities is greatest.

Our objector will say that the policy maximizer allows her choices to be ruled by the dead hand of the past, whereas he, the performance maximizer, lives and chooses in the present. But our objector is mistaken. Unable to escape the burden of choice, the performance maximizer must, choosing in the present, keep in mind that his attempt to maximize utility in the present performance is constrained by his future attempts to maximize utility on the occasion of each successive performance. He is ruled by the unborn, and perhaps never-to-be-born, hands of his possible futures. And his yoke is the worse. Maximization is the policy maximizer's goal, but the performance maximizer's fate.[7]

Before leaving our objector to that fate, let us note carefully that the reply to him does not insist that one should maximize in the long run rather than the short run. The would-be deterrer who fails to deter and who must then make good on her threat in order to carry out her

6. Bernard Williams, *Moral Luck* (Cambridge: Cambridge University Press, 1981), p. 35.

7. I expand on this point in "Response to the Paradox of Deterrence."

conditional intention, is not maximizing at all. Her reason for sticking to her guns is not to teach others by example, not to improve her prospects for successful deterrence in the future, or anything of the sort. Her reason is simply that the expected utility or payoff of her failed policy depended on her willingness to stick to her guns.

Let us suppose that each person or nation—each actor—knew (never mind how!) that but once in his life he would be in a situation in which, by convincing another actor that he would respond in a nonmaximizing way to a possible choice of the other, he could increase his expected utility by reducing the probability that the other would make that choice. Here, if the other is not deterred, carrying out the nonmaximizing response can, *ex hypothesi*, have no effect on the actor's credibility or on future deterrence. Yet he can hope to deter only if the other believes that he will, or at least may, make that nonmaximizing response. And adopting a genuine policy of deterrence may be the only way of bringing about that belief, or increasing its strength, in the other person. Even in this one-shot situation, a deterrent policy, committing one to a nonmaximizing choice should deterrence fail, may be utility maximizing. If I have convinced you of this, then I have accomplished my most important task in this essay, because only those convinced can have a proper understanding, not only of deterrence, but also of the whole range of situations, including most prominently generalized Prisoners' Dilemmas, in which policies that require nonmaximizing behavior are utility maximizing, and so rational.[8] And what these policies effect is throughout the same—to alter the probabilities of an actor's being in certain situations, facing certain choices. Only in understanding this do we begin to appreciate the true characteristics and complexity of utility-maximizing rationality.

VI

I have referred in passing to the expression of a conditional intention to *retal* as a threat. And the argument that I have advanced for the rationality of a deterrent policy is indeed an argument for the rationality of threat enforcement. If the expected gain from deterrence exceeds the expected cost of carrying out the deterrent threat, where each expectation is probability weighted, and if no less costly means of deterrence is available, then the rational actor sincerely threatens and enforces her threat should it fail to deter.

Not all threats, we may pause to note, are properly deterrent. The kidnapper threatens the parents of his victim with the death of their child should they fail to pay; it would be perverse to say that he seeks to deter them from nonpayment. But I shall not attempt an analysis of threats here. My purpose in introducing the conception of threat is to

---

8. I discuss this, although obscurely, in "Reason and Maximization," *Canadian Journal of Philosophy* 4 (1975): 427–30. Matters should be clearer in my *Morals by Agreement* (Oxford: Oxford University Press, in press), chap. 6.

broaden the perspective of our analysis so that it embraces both threatener and threatened, and in this perspective we shall find a new and problematic dimension in our argument.

If we think of nuclear retaliation as a policy of threat enforcement, yet we must note immediately that it is also a policy of threat resistance. The US threatens nuclear retaliation to deter a strike by the SU, but a strike policy, as we have described it, may center on the issuance of a credible threat of nuclear attack should some initiative be opposed, and retaliation thus embraces resistance to such a threat. In the context of nuclear deterrence each party may be viewed both as threatener and as threatened, both as a potential threat enforcer and as a potential threat resister. Not all threat situations involve this symmetry, but the standpoints of threatener and threatened are themselves significantly parallel. For each must decide whether to adopt an intention—to enforce a threat or to resist a threat. The enforcer seeks to avoid that situation in which enforcement would be required; the resister seeks to prevent that situation in which resistance would be required. The argument of Section IV may be adapted to show the rationale for both threat enforcement and threat resistance. Since, taken together, enforcement and resistance make threat behavior unprofitable, the existence of parallel rationales may cast doubt on the rationality of any policy involving threats, and so on a policy of deterrence.

Let us consider briefly how the argument of Section IV applies to enforcement and resistance. Both the would-be threat enforcer and the would-be threat resister seek to reduce the probability of being in an undesirable situation (having one's threat ignored/facing a credible threat) by expressing a conditional intention to respond in a mutually costly way in that situation. Enforcement/resistance success lies in avoiding the undesirable situation; enforcement/resistance failure lies in having to carry out one's conditional intention. The minimum required probability for enforcement/resistance success is defined as the probability of that success in the lottery between success and failure that the enforcer/resister considers indifferent to no enforcement/no resistance. A policy of threat enforcement/ threat resistance is rational only if the proportionate decrease that it effects in the probability of having one's threat ignored/facing a credible threat is greater than the minimum required probability for enforcement/ resistance success.

The parallel rationales that can be constructed for threat enforcement and threat resistance may seem to show the overall irrationality of threat behavior. For if both enforcement and resistance are rational, then either the worst case prevails, in which a threat is issued, ignored, and executed, or the prethreat situation prevails, no threat being issued since, if it were, it would be ignored and then executed. But although there is a deep irrationality in threat behavior, the parallel rationales do not themselves suffice to demonstrate it. For they show only that the structure of the argument for enforcement is the same as that for resistance. They do not show that, in a given situation, threat enforcement and threat resistance are equally rational or irrational.

We may illustrate this by our core example—nuclear deterrence. Suppose that the SU were to announce a policy of deterrence-resistance. It will carry out, or threaten, a nuclear strike if it considers that a retaliatory response would be costly to the US—if it believes that the maximizing US response would be acquiescence or submission.

As we noted in Section III, the SU prefers strike and no retaliation to no strike, and no strike to strike and retaliation. A policy of deterrence-resistance is rational for the SU only if the proportionate decrease that it effects in the probability of a US policy of retaliation is greater than the minimum required probability for the success of deterrence-resistance. But this is the probability of strike and no retaliation in that lottery between strike and no retaliation and strike and retaliation that the SU finds indifferent to the certainty of no strike. No strike represents, in effect, acceptance of the status quo; we may plausibly suppose that the SU would require a very high probability of gain—of the US acquiescence entailed in strike and no retaliation—and a correspondingly low probability of loss—of the nuclear exchange entailed in strike and retaliation—before it would be indifferent between such a lottery and the status quo. We may plausibly suppose that deterrence-resistance will not seem to the SU to be a utility-maximizing policy.

The US, as we also noted in Section III, prefers no strike to strike and no retaliation, and strike and no retaliation to strike and retaliation. Thus as we established in Section IV, deterrence is a rational policy for the US only if the proportionate decrease that it effects in the probability of a strike policy by the SU is greater than the probability of no strike in the lottery between no strike and strike and retaliation that the US finds indifferent to the certainty of strike and no retaliation. Although we have refrained from attempting to estimate this probability, except to suggest that it is likely to be high, yet we may note that strike and no retaliation represents, not the status quo, but a real worsening of the situation of the US. Even though a nuclear exchange is a greater worsening, yet we may plausibly suppose that the US would not require a very high probability of maintaining the status quo implicit in no strike, and a very low corresponding probability of loss through nuclear exchange, to be indifferent between such a lottery and the loss implicit in no retaliation. Although any firm judgment must be beyond armchair competence, it may well be the case that nuclear retaliation is a rational policy for the US, although resistance to deterrence is not a rational policy for the SU.

Thus the parallel between the rationales for threat enforcement and threat resistance does not in itself show the irrationality of a policy of deterrence. However, even if threat behavior is rationally justifiable from the standpoint of a particular actor, there is a need for mutually agreed measures to remove the threat-inviting context. Fundamental to Hobbes's analysis of the state of nature is the need to exit through the acceptance of mutual constraints.[9] The state of nations and, more especially, of nuclear powers is our nearest analogue to the state of nature, and Hobbes's advice applies to it. The need to rely on deterrence is a sign of the presence of peril sufficient to justify an agreement removing or minimizing the need. This will be my final theme in this paper; even if deterrence not only may be, but is, a rational policy for the US, the nuclear status quo that demands deterrence is not a rational state of affairs.

VII

Threat behavior is nonproductive, and indeed counterproductive, if we take its effects on all persons into account. This does not result directly from the intentions of the actors involved. The person who issues a threat seeks to increase her expectation of benefit, but only by reducing the expectation of the party threatened. The threat enforcer's willingness to risk an unfavorable outcome lowers the prospects of the person threatened and thus brings about a redistribution of benefits and costs. But a redistribution need not be a reduction of net benefit. The threat resister simply seeks a restoration of the status quo; given a threat, his strategy is redistributive, but taken in a larger context, it is intended as a counter that renders threats ineffective. The threat resister, through his willingness to risk an unfavorable outcome, seeks to restore his initial expectation of benefit, but not by reducing the prethreat expectation of the prospective threatener. Again, there need be no reduction in net benefit.

However, if in an ideal world threat behavior might avoid mutual costs, yet in the real world we must expect that from time to time either a threat enforcer or a threat resister will be called on to make good on a conditional nonmaximizing intention. And when this occurs, the result is suboptimal. The payoff from a failed threat, or from failed threat resistance, is less desirable, to each party, than either the payoff expected in the absence of any threat or the redistributed payoff resulting from a successful threat. Insofar as threat behavior involves a real risk of such a suboptimal result, it must be regarded as ex ante disadvantageous from the standpoint of any actor who is sufficiently uncertain about future prospects. Only someone who could expect to be especially favorably placed with respect to successful threatening would lack ex ante reason to agree to eschew threat behavior. Rational persons will therefore find the mutual avoidance of threat behavior to be an appropriate matter for agreement.

We should note here a contrast between threat situations and collective-goods situations. Where the possibility of providing collective goods is present, rational persons can expect to benefit from mutual agreement to assure the optimal provision of these goods, even though such provision may require nonmaximizing behavior. For the outcome of individually maximizing behavior in such situations is typically suboptimal; each party

9. This is the import of Hobbes's second law of nature, *Leviathan*, chap. 14.

stands to gain from making and adhering to an optimizing agreement in comparison to the expected outcome of no agreement. Here non-maximizing behavior is set in a productive context. But in threat situations, the nonmaximizing behavior required to make the issuance of or resistance to threats rational is not productive. The parties to such behavior are not enabled to reach outcomes mutually preferable to those they would otherwise expect; instead, they are likely to reach outcomes mutually less preferable. Hence actors faced with the problem of providing collective goods have reason to enter into agreements calling for nonmaximizing behavior, whereas actors faced with the problem of threats have reason to enter into agreements calling for the renunciation of policies with nonmaximizing threat components. Faced with collective goods problems, rational actors will agree mutually to constrain their directly maximizing dispositions. Faced with threat problems, rational actors will agree mutually not to constrain their directly maximizing dispositions in ways that would make credible threats possible.

Deterrence, as a typical policy of threat enforcement and threat resistance, is itself clearly unproductive. But in considering the terms on which it should rationally be renounced, it is essential to recognize its role in stabilizing human interaction. For the threat implicit in nuclear deterrence is not a threat against social order but, rather, a threat intended to maintain the conditions under which viable and fair social order is possible.

We may appeal here to a normative idea clearly formulated by John Rawls, that society is "a cooperative venture for mutual advantage."[10] This idea immediately suggests a baseline condition for social interaction: no person or other social actor is entitled to benefit at the expense or cost of another, where both benefit and cost are measured against a no-interaction baseline. That is, no actor is entitled to make himself or herself better off than could be expected in the absence of interaction, by policies or performances that render other actors worse off than they would expect to be in the absence of interaction. A refusal to accept or abide by this condition is an indication of an unwillingness to interact cooperatively with others—an unwillingness, in Hobbesian language, to seek peace and follow it.

Now a policy that includes a willingness to resort to an initial nuclear strike, even if only in the event of a failed threat, is clearly ruled out by this condition. For the effect of such a policy is clearly to worsen the situation of the victim in a way that exceeds what he could expect in the absence of interaction. And the policy cannot itself be treated as defensive, as merely preventing the actor from having his own position worsened through interaction with the victim. An aggressive strike policy is one that seeks to better the condition of its holder through measures that

10. John Rawls, *A Theory of Justice* (Cambridge, Mass.: Harvard University Press, 1971), p. 4.

worsen the condition of those against whom it is directed. To resort to such a policy is to reject the prospect of cooperative interaction with others.

Nuclear retaliation, as a deterrent policy, is directed at protecting the retaliator from being victimized by any actor willing to engage in a first strike. It is, then, not to seek to redistribute benefits in a way more favorable to the would-be deterrer than could be expected in the absence of interaction but, rather, to ensure that her situation is not worsened in terms of that baseline. It is directed at upholding, rather than subverting, the requirement that human society be a cooperative venture for mutual advantage.

In itself, of course, nothing could be less cooperative, less directed at mutual advantage, than the use of nuclear weapons. But a retaliatory, deterrent policy is directed at preventing such use—directed at maintaining those conditions in which societies may be brought to recognize the benefits of cooperation. A policy of nuclear deterrence clearly has failed if a nuclear exchange occurs. But the serious alternative to such a policy, in the absence of agreement to eschew all threat behavior, can only be the willingness to accept victimization, to suffer passively a nuclear strike or to acquiesce in whatever the potential striker demands as the price of its avoidance.

Morality, in my view, follows rationality. Practical rationality is concerned with the maximization of benefit; the primary requirements of morality are that in maximizing benefit, advantage must not be taken and need not be given.[11] Nuclear deterrence, despite its horrific character, is then a moral policy—a policy aimed at encouraging the conditions under which morally acceptable and rational interaction among nations may occur. If we agree that the idea of society as a cooperative venture for mutual advantage, and the related proviso against benefiting through interaction that worsens the condition of others, express a fundamental moral ideal, then the willingness to maintain those conditions under which this ideal may be realized, and the refusal to acquiesce in measures that would subvert it, must themselves be the objects of moral approval rather than censure.

Rational nations, recognizing the need to seek peace and follow it given the costs of war, can unilaterally renounce the first use of nuclear weapons and thereby end all strike policies. Rational nations can mutually agree to destroy their holdings of nuclear weapons, at least insofar as these weapons are directed against each other, and so can end all deterrent policies. Since the knowledge that brought nuclear weapons into being will not disappear, we cannot expect a world fully free of nuclear threats. We can only minimize a peril that cannot be exorcised. But to understand the conditions under which we may rationally agree to the mutual aban-

11. Neither utilitarians nor Kantians will find this conception of morality to their taste. I cannot defend it here, but see Gauthier, *Morals by Agreement*.

donment of deterrent and other threat policies, we must first understand the rationale of deterrent policies and the role of these policies in maintaining the conditions of acceptable international interaction. Hobbes conjoins two fundamental requirements in relating the law and the right of nature: "To seek Peace, and follow it" and "by all means we can, to defend our selves."[12] Hobbes understands that these requirements are mutually supportive; a correct understanding of nuclear deterrence supports his view.

Between Assured Destruction and Nuclear Victory: The Case for the "Mad-Plus" Posture*

Robert J. Art

Nuclear strategy and nuclear war are neither pleasant nor easy to contemplate. They require thinking about the possibility of a horrendous loss of life, planning for an eventuality for which we have had no experience, and confronting a sequence of events that could destroy humanity. Over the years, contemplation of such matters has led many citizens to condemn nuclear deterrence as immoral and to call for the abolition of nuclear weapons. Modern day strategists have rejected nuclear abolition as both naive and dangerous. The knowledge of how to construct nuclear weapons, they have argued, cannot be uninvented even if their physical presence could be abolished; nor do the international political conditions exist that would permit their abolition. Unilateral nuclear disarmament could too easily subject the disarming nation to the political sway of another nuclear power. And even if each nation that had them were to abolish its nuclear weapons, all would still have to worry about the ever-present possibility of a covert attempt by others to rearm with them. This continuous danger would necessitate an international institution to police a nuclear disarmament pact, but historically the nations of the world have not proved capable of devising viable international political institutions of control.

Rather than reject nuclear weapons, strategists since World War II have divided into two distinct camps in their attempts to wrestle with nuclear strategy—the finite deterrers and the flexible responders.[1] The former are commonly associated with assured destruction, countervalue or countercity targeting, and small nuclear forces; the latter, with war waging, limited nuclear options, counterforce targeting, and large nuclear forces. Finite deterrers have held to the position that what makes nuclear deterrence stable is the threat to destroy the cities of an adversary in a

* I wish to thank Robert O. Keohane, Susan Okin, and Stephen Van Evera for helpful comments on an earlier draft of this piece. But especially I thank John Mearsheimer for pushing me to think about what I really wanted to say, for forcing me to reconceptualize the first draft and for carefully reading two subsequent drafts.

1. The best treatment of this distinction is by Robert Jervis, "Why Nuclear Superiority Doesn't Matter," *Political Science Quarterly* 4 (1979–80): 617–33.

retaliatory blow. Because a second strike countervalue blow is sufficient, nuclear deterrence requires no counterforce capabilities and only a small number of nuclear weapons, as long as a portion of them are invulnerable to a first strike. The threat to devastate a potential attacker's cities, even only a small number of them, is all that is required to dissuade him from attacking. And when both sides have an assured destruction capability, mutual assured destruction, or MAD, obtains and makes nuclear deterrence quite stable. Flexible responders argue that the threat to destroy cities in retaliation, when the adversary can do the same to the retaliator, has lost its credibility for dealing with a wide range of political/military contingencies and, therefore, that a range of options short of countercity blows is required to strengthen deterrence.

The finite deterrent position stresses that, because a nuclear war will likely get quickly out of control and involve massive numbers of explosions, limited nuclear options are superfluous at best and dangerous at worst. They are superfluous because they will have no utility in such an all-out war. They could not prevent cities from being devastated and can, therefore, serve no useful military or political purpose. They are dangerous because they foster the belief that nuclear war can be limited and, as a consequence, could make it appear less horrendous and hence more likely. The flexible response position stresses two counterpoints: first, in the era of mutual assured destruction, threats to retaliate massively against an adversary's cities lack sufficient credibility to deter him from undertaking hostile acts against one's allies; second, the threat of a retaliatory countercity blow, if it had to be implemented, would end all hope of quickly limiting and ending such a war short of total devastation to both.

In the last few years, as both the Americans and Russians have developed highly accurate, sophisticated, and ever larger numbers of nuclear forces, the difference between the two traditional camps has widened. The advance of technology and the growth in numbers have widened the gap because the flexible responders want to exploit further the potentialities for greater flexibility, while the finite deterrers fear a lowering of the restraints on nuclear use that the additional exploitation of flexibility could bring.

As a consequence, many finite deterrers no longer argue simply that a small number of nuclear weapons delivered on cities is sufficient for the stability of deterrence. Many now take the position that the *only* utility nuclear weapons possess is to deter the use of other nuclear weapons. Former Secretary of Defense Robert McNamara has forcefully argued this position: "Having spent seven years as Secretary of Defense dealing with the problems unleashed by the initial nuclear chain reaction forty years ago, I do not believe we can avoid serious and unacceptable risk of nuclear war until we recognize—and until we base all our military plans, defense budgets, weapons deployments, and arms negotiations on the recognition—*that nuclear weapons serve no military purpose whatsoever.*

They are totally useless—except only to deter one's opponent from using them."[2]
Similarly, several flexible responders now argue that nuclear wars can
be successfully waged and won and that the best way to deter them and
extend the American nuclear umbrella over its allies is to convince the
adversary that one can indeed fight and win them. A prominent exponent
of this view is Colin Gray, who has stated: "In order to extend deterrence
credibly on behalf of distant allies, the United States needs both to be
able to deny victory to the Soviet and—no less important—to avoid defeat
itself. These requirements add up to a requirement for a capability to
win wars."[3]

Thus, finite deterrers may be moving to the view that nuclear weapons
have very limited military, and hence almost no political, utility because
their initial use makes so little sense. Flexible responders may be turning
from war wagers into war winners. The possibilities that have developed
over the last ten years for greater flexibility in nuclear use have begun
to drive both camps from their respective centers toward the extremes
inherent in each.

In my view, both these camps miss the mark. On the one hand, finite
deterrers are naive because they do not understand the effects on *statecraft*
that the nuclear revolution has produced. Nuclear deterrence dissuades
an adversary from taking actions other than simply using his nuclear
weapons against another state that may or may not have them. Nuclear
deterrence produces restraining effects that are based on the fear of
nuclear war, but such effects extend far beyond simply dissuading initial
nuclear use. With or without the McNamara position, finite deterrence
severely downplays these larger political effects. On the other hand, the
flexible responders, when they become obsessed with flexibility and move
toward war winning, are also naive because they do not understand the
effects on *warfare* that the nuclear revolution has produced. War waging
has some specific but quite limited virtues for deterrence, escalation
control, and damage limitation. War winning, however, is impossible
precisely because of the fact that there is no defense now against all-out
nuclear use and probably not for the foreseeable future. A nuclear war
could therefore be controlled and won only if one side consciously chose
to lose the war, an event as unlikely in the future as it has been rare or
nonexistent in the past. It is not necessary to win a nuclear war in order
to deter it; one has only to ensure that both are likely to lose it.

There is a reasonable position between these two extremes. It embodies
elements of both finite deterrence and flexible response. In what follows,
I etch this position out by treating in turn, first, the political effects of

2. Robert McNamara, "The Military Role of Nuclear Weapons: Perceptions and Misperceptions," *Foreign Affairs* 62 (1983): 59–81, p. 79.

3. See Colin Gray, "War Fighting for Deterrence," *Journal of Strategic Studies* 7 (1984):
5–29, p. 11.

nuclear deterrence and, second, the irrelevance for the stability of deterrence of symmetry in counterforce capabilities. I thus will lay the groundwork for a position between these two extremes by analyzing the strengths and weaknesses of the finite deterrent and flexible response positions, respectively, in the next two sections.

In the last section of this paper, I conclude that if we think about nuclear strategy politically, we find that there is a viable position between the finite deterrent and flexible response positions that, for lack of a better term, I call the "MAD-plus" posture. It is one that relies heavily on the restraining effects of mutual assured destruction, but that favors some limited war-waging capability for both escalation-signaling and damage-limitation purposes. It favors some limited counterforce (what I later term "weak" counterforce) but not a "robust" counterforce capability that would undermine MAD. The purpose of a weak counterforce capability (which both the Americans and the Russians now have), or, better put, a targeting policy directed at soft military targets, is to avoid initial attacks on cities and thereby limit damage. The MAD-plus posture also favors some investment in command, control, communications, and intelligence (what is referred to as C^3I) to preserve control in any nuclear war that starts out limited precisely for the purpose of keeping the war limited. Some C^3I is necessary in order to maintain control over the nuclear exchanges and thereby buy enough time so that political leaders in both capitols can negotiate quickly to bring the limited war swiftly to an end. In essence, the MAD-plus posture is a hedge: it relies mainly on assured destruction but favors buying some limited options or flexibility for added insurance.

THE POLITICAL EFFECTS OF NUCLEAR DETERRENCE

Nuclear weapons have political consequences that extend far beyond their military effects. Neither the assured destructors nor the flexible responders, however, accept this premise. Because the former argue that the only thing the possession of nuclear weapons does for a state is to prevent another state from using them against it, nuclear weapons dissuade only nuclear use and therefore only a small number are needed. Because the latter argue that a small number of nuclear weapons is sufficient neither to deter a nuclear attack nor to limit damage should one occur, a state needs a large number of them to deter attacks on itself and its allies and to limit damage to both should war occur. For the finite deterrers, only the civilian population of the adversary need be held hostage; for the war wagers, in addition to civilians, the adversary's nuclear weapons, other military forces, command centers, and political control structures must be subject to devastation.

Oddly enough, from the same mistaken premise, they draw opposite conclusions. While the finite deterrers call for fewer of them and the war wagers for more of them, both share a common misunderstanding about the political role of nuclear weapons. Both have grossly underestimated the powerful restraining effects that the possession of nuclear weapons have had on superpower statecraft and on that of the other states that possess them. Nuclear weapons do things other than simply prevent other states from using them. The existence of nuclear weapons not only dissuades nuclear use but also dampens down the likelihood of the use of conventional forces against an adversary that also possesses nuclear weapons or against a close nonnuclear ally of a nuclear state. Nuclear weapons have made a general war, either conventional or nuclear, between the superpowers and their associated clients less likely. Nuclear weapons make a superpower and its associated clients that are involved in a conventional war more careful than they would otherwise be about how they conduct it for fear of going beyond the permissible limits and provoking intervention by the other superpower. The threat of retaliation, the possibility of escalation, the concomitant risk that things could get out of control, and the knowledge that if they do all is lost—it is these four factors that have forced nuclear statesmen to be more cautious than their pre-World-War-II "conventional" predecessors.

Most wars have occurred because someone miscalculated but in a very particular way—either about what the opponent would do, what he could do, or what could be done to him. Stalin may have lost twenty million Russians in World War II, but he certainly did not expect that outcome when he made his deal with Hitler. Hitler may ultimately have been mad, but he was banking on a short war and Allied weakness. Bethmann Hollweg may have sought relief from imperial Germany's political and military encirclement by deliberately launching a Continental war, but he certainly did not seek a world war. In these cases and others, miscalculations occurred because someone was more certain about what would happen than they should have been and than events ultimately warranted.

The nuclear age does not encourage such miscalculations to arise out of such supposed certainties. The threat to both parties that matters could quickly get out of control, together with the horrendous costs that would be imposed on both if they did, has built in a bias in nuclear statecraft toward a degree of caution and restraint that, although it can never eradicate miscalculation, has, nevertheless, minimized it greatly. That is all we can expect. But that is significant. Nuclear weapons have narrowed the range of matters about which statesmen can be certain because they have widened the range of those over which uncertainty reigns. *Ironically, miscalculation has decreased because uncertainty has increased.* It is the potential for loss of control through escalation that has built into nuclear diplomacy a degree of uncertainty about the course of events that is greater than what once obtained. It is not so much the destruction that is assured, but that which *could* occur if matters got out of control, that is the basis for the MAD world in which we live today.

The existence of nuclear weapons has thus introduced a clear and pronounced restraint into the conduct of superpower diplomacy that has affected world politics generally. Wars have continued to occur, certainly; but they have not escalated into a general one between the superpowers. Clearly crises have occurred because risks have been taken by the superpowers. We do not live in a risk-free world. But when excessive risk taking has resulted in crises, the potential for escalation has worked to defuse them. The Cuban missile crisis is a case in point. Khrushchev would clearly not have put offensive missiles into Cuba had he known that Kennedy would have reacted as forcefully as he did. He would not have knowingly and willingly put himself and his nation into the position of being humiliated, as both subsequently were. Once he saw how strong a stance Kennedy took, he backed down. But Kennedy, though insistent on getting the missiles out, also acted with restraint: he started with the least bellicose action to get the missiles out (the blockade) and did all that he could to help Khrushchev save some semblance of face, both done from his awareness of what a single misstep could bring.

The Cuban missile crisis must therefore be seen as the exception that proves the rule. Superpower statesmen have to calculate carefully because the costs of miscalculation are potentially so horrendous. Sometimes they make mistakes. But the last forty years of American-Russian relations have seen only one grievous one. And when one occurs, both nations have acted quickly to rectify it because each has a shared interest in avoiding an all-out confrontation. Each superpower will not cease testing the other, to see what it can get away with. But it will calculate as carefully as it can before it probes because it has to. Thus, nuclear deterrence can work to produce more probing actions but quick retreat if the probe hits steel. Since 1945, the "stability-instability paradox," well known to nuclear strategists, has worked more to dampen down undue risk taking by the superpowers with respect to whether they provoke crises and how they manage them than it has to embolden either to careless adventurism.[4]

Thus, because significant political effects flow from the possession of nuclear weapons, it is wrongheaded to argue either that the only function of nuclear weapons is to deter their use by another, *or* to assert that the capability to wage and win a nuclear war is necessary to deter it. Therefore, Robert McNamara is clearly wrong when he argues that nuclear weapons are "totally useless" except to deter another state from using them. The dampening down of risk-taking behavior in general, not simply initial nuclear use, flows from the existence of nuclear deterrence. So, too, is Colin Gray wrong when he argues that a denial of a Russian victory requires an American one. It is sufficient to demonstrate simply that the Soviet Union could not win a war and could suffer terribly if it persisted, even if the United States also lost it, to deter the Soviet Union. In the nuclear era, one nation does not have to win for the other

---

4. The term was first introduced by Glenn H. Snyder, "The Balance of Power and the Balance of Terror," in *The Balance of Power*, ed. Paul Seabury (San Francisco: Chandler Publishing Co., 1965). It refers to the fact that stability at the level of all-out nuclear war can produce instability at lower levels of violence.

to lose. Both can lose and therefore decide the risks are not worth taking. Thus, it is the generalized caution imposed on the superpowers by their mutual possession of a retaliatory capability that invalidates the claims of both the finite deterrers and the war wagers.[5]

The fear that things could quickly get out of control, together with the costs involved if they do—these are what work to dissuade nuclear statesmen from taking undue risks. If escalation could be controlled, there would be no risk in escalating. In the nuclear era, it is precisely the potential for the loss of control that is the keystone of restraint and the essence of deterrence. In his final work, *War and Politics,* Bernard Brodie put the case well when he argued:

> We have ample reason to feel now that nuclear weapons do act critically to deter wars between the major powers, and not nuclear wars alone but any wars. That is really a very great gain. We should no doubt be hesitant about relinquishing it even if we could. We should not complain too much because the guarantee is not ironclad. It is the curious paradox of our time that one of the foremost factors making deterrence really work and work well is the lurking fear that in some massive confrontation crisis it might fail. Under these circumstances one does not tempt fate. If we were absolutely certain that nuclear deterrence would be 100 per cent effective against nuclear attack, then it would cease to have much if any deterrence value against non-nuclear wars, and the arguments of the conventional buildup schools would indeed finally make sense.[6]

In short, what makes nuclear deterrence extend so far is the fear that it might not.

Finally, if nuclear weapons have these political effects, it is because of the destruction they can wreak and the way that they can do it. As Thomas Schelling put it many years ago, "Victory is no longer a prerequisite for hurting the enemy."[7] One can now destroy the enemy without having first vanquished him. Nuclear weapons have therefore separated the power to hurt from the power to defeat, what Schelling called, respectively, "coercive power" and "brute force." Because each superpower has it within its power to absorb a first strike from the other and still retaliate with a large number of warheads, the incentive for striking first is low. Each, therefore, can destroy, but not disarm, the other. What is balanced in the nuclear age is the power to hurt, not the power to disarm. What has ultimately ended all wars, as Schelling reminded us, was not the military

5. For more on these points, see Robert J. Art, "To What Ends Military Power?" *International Security* (1980): 3–35; Kenneth N. Waltz, *The Spread of Nuclear Weapons: More May Be Better,* Adelphi Paper 171 (London: International Institute of Strategic Studies, 1981).

6. Bernard Brodie, *War and Politics* (New York: Macmillan Publishing Co., 1973), pp. 430–31.

7. Thomas C. Schelling, *Arms and Influence* (New Haven, Conn.: Yale University Press, 1966), p. 22.

defeat of the adversary but the ability to threaten credibly to destroy him after he was defeated militarily unless he surrendered. The outcome of the brute-force exchange had to occur first before the exercise of coercive power to bring surrender could come into play. What nuclear weapons have done is to reverse permanently the traditional sequence of warfare: it is no longer necessary to vanquish the enemy in order to be in the position of threatening to destroy him. The latter can be done now without the former.

This condition, assured destruction, leads to the following three propositions:

First, if you do not have to destroy the other fellow's nuclear forces to devastate him, why bother?

Second, if you cannot destroy the other fellow's capability to devastate you, why try?

Third, great disparities in offensive forces can be safely tolerated when the power to hurt, not the power to disarm, is what is being balanced. The balancing of terror, that is, is not highly sensitive to changes in the quantitative balance of forces as long as the attacker-to-target ratio is greater than one to one.[8] With populations vulnerable, force ratios have less "force" than they once did. From a military standpoint, then, force ratio disparities are not worrisome. Militarily, it is not necessary to match forces; but, I shall argue later, there are political reasons for doing so—for having a rough parity in numbers of offensive forces.

Thus, the virtue of the assured destruction or finite deterrent school is that it reminds us of the fundamental condition of the nuclear era: as long as defense of populations is impossible, matching the adversary in the number of forces he has is not necessary. Its vice is that it is far too restrictive in its view of what nuclear weapons do in fact restrain and deter.

THE IRRELEVANCE OF COUNTERFORCE SYMMETRY

Is the flexible responder's world, with its emphasis on war waging (if not winning) and counterforce targeting better than the finite deterrers MAD world, with its emphasis on limited forces and countervalue targeting? Is it better to be able to target only cities rather than to be able to knock out military forces? The answer is, It depends on what one means by counterforce, on what types of forces one wishes to knock out. If by a counterforce world we mean one in which any nuclear power possessed a first strike capability against any other nuclear power's nuclear forces,

8. Bernard Brodie implicitly pointed this out in his *The Absolute Weapon: Atomic Power and World Order* (New York: Harcourt, Brace & Co., 1946), when he stated that "superiority in numbers of bombs is not in itself a guarantee of strategic superiority in atomic bomb warfare" (p. 46). But the first person in the public literature to develop the point fully was Glenn H. Snyder, *Deterrence and Defense: Toward a Theory of National Security* (Princeton, N.J.: Princeton University Press, 1961), pp. 42–46, 104–10.

clearly a MAD world is preferable. A true or "fully robust" counterforce world would be one in which all nuclear powers felt that each had an effective disarming capability. In a surprise attack, one adversary could knock out the other's offensive (and potential retaliatory) forces. If we are interested in preventing the use of nuclear weapons, which we should be, the attempt to attain such a capability is insane. As Schelling once put it, "Military technology that puts a premium on haste in a crisis puts a premium on war itself."[9] A counterforce world would encourage speedy decisions, hasty actions, preemptive strategies, grandiose ambitions, aggressive foreign policies, and the like.[10] Clearly a counterforce world lessens the political restraints on the physical use of nuclear force. It is desirable, therefore, that nuclear statemen continue to feel insecure about defense against nuclear attack and about their own first strike capabilities and secure only about their own and their adversary's retaliatory capabilities.

If a fully robust counterforce world is not desirable, is something short of it, what we might term a "weak" counterforce world, also undesirable? Is a world, that is, in which both sides possess considerable counterforce capabilities, but those still well short of a disarming capability, destabilizing? The answer to this question should be no simply because, no matter how extensive their counterforce capabilities are and no matter how great the asymmetry between them may be in this regard, neither side would be emboldened to strike first when the other would retain the capability to retaliate on its cities. Weak counterforce capabilities can and do exist in a MAD world. But that does not alter the fundamental condition of mutual vulnerability to which both superpowers are subject.

In order to develop this argument more fully, I will attack the position, first developed by Paul Nitze in 1976, that asserts that a perceived asymmetry in counterforce capability (in Russia's favor) both weakens deterrence and puts the United States at a disadvantage in crises and intense bargaining situations. His argument received wide currency in the United States and was reflected in the Carter administration's PD-59 and "countervailing strategy" pronouncements.[11] As explained by then Secretary of Defense Harold Brown, the countervailing strategy held to the view that, although the United States did not believe that either nation could prevail militarily in a nuclear war, nevertheless, for the stability of deterrence and the advantageous resolution of crises, the United States had to strengthen significantly its own war-waging posture and thus "countervail" against the Soviet Union.[12]

9. Schelling, p. 225.
10. Steven Van Evera has persuasively argued this case for Europe on the eve of war in 1914. He nicely shows how a belief in the disarming power of the offensive lessened the restraints on statecraft and helped bring on the war. See his "The Cult of the Offensive and the Origins of the First World War," *International Security* 9 (1984): 58–108.
11. For an excellent critique of America's countervailing strategy, see Robert Jervis, *The Illogic of American Nuclear Strategy* (Ithaca, N.Y.: Cornell University Press, 1984).
12. The best short description of the countervailing strategy appears in Harold Brown's fiscal year 1982 posture statement. See *The Report of the Secretary of Defense to the Congress*

I begin with Nitze's argument because he stated the asymmetry position in the most extreme form. In his influential article, he argued:

> In sum, the ability of U.S. nuclear power to destroy without question the bulk of Soviet industry and a large proportion of the Soviet population is by no means as clear as it once was, even if one assumes most of U.S. striking power to be available and directed to this end.
>
> A more crucial test, however, is to consider the possible results of a large-scale nuclear exchange in which one side sought to destroy as much of the other side's striking power as possible, in order to leave itself in the strongest possible position after the exchange.[13]

Nitze was concerned about the potential postattack position of the United States vis-à-vis the Soviet Union. If the Russians could wipe out most of America's land-based missile forces in a first strike and if the Americans did not have the same capability to wipe out most of Russia's land-based missiles in a first strike, then the Soviet leaders might be tempted to launch an attack on America's land forces, but they would more likely be emboldened to take risks that they otherwise would not because they would be acting from a supposedly superior position. In short, argued Nitze, asymmetries in counterforce capabilities, even if MAD still obtained, could be destabilizing and produce a more dangerous world for the United States. The countervailing strategy picked up this line of reasoning when it argued:

> The Soviet Union should entertain no illusion that by attacking our strategic nuclear forces, it could significantly reduce the damage it would suffer. Nonetheless, the state of the strategic balance after an initial exchange—measured both in absolute terms and in relation to the balance prior to the exchange—could be an important factor in the decision by one side to initiate a nuclear exchange. Thus, it is important—for the sake of deterrence—to be able to deny to the potential aggressor a fundamental and favorable shift in the strategic balance as a result of a nuclear exchange.[14]

Why, however, would asymmetries in counterforce capabilities be destabilizing if neither side had a robust or truly disarming counterforce capability? Why would the Russians attack land-based missiles when they could not get at the sea-based ones? Did the fact that the latter were invulnerable to a disarming attack not make the former, in effect, invulnerable also? The crux of Nitze's and presumably Brown's worry was this: the United States would be "self-deterred" from retaliating against Russian cities once it had suffered a massive strike against its land-based

---

on the FY 1982 Budget (Washington, D.C.: Government Printing Office, January 19, 1981), pp. 38–43.

13. See Paul Nitze, "Assuring Strategic Stability in an Era of Detente," *Foreign Affairs* 54 (1976): 207–233, p. 223.

14. Brown, p. 40.

forces. It would not hit back at Russian cities because that would cause a retaliatory Russian strike against American cities. The United States would be left in the same position many argued it once was in the fifties with its policy of massive retaliation: shoot off everything or do nothing. After its disarming blow against the land-based forces then, the Soviet Union would be in a position to intimidate the United States. In order to remedy this potential for "self-deterrence," the United States had to develop counterforce capabilities symmetrical to what the Soviet Union already had. America had, in short, to develop more of a war-waging capability in order to bolster deterrence.

The Nitze scenario and variants on it—and especially his call for the United States to develop a more formidable war-waging capability—received firm support from President Reagan's Commission on Strategic Forces in its April 1983 report:

> In order to deter such Soviet threats we must be able to put at risk those types of Soviet targets—including hardened ones such as military command bunkers and facilities, missile silos, nuclear weapons and other storage, and the rest—which the Soviet leaders have given every indication by their actions they value most, and which constitute their tools of control and power.
>
> Effective deterrence of any Soviet temptation to threaten or launch a massive conventional or limited nuclear war thus requires us to have a comparable ability to destroy Soviet military targets, hardened and otherwise. . . . A one-sided strategic condition in which the Soviet Union could effectively destroy the whole range of strategic targets in the United States, but we could not effectively destroy a similar range of targets in the Soviet Union, would be extremely unstable over the long run.
>
> . . . We must have a credible capability for controlled, prompt, limited attacks on hard targets ourselves. This capability casts a shadow over the calculus of Soviet risk-taking at any level of confrontation with the West.[15]

Early in the Reagan administration, Secretary of Defense Weinberger's call for the United States to be able to wage a "protracted" nuclear war through to a successful conclusion signified the final step in this line of reasoning. Under the early Reagan, America's policy shifted from countervailing to prevailing, from war waging to war winning. The later Reagan administration backed off from war winning in its subsequent pronouncements, but it continued to invest considerable sums to procure a formidable war-waging capability. But whether it be for war waging or war winning, the rationale has been that because they (the Russians) have it, we need it. Is this the case? Why should symmetry in counterforce capabilities be necessary? Why must we be able to wage a nuclear war as effectively as some argue the Russians can and/or intend in order to

15. "Report of the President's Commission on Strategic Forces" (April 1983, mimeographed), pp. 6, 16, 17.

deter it or in order to limit damage in it if it should occur? Is symmetry in war-fighting capabilities between the Russians and the Americans necessary for nuclear stability?

My judgment is no. I should like to offer seven reasons why I think the Nitze counterforce scenario, its many variants, and the entire symmetry-in-war-waging argument makes little military, and even less political, sense.

1. If the war wagers and counterforcers can argue that the United States would be deterred from attacking Russian cities in retaliation for a Russian first strike counterforce blow against America's Minuteman force, why can the "MAD men" not argue that, similarly, they would likely be deterred from attacking the Minuteman missiles in the first place because they cannot be certain that we would not retaliate against any, a few, or all of their cities? If self-deterrence works to prevent us from retaliating, would not self-deterrence also work to prevent them from attacking? Why does self-deterrence work only for us and not for them?

2. If neither the United States nor the Soviet Union is prepared to threaten to attack cities, *even if neither would ever want to execute that threat,* then each cannot deter the other, no matter how effective their war-fighting capabilities are. To repeat, what provides restraint is the fear that things will get out of control and that all could be lost—both sides' cities, that is,—if caution is abandoned. The war wagers, however, argue that the Soviet leaders value their machinery and their mechanisms of political control more than they do their populace. They do not accept the MAD world logic. The conclusion, they assert, is that our threat to devastate their population carries little weight with them.

How, however, in reality, can that conclusion make any military or political sense? First, a significant percentage of Russian hard targets are located in or near cities so that extensive counterforce attacks would produce civilian casualities that would likely be indistinguishable from purely countervalue attacks.[16] Colin Gray, for example, admits as much when he states: "Not only would one be assaulting the highest of Soviet values by counter-military targeting, and thereby minimizing if not removing entirely any Soviet incentives to exercise restraint, also one would be licensing a campaign that—if it were to be waged efficiently on both sides—would have to produce a vast amount of civilian damage. Both superpowers have very many military assets co-located with civilian society."[17] If extensive counterforce attacks would have much the same results for civilians as would pure population attacks, why do we need to fine tune our forces for hard target kills when we cannot avoid extensive civilian damage in the process? And would that be the best way for the

---

16. See Desmond Ball, "Research Note: Soviet ICBM Deployment," *Survival* (July/August 1980), pp. 167–70.

17. Gray, p. 23.

United States to limit damage to its civilians when the Russians know that American leaders value their populace highly? Second, would it not be extremely difficult to convince the Soviet leaders that limited counterforce strikes against military targets so colocated were aimed, not at their populace, but at them (or vice versa)? Is an attack on Moscow (or Washington) meant to be "only" decapitating, the precursor to a rolling or tit-for-tat exchange, or merely a one-time shot to show that we (or they) mean business? How could they (or we) know which was the case?

Third, finally, either extensive countervalue attacks or extensive counterforce attacks against the Soviet political mechanisms would kill so many Russian civilians that there would be little left to control! Political leaders do not value political control mechanisms per se; they value the power over others that such mechanisms yield. If there is no one left (or very few) to control, what, precisely, can be the point of the machinery for control? Surely mechanisms for control, apart from the objects of control, have little political meaning to those who possess them. Either type of attack, therefore, will eradicate the civilians. And since the leaders need the civilians to control, why go after them the hard way (counterforce) rather than the easy way (countervalue)? If there is logic to this argument, then the Soviet leaders must value their populace as much as American leaders do, even if they do so for different reasons. Thus, even the war wagers' emphasis on control mechanisms leads one inexorably back to populations and to the logic of MAD.

3. Third, what will end the nuclear war as well as prevent it is the threat of wiping out cities. Who has more weapons left over after an extensive brute-force exchange or after a series of small exchanges is irrelevant to the conclusion of the war as long as each party can still devastate the other. Postattack calculations about throw weight ratios, warhead ratios, missile ratios, and the like, make little sense. What has always brought a war to a successful conclusion for one party or a draw for both is the need to settle in order to avoid further or extensive civilian deaths. It is hard to see how disparities in force sizes, however measured, will make any difference to war termination when both will surely retain enough forces to threaten however many cities each still retains intact.

4. The Nitze scenario of an extensive Russian first strike against American's Minuteman force, although theoretically possible, glosses over the real and intractable operational difficulties the Soviet Union would have in executing such an attack. The fratricide problem alone makes the timing of such an attack inordinately complicated.[18] Although no one would advocate such a posture unless there were no choice, the United States could always resort to a launch-on-warning or -on-attack posture. It is difficult to imagine a Communist Party chairman of the Soviet Union imagining that an American president would simply watch

18. On this point, see John Steinbruner and Thomas Garwin, "Between Deterrence and Strategic Paranoia," *International Security* 1 (Summer 1976): 138–81.

the Russian missiles rain down on the United States. Would he not have to calculate that, if he shot at all of America's land-based silos, he might in effect be shooting at empty ones?

5. A massive disarming strike against America's Minuteman force would require something approaching 2,000 separate explosions. Would that be a truly limited and containable strike? Would a decision by the Soviet leaders to launch an attack of such magnitude not be equivalent to a declaration of World War III? Why would they go after America's land-based forces when America's sea-based forces remained intact? Are not land-based systems invulnerable because the sea-based ones are? Given the civilian casualties that an attack of such magnitude would have for the United States, could the Russian leaders seriously think that an American president would leave Russian cities intact? Why would they take such a risk? Why would they feel more emboldened in a crisis when such presumed capability carries such a high risk of an American counterresponse?

6. The United States today already possesses considerable counterforce capabilities and will, shortly, have even more. If these are to be used intelligently, that is, for deterrent purposes, they should be directed in our declaratory posture toward soft, not hard, military targets. If we ever need actually show that we are serious about escalation and if we want to hold our cities and theirs in hostage in the early phases of a nuclear war, surely limited counterforce attacks against credible, but containable, soft military targets is the least destabilizing counterforce posture available. If they ever were to occur, counterforce attacks should be limited and undertaken, not to disarm or to sever political control, but to demonstrate resolve in a way that still manages to limit the damage done.

7. Most of the above points have been directed to prewar deterrence. Should such a war occur, the best way to limit damage is not to institute extensive and wide-ranging counterforce attacks but, rather, to negotiate to stop the war immediately. The next best way is to limit any exchanges that may occur. The worst way to attempt to stop the war is to engage in massive counterforce exchanges that will heighten the incentives to preempt and that will, in any case, bring horrendous civilian deaths. And the deliberate, extensive targeting of Russian command, communications, control, and intelligence facilities is absurd. We (and they) need someone who is in control and with whom we can negotiate. We and they both require that someone remain in charge to limit the exchanges. In short, damage limitation does not require an extensive counterforce targeting capability. The execution of such a strategy on a large scale would likely produce the very results that it is intended to prevent—namely, extensive damage.

Beyond all these points lies a final one that renders the attempt to acquire a war-winning posture illusory. If a full-scale nuclear war is inherently uncontrollable, it is wasteful, if not absurd, to try to develop fully the means to control it. Selectivity, protractedness, fine tuning, discrimination—all these are entities not likely to exist or persevere in a protracted nuclear war of any size. Desmond Ball has persuasively shown that command, control, and communications systems are inherently more vulnerable than the strategic forces themselves, for both the Americans and the Russians, and will likely remain so for the foreseeable future. The consequence of this fact is that "the capability to exercise strict control and co-ordination would inevitably be lost relatively early in a nuclear exchange."[19] Any nuclear war, then, once it begins and if it continues, is likely to get out of hand. As long as that condition obtains, the pursuit of the ability to conduct a fully controlled and sizeable nuclear war is a fool's chase. It is not that we should not take precautions to preserve some options for selectivity and controllability. These are prudent measures. But to believe that matters can, in fact, be controlled and to operate under that assumption is wrong. The probability that things will get quickly out of control remains uncertain enough that gambling it will not is foolhardy. Because that is so, we are driven back to the MAD world of deterrence, almost, that is, but not quite.

THE CASE FOR THE "MAD-PLUS" POSTURE

Is there, then, nothing at all to be said for war waging, even after we have thrown out both war winning and symmetry in counterforce capabilities? Is finite deterrence, with its emphasis on small nuclear forces and countervalue targeting, the only sensible posture to take? Are there valid reasons why it is sensible not to have a nuclear force that is dramatically smaller in size than one's adversary's? Are there valid reasons to have some limited war-waging capabilities? I believe there are valid reasons both to match roughly one's adversary in numbers and to have a limited war-waging capability, though I stress the word "limited." I offer three reasons.

First, what makes military sense in the nuclear age—the absence of a compelling need to match exactly the adversary in the number of nuclear forces he possesses—makes little political sense for the two superpowers because their nuclear forces are used to protect territories other than merely their own. The logic of finite deterrence is impeccable for the restricted case of an attack on a superpower's homeland. (This is often referred to as type 1 deterrence, deterrence of an attack only on one's own territory.) For as long as a percentage of one's forces is invulnerable to a first strike, the adversary's cities can be held hostage to retaliation by a relatively small number of weapons. To deter one su-

19. Desmond Ball, *Can Nuclear War Be Controlled?* Adelphi Paper 169 (London: International Institute of Strategic Studies, Autumn 1981), p. 37. See also U.S. Congress, *Strategic Command, Control, and Communications: Alternative Approaches for Modernization,* a Congressional Budget Office study (October 1981); and Paul Bracken, *The Command and Control of Nuclear Forces* (New Haven, Conn.: Yale University Press, 1983).

perpower from attacking only it directly, therefore, the other superpower needs to have a force merely some fractional size of the former's.

What works for type 1 deterrence, however, has not proved politically feasible for type 2 deterrence. The latter encompasses the difficult problem of "extended deterrence," that is, extending the protection of each superpower's nuclear umbrella over its nonnuclear and small nuclear allies. The political imperatives that are rooted in these type 2 deterrent uses of their nuclear forces have pushed the superpowers to maintain a rough equivalence in the sizes of their forces and sometimes to strive for a superiority, that is, for a disarming or robust counterforce capability. For extended deterrent purposes, like it or not, if one superpower has a force dramatically smaller than the other, it looks weaker to the allies over whom the superpower's nuclear umbrella is being extended. Simply put, America's allies, especially the NATO allies, would feel better with an American superiority, bad with an American inferiority, and can tolerate an American equality with the Soviet Union. For the superpowers who have extended deterrent uses for their nuclear forces, the military logic of finite deterrence for the type 1 case is not sufficient for the political logic of alliance management inherent in the type 2 case, no matter how "illogical" the logic of the extended deterrent world may seem. Political concerns, therefore, dictate that having a small nuclear force when one's superpower adversary has a large one is politically disadvantageous and hence untenable. One of the underpinnings of finite deterrence—that large disparities in force sizes do not matter—does not hold.[20]

Second, finite deterrence has difficulties handling escalation scenarios that involve competitions in risk taking. Although it is true that, strictly speaking, what happens on the battlefield is not central to the outcome of any nuclear war that may begin, it is not totally irrelevant. To see the force of this argument, we must distinguish between how nuclear weapons are initially used and what subsequently happens on the battlefield.

In the nuclear era, it is the case that defeat on the battlefield cannot easily, if at all, be translated into victory in the war simply because the side that has suffered a temporary battlefield loss can always up the ante

20. I do not accept the converse, however: that an American nuclear superiority—a robust or disarming counterforce capability—would "solve" the problems inherent in extended deterrence. First of all, neither superpower would allow the other to acquire such a capability, which makes the issue academic. Second of all, for the NATO alliance at least, even when the United States was perceived by its allies to be ahead, in the fifties and sixties, still they were not satisfied. The United States in its era of nuclear advantage had to take many additional actions *in the theater* (within Western Europe) to assuage its allies, such as permanently stationing 300,000 American troops there. For lack of space, I simply assert this proposition: extended deterrent problems cannot be solved by seeking superiority or advantageous positions with central strategic systems; they must be handled with in-theater solutions. The way to extend deterrence, that is, is to make the territory being protected look sufficiently important to the United States such that its extension of its nuclear umbrella over it looks credible. See my forthcoming *NATO in the Era of Parity: Extended Deterrence and Alliance Politics* (Washington, D.C.: Brookings Institution, 1985) for a full treatment of this issue.

and go to a higher level of violence if he deems what he is fighting for worth the escalation. Battlefield victories have little meaning if the adversary can still destroy you after suffering them. In the nuclear era, "escalation dominance"—the ability to contain or defeat an adversary at all levels of violence except at the highest (all-out nuclear war)—is not feasible simply because the adversary can suffer defeat at one level and go to the next higher one.[21] It is not the military outcomes of battles that will determine how intensely the war is waged and when it will stop. Rather, it is how much each adversary values what he is fighting for that will determine the scope, scale, and intensity of the conflict. Resolve, not battlefield victory, is the crucial element in any competitive risk-taking situation. Each party has a shared interest in avoiding an escalation to all-out war where they both would be destroyed. Each will be forced to weigh how much he and his adversary value what both are fighting for in order to determine how firm to stand. As has been pointed out many times before, this is the proverbial game of chicken. Ultimately, one side is likely to give way to avoid devastation. It is true, therefore, that when defense of populations is not possible, escalation dominance loses its utility.

What happens on the battlefield, however, can have meaning for structuring the dynamics of competitive risk-taking situations. Battlefield actions are important for what they signal about resolve, not whether they defeat the adversary. How battles are started can affect both the perceptions of resolve and the subsequent dynamics of a competitive risk-taking situation. It is not sufficient to argue, therefore, that escalation involves a competition in risk taking and simply leave matters at that. How, exactly, does one demonstrate resolve if one has to fire one or several nuclear weapons? Are demonstration shots—those that involve explosions in remote areas where there are no military forces and civilians— demonstrations of one's resolve to use nuclear weapons or of one's fear of using them? Is it sufficient simply to fire one off to a place where its military effects are harmless? Or does one need to make a significant military statement by the initial use of one's nuclear forces, *knowing full well that any military gain thereby achieved is only temporary if the adversary decides to reciprocate*? Does it make sense to use such forces initially against the adversary's cities, even if only one small city is destroyed? That may demonstrate resolve all right, but will it not overly provoke the adversary and cause him to return the blow, when in fact the point of one's initial use was to cause him to stop his military action?

These questions are perplexing. The initial use of nuclear weapons in small numbers involves what Schelling once called "threats that leave something to chance."[22] The line between deliberate escalation in order

---

21. The best recent, if not the best, discussion of the difference between escalation dominance and the competition in risk taking, is to be found in Jervis, *The Illogic of American Nuclear Strategy*, chap. 5. I have benefited enormously from this chapter and book.

22. See Thomas C. Schelling, *The Strategy of Conflict* (Cambridge, Mass.: Harvard University Press, 1960), chap. 8.

to stop a war and escalation that gets out of control is a fine one, indeed. By definition, escalatory actions that are taken to manipulate risk involve the chance that they will get out of control. If they could not, there would be no risk, escalation could be controlled, and escalation to manipulate risk would turn into escalation dominance. In competitions in risk taking, the effectiveness of escalatory threats lies precisely in the fact that they can get out of control. Because that is the case, one must worry about how to walk the fine line, how to signal the adversary politically, how to get him to stop, and how to avoid provoking him into his own escalation.

There can be no definitive answers to the questions asked above. But surely common sense dictates that soft counterforce targets—divisions, transportation nodes, and the like—make more sense to threaten initially than countervalue ones if one is trying both to signal resolve and yet not overly to provoke one's adversary. And if that be the case, escalatory threats designed to signal politically must have *some* military effect if they are to have a chance of succeeding. Hence, hitting military targets can make great political sense. Thus, a second underpinning of finite deterrence, an exclusive reliance on countervalue targeting, no longer holds.

Third, finally, surely some war-waging capability is desirable for rapid war termination. Finite deterrers provide a partial answer when they argue that the best way to limit damage in any nuclear war that begins small is to stop it as quickly as possible. But, again, it is not sufficient to leave matters there. We must ask what is required of one's forces and command and control facilities for this to happen. In order to limit damage, two requirements have to be met: first, someone must be in command who has the will and desire to terminate the war; second, he must have control over his forces to limit their use. If a nuclear war begins (and ends) as an all-out spasm response by both sides, the matter of control is academic. But if it begins with a severely limited use of nuclear weapons, we must take some precautions to do what we can to maintain control in order to keep use severely limited. This requires soft counterforce targeting and sufficient investment in command, control, and intelligence capabilities such that we can have reasonable confidence that the national command authority can survive for a few limited exchanges of blows.

What is required for damage limitation in the event a limited nuclear war begins, therefore, is some prudent investment in controllability. What is not required, however, is an investment to endure a protracted and extensive nuclear war. That is beyond the pale of feasibility. Nor is it desirable to engage in extensive counterforce exchanges against hardened targets—the adversary's command and control centers and his nuclear forces—for the reasons outlined earlier. What we should procure are war-waging capabilities that are designed to end the war quickly with severely limited nuclear use. What we must avoid are war-waging capabilities that are designed for long endurance and extensive use. If this be so, that some very limited war-waging flexibility is desired, then the third tenet of the assured destruction school—an opposition to flexibility—also is no longer tenable.

There is a final point that needs to be made. In the mid-eighties, we may be on the verge of a race to build effective population defenses. The MAD-plus position clearly does not call for this type of insurance and in fact finds it dangerous. Is a world in which both superpowers have an assured defense of populations preferable to the one in which they do not? Is the BAD world (Both Assured of Defense) better than the MAD-plus world?

There can be no definitive answer to this question, but informed speculation is in order.[23] A MAD-plus world is one in which the leaders of both superpowers know that, if they do not calculate correctly and tread carefully, events could get out of control. In a MAD world, escalation and loss of control are ever-present contingencies, even if they are almost never ever-present occurrences. As argued above, it is this knowledge that makes MAD nuclear statesmen cautious, restrained, and careful calculators. In a BAD world, however, these restraints would be relaxed. If their populations were thought defendable or invulnerable to retaliatory strikes, BAD statesmen would be more likely to take greater risks. As then Secretary of Defense Harold Brown put it in 1979: "I have always been concerned about massive ABM systems because I have always felt there was some possibility that some clever briefer could delude a political decision maker into thinking that they were going to work."[24] The costs of guessing wrong would presumably be less than in a MAD world if the safety net of population defense worked. A MAD world discourages unwarranted risk taking; a BAD world would not. A MAD world balances terror; a BAD world does not. A MAD world has little or no safety net for bad judgment; a BAD world presumably does.

If, however, a BAD world turns out to be one in which a credible population defense is not really feasible and one in which risk taking is not restrained, then the costs would be horrendous. Historically, for every offensive innovation, there developed a defensive response. But in the past, no weapon possessed the speed and destructive power of nuclear weapons. Population defenses require a degree of perfection to be effective that offensive forces do not. They must be held to a higher standard of workability. There is therefore a gross asymmetry between how well nuclear offenses and defenses have to work in order to be effective that tips the balance toward the offense. Even if the population defense is nearly perfect, it is still not perfect and enough missiles will get through to assure population devastation. For the foreseeable future, therefore,

23. For more on the likely instabilities of a BAD world, see Robert J. Art, "The Role of Military Power in International Relations," in *National Security Affairs: Theoretical Perspectives and Contemporary Issues,* ed. Thomas B. Trout and James E. Harf (New Brunswick, N.J.: Transaction Books, 1982), pp. 13–27; and Charles S. Glaser, "Why Even Good Defenses May Be Bad," *International Security* 9 (1984): 92–123.

24. Harold Brown, quoted in the *Wall Street Journal* (September 28, 1984), p. 10.

the offense will always get through, either ballistically or in some other fashion.[25]

A 100 percent population defense would be nice to have but so, too, would immortality. If a credible population defense is not presently and foreseeably feasible and if neither superpower would, anyway, sit still and permit its offensive forces to be so stymied, is it not better to live in a world in which the risks of using nuclear weapons are thought to be great, not small? Is the best restraint on nuclear weapons use not fear of the uncertainties surrounding their use? And in this "MAD" world of ours, is it not better to purchase a little bit of extra insurance along the lines of the MAD-plus posture described above?

25. For the technical details of why this is so, see Ashton B. Carter, *Directed Energy Missile Defense in Space,* Office of Technology Assessment (Washington, D.C.: Government Printing Office, April 1984); and *Space-based Missile Defense,* A Report by the Union of Concerned Scientists (Cambridge, Mass., March 1984).

Deterrence and Deontology*

Jeff McMahan

The most familiar and probably the most widely accepted moral objection to the policy of nuclear deterrence is that it involves a conditional intention to use nuclear weapons in ways that would be immoral. Because it requires this intention, which is itself held to be wrongful, nuclear deterrence is deemed to be immoral, even if it is successful and nuclear weapons are never used.

This "Deontologist's Argument" is one which makes many of those who are skeptical about the morality of nuclear deterrence uncomfortable. For, obviously, one can (as I do) believe both that there are strong moral arguments against nuclear deterrence and that this particular argument is not among them. Yet in rejecting the argument one not only risks giving the impression that it is fine to intend to commit mass murder but also risks losing important allies in the antinuclear movement (particularly in theological circles) whose faith in this particular argument is the sole basis of their opposition to nuclear deterrence.

In spite of these risks, my aim here will be to expose the source of the not uncommon dissatisfaction with the Deontologist's Argument. My hope is that those who have been persuaded by this argument will discover that it does not in fact articulate the intuitive basis of their opposition to nuclear deterrence, so that their opposition to nuclear deterrence will survive even if their acceptance of this particular argument does not.

I

The Deontologist's Argument involves three claims. The first is that the actual use of nuclear weapons would be wrong. Normally the ground for this first claim is that the use of nuclear weapons would inevitably violate one or both of the traditional "just war" criteria for determining what types of action are permissible in warfare. These two criteria are:

1. *The Criterion of Proportionality.*—This states that the level of force employed must be proportional to the good it is intended to achieve.

* An earlier version of this paper was read at University College, Cardiff. I have benefited from comments on the earlier draft by Gerald Dworkin, Robert Goodin, David Hendrickson, Catherine Kelleher, Steven Lee, Neil Shimmield, Johann Somerville, and Walter Stein, and from discussions about the morality of nuclear deterrence with Paul Russell and Jorge Secada.

In other words, for an act to be justified, the good it is intended to achieve must, when probabilities are taken into account, outweigh any bad consequences which might also be caused.

2. *The Criterion of Discrimination.*—This states that force should be used in a way which respects the distinction between combatants and noncombatants. In particular, the intentional killing of non-combatants is forbidden.

These are plausible principles, though each suffers from a certain indeterminacy. The Criterion of Proportionality, for example, requires us to maintain a relation of proportionality between good and bad consequences which it may be impossible to compare with any precision. How, for example, does sacrificing the lives of x number of people compare with preserving the liberty and independence of y? And the Criterion of Discrimination suffers from the fact that there is no generally accepted test for determining whether certain consequences of an act are to count as intended or as merely foreseen but unintended. Suppose, for example, that tactical nuclear weapons were to be used on the battlefield in Europe, with the predictable consequence that large numbers of civilians living in nearby areas would be killed. Would the deaths of these noncombatants be an intended consequence of the use of tactical nuclear weapons, so that the use of these weapons would in this case violate the Criterion of Discrimination? The authors of one recent study contend that the Criterion of Discrimination would be violated since "these deaths are not the accidental or incidental result of lawful military action, but are what one is aiming to do in choosing to fight with this type of weapon."[1] Others, however, would claim that the deaths were not intended and that this is shown by the fact that the aims of the armies using tactical nuclear weapons would not have been less well achieved if, miraculously, no civilians had been around to be killed. According to this view, the use of tactical nuclear weapons in these circumstances would not be ruled out by the Criterion of Discrimination (though of course it might be by the Criterion of Proportionality).[2]

Despite these problems, the two criteria seem plausible as rough guides to the limits of permissible conduct in warfare. It also seems clear that most uses of nuclear weapons would violate one or both of these criteria. Certainly a direct, punitive strike against a city would violate the Criterion of Discrimination, and most other uses would be too destructive to be considered proportionate. Yet there are certain uses of nuclear weapons which might not violate either criterion. Limited counterforce

---

1. *The Church and the Bomb: Nuclear Weapons and the Christian Conscience* (London: Hodder & Stoughton with CIO Publishing, 1982), pp. 96–97; cf. G. E. M. Anscombe, "War and Murder," in *Nuclear Weapons: A Catholic Response,* ed. Walter Stein (London: Merlin Press, 1965).

2. On the difficulty of determining when a consequence is intended, see the third lecture in Jonathan Bennett's "Morality and Consequences," in *The Tanner Lectures on Human Values, 1981,* ed. Stirling McMurrin (Cambridge: Cambridge University Press, 1981).

strikes against remote military installations might be discriminate, in that they would not be intended to kill noncombatants, and they could conceivably be considered proportionate, in that, for example, they could reasonably be expected to lead to a favorable settlement of some military conflict.

On the other hand, it is sometimes suggested that the overwhelming likelihood of uncontrollable escalation following even the most limited use of nuclear weapons means that the probable bad consequences of virtually any use of nuclear weapons would outweigh any good that might be achieved and that virtually any use of nuclear weapons would therefore violate the Criterion of Proportionality. This claim has considerable plausibility—though of course there remain certain conceivable cases in which escalation would be very unlikely. What does seem true is that virtually all of the uses of nuclear weapons contemplated by strategists as realistic possibilities, and in particular those which constitute the ultimate sanction in any viable policy of nuclear deterrence, would violate either the Criterion of Discrimination or the Criterion of Proportionality—in the latter case either by directly causing a disproportionate amount of violence or by posing a high risk of escalation to a level of violence that would be disproportionate. Indeed, in virtually every case that could be considered realistic, it is precisely the possibility of escalation which makes the threat of "limited" use credible as a deterrent. Thus I shall assume—and this is all that the argument requires—that those uses of nuclear weapons which have to be threatened in order to maintain a viable policy of deterrence would be wrong. (Perhaps surprisingly, this assumption is not uncontroversial. There are those, such as the present bishop of London, who appear to believe that the intentional mass killing of the innocent with nuclear weapons could be "morally acceptable, as a way of exercising our moral responsibility in a fallen world.")[3]

II

While the first premise of the argument thus seems plausible, other premises are required in order to generate the conclusion that it is wrong to possess nuclear weapons for purposes of deterrence. For, as advocates of nuclear deterrence point out, as long as the policy is successful, nuclear weapons will never actually be used. Therefore the next stage in the argument normally involves an appeal to one or the other of the following two principles.

   a) It is wrong to threaten to do that which it would be wrong to do.
   b) It is wrong to intend, even conditionally, to do that which it would be wrong to do.

3. Graham Leonard, quoted in the *Guardian* (London) (November 4, 1982). The fact that Leonard favors the retention of Britain's "independent deterrent," which is at present a "countercity" force, suggests that he means to include the destruction of cities among the morally acceptable uses of nuclear weapons.

The difference between these two principles is that the second, but not the first, would allow one to threaten to do something which it would be wrong to do, provided that one was bluffing (i.e., if one really intended not to fulfill one's threat) or provided that one had simply not decided whether or not one would fulfill one's threat. Is it plausible to forbid threats of these sorts? Bluffing, of course, involves deceit, and there is a moral presumption against that; but it would seem absurd to object to a policy of nuclear deterrence based entirely on a bluff on the ground that it would involve deceit. One could make a more convincing case against a policy of nuclear deterrence based on the second type of threat, for to make a threat without having decided whether one would fulfill it is to run a risk that one may indeed fulfill it. But I shall shortly suggest that there is no reason for supposing that any actual policy of deterrence is based on this type of threat (or indeed on a bluff). So, while the first of these two principles has some plausibility, it would contribute nothing to the argument against nuclear deterrence which would not also be provided by the second.

The second principle covers only those threats which one intends to fulfill or which one intends to fulfill if certain conditions obtain. It is a widely accepted principle—though how it is interpreted and what its grounds are are matters of dispute. Some writers ground the principle on consequentialist considerations. They argue that the reason it is wrong to intend to do what, for consequentialist reasons, it would be wrong to do is simply that the formation of the intention increases the probability that the wrongful act will be done. This is true of conditional as well as unconditional intentions.[4]

This is a perfectly valid point; but the problem is that it tends to obscure the fact that, in the case of nuclear deterrence, there may be consequentialist reasons in favor of forming a conditional intention to do what, if the relevant conditions were ever to obtain, it would certainly be wrong to do (for both consequentialist and nonconsequentialist reasons). For it is at least arguable that a policy of nuclear deterrence based on the conditional intention to use nuclear weapons would in certain circumstances have the joint effects of preventing the use of nuclear weapons and preventing the forceful domination of one country by another—both admirable consequentialist aims. Thus, in consequentialist terms, whether it would be wrong to form the conditional intention to use nuclear weapons will always depend on questions concerning the evaluation of outcomes and the assessment of probabilities. Indeed, the question about the conditional intention and its effects simply gets absorbed into this reasoning about outcomes and probabilities, and hence it is misleading for a consequentialist to give it as much prominence as the argument I

4. See Douglas Lackey, "The Intentions of Deterrence," in *Nuclear Weapons and the Future of Humanity: The Fundamental Questions*, ed. Steven Lee and Avner Cohen (Totowa, N.J.: Rowman & Allanheld, 1984); and Robert McKim, "An Examination of a Moral Argument against Nuclear Deterrence," *Journal of Religious Ethics* (in press).

am considering does. In short, while the argument I am considering has a consequentialist interpretation, it is nevertheless incomplete as a consequentialist argument and would in fact be swallowed up by and disappear in a complete argument of that sort. Hence, if the argument is to stand on its own, the premise about intentions must be given a nonconsequentialist interpretation.

A second interpretation of the principle about intentions which has been advanced by various writers holds that to form an intention, whether conditional or unconditional, to do what it would be wrong to do is itself wrong because it is morally corrupting or dehumanizing. Thus Stanley Benn argues that, in the case of nuclear deterrence, the formation of the required conditional intention to use nuclear weapons by the persons responsible for implementing the strategy would "do violence to their moral natures." Moreover, he contends, "the sacrifice would need to be very general indeed if the public support necessary for the credibility [of the deterrent threat] is to be sustained—so general as to amount to a corruption of society."[5] In short, the conditional intention to use nuclear weapons is morally corrupting in those who adopt it, and hence consent by the wider public to a policy which requires the adoption of such an intention is itself both wrong and morally corrosive.

What is bizarre about this interpretation of the principle about intentions is that, in the case of nuclear deterrence, it treats the *offenders*—namely, those responsible for the implementation of the policy—as the *victims* of the operation of the policy. It hardly seems plausible to object to nuclear deterrence on the ground that maintaining the policy is harmful to President Reagan or Mrs. Thatcher. Nuclear deterrence clearly has present victims—for example, those who are psychologically damaged by being held hostage by rival nuclear powers and those who are economically deprived as a result, in part, of the diversion of resources to the development and deployment of nuclear weapons. But the primary victims of deterrence are the potential victims of the policy's potential failure. These, rather than those who now run the policy, are the people about whom we should be concerned.

Even this second interpretation of the principle about intentions has its consequentialist aspect. This shows up quite clearly in the way the principle is used by those who interpret it in this way. J. E. Hare and Carey Joynt, for example, see having the conditional intention to use nuclear weapons as bad for the person who has it; thus a person's having the intention is an undesirable state of affairs which, other things being equal, must be minimized. Focusing on the case of the aircraft crews who dropped the bombs on Hiroshima and Nagasaki, Hare and Joynt write that "those men had undoubtedly formed the conditional intention, when they entered the aircraft, to drop the bombs. Their mental health was

5. S. I. Benn, "Deterrence or Appeasement? or, On Trying to Be Rational about Nuclear War," *Journal of Applied Philosophy* 1 (1984): 5–19, p. 15.

in a sense sacrificed to the general welfare. . . . [One] is forced to weigh the wrong to them against the benefits of a deterrence policy in general."[6] This passage requires some tidying up: for the bombings of Hiroshima and Nagasaki were not part of a policy of deterrence, the intentions of the crews were not conditional, and the corruption of the crews consisted not just in their intending to drop the bombs but also in their actually dropping them. Nevertheless, the point which this passage makes illustrates nicely the absurdity of the second interpretation of the principle about intentions as it appears in the argument against nuclear deterrence. By picking out the alleged victimization of a handful of war criminals as something which must be weighed against the supposed benefits of the bombings while saying nothing at all about the hundreds of thousands of innocent people who perished in agony under the nuclear fireballs or who later died lingering deaths from mutilation or radiation poisoning, Hare and Joynt display a certain insensitivity to the facts of moral salience. This is not a native insensitivity but an insensitivity engendered by taking seriously their own theorizing about intentions. The point is that, in this case as in other cases in which the use of nuclear weapons is at issue, the moral corruption of a relatively small number of individuals seems, comparatively speaking, so insignificant as almost not to rate among the morally relevant considerations. The case of nuclear deterrence is no exception. (Benn's claim that nuclear deterrence involves the moral corruption not just of a few people but also of the entire society which practices it is greatly overstated: only a relatively small number of people are required to have the relevant conditional intention in order for the policy to function. For the rest of society, it is sufficient if people simply give no thought to the policy, which is in fact what most people do.)

Suppose that we nevertheless think that to intend to do what it would be wrong to do is morally corrupting. If we are right, the most plausible explanation of why it is corrupting is presumably that having such an intention is wrong in itself. Rather than saying that having such an intention is corrupting, one might say that it indicates corruption. For

6. J. E. Hare and Carey B. Joynt, *Ethics and International Affairs* (London: Macmillan, 1982), p. 112. The survivors of Hiroshima and Nagasaki may be pardoned for wondering what beneficial effects the bombings had on the "general welfare." It is often claimed that the bombings saved more lives than they cost since they rendered unnecessary an American invasion of Japan in which perhaps half a million people would have died. But the idea that an invasion and occupation would otherwise have been necessary takes for granted the American aim of securing unconditional surrender. Had the United States not insisted on an unconditional surrender, an invasion would not have been required. (The United States, incidentally, had no right to require unconditional surrender. As Anthony Kenny has argued, "Spelling out the particular wrong which justifies one's taking up arms is *eo ipso* to spell out the conditions on which one ought to be ready to accept surrender [plus whatever extra conditions are necessary in order to ensure that the terms of surrender are observed]. . . . This means that the unconditional surrender of an enemy is not a legitimate objective of war" [see his " 'Better Dead than Red,' " in *Objections to Nuclear Defence*, ed. Nigel Blake and Kay Pole (London: Routledge & Kegan Paul, 1984), pp. 13–27; and also Michael Dummett, "Nuclear Warfare," in Blake and Pole, eds., pp. 28–40].)

in intending to act in a certain way one commits oneself to the act in the same way one would in actually doing it. Thus if a person intends to act in a way which is wrong but is prevented by external circumstances from doing so, he is still regarded as culpable, as having done something wrong.[7] (Whether he is as culpable as he would have been had he not been prevented from acting on the intention may depend in part on our view of what Bernard Williams calls "moral luck.")[8]

This example suggests that the principle about intentions has some plausibility, at least insofar as the plausibility of a principle is attested to by its ability to explain our beliefs. Furthermore, the example indicates why, if we believe that unconditional intentions to do wrong are themselves wrong, we should then believe that conditional intentions to do wrong are also wrong. For a conditional intention involves the same commitment; if it is never acted on, this is only because of the intervention of external circumstances which the agent cannot fully control.

Thus if intending to do what it would be wrong to do is morally corrupting or, rather, indicative of corruption, that is because it is wrong in itself, and this intrinsic wrongness, rather than the concomitant corruption, should be the focus of our concern. This is, indeed, the way the principle about intentions is normally understood by proponents of the Deontologist's Argument, and this in turn is what gives the argument its distinctly deontological character. Henceforth I shall therefore assume that the principle is to be understood in this way.

III

If we accept that it is wrong to intend, even conditionally, to do that which it would be wrong to do, and if we also accept that it would be wrong to use nuclear weapons in ways that have to be threatened in order to maintain deterrence, then we are only one step away from the conclusion that nuclear deterrence is wrong. The third and final step in the Deontologist's Argument, which brings us to this conclusion, consists in the claim that any credible policy of nuclear deterrence must be based on the conditional intention to use nuclear weapons.

Some defenders of nuclear deterrence accept the first two premises of the Deontologist's Argument (i.e., they accept that it is wrong conditionally to intend to use nuclear weapons) while rejecting the third (i.e., they do not accept that nuclear deterrence must involve a conditional intention to use nuclear weapons). This position is supported by an appeal to one or the other of two possibilities: that the deterrent threat is a bluff or that the national leaders whose decision it would be to fire the weapons in the event of an attack have simply not decided whether they would do so. In either case, it is claimed, the mere fact that the

7. This example is taken from Gregory S. Kavka, "Some Paradoxes of Deterrence," *Journal of Philosophy* 75 (1978): 285–302, p. 289.

8. Bernard Williams, "Moral Luck," *Proceedings of the Aristotelian Society* 50, suppl. (1976): 115–35.

leaders would have the capability to use nuclear weapons, together with the absence of any overt and decisive indication that they would not use them, would create sufficient uncertainty in the minds of potential adversaries to guarantee deterrence.

Both of these suggestions share certain faults, and the arguments against them run parallel. First, neither of the possibilities mentioned is relevant as long as it remains a mere possibility. There must be reason to believe that one or the other possibility is actually the basis of the policy. Is there any such reason in the case of present American policy? Certainly there are no grounds for supposing that Ronald Reagan has been led by moral scruples either to bluff or to remain undecided about the use of nuclear weapons. After all, his administration has for years been engaged, without any qualms, in sponsoring the mass killing of the innocent in various parts of the world (most notably in El Salvador) and has been content to allow hundreds of thousands of people to die of starvation when they could easily have been saved for less than the cost of just one of the many new American nuclear weapons programs.[9] (In Ethiopia, five million people now face starvation. The Reagan administration is unwilling to lift a finger to help them because their government happens to be on the wrong side in the Cold War.) Americans have a regrettable tendency to assume that their elected leaders are unique in history in being incapable of perpetrating atrocities. It is therefore salutary to recall that, on the only occasions when nuclear weapons have actually been used, it was an American president who gave the order. Indeed, Truman, who was in some ways a morally more sensitive person than Reagan is, ordered the nuclear destruction of two Japanese cities in response to provocation that was far less serious than that to which the United States would be subjected in the situations in which Reagan has threatened to use nuclear weapons. It is, in short, not credible to suppose that Reagan would be restrained by moral considerations from retaliating or, a fortiori, from intending to retaliate.

Suppose for the sake of argument, however, that Reagan might wish to bluff, or to remain undecided about the use of nuclear weapons. That would still not be sufficient to enable the United States to run a policy of nuclear deterrence free from the taint of the conditional intention to use nuclear weapons. For nuclear deterrence requires a lengthy chain of command controlling the firing of nuclear weapons, and it is not possible for the policy to function without at least those lower down in the chain of command having the intention to use nuclear weapons if instructed to do so. For an attempt to run the policy on the basis of bluffing or uncertainty *at every level* would soon be discovered by potential adversaries, and deterrence would be undermined. Hence those in the military chain of command must be selected in part for their willingness to obey orders

---

9. For a review of the Reagan administration's record of respect for human life, see my *Reagan and the World: Imperial Policy in the New Cold War* (London: Pluto Press, 1984).

and trained to fire their weapons on receiving the command to do so. They, at least, must have the conditional intention to use nuclear weapons.[10]

So, even if a policy of deterrence could in principle be maintained without anyone conditionally intending to use nuclear weapons, there is no actual policy which is maintained in this way. It is, moreover, not practically possible that a policy of nuclear deterrence could be instituted on this basis—at least not in a way that would be compatible with democracy. Politicians could not run for office on a pledge to bluff or to avoid deciding beforehand what they would do in the event of an attack. Nor could it be suggested that officers in the military would be instructed simply not to think about what they would do if they were commanded to fire their nuclear weapons. This would obviously undermine deterrence. Thus, if the citizens in a democracy support a policy of nuclear deterrence, they are necessarily authorizing their political and military leaders to intend conditionally to use nuclear weapons (and also, of course, to use nuclear weapons in certain conditions), and they cannot assume that their leaders will not have such an intention.

Defenders of nuclear deterrence have tried other ways of getting around the Deontologist's Argument. Most simply ignore it—as does Lord Zuckerman when he genuflects before "the moral argument, to which there can be no answer," but then goes on to embrace the doctrine of deterrence and to defend it against other objections.[11] Others have defended the policy of deterrence on the ground that it provides the most effective means of ensuring that nuclear weapons will never actually be used. If what is meant is that the policy is more likely than any other to prevent the use of nuclear weapons by anyone, then the claim may be true—though I doubt it.[12] But we need not pursue this point here, for this objection to the Deontologist's Argument is beside the point. The objection does not directly address the Deontologist's Argument, for it amounts to little more than an assertion of the view that evil may be done that good may come. In short, it simply asserts that the Deontologist's Argument cannot be absolutist in character, but it offers no argument to support this claim.

It is sometimes suggested that nuclear deterrence provides the most effective means of ensuring that *we* will never use nuclear weapons. Thus Michael Walzer writes that "we threaten evil in order not to do it, and the doing of it would be so terrible that the threat seems in comparison to be morally defensible," while Sir Arthur Hockaday claims that deterrence constitutes "the most likely means of securing . . . that nuclear weapons

---

10. Compare Roger Ruston, *Nuclear Deterrence—Right or Wrong?* (Abbots Langley: Catholic Information Services, 1981), p. 61; and Steven Lee, "Nuclear Deterrence: Hostage Holding and Consequences," in this volume.

11. Solly Zuckerman, *Nuclear Illusion and Reality* (London: Collins, 1982), p. 140.

12. For some speculation about whether the probability that nuclear weapons will be used is higher under a policy of nuclear deterrence or under a policy of nonnuclear defense, see my "Nuclear Deterrence and Future Generations," in Lee and Cohen, eds.

shall not be used, either by myself or by others."[13] I take these claims to be evidently absurd, for, while deterrence enables us to use nuclear weapons, we could not use them if we were to abandon them and, with them, the doctrine of deterrence. I mention this idea, that deterrence itself prevents us from wrongdoing, only because it is so puzzlingly common.

IV

As the foregoing survey shows, many of the commonest objections to the Deontologist's Argument are absurdly casuistic and unconvincing, and none seems to locate the real source of many people's dissatisfaction with the argument. In what follows I shall present several objections which I hope will expose the argument's real weaknesses. My initial challenge will take the form of a dilemma: depending on how the second premise (i.e., the principle about intentions) is interpreted, either the argument has little force, or it has implications which are absurd. After posing this dilemma, I shall present two counterexamples which will reinforce my claim that the argument is implausible and may help to reveal where the argument has gone wrong. I shall conclude by suggesting that there is a different, though related, deontological argument against nuclear deterrence which better accommodates people's intuitions and is considerably more convincing.

The dilemma which the defender of the Deontologist's Argument faces concerns the question whether the prohibition on conditionally intending to use nuclear weapons is an absolute prohibition. As it is normally understood by proponents of the Deontologist's Argument, the prohibition on actually using nuclear weapons (at least in ways which would violate just war criteria) *is* absolute. (For the consequentialist, too, the ban on using nuclear weapons is arguably absolute for all practical purposes, for there may be no realistic conditions in which the use of nuclear weapons would be justifiable in consequentialist terms.) The question, then, is whether the absolute prohibition on the act extends also to the intention to act. Suppose that we think it does not and thus that, while it is wrong conditionally to intend to use nuclear weapons, it is not absolutely forbidden, even though it *is* absolutely forbidden actually to use nuclear weapons. If this is our view, it then becomes an open question to what extent it is wrong to pursue a policy which involves the conditional intention to use nuclear weapons, and the consideration of consequences becomes relevant in determining whether it is permissible to pursue such a policy. It is then open to defenders of nuclear deterrence

13. Michael Walzer, *Just and Unjust Wars* (Harmondsworth: Penguin Books, 1977), p. 274; Sir Arthur Hockaday, "In Defence of Deterrence," in *Ethics and Nuclear Deterrence*, ed. Geoffrey Goodwin (London: Croom Helm, 1982), pp. 68–93, p. 85. Compare Michael Novak's assertion that "the fundamental moral intention in nuclear deterrence is never to have to use the deterrent force" ("Moral Clarity in the Nuclear Age," *National Review* [April 1, 1983], pp. 354–92, p. 384). This should be an easy intention to fulfill since no one can force us to use the "deterrent" against our will.

to claim that the policy is the lesser of two evils: that, while having the conditional intention to use nuclear weapons is an evil and thus would normally be wrong, nevertheless having it is "a morally acceptable price to pay" to secure the benefits of peace and freedom.[14] This objection has been well stated by Anthony Kenny: "Defenders of the deterrent will argue that the conditional willingness to engage in massacre which is an essential element of the policy is a slight and almost metaphysical evil to weigh in the balance against the good of preserving peace. The moral blemish which this may taint us with in the eyes of the fastidious is at best [*sic*] something to be put on the debit side, along with the financial cost of the weapons system, against the massive credit of maintaining our independence and our security from nuclear attack."[15] Kenny rejects this reply; but *if* it is not absolutely forbidden conditionally to intend to use nuclear weapons, and *if* the policy of nuclear deterrence does, as many people believe, offer the best hope of maintaining both peace and freedom, then the reply seems quite cogent. (Of course, the deontologist can argue that this objection rests on a mistaken assessment of the comparative expected consequences of nuclear deterrence and the alternative to it; but then he will be pressing a consequentialist objection to deterrence, in which case his own argument may seem superfluous.)[16]

In short, if the wrongness of having the conditional intention to use nuclear weapons is not absolute, then it seems that the presumption against a policy which involves people having this intention could be overridden by a consideration of consequences. But suppose, on the other hand, that the prohibition against conditionally intending to do what it is absolutely forbidden to do is itself absolute. In that case the Deontologist's Argument yields the conclusion which it is normally supposed to have: that nuclear deterrence is ruled out, whatever the consequences.

There is, however, a price to be paid for deriving the conclusion in this way; for, given this interpretation of the second premise, the argument has implausible implications. In particular, it implies that to follow a policy of nuclear deterrence, even if the policy is successful and nuclear weapons are never used, is equally wrong as actually using nuclear weapons would be.[17]

14. Hockaday, p. 84.

15. Kenny.

16. Here and elsewhere in this article, "he" and "his," when not used to refer to a specific person, should be understood to mean "he or she" and "his or her."

17. Compare Bernard Williams's claim that the Deontologist's Argument implies "that there is no moral difference between running a deterrent strategy on the one hand, and intentionally—indeed, wantonly—starting a nuclear war on the other; so that the first is as totally evil as the second" ("How to Think Sceptically about the Bomb," *New Society* [November 18, 1982], p. 289). Williams's point is, I take it, the same as mine; though, for reasons which will soon become evident, I think it is infelicitously expressed. Williams regards the point as a reductio of the Deontologist's Argument; but some of the argument's proponents seem willing to bite the bullet. Thus J. Bryan Hehir notes that traditional

This claim assumes that all violations of absolute prohibitions are absolutely and therefore equally wrong. This will be true if there is, as one would expect, a strict correlation between the strength of a particular duty, the degree of wrongness of violating the duty, and the stringency of the conditions which would release one from the necessity of fulfilling the duty. To take an uncontroversial example, we believe that the duty not to murder is stronger than the duty not to lie. Other things being equal, we can infer from this both that it is less wrong to lie than it is to murder and that the conditions, if any, which would release a person from the duty not to murder would also release him from the duty not to lie, though not all the conditions which would release him from the duty not to lie would also release him from the duty not to murder. The same general claims will hold true even in the case of a hierarchy of duties in which the ordering of the duties is not correlated with the consequences of fulfilling or violating the duties. (For example, in such a hierarchy, the duty not to lie might always override the duty to help others.) In general, then, if (1) the duty to do x is stronger than the duty to do y, then it follows (2) that it is less wrong not to do y than it is not to do x, (3) that, in cases of conflict, one may fail to do y in order to do x, though one may not fail to do x in order to do y, and (4) that any conditions which would release one from the duty to do x would also be sufficient to release one from the duty to do y, though not all the conditions which would release one from the duty to do y would release one from the duty to do x.

From any one of these claims—claims about the relative strengths of certain duties, the relative degrees of wrongness of violating the various duties, and the conditions under which one would be released from performing them—one could infer the others. Thus, if the conditions which would release one from the performance of one duty are the same as those which would release one from the performance of another duty, then it follows that both duties are equally strong and that it would be equally wrong to violate either. In the case of absolutes, the conditions which would release one from the necessity of obeying them are, in a sense, always the same: for, in the case of absolutes, there are *no* excusing conditions. Thus, if I am right that there is a strict correlation between the excusing conditions for a certain duty and the degree of wrongness of violating the duty, then it follows that the violation of any absolute prohibition is equally wrong as the violation of any other.

Of course, from the fact that the violation of one duty is equally wrong as the violation of another, it does not follow that the two acts

<hr>

"moral theology asserts that a formed intention to do evil carries the same degree of culpability as the doing of evil" ("The Just War Ethic," in *War or Peace? The Search for New Answers*, ed. Thomas Shannon [Maryknoll, N.Y.: Orbis Books, 1980], pp. 27–28, quoted in McKim). Barrie Paskins notes: "I doubt . . . whether deterrence can be defended by claiming that it is 'less immoral than' all-out nuclear war" ("Deep Cuts Are Morally Imperative," in Goodwin, ed., pp. 94–116).

must be in every respect morally equivalent. For example, an absolutist seems committed to the claim that it is equally wrong to murder one person as it is to murder a hundred. But that does not exclude the possibility that killing a hundred people may be worse, or more evil, or even more culpable, than killing only one.

It might be thought that this admission undermines the attempted reductio ad absurdum of the Deontologist's Argument. For it concedes to the defender of the argument the reply that, while pursuing a policy of nuclear deterrence is indeed equally wrong as actually using nuclear weapons would be, the two are nevertheless not morally equivalent. Just as killing a hundred people is worse than killing one, so using nuclear weapons would be worse, or more evil, or more culpable, than pursuing a policy of nuclear deterrence is. And, as long as the defender of the argument can thus avoid being committed to the view that conditionally intending to use nuclear weapons and actually using them are morally equivalent, he need not be embarrassed by the implication that the two are equally wrong. For, it might be claimed, the reductio has force only if we illegitimately conflate equal wrongness with complete moral equivalence.

This reply, while undeniably forceful, cannot rescue the Deontologist's Argument. The act of using nuclear weapons would be worse than the successful pursuit of deterrence because its probable consequences would be worse. It would also be more evil, or more culpable, in that it would indicate a greater degree of moral corruption or depravity in the agent. Both a concern with consequences and a concern with the evaluation of agents are, moreover, certainly relevant to any moral comparison between using nuclear weapons and running a deterrent strategy. These modes of evaluation are accessible to the deontologist and are compatible with his view. But they are extraneous to the core of that view. Deontology, and a fortiori the Deontologist's Argument, are concerned with the intrinsic moral character of action. And in *this* respect—that is, in terms of their intrinsic natures—using nuclear weapons and running a successful deterrent strategy *are* held by the argument to be morally equivalent. This conclusion alone is sufficiently absurd to condemn the absolutist version of the Deontologist's Argument.

That this implication of the argument is unacceptable is attested to by the fact that many of the argument's own defenders do not seem to accept it. Their inability to accept the implication is, I think, evident in the more startling fact that they do not even embrace the explicit conclusion of the argument—namely, that the policy of nuclear deterrence is ruled out absolutely. The argument's defenders are formally committed to support unilateral nuclear disarmament, not just as a long-term goal, but as an immediate imperative, beginning with an announcement by the government that it will not use its nuclear weapons for retaliatory or any other purposes. Any other stance on the question of deterrence admits the relevance of consequences in determining what ought to be done, and this is inconsistent with the absolute character of the prohibition implied by the argument.

Consider, however, the position of the American Catholic bishops. Arguing within a traditional absolutist framework, they assert that "it is not morally acceptable to intend to kill the innocent as part of a strategy of deterring nuclear war." They go on, moreover, to argue that, even though American officials had assured them that "it is not U.S. strategic policy to target the Soviet civilian population as such," the fact that planned uses of nuclear weapons by the United States would violate the Criterion of Proportionality means that "we cannot be satisfied that the assertion of an intention not to strike civilians directly or even the most honest effort to implement that intention by itself constitutes a 'moral policy' for the use of nuclear weapons." Thus, even though they do not explicitly endorse the Deontologist's Argument, they do seem to accept both the principle about intentions and the fact that some of the uses of nuclear weapons conditionally intended by American leaders would violate at least one and possibly both of the criteria of *jus in bello.* Surprisingly, however, they then assert that "we do not advocate a policy of unilateral [nuclear] disarmament" but go on instead to agree on "a strictly conditioned moral acceptance of nuclear deterrence."[18]

Similarly, Barrie Paskins argues that "the Soviet and Western deterrents are rightly characterised in terms of the conditional intention to wage, *in extremis,* all-out nuclear war; and [hence] they as well as all-out nuclear war are immoral." He does not, however, recommend abandoning deterrence immediately but instead argues for "deep unilateral cuts in the West's deterrent," conceding thereby the permissibility of continuing to engage in nuclear deterrence, at least as a short-term policy. He defends this position by appealing to an analogy with the case of a man engaged in an adulterous affair with a "mistress . . . suicidally dependent on the relationship," noting that, although the affair is immoral, it would be wrong to end it abruptly. "The ending of our conditional intention to wage all-out nuclear war seems to involve the complexities of the [case of adultery], not least because there are no God-given rules of disengagement. Hence all-too-fallible prudence as well as moral principle must guide us in withdrawing from our morally untenable position."[19]

---

18. *The Challenge of Peace: God's Promise and Our Response: The U.S. Bishops' Pastoral Letter on War and Peace in the Nuclear Age* (London: Catholic Truth Society and SPCK Press, 1983), pp. 51, 53, 59.

19. Paskins, pp. 99–100. Part of the force of Paskins's analogy may derive from the fact that many of us do not consider adultery to be absolutely forbidden, so we admit that a consideration of consequences can qualify the imperative to end an adulterous relation. Paskins, however, appears to be working within an absolutist framework, and thus the prohibition of adultery must be absolute for the analogy to be valid. That he is working within an absolutist framework is suggested (though not entailed) by his explicit denial, cited in n. 17, that running a deterrent strategy could be "less immoral than" waging all-out nuclear war.

The fact that these proponents of the Deontologist's Argument do not accept the imperative to abandon immediately the policy of deterrence indicates that they do not really believe that pursuing such a policy is equally wrong as using nuclear weapons would be. For, if the two were equally wrong, it would be equally imperative not to engage in deterrence as it would be not to use nuclear weapons. (This is true even if engaging in deterrence would be less *evil*. Consider the following analogy. Unpremeditated murder is less evil than premeditated murder, though the two are equally *wrong*. The fact that unpremeditated murder is less evil does not, however, imply that the imperative to avoid it is weaker.) If these proponents of the Deontologist's Argument believed that it was equally imperative not to engage in deterrence as it is not to use nuclear weapons, then they would not, I trust, be so casual about assenting to the permissibility of continuing to practice deterrence. The American bishops would not (and indeed do not) accept "a strictly conditioned moral acceptance" of the nuclear incineration of cities. Nor would Paskins allow that we could gradually extricate ourselves from a policy of nuclear genocide. It follows that they cannot really believe that nuclear deterrence is equally wrong as waging all-out nuclear war would be. Yet that is what their argument implies.

V

What seems wrong about the Deontologist's Argument is not just that it is (as it is ordinarily understood) implausibly absolutist in form; it is also that it focuses on the presence or absence of the conditional intention as the crucial moral fact about nuclear deterrence. Perhaps some of its defenders have been led to acquiesce in this assessment at least in part because they have assumed that the presence or absence of the conditional intention is necessarily and closely connected to the probability that the agents who have the intention will actually use nuclear weapons. It may be this assumption which lends credibility to the focus on the conditional intention. If so, the credibility is specious, for considerations of intention and the probability of use can come apart. To test our intuitions, let us examine a case in which they do come apart.

Suppose that there are two countries, both of which are threatened by a hostile nuclear power. Unless each of these countries maintains a policy of nuclear deterrence, there will be a high probability that it will be attacked with nuclear weapons. If, on the other hand, each maintains a policy of nuclear deterrence, the probability that it will be attacked will be very considerably less. Because of these conditions, each country does pursue a policy of deterrence. In both countries, the number of nuclear weapons required to maintain deterrence is small, and thus the number of persons who control the firing of the weapons is also small. Neither country is a democracy.

In one country, Sinceria, the political and military leaders have the conditional intention to use nuclear weapons in the event of an attack.

The leaders in the other country, Incertia, are, however, more sensitive to the demands of morality. Having been exposed to the Deontologist's Argument, they have deliberately refrained from making a decision about what they would do in the event of an attack. They do not now know, and cannot even predict, what they would do in that situation. (Because they are few, and their country undemocratic, they are able to maintain a policy of deterrence on this basis.) Of course, having accepted the Deontologist's Argument, they believe that it would be wrong to use nuclear weapons, even in retaliation. But they also know that, given the intense pressures they would be under in the event of an attack, there is a significant probability that they might launch their nuclear weapons in spite of their moral beliefs.

While the leaders in Incertia have attempted to conceal from their adversaries the fact that they have not formed the conditional intention to use nuclear weapons, it is not possible to conceal this entirely, and their adversaries have sensed that they are not fully resolved to retaliate. As a consequence, Incertia's deterrent threats are less credible than those of Sinceria are, and Incertia is therefore more likely to be attacked. Because the leaders of Incertia are thus more likely to find themselves in circumstances in which they might use nuclear weapons, they are on balance more likely actually to use nuclear weapons than the leaders of Sinceria are, even though they are less likely than the leaders of Sinceria are to use nuclear weapons *in those circumstances.*

The Deontologist's Argument does not condemn the policy of deterrence as practiced by Incertia since that policy does not involve the conditional intention to use nuclear weapons, though the argument does condemn the policy as practiced by Sinceria—even though, as a result of their policy, the leaders of Incertia are more likely than the leaders of Sinceria are to use nuclear weapons. This seems absurd.

In this example, the absence of the conditional intention does not reduce the risk that the leaders of Incertia will use nuclear weapons. On the contrary, if they were to form the conditional intention, the probability of their deliberately using nuclear weapons would be decreased. Still, while the presence of the conditional intention is in this case not correlated with an increase in the probability of use, nor its absence with a decrease in that probability, the presence of the conditional intention is nevertheless connected with the possibility of use. There is a temptation to assume that the presence of the conditional intention to use nuclear weapons in the event of an attack (which presupposes the possession of nuclear weapons) is always a sufficient condition for there being some likelihood of deliberate use. It may be that the Deontologist's Argument derives some of its apparent plausibility from this assumption.

Consider the following case. Suppose that I have been elected the head of state of some nuclear-armed country and have been granted broad discretionary powers by the electorate. In particular, I can decide whether or not to maintain a policy of nuclear deterrence until the end of my tenure in office (or until I die or become incapacitated), at which time a referendum on the subject will be held. (Thus my decision will not determine whether nuclear deterrence will be practiced by my successors.) I know that, if I reject the policy of nuclear deterrence, there will be a high probability, whatever else I may do, that my country will be attacked with nuclear weapons by an ideologically and implacably hostile adversary. If, on the other hand, I choose to maintain a nuclear deterrent threat, the probability that my country will be attacked will be negligible. I firmly believe that the use of nuclear weapons would be wrong—indeed, I find the thought of using them so utterly abhorrent that I can confidently predict that I would never, under any circumstances, actually use them. So, if I were to pursue a policy of deterrence, it would be based on a bluff. I would have no intention of using the nuclear weapons under my command. Moreover, I alone would have the authority and the physical power to release the weapons, and thus there would be no possibility of their being used without my consent. The fact that no one else would be involved in the nuclear decision-making process would also mean that I could easily conceal the fact that my deterrent threat would be a bluff. On the other hand, in order to protect the secret that my threat would be a bluff, I would have to deceive the people in the military chain of command who would be responsible for implementing the decision to use nuclear weapons were that decision to be taken. They, along with my country's adversaries, would believe in the sincerity of my deterrent threat.

Should I pursue a policy of deterrence? Pursuing the policy would probably have the effect of preventing my country from being attacked with nuclear weapons. It would thus save the lives of millions of innocent people. Moreover, the pursuit of the policy would not entail a risk that the weapons would actually be used. (Assume that, for whatever reason, whether or not I follow the policy will have no effect on the voting in the later referendum.) In spite of all this, the Deontologist's Argument implies that it would be wrong for me to pursue a policy of deterrence. For the people in the military chain of command would have the conditional intention to fire the nuclear weapons on receiving the command from me. Thus, according to this argument, the policy would inevitably involve the transgression of an absolute prohibition. Again this conclusion seems absurd. For not only does it not seem wrong for me to pursue a policy of nuclear deterrence in these circumstances, but it would also seem to be my duty to do so.

It might be objected here that the Deontologist's Argument does not in fact condemn my adopting a policy of nuclear deterrence since I would be bluffing and would not, therefore, be doing anything which is absolutely forbidden. The argument would of course condemn the persons in the military chain of command for having the conditional intention to use nuclear weapons, but that is another matter. They are free and autonomous agents, and hence my action cannot be condemned because of what they do.

Notice, however, that my position in this example vis-à-vis the persons in the military chain of command is exactly analogous to that of the citizens in a democracy vis-à-vis their elected leaders. If it is not wrong for me to cause military commanders to have the conditional intention to use nuclear weapons, then it is also not wrong for the citizens in a democracy to demand a policy of deterrence, thereby requiring their leaders to have the offending intention. In short, unless the Deontologist's Argument rules out my implementing a deterrent strategy in our hypothetical example, it will then permit the citizens in a democracy to support, indeed, insist on, a policy of nuclear deterrence—though it will of course condemn the action of their leaders who will be required, in implementing the policy, to form the conditional intention to use nuclear weapons.

In both cases some further principle may be necessary to bridge the gap between the wrongdoing of those who have the conditional intention and the wrongdoing of those who cause the others to have the intention. Such a principle would condemn as wrong the causing of another to do wrong or to intend to do wrong—though the precise nature and scope of the principle need not detain us here.[20] We do not, for example, need to determine whether such a principle would absolutely forbid causing another to do what would be absolutely forbidden. In the hypothetical case sketched above, even if what *I* do in implementing the policy is not absolutely ruled out, the policy itself is since it cannot be implemented without the violation of an absolute prohibition.

This example brings out quite vividly the way in which the Deontologist's Argument has gone wrong. It shows, I think, that it is a mistake to locate the wrongness of deterrence in the supposed intrinsic wrongness of the conditional intention rather than in the fact that following a policy of deterrence normally entails a risk of deliberately using nuclear weapons. Thus the argument implies that nuclear deterrence is wrong in cases, such as the present one, in which there is no possibility that possessing nuclear weapons for purposes of deterrence will lead to their being used, while it does not imply that the policy is wrong in other cases, such as that of Incertia, even though in those cases the policy carries a substantial risk that the weapons will be deliberately used.

VI

While the Deontologist's Argument seems clearly mistaken, the foregoing critique suggests that it may be possible to construct a more powerful

---

20. Compare Walter Stein, "The Limits of Nuclear War: Is a Just Deterrence Strategy Possible?" in *Peace, the Churches, and the Bomb*, ed. James Finn (New York: Council on Religion and International Affairs, 1965), pp. 82–83.

argument against nuclear deterrence within a deontological framework. This argument would retain the claim that it would be wrong to use nuclear weapons in the ways that have to be threatened to maintain deterrence but would have as its second premise a principle similar to the "bridge principle" suggested in the last section. This similar principle is that it is wrong, other things being equal, to risk doing that which it would be wrong to do[21] and wrong to support a policy which carries a risk of wrongdoing—in particular a policy which makes it possible for wrong to be done in one's name or with one's authorization. The argument's third premise would then be that any policy of nuclear deterrence which it would be possible for citizens in a democracy to support would involve a risk that nuclear weapons would be used with their authorization. It follows from these three claims that it would be wrong for citizens in a democracy to support a policy of nuclear deterrence.

This is a powerful argument. It is not in the least implausible to suppose that it is wrong to risk having the horrendous crime of genocide perpetrated by one's representatives, on one's behalf, and with one's authorization—even if the aim is to protect one's own life and liberty. Can we really in good conscience defend our lives and liberty by taking a calculated risk that millions of innocent people will be murdered in our name?

The argument also has the right focus. It would not draw a radical moral distinction between the policy followed by Sinceria and that followed by Incertia. Nor would it, in the circumstances envisaged in my second example, rule out my following a policy of bluff (though, paradoxically, it would rule out my citizens being able to support my deterrent policy). The argument would not, moreover, need to be absolutist in form in order to provide a strong objection to nuclear deterrence. Because it would locate the wrongness of deterrence not in the intrinsic wrongness of having certain intentions but in the obviously important fact that the policy risks the deliberate use of nuclear weapons in ways which would be wrong, the objection to nuclear deterrence will remain quite strong even if it is conceded that it is not absolutely forbidden to risk doing what it would be wrong to do. (This being the case, it is also unnecessary to insist that the prohibition on using nuclear weapons should itself be absolute.) Finally, since the second premise need not be interpreted as an absolute principle, the argument does not imply that the pursuit of

---

21. It may seem odd to suppose that one can risk deliberately doing something which it is within the power of one's will either to do or not to do. But a few examples will suffice to show that there is sense in the notion of risking that one will act in certain ways. For some people, taking a drink is to risk acting aggressively. Placing oneself in the company of someone that one finds provoking is to risk behaving rudely. For persons of a violent or explosive temperament, to buy a gun is to risk killing someone. Similarly, to set up an arsenal of potentially genocidal destructiveness, even if one's sole aim is to deter aggression against oneself, is normally to risk committing genocide.

a policy of deterrence must be equally wrong as the actual use of nuclear weapons.

Since the argument is not absolutist, it can, like the nonabsolutist version of the Deontologist's Argument, be challenged by an appeal to consequences. If the expected consequences of abandoning nuclear deterrence would be very much worse than those of carrying on with deterrence would be, then the deontological constraint on practicing deterrence may be overridden. Therefore whether it is wrong, all things considered, to risk having nuclear weapons used with one's authorization depends on, among other things, how great that risk is.

The argument does not, therefore, allow us to ignore considerations of consequences. Nor would it be plausible if it did so. Nevertheless, it should be stressed that the argument itself is strictly deontological in character. It is concerned with what one *does* rather than simply with what *happens*. What the argument requires (leaving aside for the moment the question of intention) is that one must not oneself use nuclear weapons, not that one should aim to prevent their use by anyone. That one should aim to prevent the use of nuclear weapons by anyone is also a requirement of morality, but it is not implied by this particular argument.

I suspect that an argument of this sort may better accommodate those moral intuitions which people may have mistakenly thought to be articulated by the Deontologist's Argument. If so, perhaps we can look forward to a more careful development and defense of such an argument by those whose opposition to deterrence has hitherto been based on the Deontologist's Argument. That, in any case, is my hope.

Nuclear Deterrence and Self-Defense*

Thomas Donaldson

It has been said that, in discussions of nuclear arms, consequences over-whelm principles, that considerations of ten or twenty or forty million human dead overwhelm those of abstract rights and principles. Hence, most discussions of the morality of U.S. nuclear deterrence policy have focused on the issue of whether deterrence does in fact deter. That is, they focus on whether deterrence discourages the awesome consequences of nuclear war.[1] But what if it could be shown that nuclear deterrence is a moral failure apart from the sheer number of casualties resulting from a nuclear war? In this essay I show that the structure of the moral argument for nuclear deterrence is flawed owing to straightforward con-siderations of the principle of self-defense. I analyze the concept of a right to self-defense by isolating a set of limiting conditions on its exercise; I then map individual analogues to a policy of national nuclear deterrence to show that deterrence fails to meet these conditions. Because the position I defend regards nuclear deterrence as morally unacceptable, it does not tolerate nuclear threats even when considered as an interim solution along the road to disarmament.

I want to define nuclear deterrence as a policy implemented for the purpose of avoiding enemy attack involving the maintenance of a strategic

* This paper is indebted to the participants in the Ethics, Politics and Arms Control Seminar at the University of Chicago, including Russell Hardin, Duncan Snidal, Gerald Dworkin, Robin Lovin, Ruth Adams, James Gustafson, Robert Sachs, Charles Lipson, and John Mearsheimer.

1. Douglas Lackey has argued that unilateral nuclear disarmament is defensible both on consequentialist and on prudential grounds in "Missiles and Morals: A Utilitarian Look at Nuclear Deterrence," *Philosophy & Public Affairs* 11 (1982): 189–231; while Russell Hardin—disagreeing with Lackey—has mapped many important complexities inherent in game-theoretic analyses of nuclear strategy in "Unilateral versus Mutual Disarmament," *Philosophy & Public Affairs* 12 (1983): 236–54. For some classic and well-known discussions of the issue of nuclear deterrence, see Geoffrey Goodwin, *Ethics and Nuclear Deterrence* (New York: St. Martin's Press, 1982); Philip Green, *Deadly Logic: The Theory of Nuclear Deterrence* (Columbus: Ohio State University Press, 1966); Harvard Nuclear Study Group, *Living with Nuclear Weapons* (New York: Bantam Books, 1983); Roy E. Jones, *Nuclear Deterrence: A Short Political Analysis* (London: Routledge & Kegan Paul, 1968); Patrick Morgan, *Deterrence: A Conceptual Analysis* (Beverly Hills, Calif.: Sage Publications, 1977); Emma Rothschild, "The Delusions of Deterrence," *New York Review of Books* 30 (April 14, 1983): 40–49; and U.S. Catholic Bishops, *The Challenge of Peace: God's Call and Our Response* (Washington, D.C.: U.S. Catholic Conference, Office of Publishing Services, 1983) (the final version of the pastoral letter).

system of megaton-level, thermonuclear warheads and delivery vehicles targeted on the enemy, with the express intent to use such weapons in the event of enemy attack. I have in mind, then, the very sort of strategic nuclear weapons systems now possessed by the superpowers. For present purposes it makes no difference whether or not we limit the enemy attack to the nuclear kind, thus adopting a no-first-use policy.

One should distinguish between a policy that is a bluff and one that is not. For present purposes I am concerned with only "reliable threats," that is, ones backed by the sincere intent to use nuclear arms in the event of attack. As are most students of the arms race, I am convinced that considerations of technology, strategic policy, and counterintelligence make a bluff policy unworkable, but I shall not argue that here.

What is special about nuclear arms? Many weapons have been condemned as representing a qualitatively new, unacceptable stage of evil. Critics complained about the introduction of Gatling and machine guns. Still earlier, the introduction of chariots, iron weapons, horse armor, stirrups, and gunpowder escalated war's capacity for destruction. Yet such advances have proven essential for the defense of civilized societies. Are not nuclear weapons the next step in a relatively smooth continuum of war's advancing destructiveness, regrettable in their awesome ability but necessary in their deterrent capability?

I think not. Indeed, one may grant—and I shall—that, when the earlier definition of deterrence is altered to refer to the maintenance of conventional rather than nuclear weapons, deterrence may be morally justified. This is not to say that any sort of deterrence policy involving conventional weapons is morally justified; it is only to say that certain forms of conventional deterrence can be. The shift to nuclear from nonnuclear weapons systems, however, rules out the possibility of justifying a deterrence strategy.

For most defenders of deterrence, it is primarily the enormity of the threat to human life posed by an enemy possessing nuclear weapons that justifies the risks inherent in a policy of deterrence. Conversely, it has been the enormity of the threat posed by the mere possession of nuclear weapons on both sides, including the possibility of fail-safe failures, that has been used to argue against the policy of deterrence. In this way, arguments pro and con tend to be consequentialist. Evils are weighed against evils in terms of their magnitude. We might phrase a simplistic consequential argument in a single proposition:

> Adopting a policy of deterrence reduces the likelihood of enemy attack.

Let us assume that the damage inflicted on the enemy in the event of a nuclear counterattack in consequential terms is roughly equal to the damage inflicted by the enemy. (This assumption, by the way, seems reasonable in light of current knowledge.) Let us note with Douglas Lackey that, all other things being equal, and considering only the issue of total casualties, the probability of an enemy attack under a policy of deterrence must be half or less that of an attack under a policy of unilateral disarmament.[2] That is, since the policy of deterrence involves nuclear response in the event of attack, and since the damage in consequential terms would in this event be twice as great, it follows that, in order to be morally justifiable, the posture of deterrence must make the chance of attack twice as unlikely as it is with a policy of unilateral disarmament. The requirement that the likelihood of attack be halved places a substantial burden on defenders of deterrence who wish to use straightforward consequential arguments.

Indeed this is one reason why most sophisticated defenders of deterrence never adopt such straightforwardly consequential positions. Another is that simply adding up the amount of potential harm overlooks accepted moral priorities. In particular, because consequentialism typically assumes that each person counts for one and no more than one it discourages a nation's favoring its own safety over that of the enemy and, in turn, treating an aggressor with less sympathy than his victim.

A stronger argument for deterrence buttresses consequential considerations by reference to a right to self-defense. For present purposes let us assume that an individual is justified in killing in self-defense.[3] It seems to follow that nations too have such a right. Indeed, traditional justifications of the right to self-defense on the part of nations have turned on the so-called domestic analogy. As Michael Walzer puts it: "A man has certain rights in his home . . . because neither his life nor his liberty is secure unless there exists some physical space in which he is safe from intrusion. Similarly again, the right of a nation or people not to be invaded derives from the common life its members have made."[4]

To see the importance of the introduction of the right to self-defense in the deterrence argument, consider two hypothetical cases. Under the first, a country knows that a policy of nuclear deterrence that targets the enemy country will reduce the chances of nuclear enemy aggression by 50 percent. Under the second, the same country knows that targeting a completely innocent country will lessen the chances of enemy nuclear aggression by 70 percent. Clearly, the first case is morally preferable to the second despite the enhancement of deterrence. Here we are reminded of Paul Ramsey's point that, even if it turned out that one could eliminate fifty thousand annual holiday accident fatalities in the United States by tying babies to the bumpers of traveling automobiles, the practice is morally unacceptable. By augmenting consequential considerations by the notion of self-defense, supporters of deterrence are thus able to

2. Lackey.
3. It is worth noting that the existence of a right to kill another in self-defense is not an open-and-shut moral issue. Though the majority of humanity accepts such a right, many respected moral authorities do not. The very existence of the doctrine of pacifism implies disagreement.
4. Michael Walzer, *Just and Unjust Wars* (New York: Basic Books, 1977), p. 55.

accommodate the presumption that, in exercising the right to self-defense, harm to an aggressor, but not harm to a nonaggressor, is justified.

There are further ramifications of the concept of self-defense. Michael Walzer's brief argument on behalf of deterrence in his *Just and Unjust Wars* concludes that the harm threatened by an enemy intending to use nuclear weapons is sufficiently severe that the threat justifies a counter– nuclear threat in order to prevent such harm. And we must agree with Walzer that, ceteris paribus, the greater the harm threatened, the greater the morally justified harm that may be threatened in response. Unarmed robbery is to be distinguished from armed robbery, and the justification for using a gun to deter an armed burglar is greater than is the justification for using a gun to deter an unarmed burglar. It seems to follow, then, that nuclear threats are justified against nuclear enemies.

Yet even assuming the domestic analogy is correct, specific limitations on the exercise of self-defense must be acknowledged. International covenants and treaties consistently affirm such limitations, as when article 22 of the Hague Regulations states that "the right of belligerents to adopt means of injuring the enemy is not unlimited."[5] Walzer himself grants that nothing but aggression can justify war: "There must," he says, "actually have been a wrong."[6] The point is worth emphasizing. Self-defense is distinct from self-preservation, and harming another in self-defense is not justified if the party harmed is innocent. Sentenced to die in the electric chair, John Gacy, the mass murderer, may possess the Hobbesian right to attempt to escape as an act of self-preservation, but he does not have the right to kill his jailor. One may harm an attacker who is harming, or about to harm, oneself, but not unless that person is morally culpable or—at a minimum—insane.

Still further, the right of self-defense is limited by a principle of proportionality. Force must be proportional to its ends, and this means not only that no more force must be used than is necessary to achieve a given end but also that the value of the end must outweigh the disvalue of the means. Using a gun in self-defense is morally justified only if the gun is actually needed for self-defense and if the harm caused by the gun is roughly proportional to the harm avoided.

Thus three limiting conditions for the right to self-defense emerge.

1. One should avoid harming persons who are neither inflicting nor about to inflict harm.
2. The force one intends to use should be proportional to its ends.
3. One should avoid harming persons who are neither culpable nor insane.

5. For an account of the impact of international law on the arms race, see Milan Sahovic, "Disarmament and International Law," in *The Dynamics of the Arms Race*, ed. Carl Carlton and Carlo Schaerf (New York: John Wiley & Sons, 1975), pp. 160–70.
6. Walzer, pp. 61–62.

The critical moral feature of nuclear weapons systems that frustrates the above conditions might be called "technological recalcitrance." That is to say, at present levels of technology, such weapons systems are recalcitrant to the intentions of their users: they are relatively uncontrollable, subject to accidents, and strikingly indiscriminate in the scope of their damage.

Let us sketch the outward shape of the problem of technological recalcitrance manifested in nuclear weapons systems. It is a feature of such systems that the time between decision and delivery is extremely short. The delivery time of the new Pershing missiles in Europe is about nine minutes. Countering such an immediately present danger means abandoning the luxury of even modest deliberation time. Defense strategists are driven to employ increasingly complex, hair-triggered control systems capable of launching hundreds of nuclear weapons at a moment's notice. Nuclear weapons systems, thus, become technologically "slippery."

Technologically slippery systems increase the risk of accidental attack and hence the risk of violating principles 1 and 3. The ever-present possibility of human error is aggravated by the use of independent automated delivery mechanisms. Almost every traditional weapons system lacked this feature. The sword, the spear, the cavalry, were relatively accident free. When Marcus Aurelius considered marching on Partha, he could be confident his attack was the result of human intention. A nuclear counterattack may occur as a consequence of technological accident, or it may occur in response to a limited, accidental launch by the other side. In neither case could the enemy be regarded as either culpable or insane.

Furthermore, the very character of nuclear weapons systems implies increased harm to noncombatants—to persons who are neither harming nor about to harm us. Nuclear weapons systems are quite different from single nuclear weapons. In such systems individual weapons occur as parts of complex attack plans designed to explode thousands of bombs in a given order and pattern. This, coupled with the indiscriminate character of the hydrogen nuclear explosion, means that civilian casualties in the event of a nuclear attack by the superpowers would be substantial. It explains why even theories designed to justify war, such as the *jus ad bellum* and *jus in bello* doctrines, have difficulty justifying the inevitable harm to noncombatants resulting from nuclear warfare.[7] A nuclear strike

---

7. The *jus ad bellum* and *jus in bello* doctrines were introduced by medieval writers. The former addresses the issue of whether a particular war or act of self-defense is justified, while the latter addresses the issue of whether a particular action in a given war is justified. For interpretations of just war theories, see Iris Claude, Jr., "Just Wars: Doctrines and Institutions," *Political Science Quarterly* 95 (1980): 83–96; James T. Johnson, *Just War Tradition and the Restraint of War: A Moral and Historical Inquiry* (Princeton, N.J.: Princeton University Press, 1981); William V. O'Brien, *The Conduct of Just and Limited War* (New York: Praeger Publishers, 1981); Thomas D. O'Connor, "A Reappraisal of the Just War Tradition," *Ethics* 84 (1974): 161–73; Paul Ramsey, *The Just War: Force and Political Responsibility* (New York:

would bring about as a matter of certainty the deaths of thousands of persons who could in no way be regarded as culpable. Even if one includes the ordinary Soviet citizen along with Soviet leaders as culpable agents, thousands of children under the age of six would be killed. A nuclear exchange may also harm innocents living beyond the boundaries of targeted nations. Indeed, Jonathan Schell has argued that nuclear weapons are unique in threatening the very existence of the human species.[8]

Next, a nuclear weapons system tends to foreclose options to negotiate and thus to frustrate the principle of proportionality. A delivery time of seven or twenty minutes forecloses the possibility of allowing the other side to respond to the initiation of hostilities and consider peace negotiations. This drawback is critical since, whether in the resolution of strikes or war, compromise is more likely the closer one moves to the brink of disaster. With conventional warfare, the steady advance of pain and death tends to weaken the idealism of its participants and bring home the costs of the struggle. With nuclear warfare, there are no costs until the final terrible moment—and then everything becomes due at once. Again, traditional weapons were more accommodating. When Louis XIV began a march against the enemy, the enemy had days or weeks to reconsider the issue in contention; and so did Louis.[9]

Thus nuclear weapons systems are distinguished by the feature of technological recalcitrance. This recalcitrance to human intention, spawned by the technical properties of the weapon itself, means that the maintenance of such systems is an action with double effect. In addition to the (hoped-for) effect of decreasing the likelihood of enemy attack, there is the increased probability of accidental or unwanted destruction and, in turn, of a violation of the conditions limiting the right to self-defense.[10]

But surely, critics will reply, the matter cannot be so simple. The issue of noncombatant immunity is the subject of a growing literature which reveals the difficulties of simplistic proscriptions against noncombatant harm in the context of modern warfare. The proscription against the killing of innocents, called the principle of "discrimination" in the *jus in bello* tradition, is a subject of vigorous controversy. For example, William O'Brien writes that "the literal application of noncombatant immunity is incompatible with modern war, wherein much of the hostilities are carried out by weapons of great ranges and destructive powers. If discrimination means no direct intentional killing of noncombatants in the sense that no such killing would be foreseeable in using the modern

Charles Scribner's Sons, 1968); and James Childress, "Just War Theories," in *War or Peace? The Search for New Answers,* ed. Thomas A. Shannon (New York: Orbis Books, 1980).

8. Jonathan Schell, *The Fate of the Earth* (New York: Alfred A. Knopf, Inc., 1982).

9. Only with the beginning of World War I did humanity witness an erosion of the opportunity to negotiate at the brink of disaster, as mobilization systems became sufficiently elaborate that, once started, their reversal was almost impossible.

10. This feature may, of course, be shared by other nonnuclear weapons, e.g., large conventional bombs, poison gases, and weapons of biological warfare.

weapons of war, no warfare waged in an environment including non-combatants and civilian targets would be morally permissible."[11] O'Brien concludes that respect for the right of legitimate self-defense implies a rejection of what he calls the "pacifist position," that is, a strict interpretation of the principle of noncombatant immunity. Discrimination cannot be viewed as an ironclad principle; instead it must be seen as a relative prescription enjoining us to concentrate our attacks on military objectives and to minimize our destruction of noncombatants and civilian targets.[12] The upper limit of damage to noncombatants should be established, O'Brien adds, by reference to the principle of proportionality.

Let us set aside for the moment the issue of whether O'Brien exaggerates the technological recalcitrance of modern, nonnuclear weaponry. His primary challenge is to a strict interpretation of what earlier were asserted to be two limiting conditions on the right to self-defense: (1) one should avoid harming persons who are neither inflicting nor about to inflict harm and (2) one should avoid harming agents who are neither culpable nor insane. Serious problems, however, arise for O'Brien's analysis.

To conclude that the principle of discrimination means merely a "minimization" of noncombatant deaths leaves open the question of what counts as an acceptable minimum. To answer the question by reference to the principle of proportionality has the effect of reducing the principle of discrimination to the principle of proportionality, and this is an effect which flies in the face of the traditional insight that noncombatant immunity is a prior and limiting principle governing any weighing of costs and benefits.

Worse, however, is the circularity that arises. Clearly, it is not an argument against a strict interpretation of noncombatant immunity to say that modern warfare as we know it would be impossible, for what is at stake is precisely the permissibility of certain aspects of modern warfare. Nor is it an argument against a strict interpretation to appeal to the right of self-defense, for, again, it is the character of the limiting conditions on the exercise of the right to self-defense that is at issue.

Instead of beginning with the complex realities of global arsenals and strategies, it helps to begin with the home territory of the self-defense analogy, namely, the right of individuals to defend themselves against harm from others. This is the basis of the domestic analogy and the basis, in turn, of the moral justification of threats by nations to use nuclear arms in self-defense. A bit of moral geometry, utilizing parameters drawn from instances of self-defense in ordinary moral life, will show that there is no instance of domestic self-defense in which the parameters resemble those of nuclear deterrence and in which one is justified in adopting the deterrence posture in question. It shows, in short, that the domestic

11. William O'Brien, "Just War Doctrine in a Nuclear Context," *Theological Studies* 44 (1983): 191–220.
12. Ibid., p. 211.

analogy cannot provide a justification for nuclear deterrence because "domestic" situations are unambiguous with respect to the issue of harm to innocents.

Let us consider the parameters of domestic situations in more detail. If an individual, A, adopts a policy of deterrence that includes the sincere intent to harm B in the event B attempts to initiate harm, then the justifiability of A's policy of deterrence is a function of at least three variables: level of risk to A, probability of harm to innocents, and level of harm to B. As risk to A increases, ceteris paribus, so does the force of the moral argument on behalf of the policy of deterrence. For example, if B has not threatened A, or if B is not in a position to inflict significant harm on A, then A's justification for threatening harm to B loses force. As the probability of harm to innocents increases, however, the reverse is true, that is, the moral argument on behalf of the deterrent threat is weakened. For example, one's belief that adopting a policy of deterrence places no innocent persons at risk would be reason weighing heavily on behalf of the policy. Finally, as the level of sincerely threatened harm to the aggressor increases, the moral support for a policy of deterrence decreases. Since harm is a prima facie evil, and because greater harm implies greater evil, threatening more harm requires a stronger justification than threatening less does. Thus as A threatens to inflict increasing levels of harm to B, the justifiability of A's threat decreases; yet the point at which A is no longer justified in making the threat will be affected by the level of harm that B is threatening in turn.

Utilizing the three variables isolated above, it becomes possible to map analogues to a policy of nuclear deterrence in ordinary moral life. A policy of nuclear deterrence is analogous to domestic situations where the risk to A is extremely high, where the level of threatened harm to B is at least equally high, and where the probability not only of harming but also of killing innocents as a result of A's policy of deterrence is nonnegligible, that is, significant. Now the first factor speaks strongly on behalf of a deterrence policy, while the second and third speak against it. And yet—and here is the crucial point—the third factor is decisive in a manner which makes it impossible for us to imagine a relevantly similar case of self-defense drawn from domestic moral life in which the probability of killing innocents is significant and deterrence is justified. So low is the threshhold at which the probability of such killing triggers our moral indignation that we condemn sincere threats to kill aggressors made by individuals in everyday situations of self-defense when the probability of killing innocents rises above insignificance.

Let us clarify this point by constructing two hypothetical cases of persons adopting "deterrence" policies where the three relevant variables are the same as those operating at the level of national nuclear deterrence. In other words, let us construct cases on the level of individual or family self-defense that are analogous to that of national nuclear defense. It will be helpful in the following examples to assume the absence of police force or national government, that is, to assume a kind of state of nature, to mirror the absence of global authority at the international level.

Scenario 1.—A undertakes to protect himself (or his family) against the threat of armed aggressors. A possesses a remarkable gun, one that kills when pointed in the general vicinity of an assailant and operates on the principle of identifying the assailant's chromosomal structure. Its drawback is that it also destroys all other persons with the same chromosomal structure within a one-hundred-mile radius.

Scenario 2.—A has received a threat from Murder, Inc. A undertakes to protect himself (or his family) through the use of nitroglycerin stored in A's home. Signs are posted in A's window reading "Warning: High Explosives on Hair Trigger, Intruders Will Be Destroyed!" Although the nitroglycerin can be triggered by moving one of the many trip wires positioned around the house, it can also be triggered by accident, for example, by an earthquake. The amount of nitroglycerin is sufficient also to destroy the homes of surrounding neighbors.

Scenario 1 reflects the indiscriminate effects of the use of a nuclear weapons system through the indiscriminate targeting effects of the chromosome gun. Scenario 2, on the other hand, reflects not only the indiscriminate effects of the use of such weapons but also their accident-prone tendencies. In both scenarios 1 and 2, three key variables are relevantly similar to those at the level of national nuclear deterrence: that is to say, risk to A is extremely high, level of threatened harm to B is at least equally high, and the probability of harm to innocents as a result of adoption of the policy of deterrence is significant. (When speaking of possible harm to innocents, we are focusing not on the actual carrying out of the threat—where the probability of harm to innocents, of course, would be close to 1.0—but on the adoption of the policy of deterrence. In scenarios 1 and 2 even the sincere adoption of the deterrence policies in question poses risk to innocents.)[13]

Would the rigging of one's home with nitroglycerin or the making of a sincere threat to use a chromosome gun be justified even if doing so had a stronger deterrent effect than alternate threats? Would either policy be justified even if the scruples of one's enemy allowed the use of such threats?[14] No one, I think, could make a convincing case for such policies of deterrence; and the difficulty of making a convincing case stems from more than the inherent power of the weapons in question

13. The importance of separating the morality of the use of nuclear weapons from the morality of the threat to use nuclear weapons is underscored in Jeff McMahan's "Deterrence and Deontology," in this volume.

14. The fact that a man standing in a crowded elevator is about to shoot someone standing outside the elevator does not justify the person outside, however innocent, in throwing a grenade into the elevator.

or the sheer number of potential casualties. The problem, rather, is with whom the weapons might kill and under what conditions.

If A were protecting his family rather than himself, we might sympathize more with his desire to make such threats. But the threats themselves would not thereby become permissible. It is common when discussing fiduciary and managerial responsibility to point out that one's duties to serve the interests of others fail to excuse the violation of standard moral norms.[15] This point has special force, moreover, when the moral norms in question are relatively exceptionless, for example, the prohibition on the killing of innocents.

It follows that a national policy of nuclear deterrence cannot be justified by appeal to some type of domestic analogy. The domestic analogy fails to justify the exercise of self-defense through the use of nuclear weapons systems on the national level since relevantly similar analogues on the domestic level clash with common moral intuition. The limiting conditions for self-defense are not fulfilled. If there is some right of self-defense possessed by nations that does not derive from our more fundamental convictions about individual self-defense, then the conclusion of the foregoing analysis may be questioned. But I cannot imagine what such a right would look like.

Although the argument so far is deontological in form, it need not neglect morally relevant probabilities. For example, our condemnation of the threat in scenario 1 undoubtedly presumes that it is not the case that the surrounding area is sparsely populated and that only one in ten million persons shares the chromosomal structure targeted by the gun. Were this true, the chances of killing an innocent person would be negligible, and we might well retract our condemnation of the threat. Similarly, in the context of national policies of deterrence the critical value of deterring enemy attack establishes as a necessary condition for declaring a policy impermissible that both the number of innocents likely to be harmed and the risk of harming them be significant. This is nothing other than the application of the principle of proportionality identified earlier as a limiting condition on the exercise of self-defense.[16] Disputes over what should and should not count as "significant" are inevitable, but it seems likely that even low numbers will count and that present policies of nuclear deterrence satisfy the condition. In its recognition of even low probabilities, the analysis of nuclear permissibility resembles

---

15. For a discussion of this point, see Thomas Donaldson, *Corporations and Morality* (Englewood Cliffs, N.J.: Prentice-Hall, Inc., 1982), esp. chap. 5.

16. Here the issue of national self-defense differs from that of individual self-defense. Since in individual self-defense only a single life is being defended from attack, any risk undertaken in the act of self-defense to a single additional innocent person is sufficient, ceteris paribus, to violate the proportionality criterion. But in the instance of national self-defense, millions of lives are typically being defended. Hence it does not follow that a risk undertaken in the act of national self-defense to a single innocent individual—or even a handful of individuals—will necessarily violate the principle of proportionality.

that of recklessness in the law. If a person picks up a pistol from a table containing six pistols, one of which he knows is loaded, then aims it at a total stranger and pulls the trigger, the person is guilty of recklessness. And the label of recklessness applies no less when the probabilities are much smaller and the table contains, not six, but sixty pistols.[17] Nonetheless, were it possible, owing to special empirical features of the deterrence context (involving, say, remarkably low yield nuclear weapons with pinpoint accuracy), to demonstrate that either the number of innocents to be harmed or the risk of harming them were truly insignificant, then one might successfully rebut charges of moral impermissibility.

That the present analysis includes an assessment of at least hypothetical probabilities does not render its form consequential rather than deontological. The emphasis remains with the principles limiting the exercise of self-defense. Rather, the application of the principles requires a healthy sense of realism. Consider again the analogy of recklessness. Recklessness is wrong on principle yet requires probabilistic assessments for its application. The answer to the question of whether it is reckless to carry about a dynamite cap in one's briefcase depends on the empirical characteristics of dynamite caps, their likelihood of exploding under certain conditions, and so on. Were threats by nations to use powerful weapons of indiscriminate destruction never fulfilled, then categorical denunciations of such threats would be harder to justify. Even Kant speaks of the "empirical spring" necessary to apply the Categorical Imperative.

The peculiarly deontological character of the present argument is reflected not only in its emphasis on principles but also in its insistence that in thinking about nuclear deterrence, more than consequences matter. Not only the predicted consequences of either intentionally adopting the policy or undertaking an eventual strike are evil—though these are awesome enough—but also the intentional performance of the actions themselves. Some actions ought not be done; some risks ought not be assumed; and they ought not be done or assumed as a matter of principle.

If, as I have suggested, nuclear deterrence ultimately lacks a viable moral defense, either from a domestic analogy or elsewhere, is one forced to recommend surrender to the Soviets? No such recommendation is entailed by the impermissibility of making sincere threats to launch a nuclear strike. Even assuming the implausibility of some variation of the

17. Legal theorists acknowledge that the matter is different when the person's action is part of a practice that serves a valid human end and when the innocents placed at risk generally stand to benefit. When we step into our automobiles and confront the small but existing probability that we will injure another motorist or pedestrian, the risks must be weighed against the general benefits of automobile transportation, benefits which accrue to the public at large. When drunk or driving an automobile with bad steering, the risks are too great; under normal conditions they are not. Nuclear deterrence is difficult to subsume under this exception, however, since it seems implausible that, e.g., our nuclear threat against the Soviet Union benefits innocent Soviet citizens. For a classical analysis of recklessness in the law, see Glanville L. Williams, *Criminal Law: The General Part* (London: Stevens & Sons, 1953), pp. 49–59.

"bluff" strategy, the obvious alternatives to unilateral nuclear disarmament are multilateral or bilateral nuclear disarmament. There exists also the option of substituting conventional for nuclear weapons, which many believe would provide an adequate deterrence and one less dangerous than what we presently possess.[18] Even were this not the case, a unilateral decision by the United States to back out of the superpower rivalry would not entail the Soviet occupation of Detroit; indeed, it is a decision which some believe would enhance rather than harm the long-term self-interest of the U.S. citizenry.

This is not the place to defend or debate these empirical matters, and in the most important sense the outcome of such a debate is irrelevant to the article's conclusion. If risking the launch of nuclear missiles—a launch which would have as one of its foreseeable consequences the deaths of untold innocents—is impermissible, then it is impermissible whether national self-interest is enhanced or not. It is no surprise that morality sometimes requires the conscious assumption of risk. In the present context, however, it may help to recognize that even the existence of risk to ourselves from the abandonment of our present policies, much less its degree, is a matter of dispute.

Our conclusion, then, is in keeping with the spirit of *jus in bello* and *jus ad bellum* doctrines insofar as it condemns nuclear deterrence by an appeal to moral principle; again, the problem is not only the enormity of the horror but also the kind of horror. In contrast to such theories, however, the conclusion has been reached through an analysis not of specific acts of war, for example, area bombing, but of moral analogues to policies of national nuclear deterrence on a domestic level. Nuclear deterrence finds its strongest rationale in arguments that supplement consequential considerations by an appeal to the right of self-defense. But the right of society to its self-defense, like its right to imprison lawbreakers, requires limiting conditions for its exercise. The very technological recalcitrance of nuclear weapons systems places the fulfillment of these conditions at significant risk. In this instance, the risks are too high, and they are too high as a matter of principle.

18. For a discussion of this issue, see George H. Quester, "Substituting Conventional for Nuclear Weapons: Some Problems and Some Possibilities," in this volume.

The Morality of Nuclear Deterrence: Hostage Holding and Consequences*

Steven Lee

I

Philosophical analyses of practical moral issues frequently take into account both consequentialist and nonconsequentialist moral perspectives. Consideration is given not only to the value of the consequences of alternative actions or policies but also to the extent to which the alternatives are fair, just, respectful of human rights, and so forth, and both kinds of factors are taken into account in the overall evaluation. Nuclear deterrence, perhaps the central moral issue of our time, has only belatedly come to the attention of philosophers. But the work that has been done by philosophers on the morality of nuclear deterrence too often has considered the topic from only one or the other of these two moral perspectives.[1] This is unfortunate. Because there are both consequentialist and nonconsequentialist implications for nuclear deterrence of great importance, and because these implications are not guaranteed to converge, both perspectives should be considered in the moral evaluation. In this essay, I attempt to further the moral analysis of nuclear deterrence by examining some of the implications of the consideration of both moral perspectives.

First, some words about how nuclear deterrence is understood here. Nuclear deterrence is a policy of threats. Threats may be schematically represented as such:

TS: A expresses an intention (explicitly or implicitly) to do x (something harmful) to B if B does y.

What distinguishes nuclear deterrence within the general class of threats is that x involves an attack with nuclear weapons and A and B are nations. But there are different kinds of nuclear deterrence policies, depending on the specific values of x and y. This is too often ignored in discussions

* I wish to thank the following persons, who provided me with comments on earlier versions of this paper: Gregory Kavka, Russell Hardin, John Stevens, Scott Brophy, Jeff McMahan, Robert Goodin, and Larry Alexander.

1. An important exception to this is the early essay by Douglas Lackey, "Ethics and Nuclear Deterrence," in *Moral Problems,* ed. James Rachels, 2d ed. (New York: Harper & Row, 1975), pp. 332–45.

by philosophers. Later in this essay, the moral relevance of the values of x and y will be considered. For the time being, however, we can understand nuclear deterrence in the generic sense, where the value of x is simply an attack with nuclear weapons and the value of y is left undetermined.[2]

To consider how both the consequentialist and the nonconsequentialist perspectives should be taken into account in the moral evaluation of nuclear deterrence, we might consider how this is normally done in the case of an individual action. In most cases, the fact that an action is, for example, a case of injustice or a rights violation is sufficient to show that it is not morally justified. Such actions may be justified by the valuable consequences (social benefit) they achieve, but only if the amount of social benefit is large. Anything less than a large amount of social benefit is not enough to override the moral objection to the action on the basis of its being a violation of nonconsequentialist rules. Priority is given to nonconsequentialist factors in judging the morality of an individual action, with the exception of those cases in which there is a great deal at stake in terms of the action's consequences.[3]

But nuclear deterrence is not, of course, an individual action. It is not an isolated deterrent act but a large-scale, ongoing public policy involving thousands of persons in various roles. It is, in other words, a social institution.[4] How can the method of moral evaluation of an individual action be applied as a model in judging the moral status of a social institution? Any institution is liable to involve some isolated violations of nonconsequentialist rules, and when it does, the method of moral evaluation of an individual action can be applied in a straightforward manner: if the institution achieves sufficient social benefit to override the violations, then it may be morally justified despite them. But some institutions involve not merely isolated violations of nonconsequentialist rules but systematic violations of such rules. This occurs when injustice or disrespect for rights, for example, is essential to, or characteristic of, the institution's functioning. In this case the moral objection to the institution on nonconsequentialist grounds is so much stronger than when violations are isolated that no amount of social benefit the institution could be expected to achieve would be sufficient to override its nonconsequentialist unac-

2. In addition, y is usually understood to be a commission rather than an omission. Deterrence seeks to get a party to refrain from some action rather than to perform some action.

3. If it is assumed that there is no overarching moral principle for determining specifically when consequentialist factors override nonconsequentialist factors, the moral theory supporting such moral evaluation would be a form of intuitionism (see John Rawls, *A Theory of Justice* [Cambridge, Mass.: Harvard University Press, 1970], pp. 34–40).

4. The contrast between deterrence as isolated act and as social policy is discussed by David Hoekema, "Intentions, Threats, and Nuclear Deterrence," in *The Applied Turn in Contemporary Philosophy,* ed. Michael Bradie, Thomas Attig, and Nicholas Rescher, Bowling Green Studies in Applied Philosophy, vol. 5 (Bowling Green, Ohio: Bowling Green State University, Department of Philosophy, 1983), pp. 111–25.

ceptability. For example, a slave-based economy would not be justified even by great economic productivity. As a result, lack of systematic non-consequentialist rule violations becomes, in practice, a necessary condition for the moral justifiability of social institutions. This idea may be called the principle of the morality of social institutions (PMSI):

> PMSI: Social institutions are morally justified only if they achieve their social benefit in a way that does not systematically violate nonconsequentialist rules, such as those of justice and respect for rights.

The issue of the morality of punishment is a good example of the principle at work. The institution of legal punishment is morally justified not only in terms of the social benefit of its deterrent effects but also in terms of its conformity to nonconsequentialist rules of retributive justice. H. L. A. Hart has clearly expressed the point that deterrent effects justify punishment only if the burdens of the system are distributed in a retributively just manner, in accordance with desert.[5] The lack of systematic nonconsequentialist rule violations is, then, a necessary condition on the moral justifiability of this institution. But a justified system of punishment may involve isolated injustices, as when occasional mistakes occur in the operation of the system, resulting in miscarriages of justice.

But if there were a system of punishment which systematically violated principles of retributive justice, that system would not be morally justified despite its deterrent effects. A system of vicarious punishment would be of this kind. In such a system it is not the lawbreakers who are punished but other persons, such as members of the lawbreakers' families. One thing wrong with this, of course, is that the persons punished are innocent parties and do not deserve punishment. But more than the actual punishment of innocent persons is wrong with vicarious punishment. Innocent persons are threatened with punishment, whether they are actually punished or not, and they are thereby held hostage to the lawful behavior of the potential lawbreakers. The institution which threatens them is an institution of systematic hostage holding. Such hostage holding clearly violates nonconsequentialist rules, whether it is regarded as an unjust distribution of the institution's burdens, as a case of violating the rights of the innocent persons threatened, or simply as a process that treats persons as mere means rather than as ends. Vicarious punishment, despite its deterrent effects, is morally unacceptable because it is systematic hostage holding.

But our interest is in the institution of nuclear deterrence. Nuclear deterrence must accord with PMSI if it is to be morally justified. In order to determine whether it so accords, we should begin by examining it from a nonconsequentialist perspective.

---

5. H. L. A. Hart, *Punishment and Responsibility* (Oxford: Oxford University Press, 1968), pp. 1–27.

II

Nuclear deterrence is frequently claimed to be unacceptable from a non-consequentialist perspective on the following argument: it is wrong to kill innocent persons; because retaliation with nuclear weapons would inevitably kill innocent persons, nuclear deterrence involves the intention to kill innocent persons; but it is wrong to intend what it would be wrong to do; therefore nuclear deterrence is morally unacceptable.

A number of problems with this argument have been raised. One is that the argument assumes that nuclear deterrence involves an intention to retaliate, when in fact the policy may be one of bluff. Of course, it is possible that nuclear deterrence is a policy of bluff, but there is strong reason to think that in fact it is not.[6] Deterrence works only if it is credible, which requires that it create in the mind of the opponent a firm belief that retaliation would occur. For this, bluff is not enough. A reality contrary to the appearance would tend to undermine the appearance to too great an extent. Nuclear deterrence is the policy of a large organization. A single agent who threatens, and who is a good actor, can often engage in bluff without diminishing the credibility of the threat. But a large organization engaging in a policy of threat is not as able to do this. For if such a threat were bluff, bureaucratic provisions would have to be made, contrary to the public posture, not to carry out the threat should it fail. The difference between an intention to carry out the threat and bluff would go beyond a difference in disposition of a single individual to a difference in dispositions of a number of individuals and to a difference in organizational structure. At the organizational level, a policy of threats which is bluff is too likely to be discovered or suspected to be such and so to be less effective. Thus an effective policy of nuclear deterrence must involve the intention to retaliate.

However, there are other problems with this argument against nuclear deterrence that are not so easily dismissed. Consider two objections. First, the premise that it is wrong to intend what it would be wrong to do may not be acceptable. This premise, which Gregory Kavka has referred to as the wrongful-intentions principle,[7] seems especially problematic given that the intention involved in deterrence is conditional rather than categorical. Second, A may deter by threatening to use nuclear weapons in such a way that its intention is not to kill innocent persons. If the weapons are intended for use against B's military targets rather than against its population centers, then, it is argued, A has no intention to kill innocent persons, and the wrongful-intentions principle simply does not apply.

Without entering into the debate over these two objections, we can see the advantage there would be in a nonconsequentialist argument

6. For a contrary view, see John Hare, "Credibility and Bluff," in *Nuclear Weapons and the Future of Humanity: The Fundamental Questions*, ed. Avner Cohen and Steven Lee (Totowa, N.J.: Rowman & Allanheld, 1985).

7. Gregory Kavka, "Some Paradoxes of Deterrence," *Journal of Philosophy* 75 (1978): 285–302, p. 289.

against nuclear deterrence that avoided them. There is such an argument. It can be found by attending not to the moral status of the intentions involved in the policy of nuclear deterrence but directly to the moral status of the activity that involves having those intentions. This is an activity of threatening, but threatening of a special kind. The threat is largely against innocent third parties, persons who would not be responsible for the actions prompting the nuclear retaliation. The persons whose behavior the threat seeks to control, the opponent's military and political leaders, are for the most part not the persons on whom harm would be visited should the threat be carried out. This kind of threat may be referred to as a third-party threat. The making of a third-party threat is the holding of hostages, and nuclear deterrence, like vicarious punishment, is an institution of hostage holding.[8] It is often noted that nuclear deterrence is a policy of holding hostage the population of one's opponent to the good behavior of its leaders, but the moral implications of this have not always been fully appreciated.[9]

What is morally wrong with hostage holding? The basis of the non-consequentialist objection to hostage holding can be seen in the following terms. Hostages are persons threatened with harm without their consent in order to control the behavior of some other person or group. First, central to the moral wrongness of hostage holding is that the persons threatened are not the same as the persons whose behavior the threatener seeks to control (i.e., the threat is a third-party threat). Those threatened are innocent in the sense that they generally have no control over, nor responsibility for, the behavior of the persons the threatener seeks to control. It is this feature of innocence and not the illegitimacy of the threatener's demands that makes hostage holding wrong. If the tax man threatens your spouse unless you surrender your money, this is just as much a case of hostage holding as if a gunman does the same thing.

Second, hostages are persons who are threatened, and the moral wrongness of hostage holding results from the fact that they are threatened, whether or not the threat is carried out. What is wrong with the mere threat is that it imposes a risk of harm on the hostages, whether or not the potential harm is actualized through the threat's being carried out. Otherwise, the moral wrongness of hostage holding would be dissolved by the success of the threat, which is absurd. Just as it is wrong to harm someone who is not deserving of harm, it is wrong to create or increase the risk that such a person will be harmed. Third, hostages are those on whom a risk of harm is imposed without their consent. Third-party threats are morally wrong only insofar as the third parties have not consented to the imposition of the threat. If I pledge someone else's fidelity with my life or put up bail for someone else in jail, I have consented

8. Michael Walzer also makes the comparison between vicarious punishment and nuclear deterrence in *Just and Unjust Wars* (New York: Basic Books, 1977), p. 272.

9. One who does appreciate the moral implications of regarding nuclear deterrence as hostage holding is Douglas Lackey. This part of the argument owes much to his discussion.

to the threat imposed on me by the authorities to control the behavior of that other person. I am not being held hostage, and there may be nothing wrong with a third-party threat in this kind of case.

So, the three features of hostage holding necessary (and jointly sufficient) for its moral wrongness are that (1) innocent third parties (2) have imposed on them a risk of harm (3) without their consent. Nuclear deterrence fits all three of these conditions.

First, the vast majority of persons whose lives and well-being are threatened by a policy of nuclear deterrence are innocent third parties who have no direct causal connection with, or responsibility for, the behavior of the political and military leaders that the threat seeks to control. Given the global effects of multiple nuclear explosions, many of the persons threatened are not even citizens of the nation that would be the object of the retaliation. The traditional problem of where one draws the line between innocent and noninnocent persons in military contexts is largely irrelevant since so many persons are likely to be killed in a nuclear retaliatory strike that there would be a very large number of innocent persons among that group on anyone's criterion of innocence. To deny this is to presuppose an unacceptable theory of collective responsibility.

Second, nuclear deterrence imposes on the innocent persons whose lives and well-being it threatens a substantial risk of harm. The risk is real, for the policy is not guaranteed success. It might fail through deliberation or through accident, and the probability of its failure, even if small, is not negligible. Given the nonnegligible probability of failure and the extent of harm failure would bring to innocent persons, the policy imposes a substantial risk of harm on those persons. This is the same way in which cancer is said to impose a substantial risk to each person: the chances of a given person's getting cancer may be small, but the extent of harm caused if cancer does strike is great. Even if deterrence policy never fails, this would not falsify the claim that it imposes a substantial risk of harm.

Third, the risk of harm imposed by nuclear deterrence on innocent persons is imposed without their consent. No nation seeks the consent of its opponent's citizens before instituting a policy of nuclear deterrence. But the obvious response here is that it is certainly not a realistic demand that explicit consent to the imposition of risk be required for the moral justifiability of social institutions. Many institutions and activities impose risk on innocent persons, and whether this risk is justifiably imposed does not seem to depend on whether these persons have given consent. For example, automobile driving imposes a risk on innocent persons without their consent, but we presumably regard such risk as justified.[10]

10. This example is discussed by Douglas Lackey in "Intention and Risk, Deterrence and Holocaust" (1983, typescript).

So the risk imposed by nuclear deterrence might be justified even though there is no consent.

This response may be met by introducing the notion of hypothetical consent.[11] It may be granted that no institutional policy or practice imposing risk on innocent persons can satisfy a demand for explicit consent from all those persons. But if those persons benefit significantly from the policy, and if it would be rational for them to accept for that benefit the degree of risk the policy or practice imposes, they may be regarded as hypothetically consenting to the risk. Hypothetical consent may be regarded as replacing explicit consent in the justification of the risks imposed by social practices and institutions. Since all persons in a society receive great economic benefit from the practice of automobile driving (whether or not they themselves drive), they may be regarded as hypothetically consenting to the risk the practice imposes on them, and this makes automobile driving justified. But there is no such hypothetical consent in the case of nuclear deterrence. A's policy of threatening nuclear retaliation against B does not benefit the citizens of B; they would be far better off if A abandoned its policy, for then there would be no nuclear weapons pointed at them.

This whole line of argument, however, would be rejected by some on the grounds that it is incorrect to characterize nuclear deterrence as hostage holding. A hostage, they would maintain, is one whose liberty is constrained, and deterrence does not constrain the liberty of those threatened. But whether constraint of liberty is a necessary condition for someone's being a hostage is an irrelevant, verbal matter. The important point is that it is morally wrong to threaten innocent third parties without their consent, whether or not we label such behavior "hostage holding." Nor does the moral wrongness of this behavior depend on any harm (such as psychological trauma) being caused to the innocent persons by their knowledge of the threat. Constraint of liberty and the causing of psychological trauma are, when present, additional reasons for condemning hostage holding, but it is wrong even in their absence.[12]

Let me show how the argument against nuclear deterrence as a form of hostage holding avoids the two objections mentioned earlier to the more familiar antideterrence argument that is based on the moral status of the policy's intentions. First, the argument in terms of hostage holding does not need to appeal, as the other argument does, to the controversial wrongful-intentions principle. The argument in terms of hostage holding shows why it is wrong to intend to inflict undeserved harm: having the intention creates the risk of the harm that the carrying out of the intention would inflict. The argument thus needs no support from the general

11. For a discussion of hypothetical consent to the imposition of risk, see Douglas MacLean, "Risk and Consent: Philosophical Issues for Centralized Decisions," *Risk Analysis* 2 (1982): 59–67.

12. Walzer (p. 272) seems to miss this point.

wrongful-intentions principle, which may or may not hold in the case of other kinds of moral wrongs.

Second, the argument in terms of hostage holding applies even when the retaliatory intention is directed against military rather than civilian targets. Hostages include all innocent persons who, without their consent, are directly put at risk of harm by a threat, whether the threatener's harm of them would be directly intended or merely foreseen (or whether the risk to them is believed by the threatener to be instrumental to the success of the threat). If a terrorist threatens to blow up an airplane, all aboard the plane are hostages even if the terrorist believes that the threat to destroy the plane itself is sufficient for his or her demands to be met. Given the widespread harmful effects of nuclear explosions, even retaliation against military targets would kill a very large number of innocent persons. So a deterrence policy of threatening nuclear retaliation against military targets also holds hostages.

The conclusion is that nuclear deterrence involves in its treatment of innocent persons systematic violation of nonconsequentialist moral rules. According to PMSI, then, nuclear deterrence is morally unacceptable.

III

But can such a judgment be allowed to stand when so much is at stake? When the consequence of abandoning an institution is a substantial risk of grave disaster, should not an exception be allowed to the principle of the morality of social institutions? If the social benefit is of sufficiently great magnitude, the answer should perhaps be yes.

The comparison with vicarious punishment may again be helpful. We may so readily judge vicarious punishment to be morally unacceptable because we know that there is a morally acceptable alternative, ordinary nonvicarious punishment, that also secures the social benefit of deterring crime. But imagine a world in which the threat of ordinary punishment is not a deterrent but the threat of third-party punishment is. In such a world, the immense social benefit of crime control would be achievable only by vicarious punishment, and this would, it seems, morally justify such an institution despite its systematic injustice.[13] But perhaps our world is like this imaginary world when the institution in question is nuclear deterrence: there is immense social benefit from this institution that only it can achieve.

. Should it be granted that nuclear deterrence achieves immense social benefit when compared with the alternative policy of unilateral nuclear disarmament? Despite the apparent plausibility of this assumption, it is not difficult to raise doubts about it.[14] Since the consequences of policies

13. But in this imaginary world, vicarious punishment might also be justified on the grounds of hypothetical consent, which does not hold in the case of nuclear deterrence.
14. See, e.g., Douglas Lackey, "Missiles and Morals: A Utilitarian Look at Deterrence," *Philosophy & Public Affairs* 11 (1982): 189–231; and Jefferson McMahan, "Nuclear Deterrence and Future Generations," in Cohen and Lee, eds.

must be figured in terms of expected social benefit, not only must the kind of consequences sought from nuclear deterrence be of great social value, but also the likelihood that the policy would achieve such consequences must be substantially greater than the likelihood that the alternative policy would achieve them. Otherwise, these two factors will not yield a product large enough to override the policy's systematic violation of nonconsequentialist rules. Further, the expected social benefit must remain large enough even after the costs of deterrence policy, such as an increased likelihood of accidental nuclear war, are taken into account. Nevertheless, I shall accept the assumption for the sake of argument because I am interested in the moral difficulties of present nuclear weapons policy that follow even when the assumption is granted.

Given this assumption, the claim that the institution of nuclear deterrence should be an allowable exception to PMSI is based, like the principle itself, on the model of our moral evaluation of individual actions. Just as an individual action that violates nonconsequentialist rules may be morally justified if it achieves a great amount of social benefit, an institution that systematically violates these rules may be morally justified if its amount of social benefit is correspondingly greater. The principle was stated earlier in categorical form, without allowance for exceptions, because the amount of social benefit needed for an exception is so great that I was supposing that institutions would not be able to achieve this much. In fact, nuclear deterrence may well be the only social institution with consequences of sufficient magnitude to qualify as an exception to the principle. It is, of course, important to add that not only must the social benefit be sufficiently great but also there must be no alternative social institution without the systematic nonconsequentialist rule violation that can achieve that benefit. On our assumption, the policy alternative to nuclear deterrence, unilateral nuclear disarmament, does not achieve that benefit.

But this is a rather coarse moral analysis. The argument so far has focused only on the alternatives of nuclear deterrence and unilateral nuclear disarmament. But there are different forms of nuclear deterrence policy, and the contemporary policy debate among both members of the public and strategic theorists focuses primarily on which form should be adopted rather than on whether nuclear deterrence should be abandoned for a policy of unilateral nuclear disarmament. A finer moral analysis may allow us to enter this debate. While the different forms of nuclear deterrence may all involve systematic hostage holding, there may yet be important moral differences among them.

The example of vicarious punishment may once more be of use. As suggested earlier, in a world in which vicarious punishment is a successful deterrent of crime and nonvicarious punishment is not, a policy of vicarious punishment may be morally justified on the same grounds on which nuclear deterrence may be justified in our world. But the policymakers in that other world would still face moral choices about what form the policy should take. Two problems, in particular, they would need to consider are (1) what actions to threaten vicarious punishment for the commission of and (2) what form the acts of vicarious punishment should take and how severe they should be. The general rule in solving these problems would be to minimize the extent to which the policy is unacceptable from a nonconsequentialist perspective while yet achieving the social benefit of a substantial level of deterrence.

A similar task of moral analysis faces the policymakers in our world with regard to nuclear deterrence. The form of nuclear deterrence that should be adopted is the one that achieves the social benefit of a substantial level of deterrence in a way that is least unacceptable from a nonconsequentialist perspective. This goal can be more fully specified by formulating more precisely the conditions under which exceptions are allowed to PMSI:

> PMSI*: An institution I that systematically violates nonconsequentialist rules is morally justified only if (1) I achieves a sufficiently great social benefit, (2) no part of the social benefit that I achieves could be achieved at least substantially as well without systematic nonconsequentialist rule violation, and (3) there is no alternative institution (or no different form of the institution) that would achieve at least a substantial portion of the social benefit of I while being less unacceptable from a nonconsequentialist perspective.

Two features of this formulation need some comment. First, the formulation speaks of one policy being less unacceptable from the nonconsequentialist perspective than another would be. Such a comparison may strike some as morally irrelevant. Indeed, such a comparison of policies may be beside the point when the moral evaluation is exclusively from a nonconsequentialist perspective. For example, holding hostages at a high level of risk of harm and holding hostages at a low level of risk of harm are both morally unacceptable from a nonconsequentialist perspective, and so the question of which is more unacceptable is irrelevant to the question of moral justifiability considered from this perspective alone. But when the moral evaluation of a policy takes into account both consequentialist and nonconsequentialist factors, weighing one against the other, something like the degree of unacceptability from the nonconsequentialist perspective, however it is determined, must be considered.

Second, the formulation reflects the greater weight afforded nonconsequentialist factors over consequentialist factors in that it allows, in clauses 2 and 3, that, when some improvement from the nonconsequentialist perspective can be purchased with a loss in the value of the consequences that is not too disproportionately great, the bargain should be struck. When an institution can become more just or respectful of rights at the expense of some loss of efficiency, such a change should generally be made. This is, of course, the basis for the respect our criminal justice system shows for the rights of defendants.

IV

The different forms of nuclear deterrence policy to be compared in our finer moral analysis will be those generated by different values for *x* and *y* in the threat schema presented earlier:

> TS: A expresses an intention (explicitly or implicitly) to do *x* (something harmful) to B if B does *y*.

For simplicity, I shall consider only two different values for each variable. For *x*, the two values are (1) an attack on civilian and economic targets and (2) an attack on military targets, including strategic nuclear forces. The form of nuclear deterrence generated by the first value of *x* is "countercity deterrence," and the form generated by the second value is "counterforce deterrence." The value of *y* concerns the kinds of behavior on B's part that A seeks to control, and it may vary over a wide range. Dividing this range in two, the values I will take for *y* are (1) B's attacking A or A's allies with nuclear weapons and (2) any other forms of B's behavior A seeks to deter through threat of nuclear retaliation. The form of nuclear deterrence generated by the first value of *y* is "nonextended deterrence," and the form generated by the second value is "extended deterrence."[15]

While these pairs of values for *x* and *y* generate four possible forms of nuclear deterrence, in practice *x* and *y* are not independent variables, and there are only two forms to consider. Policies of counterforce deterrence tend also to be policies of extended deterrence. The reason seems to be that the broader range of retaliatory options afforded by the weapons deployed under a counterforce policy naturally leads a nation to attempt to use nuclear threats to control a broader range of the opponent's behavior; and an extended-deterrence threat seeking to restrain a broader range of behavior requires for credibility a broader range of retaliatory options. The same kind of reasoning connects countercity deterrence and nonextended deterrence, at least when one's opponent also has many nuclear weapons: countercity policy does not permit a sufficient range of retaliatory options to support extended deterrence, and nonextended deterrence does not require a broad range of retaliatory options. The two basic forms of nuclear deterrence are, thus, counterforce-extended deterrence and countercity-nonextended deterrence.

Present U.S. nuclear deterrence policy is not, however, purely one or the other of these two forms. United States policy has been moving in a counterforce direction for a number of years, largely following the development of greater accuracy in missile guidance systems, which is a technological prerequisite for an effective counterforce policy. But U.S.

---

15. By including deterring nuclear attacks on allies as part of nonextended deterrence, I am drawing the extended/nonextended distinction differently from the way it is often drawn. My concern is to separate deterrence of the use of nuclear weapons from deterrence of other kinds of behavior.

policy is not purely counterforce, for the threat to civilian and economic targets has been retained, while the threat to military targets has been added. The policy, officially known as countervailing strategy, is, in effect, a combination of countercity and counterforce forms of deterrence. The counterforce elements, however, assure the policy an extended deterrence form.[16] In fact, one interpretation of the development of the counterforce elements in U.S. policy sees them as necessary to maintain extended deterrence in the face of the Soviet buildup to nuclear parity. For as a result of this buildup, extended deterrence could no longer be achieved with countercity threats alone as it could in the 1950s, when Soviet nuclear strength was greatly inferior.

The discussion below will be a moral comparison of present U.S. policy, with its increasing counterforce emphasis, and a purely countercity policy, although most of the criticisms offered of present policy would apply as well to a purely counterforce policy. The opposition between present policy and a purely countercity policy captures much of the contemporary debate over deterrence policy between those who are proponents of the new, more accurate weapons systems and the doctrinal ideas such as escalation dominance and nuclear war fighting and those who argue against the new weapons and for disarmament to a level of "minimum deterrence." Any moral comparison of different deterrence policies must, of course, take account of debates in strategic theory. The discussion below, however, attempts not to contribute new strategic insights but rather to show the relevance of moral considerations.

V

In determining whether present policy or countercity policy is an allowable exception to the principle of the morality of social institutions, two questions need to be considered. First, is it morally preferable to have nuclear deterrence policy extended or nonextended? Second, is it morally preferable to have nuclear deterrence policy counterforce or countercity? Both questions must be answered in the light of PMSI*.

One moral argument in favor of extended over nonextended deterrence is the consequentialist argument that extended deterrence, in restraining a greater range of the opponent's behavior, produces a greater amount of social benefit than nonextended deterrence would. An immediate problem with this argument, of course, is that it identifies what is in the interests of one nation with what is of social benefit overall, and such an identification is almost always problematic. But there is another problem. Because policies of extended deterrence and nonextended deterrence both involve systematic hostage holding, they can be morally

16. For example, a U.S. government publication on countervailing strategy speaks of the need for "deterrence of all types of attacks . . . including the potential use of strategic nuclear weapons to deter conventional attacks" (*Countervailing Strategy Demands Revision of Strategic Force Acquision Plans,* Government Accounting Office publication MASAD-81-35 [Washington, D.C.: General Accounting Office, 1981], p. 11).

compared, and their pursuit of social benefit morally justified, only in the light of PMSI*. PMSI* has an important implication concerning the greater social benefit claimed for extended deterrence. Clause 2 requires that, if an institution involves systematic hostage holding, no part of its social benefit be achievable at least substantially as well in a way that does not involve nonconsequentialist rule violation. Does the social benefit of extended deterrence satisfy this condition?

What are the specific social benefits that extended deterrence seeks to achieve? A typical example of a claim made by strategists about extended deterrence is that U.S. nuclear forces "are intended to support U.S. foreign policy, as reflected, for example, in the commitment to preserve Western Europe against aggression."[17] Certainly the deterrence of a Soviet conventional attack on Western Europe is the most important and best known goal of extended deterrence, but how many other U.S. foreign policy goals are nuclear weapons under extended deterrence meant to help to achieve? No definite answer seems to be available. But there appears under present policy to be a general tendency, beyond using nuclear weapons to deter nuclear attack, to use them (and to seek nuclear superiority to be better able to use them) to project power and to promote the national interest in the variety of ways that military force traditionally has. It is the use of nuclear weapons to serve the full range of traditional ends of military power that is under scrutiny in a moral examination of extended deterrence.

Despite the indefiniteness of the list of goals of extended deterrence, however, it can be argued that pursuit of these goals is not compatible with clause 2 of PMSI*. For it can be shown that the most important goal of extended deterrence can be achieved at least substantially as well without a nuclear threat, and this provides good reason to conclude that this is the case as well for all the lesser goals, whatever they are. The most important goal of extended deterrence is the deterring of a Soviet conventional attack on Western Europe, but this could be achieved at least almost as well by a conventional deterrent. Even those who presently see a nuclear threat here as necessary argue that it is necessary because Warsaw Pact conventional forces are superior to NATO conventional forces. They would, then, presumably agree that, if NATO conventional forces were sufficiently strong, conventional deterrence of a Soviet conventional attack would be achieved.

The general point is that the goals of extended deterrence (controlling various forms of the opponent's nonnuclear behavior) can be achieved by nonnuclear means. This is indicated by the conclusion that the most important of these goals, the defense of Western Europe against conventional attack, can be achieved by conventional deterrence. Further, nonnuclear means need not involve any systematic nonconsequentialist

17. Colin Gray and Keith Payne, "Victory Is Possible," *Foreign Policy* 39 (1980): 14–27, p. 20.

rule violation. Conventional deterrence, for example, is not systematic hostage holding because it involves a threat against attacking military forces, not civilians on the home front. As a result, the pursuit of the goals of extended deterrence by nuclear means is ruled out by clause 2 of PMSI*. This remains the case even if the nonnuclear means of deterrence are not quite as effective deterrents as the nuclear means.

The second question pertaining to the moral evaluation of present policy now needs to be addressed. Is it morally preferable to have nuclear deterrence policy countercity or counterforce? In answering this question the relevant part of PMSI* is clause 3. The question is whether counterforce policy is morally acceptable in the light of the alternative of countercity policy, and clause 3 implies that counterforce deterrence is morally acceptable in comparison with countercity policy only if countercity deterrence either would not achieve at least a substantial portion of the social benefit of counterforce policy or would be less acceptable than counterforce policy from a nonconsequentialist perspective. We must consider, then, (a) whether countercity policy produces substantially less social benefit than counterforce policy and (b) whether countercity policy is less acceptable from a nonconsequentialist perspective than is counterforce policy.

To begin with b, we should consider a frequently advanced non-consequentialist argument that counterforce policy is morally preferable to countercity policy: it is morally acceptable to threaten nuclear retaliation against military targets, as counterforce policy does, but not to threaten nuclear retaliation against civilian targets, as countercity policy does, for the former does not involve an intention to kill innocent persons, whereas the latter does.[18]

This argument loses its force to the extent that it is deployed as a defense of present policy since present policy, retaining the threat to retaliate against civilian targets, is at one with a purely countercity policy in involving an intention to kill innocent persons. But our earlier discussion shows that even a purely counterforce policy would not have the moral advantage claimed in this argument. What is morally objectionable about nuclear deterrence from a nonconsequentialist perspective is that it is systematic hostage holding, and as I argued earlier, given the indiscriminate effects of nuclear weapons, a threat to use them holds hostages whether it is directed at military or at civilian targets. Neither form of nuclear deterrence is completely acceptable from a nonconsequentialist perspective, and the direction of intention is not the relevant factor in judging which form of deterrence is more acceptable from this perspective. Just what is the relevant factor in this judgment? Proponents of counterforce might respond that the relevant factor is that counterforce retaliation would kill fewer hostages than countercity retaliation would. This is indeed one

18. One who has developed such an argument is Paul Ramsey; see his *War and Christian Conscience: How Shall Modern War Be Justly Conducted?* (Durham, N.C.: Duke University Press, 1961), and *The Just War: Force and Political Responsibility* (New York: Charles Scribner's Sons, 1968).

relevant factor, but it is not the only one. The other main factor will become clear if we turn to consideration *a*, which concerns the relative amounts of social benefit the policies produce.

A consequentialist argument advanced in favor of counterforce policy is that it works better than countercity policy: in comparison with countercity policy, counterforce policy is a more successful deterrent. One writer on strategy, speaking of countercity policy, states that "any moral claim the doctrine may have rests in the first place on the assumption that it will work," and he goes on to argue that countercity policy does not work, whereas counterforce policy does.[19] The better a policy works, the more successfully it deters and the more social benefit it is likely to achieve. One problem with this argument is, again, that it assumes that the national interest promoted by nuclear deterrence can be identified with social benefit in the consequentialist sense. But consider what other problems it has.

What is the argument that countercity policy is the worse deterrent? Countercity policy is a threat to commit suicide since any U.S. countercity retaliation on the Soviet Union would bring in response a countercity attack on the United States if this had not already occurred. As a result, countercity policy is not a credible threat to deter Soviet aggression against U.S. interests short of a countercity attack on the United States itself. If the policy is not credible, it is more likely to fail to deter. One weakness in this argument is that it receives a good deal of its force by coupling countercity policy with extended deterrence. It assumes that a countercity policy would seek to control the same broad range of Soviet behavior that counterforce policy does, and part of its point is that countercity policy is ill suited to pursue the goals of extended deterrence. It may be that a countercity policy pursuing the goals of extended deterrence would have less credibility than a counterforce policy would. But, as argued earlier, pursuit of these goals through nuclear deterrence is not morally acceptable. A countercity policy that stuck to deterring a nuclear attack against the United States or its allies would not have the sort of credibility problem alleged in this argument.

But a counterforce proponent would respond in this way: even if the United States adopted a policy of nonextended deterrence, there would still be a credibility problem for countercity policy, for it would still have to deter a limited nuclear attack against the United States or its allies. Threat of countercity retaliation is fully credible only in response to a full Soviet countercity attack. The United States might not respond with countercity retaliation to a limited nuclear attack out of fear of the Soviet countercity response, and so its threat to do so would lack some credibility.[20] Some who are concerned with this credibility problem believe

19. Patrick Glynn, "The Moral Case for the Arms Buildup," in *Nuclear Arms: Ethics, Strategy, Politics,* ed. James Woolsey (San Francisco: ICS Press, 1984), pp. 23–51, p. 30.

20. This argument, in one version, is the popular "window of vulnerability" argument.

that the real risk is not that the Soviets would actually launch a limited nuclear attack but rather that they might seek to promote their national interests in competition with those of the United States by implicit threat to do so. But if this is the worry, the concern is again with the goals of extended deterrence, and this response falls victim to the criticism in the preceding paragraph. Whether there is such an increased risk of an actual limited nuclear attack under countercity policy is a hotly debated question. But to give the benefit of the doubt to the counterforce proponent, let us assume that there is. This does not yet, however, settle the consequentialist case in favor of counterforce policy.

The claim that counterforce policy has greater credibility also cuts the other way. As many others have argued, counterforce weapons deployments are inherently ambiguous between defense and offense. They carry the potential for either role: the same weapons that can be used in retaliation against military targets can also be used in a disarming first strike against those same targets. Since one side will determine the intentions of the other largely by considering its military capabilities, a counterforce capability may lead one's opponent reasonably to suspect that one has first strike intentions. The suspicion would significantly increase the risk of nuclear attack because it would incline the opponent in a crisis to a preemptive strike out of fear that it was about to be attacked first. This is the dark side of counterforce's claim to greater credibility: if A's policy is more credible because B believes that A is more likely to use its nuclear weapons, B may come to believe that A is likely to use them first, and so B may launch a strike to preempt A's anticipated attack. This is one way, among others, that counterforce policy is argued to be destabilizing and so to increase the risk of nuclear attack.

Countercity policy, on the other hand, is unambiguously defensive and so generates no such fears of first strike intentions. Countercity policy is more stable than counterforce policy in other ways as well, such as in its tendency to discourage arms competitions. In balancing the possibility of the greater risk of a limited Soviet nuclear attack under countercity policy against the increased risk of Soviet nuclear attack under a counterforce policy due to Soviet first strike fears and other destabilizing elements of the policy, it seems clear that the risk of Soviet nuclear attack is greater for the United States under counterforce policy than under countercity policy. Counterforce policy is, then, the worse deterrent of a nuclear attack, which is the only sort of behavior that it is morally acceptable to use nuclear weapons to deter. The conclusion is that more than achieving at least substantially as much social benefit as counterforce policy, countercity policy achieves greater social benefit. But to complete the investigation of whether counterforce policy in comparison with countercity policy satisfies clause 3 of PMSI*, we must return to consideration *b:* whether countercity policy is less acceptable from a nonconsequentialist perspective than is counterforce policy.

What are the relevant factors in determining which policy is more acceptable from this perspective? If the moral wrong of nuclear deterrence is the risk of harm it imposes on innocent persons, then the relative moral acceptability of a policy from the nonconsequentialist perspective would be a function of the amount of such risk it imposes. This kind of risk is of nonconsequentialist importance because it is risk to persons who are undeserving of its imposition. The main factor in determining the amount of such risk is the degree of risk to innocent persons or the likelihood that the threat to the innocent persons will be carried out. The consequentialist argument, then, bears on the nonconsequentialist argument: a greater risk of Soviet nuclear attack results in a greater risk of U.S. nuclear retaliation, which means a greater degree of risk of harm to the policy's hostages. Thus, a greater risk of Soviet nuclear attack, which is a consequentialist concern, implies a greater risk of harm to the policy's hostages, which is the nonconsequentialist concern (and a consequentialist concern as well). In regard to the degree of risk of harm, then, countercity policy, involving a smaller risk than counterforce policy does of Soviet nuclear attack, is more acceptable from a nonconsequentialist perspective as well as from a consequentialist perspective.

There is, however, as mentioned earlier, another factor in determining the amount of risk to innocent persons. The amount of risk is a function not only of the degree of risk to innocent persons but also of the number of innocent persons who are at risk. The amount of risk would be the product of these two factors. So even though the degree of risk is greater under counterforce policy, the amount of risk under this policy would not necessarily be greater if the number of innocent persons it puts at risk is smaller. This is what is argued: counterforce policy, in focusing retaliation on military targets, creates the possibility of keeping nuclear war limited and so of doing harm to fewer innocent persons. The likelihood that a nuclear war could be kept limited is, of course, another hotly debated matter. We can make two points. First, since few would doubt that there is a substantial likelihood, even under counterforce policy, that a nuclear war could not be kept limited, the expected number of innocent persons counterforce policy puts at risk may approach closely to the number that countercity policy puts at risk. This means that the product of the two factors, the amount of risk, is still probably lower in the case of countercity policy.

The second point is that, to the extent that nuclear war is likely to be limited under counterforce policy, it is most likely to be limited when the goals pursued are those of extended deterrence, for if extended deterrence fails, not as much is at stake and the initial U.S. retaliation might itself be limited. Under nonextended deterrence, which is the form that deterrence policy is morally required to assume, those opportunities for nuclear war that under counterforce policy might be limited would simply not arise. On the other hand, the kind of Soviet nuclear attack that counterforce policy poses a greater risk of is the preemptive attack out of fear of U.S. first strike intentions. Because such an attack would almost certainly be large-scale, there is little or no chance that the resulting war would be limited. It is clear, then, that the possibility of limited nuclear war can do little to lower the expected number of innocent persons put at risk by counterforce policy in comparison with the number put at risk by countercity policy, and so the overall amount of risk of harm to innocent persons would be lower for countercity policy. Thus countercity policy is more acceptable than counterforce policy from a nonconsequentialist perspective. The result is that counterforce policy in comparison with countercity policy fails to satisfy clause 3 of PMSI*.

This completes the moral evaluation of present U.S. nuclear deterrence policy. The extended-deterrence aspect of the policy has been shown to be morally unacceptable in the light of clause 2 of PMSI*, and the counterforce aspect has been shown to be morally unacceptable in the light of clause 3. Present policy is not an allowable exception to the principle of the morality of social institutions. These same arguments show that countercity-nonextended deterrence may be morally acceptable. But this form of deterrence is morally acceptable only if our initial assumption is correct and there is no third form of nuclear deterrence that is morally preferable to it in terms of PMSI*.[21] In any case, if any form of nuclear deterrence is morally acceptable, it is not the present form of the policy.

21. A third form of nuclear deterrence that has been suggested involves having a smaller number of weapons, like countercity policy, but aiming them at military targets, like counterforce policy. It would be argued that this policy would both lower the degree of risk to innocents and put fewer innocents at risk, thereby being morally preferable to countercity policy. This case for moral preferability, however, may be undermined by the following dilemma: either the weapons would be too few, in that they may not provide an adequate deterrent against a Soviet countercity attack, or they would be too many, in that they would be perceived to threaten a first strike. In either case the policy might carry a substantially higher risk of nuclear attack than countercity policy and so increase the degree of risk to innocents.

Denuclearizing International Politics

Richard H. Ullman

THE CURSE OF NUCLEAR KNOWLEDGE

Since the dawn of the nuclear era, men and women everywhere have wished that the terrible engine of destruction represented by the device exploded in the New Mexico desert in July 1945 had never existed. In more recent years many thousands of persons in tens of countries have taken to the streets to rage against the possession of nuclear weapons — in particular, their possession by the two superpowers. However, neither rage nor grief nor mass action can rid the world of nuclear weapons. The know-how required to build them will ever remain with mankind; because that knowledge cannot be eradicated, neither we nor our heirs will ever be entirely free of fear of the blast, the firestorm, and the lethal radioactivity that lurk beneath the mushroom cloud.[1]

Yet if the nuclear genie cannot be put back into the bottle, it may still be possible largely to eliminate the threat of the use of nuclear weapons as a dominating factor in international politics. That would be the case if it came to be generally perceived that nuclear weapons were retained in national arsenals solely to deter their use by other nations. Such a perception cannot be induced simply by means of declarations or injunctions—although how governments talk about nuclear weapons is clearly of enormous importance. It might be brought about through a combination of changes in declaratory postures and careful "engineering" of the nuclear forces of the United States and the Soviet Union, the only countries currently with nuclear forces large and diverse enough to make them obviously suitable for "war fighting" as well as for deterrence. That perception would be a very long step toward the denuclearization of international politics.

It will not easily be achieved, however, for such a perception would connote a radical departure from the one on which the governments of both superpowers have grown used to relying for the past several decades. With varying assiduity at various moments, both have fostered a perception

---

1. See the persuasive argument of this point in John H. Barton, "The Proscription of Nuclear Weapons: A Third Nuclear Regime," in *Nuclear Weapons in World Politics: Alternatives for the Future,* by David C. Gompert et al., 1980s Project, Council on Foreign Relations (New York: McGraw-Hill Book Co., 1977), pp. 151–211.

of nuclear weapons as instruments for fighting wars. And even when they have not been emphasizing war-fighting roles, the American and Soviet governments, together with those of the other acknowledged nuclear weapons powers—Britain, France, the People's Republic of China, and India (which has exploded a "device" but not a "bomb")—have promoted a view of nuclear weapons as conferring on their possessors special status in the international system. That is just the reverse of denuclearization.

It is not surprising, therefore, that the early 1980s have been marked by greater anxiety about nuclear weapons than any period since the early 1960s (indeed, some observers would say by even greater anxiety): that anxiety owes much to the doctrinal approaches these national leaderships have taken toward the nuclear forces under their control. But it is also owing to the fact that all the world's nuclear forces have been undergoing substantial technological improvements that are likely to make them seem more "usable" and governments (regardless of declaratory posture) more willing to use them. All this is a long way from a world in which governments—and publics—perceive nuclear weapons as merely deterrents against other nuclear weapons.

ETHICISTS AND STRATEGISTS

This volume is both a symptom and a product of that anxiety. A shared concern for avoiding nuclear war has brought together representatives of two intellectual communities—that of the professional moral philosophers and that of the political scientists who concentrate on questions of foreign policy and military strategy. The two communities have different working methods, and they begin their analyses from different assumptions. When they have dealt with issues of nuclear war and peace their work has tended to go in quite divergent directions. The philosophers have concentrated on the ethical implications of the use or the threat of the use of nuclear weapons. Their focus has been on ends rather than on process. The strategists have focused on process of war avoidance—processes usually subsumed under the label of "arms control."

More than any other topic that "ethicists" and "strategists" might address, arms control exemplifies their differences. Arms control is preeminently about management, and most of all about the management of separate national security establishments so as to diminish both the likelihood and the costs of war. Thus it is scarcely surprising that the literature of arms control has been the province of the strategists, not the ethicists. Although it has been concerned with values—war avoidance, conflict resolution, damage limitation, and the like are generally recognized as "goods"—its discussion of values has tended to be implicit rather than explicit. And it has not been much concerned with ethical choice.

Indeed, the literature of strategy (and, within strategy, the literature of arms control) has eschewed moral questions. Within it one searches in vain for discussions of the circumstances in which it would be ethically "right" for a government to use a nuclear weapon. Some strategists (perhaps

66666

even many of them—the closets may be full) would agree with what is surely the predominant view put forward by the philosophers whose work is represented in this volume: that there are no circumstances in which the use of a nuclear weapon would be morally justified. But they have not regarded it as their job to point that out. Confronted with the clichéd choice between "Red" and "dead," they have thrown up their hands. They acknowledge that in a crisis individual citizens in those states that are potential nuclear targets are not likely ever to be able to make this choice for themselves. But rather than cope with the consequences of that conundrum, as the philosophers who have contributed to this symposium have done, they have tended to define their task as that of designing arrangements that might reduce to a minimum the probability that a rational head of government would ever make the awful decision actually to explode a nuclear weapon as an instrument of war.

That means that they have concentrated overwhelmingly on deterrence. Within that intellectual domain, however, there have been very wide disagreements. One continuing argument has focused on the size of the nuclear arsenal necessary for deterrence. At one end of a continuum are those who have espoused what has come to be called "minimum deterrence"—the view that the prospect of assured retaliatory delivery on its homeland of no more than a very small number of nuclear warheads would be sufficient to deter even a much more heavily armed adversary from a nuclear attack.[2] At the other end are those who argue that only by its possession of a finely graduated array of "nuclear options" that are perceptibly superior at every rung on the ladder of escalation can a government be confident that an adversary will be deterred. This posture has come to be called "escalation dominance."[3]

Another argument has focused on the command and control of nuclear forces. Here again there is a continuum. At one end are those who emphasize the need for a national command authority to be securely in control of the nuclear forces at its disposal. They argue that the effectiveness of deterrence depends not so much on the relative size of opposing nuclear arsenals as on the degree to which a power contemplating a first strike feels confident that it can destroy the command centers and communication links whose survival is necessary for its adversary effectively

2. See Robert Jervis, "Why Nuclear Superiority Doesn't Matter," *Political Science Quarterly* 94 (1979–80): 617–33. See also the classic formulation by McGeorge Bundy, "To Cap the Volcano," *Foreign Affairs* 48 (1969): 1–20, pp. 9–10.
3. For endorsements of "escalation dominance" by two successive secretaries of defense, Harold Brown and Caspar W. Weinberger, see Department of Defense, *Annual Report, Fiscal Year 1982* (Washington, D.C.: Government Printing Office, 1981), p. 64, and *Annual Report, Fiscal Year 1984* (Washington, D.C.: Government Printing Office, 1983), pp. 51–52, 57. For one by two policy analysts, see Colin S. Gray and Keith Payne, "Victory Is Possible," *Foreign Policy*, no. 39 (Summer 1980), pp. 14–27. For an extended critique, see Robert Jervis, *The Illogic of American Nuclear Strategy* (Ithaca, N.Y.: Cornell University Press, 1984).

to retaliate.[4] Yet other analysts contend that, because the use of a nuclear weapon even in retaliation can never be a wholly rational act, reliable deterrence requires that one's adversary know that the destruction of control networks will increase rather than decrease the probability of a retaliatory response: the system must therefore be designed so as to build in irrationality.[5]

Deterrence is by its nature probabilistic. Its successful working is conditional. And if deterrence fails, it makes likely the carrying out of an act—using nuclear weapons in retaliation—that is absolutely reprehensible morally. That is why arms control as a topic for intellectual discourse must seem to moral philosophers to offer so small a purchase. For many ethicists, disarmament—doing away with weapons of mass destruction—is much more promising, even if it must be, as Robert E. Goodin suggests in his contribution to this symposium, unilateral for the West, and at the risk of what he assumes might be "a moderate-sized increase in the probability of Soviet conquest." Since (except under the most implausible of circumstances) it takes two to make a nuclear holocaust, the renunciation of nuclear weapons by at least one of the two superpowers would reduce the probability of a holocaust to very close to zero.[6]

It is not the purpose of this essay directly to join this discussion. Yet the very fact that it does not recommend unilateral nuclear disarmament may seem to place its author among the ranks of the morally compromised. Nor does the essay discuss those situations or contingencies in which the actual use (as distinguished from the threat of the use) of nuclear weapons might be recommended. Not having to specify such circumstances is a luxury that writers on arms control have historically enjoyed. Their purpose, after all, has been to explore the design of institutional structures— ranging from unilateral force deployments to multilateral "regimes"— that hold the promise of making nuclear war, and war in general, less likely to occur.[7] That is the purpose of the discussion that follows.

---

4. For representative works, see John D. Steinbruner, "Nuclear Decapitation," *Foreign Policy,* no. 45 (Winter 1981–82), pp. 16–28; Desmond Ball, *Can Nuclear War Be Controlled?* Adelphi Papers, no. 169 (London: International Institute for Strategic Studies, 1981); Paul Bracken, *The Command and Control of Nuclear Forces* (New Haven, Conn.: Yale University Press, 1983).

5. An outstanding example of a work that makes such an argument is a Princeton University Ph.D. dissertation now in progress by Edward Rhodes, "Nuclear Weapons, Irrational Behavior, and Extended Deterrence" (expected 1985). Rhodes's central premise is that the maintenance by the United States of "extended deterrence" (i.e., the ability to deter a Soviet attack on U.S. allies in Europe) *"depends on the credible threat to behave in an irrational fashion"* (p. 3; emphasis in original).

6. Robert E. Goodin, "Nuclear Disarmament as a Moral Certainty," in this volume.

7. The goals of reducing the probability of nuclear war and reducing the probability of war of any sort may in some circumstances be antithetic. The less the likelihood of escalation to nuclear weapons, the less that governments may be deterred from initiating war with conventional weapons. For a discussion of this point, see Lawrence Freedman, *The Evolution of Nuclear Strategy* (New York: St. Martin's Press, 1981), pp. 285–302.

NUCLEAR THREATS AND NUCLEAR FEARS

Our goal is the denuclearization of international politics. But how, and to what extent, are those politics today nuclearized? We have noted that a generalized fear of nuclear war is a part of the context in which we all lead our lives. But how has that fear affected the behavior of states?

It is ironic that, while governments have popularly come to be seen as more ready to brandish their nuclear weapons for coercive purposes, no one has persuasively put forward any specific uses for them other than for deterrence. Scenarios in which nuclear weapons are used to compel desired behavior on the part of a nuclear-armed adversary all run up against the probability of a punishing nuclear response and therefore lack credibility. Scenarios in which nuclear weapons are used against a nonnuclear adversary are fully credible only if it is posited that the using state is in extremis—for example, an Israel whose cities are about to be overrun by its Arab neighbors—and therefore willing to run extraordinary risks. For a major power to threaten (let alone actually use) nuclear weapons against a nonnuclear state would open it to enormous opprobrium from the international community and perhaps even from many of its own citizens.

It would be instructive to know which governments today really fear that nuclear weapons might be used against them. The answer, surely, is not very many. Argentina, for example, undoubtedly feared that Great Britain would attack its mainland ports and bases during their 1982 war over the Falklands/Malvinas, but not with nuclear weapons. The Argentines surely knew that, even if the British suffered a catastrophic defeat, they would not use nuclear weapons against an adversary that posed no nuclear threat itself. Thus the United Kingdom's nuclear weapons had no deterrent effect in Buenos Aires. For years the United States has stockpiled nuclear weapons in South Korea against the contingency that U.S. and South Korean forces present on the peninsula might not repulse a hypothetical North Korean offensive. But does the North Korean government really worry about an American nuclear response? Its nonnuclear status must give it reassurance. Only if its offensive was being actively supported by the Soviet Union—not a likely contingency under present conditions— would it have any reason to think that Washington might violate the nuclear taboo, and even then the prospect of triggering a Soviet nuclear response is likely to have a substantial deterrent effect.

It seems likely that only two kinds of states have reason to worry seriously about being the target of a nuclear weapon. The first are the adversaries of what have sometimes been termed "crazy states"—nations led by leaders who seem fanatical in pursuit of a cause. Thus, Israel might fear a sudden nuclear attack by a "rejectionist" Arab state, particularly Colonel Qadaffi's Libya. The probabilities of such an attack are scarcely high, but they must be considerably higher than they are that in any context short of a U.S.-Soviet war the USSR might use nuclear weapons against Israel. Similarly, Iran and Iraq, locked for so long in a grim quasi-religious war, must at various moments have felt reason to fear that the other might covertly acquire and then use a nuclear weapon.

There are not many states in this category. It does not include most of those real or hypothetical conflictual couples, such as India and Pakistan, or Argentina and Chile (or Brazil), that for two decades have figured on everyone's list of probable proliferators. Some of them might indeed (as India already has) make the decision to acquire a nuclear weapons capability, but the probability that any will ever make the additional and very much more drastic decision actually to use a nuclear weapon must surely be exceedingly small.

The second category of states that have reason seriously to worry about being targets of nuclear weapons is, of course, that of the superpowers and their principal allies. For their citizens the prospect of nuclear annihilation is an omnipresent aspect of contemporary existence. Yet it is for the most part pervasive rather than acutely salient, a dull ache rather than a searing pain. Only once, in October 1962, and then briefly, have the United States and the Soviet Union really approached the brink of nuclear war. Neither liked what it saw there. Their mutually shared fear of initiating a nuclear war, with all the unknown and unknowable consequences that would entail, has over the years engendered in each a marked reluctance to press any dispute that might arise between them to the point of a confrontation in which shots might be fired. It is indeed the case that the two superpowers get substantial leverage from the threat implied by their possession of large and diverse nuclear arsenals. It is leverage of a special sort, however; as many commentators have pointed out, much more is it the power to deter than it is the power to compel or coerce. And much more is it leverage against each other (and against the other's close allies) than it is leverage against states that are not principal participants in the East-West conflict. The nuclear threat posed by the superpowers to Third World, nonnuclear states is, as has been suggested above, largely hollow.[8]

NUCLEAR WEAPONS AND INTERNATIONAL HIERARCHY

It is often argued—particularly by politicians, officials, and publicists of nonnuclear weapons states—that nuclear weapons create and define the international hierarchy. Yet it is probably more accurate to say that nuclear weapons define international conflict systems rather than hierarchy. Within the international system as a whole there are subsystems which themselves are defined by the fact of conflict among their members. Preeminent among them is the East-West conflict between the United States and the Soviet Union and their respective allies. But there are many others, such

8. This is surely what Mao Zhedong and other Chinese leaders had in mind when, on repeated occasions from the 1940s onward, they referred to the United States as a "paper tiger."

as those between the Arab states and Israel, India and Pakistan, and South Africa and its neighbors—the last, of course, an extension of the South African internal struggle.

The East-West conflict is one of two between overt nuclear weapons powers, the second being that between the Soviet Union and China. Neither was caused by nuclear weapons. In both instances the parties have had other, more fundamental issues over which to contend. In both instances the underlying conflict was, in fact, the primary cause of the acquisition of nuclear weapons by the side that initially lacked them. The USSR acquired nuclear weapons in order to offset the nuclear capability—indeed, the international monopoly—of its American adversary. China seems to have originally wanted them also in order to deter the United States, but by 1964 when it exploded its first device it had long since come to fear the Soviet Union even more. Of the other states which have developed an overt nuclear weapons capability, only India did not do so in order to deter a nuclear adversary.[9] Both the British and the French governments felt that they could not rely solely on the United States to deter a Soviet nuclear attack on them.

Although a desire for prestige undoubtedly was one factor in every instance of nuclear weapons acquisition except the American, for the USSR, the United Kingdom, and France security considerations were more important—in the case of the USSR, much more important. For India, however, it seems likely that prestige rather than security was the uppermost goal. That is why it could be met by proceeding as far as the proved "device" rather than to actual weapons.

This is scarcely an unfamiliar history. It is retold here to emphasize two points. The first is that the record thus far is one of states acquiring nuclear weapons to deter nuclear-armed adversaries, not to threaten nonnuclear states. That record is not blurred much even when one adds to it the cases of what might be called the "near-nuclear" states. Two such states, Israel and South Africa, are commonly supposed to have carried nuclear weapons research to a point where they could readily fabricate deliverable weapons; for Israel, it has been asserted, the time required would be very short. Their reasons for seeking that capability are obvious: both states regard themselves as threatened with potential annihilation by seemingly implacable and vastly more populous (but conventionally armed) neighbors. Presumably they would employ nuclear weapons in extremis, in circumstances actually quite analogous to (although superficially different from) those which would lead Britain and France to employ theirs. The two other states that deserve the label "near-nuclear,"

---

9. India, indeed, is the exception that proves the rule: had the Indian government felt significantly threatened by a nuclear weapons state, it would not have rested content merely with the explosion underground of a nuclear device designed purportedly for "peaceful" purposes. (India had once felt so threatened by China. But by 1974, while the Sino-Indian rivalry had become for New Delhi something of an annoyance, no longer did it seem potentially deadly.)

Iraq and Pakistan, are said to be seeking to produce weapons-grade fissionable material, the essential ingredient for nuclear weapons. Iraq's effort was retarded—perhaps even obliterated—by Israel's destruction of the Osirak research reactor in Baghdad in 1981. Pakistan's effort apparently moves slowly forward. Both nations' programs seem to have had their origins in a desire to keep up with nuclear (or near-nuclear) adversaries—India and Israel.

The second point that can be made on the basis of the history of the spread of nuclear weapons thus far is that they do not much enhance the status of the state that acquires them. The Soviet Union did not need them to demonstrate that it had emerged from World War II, despite the grievous costs of that war, as a power comparable only to the United States; it needed them for survival. By contrast, the search for international status undoubtedly was a factor in the British and French nuclear decisions. But who is to say that their influence would be any the less great today had they foresworn nuclear weapons and invested comparable resources in enhancing their conventional forces? The comparison with nonnuclear West Germany and Japan is instructive. If the international influence of Britain and France is greater (a questionable contention in itself), that is because Bonn and Tokyo have chosen not to acquire military forces capable of projecting power at a distance, not because they lack nuclear weapons. It seems even clearer that a demonstrated ability to produce a nuclear explosive has done nothing substantial for India's prestige. Like Brazil or South Korea, India has a large and well-developed research and industrial sector. For such societies in the late twentieth century, producing a reliable nuclear explosive device (as distinguished, e.g., from producing delivery systems capable of penetrating sophisticated defenses) is an achievement that says more about state priorities than about relative technological standing or absolute national power.

"HORIZONTAL" AND "VERTICAL" PROLIFERATION

The very slow pace at which the ranks of nuclear weapons powers have grown—the fact that in forty years the nuclear club started by the United States has enrolled only four new full members and one associate—is testimony that few governments perceive that nuclear weapons will solve their security problems. Indeed, it is likely that the overwhelming majority feel that acquiring nuclear weapons would make them less rather than more secure; since they could not afford to build either a large or an invulnerable force, what weapons they had would be tempting targets for preemptive attacks—perhaps even terrorist attacks—by fearful neighbors.

Whether the nuclear club will grow will depend at least to some degree on the behavior of the superpowers. For more than two decades— ever since the international treaty of 1963 prohibiting the testing of nuclear weapons in the atmosphere and the subsequent effort, culminating in the treaty of 1968, to ban the proliferation of nuclear weapons—

Third World governments have found it useful to argue that there is a definite link between "horizontal" and "vertical" proliferation. Additional states will make the decision to acquire nuclear weapons (horizontal proliferation), the argument runs, if the existing nuclear weapons powers continue adding to their arsenals (vertical proliferation) because the former will be impressed with how useful the latter continue to seem to find those arsenals to be. Indeed, the 1968 nonproliferation treaty gave implicit sanction to this hypothesis: its nonnuclear signers bound themselves "not to manufacture or otherwise acquire nuclear weapons or other nuclear explosive devices," while its nuclear signers (the U.S., the USSR, and the U.K.—France and China having refused to sign) undertook "to pursue negotiations in good faith on effective measures relating to cessation of the nuclear arms race at an early date and to nuclear disarmament."[10]

The slow pace of proliferation thus far suggests that there has in fact been very little linkage between the horizontal and the vertical strands: the continued enlargement and improvement of the superpower nuclear arsenals has not prompted new entrants into the club. That should not be surprising, given the technological difficulties, the great costs, and the limited apparent utility of acquiring a nuclear force. Yet the equation is changing. A larger number of states can afford the costs and master the technology. And over the past decade, as the superpowers have reduced the yields of many of their nuclear warheads, increased their accuracy, and multiplied the number and variety of their delivery vehicles, their behavior (and, indeed, much of their rhetoric) has implied that they are tending to view nuclear weapons as increasingly useful instruments of war. Since the decision to acquire nuclear weapons is nearly always a marginal one, these factors may carry decisive weight for states that until now have come down on the negative side of the balance.

That should be a source of some concern for the international community generally and for the superpowers in particular. Leaving aside the special dangers (discussed above) inherent when a "crazy state" acquires nuclear weapons, any proliferation must increase by some measure the probability that a nuclear weapon will someday be used in war. Arguably, that increment may be slight; the history of the nuclear era contains no evidence that new members of the club will not be reasonably prudent. But any increase in the probability of nuclear use must be greeted with dismay because of the unpredictable course that nuclear war, anywhere, is likely to take. For the superpowers, especially, that unpredictability holds dangers.

It is possible to imagine ways in which a nuclear weapon might be used that would not cause grievous injury—a "demonstration shot," the

10. For the text of the 1968 nonproliferation treaty, see Arms Control and Disarmament Agency, *Arms Control and Disarmament Agreements: Texts and Histories of Negotiations* (Washington, D.C.: Government Printing Office, 1982), pp. 91–95. Signatory states and dates of accession are listed on pp. 95–98. The text of the 1963 limited test ban and list of signatories are on pp. 41–43 and 44–47.

destruction of a purely military target in an otherwise unpopulated region, use against a naval vessel at sea, and the like—but the chances are that the first use in anger since 1945 of a nuclear weapon will not take so benign a form. Especially is that likely to be the case if the user is a relative newcomer to the nuclear club or is a state with only a small stockpile of warheads: for such a state, "demonstration shots" and other such uses would be sophisticated luxuries. Unable to afford them, if it shoots at all it would be likely to aim to kill, not to warn or to stun.

It may well be the case that this next use of a nuclear weapon will not presage an exchange. There might be no retaliation, either by the stricken society or by third parties. A horrified world might look on, moved but unmoving. As in 1945, the initial use may decide the conflict. More likely, however, would be retaliation of some sort and then perhaps further escalation by the state initiating the exchange. Into that process other powers might be drawn. It is easy to imagine, for example, how the superpowers might be drawn into a nascent nuclear war in the Middle East. Either might attempt to punish a client of the other and to protect a client of its own, perhaps using a nuclear weapon to do so. So drastic a measure might well bring the conflict to a close; the other superpower might remain a spectator to these events. But it might feel compelled to retaliate, thus initiating a process of escalation ending in the most feared of all outcomes, a nuclear exchange between the United States and the Soviet Union.

How likely is such an outcome? We have become accustomed to believing that the bulwarks that keep states from being swept over the brink of nuclear war are strong. Yet we should be wary of putting the structure of nuclear safety to a severe test. Our ignorance of how the international system will work under conditions of intense stress is too great. That is why it is worth exerting substantial effort to retard the process by which additional states acquire nuclear weapons. As Joseph S. Nye has effectively argued, it is more important to slow the rate of proliferation than to halt the process altogether. So long as the international system and its regional subsystems have time to adjust to the fact that another state has "gone nuclear," it is unlikely that the adjustment will be violent or traumatic. It is likely soon to be apparent that nuclear weapons are no more "usable" for the new proliferant than they have proved to be for the other members of the club. But the system might well not be able to tolerate without breakdown the abrupt addition to the ranks of nuclear powers of several states over a short interval of time.[11]

The discussion thus far suggests a conclusion that scarcely needs stating: all states have a stake in preventing the outbreak of nuclear war of any sort, but those with the greatest stakes are the superpowers. It is

11. Joseph S. Nye, "Nonproliferation: A Long-Term Strategy," *Foreign Affairs* 56 (1978): 601–23.

they who would find themselves on the upper rungs of the ladder of escalation. Their interest in halting the spread of nuclear weapons comes not, as Third World publicists often assert, because they wish to be able to threaten vulnerable weaker powers—they have ample nonnuclear means of doing so—but because they are the ones that would suffer most from a widening gyre of nuclear war. It is not surprising, therefore, that the issue on which the United States and the Soviet Union have most been able to maintain cooperation over the years, despite deep strains in their relationship, has been that of preventing proliferation. They jointly forged the 1968 treaty that continues to be the foundation of the international nonproliferation regime. And they have collaborated since the 1970s in efforts to induce states that, like themselves, export nuclear power generating equipment to do so under conditions (so-called safeguards) that do not facilitate the clandestine manufacture of nuclear weapons.

THE QUESTION OF "NO FIRST USE"

Yet the two superpowers have been strikingly unsuccessful in denuclearizing their relationship as a whole. As noted earlier, they have allowed the perception to persist that nuclear weapons are useful instruments for fighting wars, not merely for deterring the use of nuclear weapons by others. Of the two, the United States is undoubtedly the more responsible for the persistence of this perception. That is because the United States has made the threat of a nuclear response to a conventional attack the cornerstone of its strategy for defending Western Europe against Warsaw Pact forces that it and its NATO allies have always considered to be more numerous and better equipped.[12] It is the main reason why no administration in Washington has ever been willing to contemplate declaring that the United States would not use nuclear weapons in a conflict until another state had done so.

Europe is the geographic area in which U.S. policymakers have most acutely felt the need to hold out the possibility of a nuclear response to nonnuclear attack. But they have frequently defined U.S. interests elsewhere, too, in ways that led them to rely on the ultimate threat of nuclear weapons to protect them. The threat has always been implicit: it is official policy never to discuss the circumstances in which the United States might employ a nuclear weapon. As is argued above, the threat of U.S. nuclear use is no longer really credible except against the Soviet Union and its close allies. The Carter administration acknowledged that reality by de-

---

12. The problem of making that threat credible—that of so-called extended deterrence— has been endlessly discussed in the strategic literature. For a recent treatment, see Leon V. Sigal, *Nuclear Forces in Europe: Enduring Dilemmas, Present Prospects* (Washington, D.C.: Brookings Institution, 1984), pp. 7–23. For a careful analysis of the theater balance, see "The Military Balance in Central Europe," in *Challenges for U.S. National Security—Assessing the Balance: Defense Spending and Conventional Forces* (Washington, D.C.: Carnegie Endowment for International Peace, 1981), pp. 53–98.

claring that the United States would not use nuclear weapons against a state that did not itself have nuclear weapons, that did not allow them on its territory, and that was not involved in aggression in alliance with a nuclear weapons state.[13]

In contrast to the United States, the Soviet Union has declared flatly that it would not be the first to use nuclear weapons.[14] Western governments (and, indeed, Western analysts and commentators) have tended either to ignore or belittle Soviet professions regarding no first use, however.[15] One reason they have done so is that Soviet military doctrine has long seemed to contemplate the use of nuclear weapons early in a European war in order rapidly to neutralize Western defenses: for every instance of a Soviet leader proposing an agreement on nonuse or no first use, there are authoritative articles from Soviet military journals—almost entirely from the 1960s, however—seeming to take for granted that nuclear weapons would be used in any East-West war.[16] Another reason, undoubtedly, is an ideological aversion to appearing to "trust the Russians" on so important an issue.

The second reason is of course related to the first. Those who are averse to trusting pronouncements that must necessarily be taken on faith, as is the case with a declaration abjuring an action entirely within the control of the declarer, are reassured when doctrinal writings confirm their suspicions. This is particularly so when the declaration is made in the name of a state like the USSR whose overall benevolence toward the West is justifiably subject to so much doubt. Yet Western observers should consider that for Moscow a no-first-use posture makes obvious good sense. Soviet military writings and statements by political leaders have been consistently skeptical about the possibilities of limiting both the intensity and the geographic scope of a war once the nuclear threshold

13. So Secretary of State Cyrus R. Vance declared to the United Nations Special Session on Nuclear Disarmament, June 12, 1978. See *Arms Control and Disarmament Agreements*, p. 87.

14. On June 15, 1982, Soviet Minister of Foreign Affairs Andrei A. Gromyko read to the Second Special Session on Disarmament of the United Nations General Assembly a message from President Leonid I. Brezhnev stating that "the Soviet state solemnly declares the Union of Soviet Socialist Republics assumes an obligation not to be the first to use nuclear weapons." See the *New York Times* (June 16, 1982). For previous Soviet positions, see Lawrence D. Weiler, "No First Use: A History," *Bulletin of the Atomic Scientists* 39 (1983): 28–34.

15. Thus State Department officials labeled Brezhnev's June 1982 declaration as "old hat" and "a clever public relations gimmick that is perfect for the U.N." The preceding April, Secretary of State Alexander M. Haig, Jr., denounced the long-standing Soviet proposal for a mutual renunciation of first use of nuclear weapons as "tantamount to making Europe safe for conventional aggression" (*New York Times* [June 16, 1982]).

16. See Robert L. Arnett, "Soviet Attitudes towards Nuclear War: Do They Really Think They Can Win?" *Journal of Strategic Studies* 2 (1979): 172–91. Arnett points out that there is no reason to think that the 1960s writings represent current Soviet policy. See also Gerald Segal and John Baylis, "Soviet Strategy: An Introduction," in *Soviet Strategy*, ed. Gerald Segal and John Baylis (London: Croom Helm, 1981), pp. 9–51.

has been crossed. Since Warsaw Pact forces in Europe are more numerous and in some important respects better armed with conventional weapons than are their Western counterparts, they would have every reason to wait to see if NATO will fire the first nuclear shot before firing one themselves.

In doing so, they would deprive themselves of any advantage that might come from first use of nuclear weapons. One should not under-estimate the shock and the dislocation that would befall the victims of even a highly circumscribed nuclear attack aimed entirely at military targets. Yet whatever advantage that might accrue to the initiator of any sort of nuclear attack would likely be marginal at best: the forces of both alliances are well schooled in nuclear retaliation scenarios and are likely to be able to execute them even if severely crippled. Since the side that "goes first" throws away the possibility of keeping the war nonnuclear, it would need a clear notion of achievable gains in order for the decision to cross the threshold to seem even remotely reasonable. For political leaders uncertain of what a nuclear exchange might bring and relatively confident of their armed services' abilities to protect vital interests with conventional weapons, no first use is a rational and appropriate posture.

Moreover, even if only one of the parties to a potential conflict were to adopt no first use as a declaratory posture, its doing so might substantially diminish the probability of nuclear war. That is because, of all the various measures for arms control or conflict damping that might be contemplated, no first use is the least dependent on international agreement for its efficacy. A commitment to no first use by one state will in some measure affect the behavior of all others, regardless of their declaratory posture.

Thus the fact that the Soviet Union is formally committed to a policy of no first use must give U.S. decision makers at least some basis for supposing that they will not be struck with nuclear weapons so long as they do not initiate their use. (This would be the case, incidentally, even if they take a public stance of skepticism regarding the reliability of the Soviet commitment.) They would therefore have less of an incentive to use nuclear weapons to strike preemptively at Soviet nuclear forces in order to minimize the damage that they might inflict. Indeed, they would have a larger incentive not to use nuclear weapons, for if their Soviet counterparts actually did regard themselves as committed to no first use (a possibility the Americans could not dismiss), U.S. first use would free them to retaliate. Thus a no-first-use commitment undertaken unilaterally by only one party to a conflict would still serve to widen the firebreak between conventional and nuclear weapons for the conflict as a whole. And unilateral no-first-use declarations will encourage other governments to make them: the more that do so, the wider the firebreak becomes.

Whether a commitment to no first use is undertaken unilaterally or by international agreement, the consequences for individual states are exactly the same, for the commitment does not depend on international mechanisms for its enforcement. Instead, it is self-enforcing: once a state violates its pledge of no first use, others are thereby released from any commitments they might have made, subjecting the violator to the prospect of nuclear retaliation—a prospect which would be a powerful deterrent against violation. This simplicity is one of the attractive aspects of no first use as an arms control measure. It is also one of its weaknesses. A state may go back on its declared word. A government—indeed, a single national leader—may decide that a nation stands to gain more (or to lose less) from escalation to nuclear weapons, despite the retaliation that would then likely follow, than from allowing a conflict to proceed using only conventional weapons. Indeed, that very prospect of abrogation—which could never be entirely absent so long as states retain nuclear stockpiles—would in itself serve as a form of deterrent against conventional attacks. Who can say what a government might do under crisis conditions should it feel that its existence, or its vital interests, were threatened?

Such fragility is undoubtedly a drawback, but no first use is in fact no more fragile than any other arms control regime: the contemporary international system contains no mechanisms that (at least in the case of the great powers) can compel compliance. Indeed, because no first use is so directly self-enforcing, with such potentially dire consequences for abrogation, it is as relatively durable as any arms control regime can be in a world of sovereign states lacking an overarching mechanism of enforcement. In order to prevent violation, states that subscribe to the principle of no first use will nevertheless keep their own nuclear forces at whatever levels they calculate are necessary to deter nuclear attacks on them by others. As they gain confidence in the solidity of the regime, however, they might find it possible to structure their nuclear forces so as to make them self-evidently more suited to retaliatory than to initial use.[17] We will have more to say on that point below.

No first use epitomizes reduction to a minimum of the role of nuclear weapons in world politics. If all nuclear weapons powers adhered to that declaratory posture, there would be no nuclear war, regardless of the size of nuclear arsenals. But the arsenals themselves would persist, monuments to the kernel of ultimate distrust that lies at the heart of the state system. So long as state sovereignty as we know it continues, no nation can ever be entirely certain that somewhere an enemy is not preparing a nuclear weapon to use against it. In order credibly to pose the threat of retaliation against such a clandestine menace, and thus for deterrence, it must retain its own nuclear stockpile.

Stated in such terms, no first use may seem an argument for nuclear proliferation. It makes of nuclear weapons the great equalizers: like the Colt 45s of the American West, they can deter an attack with similar weapons by others.[18] The flaw in such an analogy, of course, is that in a nuclear shoot-out "others" will not be similarly armed. Under even the

17. The preceding three paragraphs are adapted from Richard H. Ullman, "No First Use of Nuclear Weapons," *Foreign Affairs* 50 (1972): 680–81.

18. For a persuasive argument to this effect, see Kenneth N. Waltz, *The Spread of Nuclear Weapons: More May Be Better*, Adelphi Papers, no. 171 (London: International Institute for Strategic Studies, 1981).

most far-reaching likely programs of arms reduction, the United States and the Soviet Union will retain a very considerable quantitative lead over the nuclear forces of other powers, such as China, France, and Britain. And those three will long have a commanding lead over other, potential nuclear powers. An effective nuclear capability—meaning not simply explosive devices but a stock of secure, invulnerable, deliverable warheads—is not cheap. Nor is it rapidly acquired.

No first use may suggest theoretical arguments favoring proliferation, but in the real world of force disparities it may well become an effective platform from which the governments of nuclear weapons states can plead the cause of nonproliferation. This would be the case especially if the leading nuclear weapons states were to combine their appeals for nonproliferation with assurances that they would themselves retaliate on behalf of non–nuclear weapons states that are victims of nuclear attacks. For such retaliation they might feel constrained to employ conventional weapons, holding their nuclear forces in reserve. Or they might define their commitments to no first use in such a manner that once another state had employed a nuclear weapon, even against a third party, they would no longer be bound not to use nuclear weapons against that state.

It is unlikely, however, that for the foreseeable future the United States, or any other present nuclear weapons state, will go much beyond the rather vaguely stated reassurances they have been willing over the years to give non–nuclear weapons states that might be threatened by a nuclear power. And as we have seen, there are good reasons—notably, the imbalance of conventional forces in Europe—which have made it difficult for the United States to adopt a posture of no first use. Indeed, it would be politically prudent for Washington to make its adoption of a no-first-use policy contingent on the successful completion of East-West negotiations for mutual and balanced conventional force reductions (MBFR) on the central front in Europe. Otherwise a no-first-use declaration might merely trigger an intensified and potentially destabilizing conventional arms competition.

There are other measures besides either no first use or nuclear reassurances which the nuclear weapons states can take to symbolize—and make actual—their own reduced dependence on nuclear arms and, thus, to make nuclear war less likely. In general, these are measures that would reduce confidence in the utility and reliability of nuclear forces in a preemptive first strike. We will specify some of them in the section that follows. These measures would all aim at a common objective: the elimination of any incentive that a nuclear weapons power might have to use those weapons in a first strike and, thus, to enforce the principle that the sole function of nuclear weapons is to deter a nuclear attack by others or to retaliate in the event an attack actually occurs.[19]

19. For an effective and inventive statement of such a posture, deemphasizing the role of nuclear weapons but retaining them in national arsenals, see Richard L. Garwin, "Reducing Dependence on Nuclear Weapons: A Second Nuclear Regime," in Gompert et al., pp. 83–147.

If ever there is to be less dependence on nuclear weapons, the United States and the Soviet Union, as the principal nuclear powers, will have to lead the way. However, it is far from certain that they will want to do so in the foreseeable future. The accepted wisdom in Washington—and perhaps in Moscow, too—is that fear of escalation to nuclear war has been a powerful force for stability that, within Europe at least, has worked to deter the outbreak of even very low levels of conventional conflict between East and West. Both governments say they want to cap the nuclear arms race and to reduce the amount they spend on ever more sophisticated nuclear forces. Yet within each country there are powerful bureaucratic and political forces aligned behind new strategic programs and complicating the process of negotiating nuclear arms limitation agreements.

FREEZING, AND THEN REDUCING, NUCLEAR WEAPONS

The increasing difficulty of negotiating strategic arms-control agreements and the momentum of the ongoing processes of weapons acquisition in both the United States and the Soviet Union are the principal arguments adduced by the proponents of a so-called freeze on the further deployment, production, and testing of nuclear weapons systems.[20] The proposal for a freeze originated in the United States among groups opposed to the administration in power and fearful that, left to themselves, the military and industrial bureaucracies—of both sides—will always undermine arms control proposals that seriously curb favored programs. The freeze is intended to put a stop to one of the most pernicious practices accompanying negotiated arms control—the tendency of political leaderships to buy the support of key political-military groups by allowing them to acquire weapons not explicitly limited.

We are quite familiar with this practice in the United States. In order to be sure that the military services and a few key members of the Senate would not oppose the SALT I agreements with the Soviet Union, the Nixon administration felt obliged to begin development of long-range cruise missiles—a system not mentioned in the agreements and therefore not limited. By so doing it formidably complicated the task of negotiating future limitations on offensive forces (owing to the ease of concealing cruise missile deployments, their existence may well be impossible to verify) and inspired a comparable weapons program in the Soviet Union. A decade earlier the Kennedy administration purchased acquiescence to the treaty with Moscow banning nuclear weapons tests by first agreeing to limit the ban to tests in the atmosphere and then by promising the armed services a program of underground testing far more vigorous (and costly) than necessary. This process of "leveling up"—of taking advantage of the partial nature of arms limitation agreements to press

20. See Randall Forsberg, "A Bilateral Nuclear-Weapon Freeze," *Scientific American* 247 (November 1982): 52–61. Forsberg is a leading figure in the freeze movement.

ahead with all programs not actually forbidden—undoubtedly has its analogues in the Soviet Union as well: we do not know the specific quid pro quos with which Khrushchev and Brezhnev secured the agreement of the Soviet military leadership for the arms-control agreements they signed, but we can be sure that they exist.

Because of the distorting effects of arms control negotiations and agreements, a theoretical (i.e., plausible) case can be made for abandoning the process, or at least for downplaying it, and instead working toward the goals of smaller, less costly, and (most important) less destabilizing military forces through unilateral actions. Freed from the constraints of the negotiating arena, President Carter could have decided not to proceed with the production of the B-1 bomber without laying himself open to accusations of dereliction for failing to trade it for a concession from the Soviet side. Then his critics would have had to respond directly to his argument that the aircraft would not provide military benefits commensurate with its cost. Similarly, in the absence of negotiations it might be easier to weigh alternate ways of coping with the problem of the increasing vulnerability of the U.S. land-based intercontinental missile force—including the option of scrapping the force entirely. In the context of ongoing negotiations such a step, without comparable "concessions" by Moscow, would be unthinkable.

These arguments are quite hypothetical, however. Even though the negotiating process is currently (late 1984) moribund, the routines and repertoires that both sides have learned over the years will not easily be unlearned. Unilateralism now signifies the breakdown, but not the abandonment, of negotiations. And unilateralism is likely to take the form of building up rather than of cutting down.

It is important to note that negotiations would surely continue under a bilateral freeze. Indeed, negotiations for substantial reductions are one of the main objectives of freeze proponents. Once the momentum behind new deployment, production, and testing of nuclear weapons was stopped, the negotiating process would be freed from much of the pressure now exerted by the military establishments of both sides. Opponents of the freeze call that a disadvantage. They argue that since a freeze would leave the Soviet Union with nuclear forces in some respects superior to those of the United States, Moscow would no longer feel compelled to negotiate. Indeed, they say, the Soviet government's endorsement of the freeze proposal is an indictor that Moscow would like to lock in its present lead.[21] That is a risk freeze proponents consider worth running. They argue that since neither side now possesses nuclear forces so clearly superior in any dimension as to give its leaders confidence that they can escape catastrophic harm if they initiate a nuclear war against the other,

---

21. Soviet leaders have proposed a bilateral freeze on several occasions. See, e.g., Yuri V. Andropov's replies to written questions from journalist Kingsbury Smith, *Current Digest of the Soviet Press* 34 (January 26, 1983): 10.

the (known) risks posed by the two forces in their current configurations will almost surely be less than the (unknown) risks inherent if the seemingly inexorable process of deploying new nuclear weapons continues.

A freeze would thus tell the military-industrial establishments of both sides that they will have no new nuclear weapons and, moreover, that their current forces are at least to some extent—the extent to which they cannot be tested or replaced—increasingly less reliable for executing war-fighting scenarios.[22] Especially if combined with assertions of the principle of no first use, a freeze would be a clear signal that the process of denuclearizing international politics had begun.

That process would almost surely include substantial reductions in the nuclear forces of the two superpowers. It is important to note, however, that reductions are not necessarily a concomitant of denuclearization. The term connotes the way in which governments plan to use (or, indeed, not to use) the nuclear forces at their disposal. Even very large and diverse forces can be reserved strictly for second strike, retaliatory roles. But the manner in which U.S. and Soviet nuclear forces are currently structured would make a regime of denuclearization much more liable to break down under the pressure of an intense crisis than either should or could be the case.

That is because, particularly in Europe, both sides currently have large numbers of vulnerable short- and intermediate-range systems deployed in a manner which suggests that, following the outbreak of war, commanders who felt that their weapons were in danger of being overrun or otherwise destroyed (and they would certainly be priority items on an attacker's target list) might be powerfully impelled to "use them or lose them." National leaderships might, of course, refuse to allow such use. But it is possible to posit circumstances in which they would be powerless to prevent it.

To make credible (and stable) a commitment toward denuclearization in Europe, NATO—either together with the Warsaw Pact or unilaterally—should take steps such as withdrawing all battlefield nuclear weapons from forward areas, removing all but at most a few of them (to be retained, perhaps, for deterrent purposes) from Europe altogether, and removing also the "quick reaction alert" aircraft programmed for nuclear missions (they would be high-priority targets). Any intermediate-range nuclear systems remaining should be highly survivable and clearly intended for second strike, retaliatory missions, such as missiles on submarines in coastal waters.[23]

Deployment changes such as these would be enormously valuable for their own sake. At one stroke they would defuse what one analyst

22. Some versions of the freeze proposal allow for reliability testing and replacement of existing weapons systems as they age; some are more restrictive. See Forsberg, p. 56.

23. See Johan Jørgen Holst, "Moving toward No First Use in Practice," in *Alliance Security and the No-First-Use Question,* ed. John D. Steinbruner and Leon V. Sigal (Washington, D.C.: Brookings Institution, 1983), pp. 173–96.

has trenchantly called "the unacknowledged probabilistic Doomsday Machine" of current American nuclear deployments in Europe.[24] If reciprocated, they would contribute significantly toward creating a climate for productive U.S.-Soviet negotiations aimed at achieving deep reductions of strategic nuclear forces.

This is not the place for a detailed discussion of the kinds of strategic forces the superpowers should retain in the context of a truly denuclearized international political environment. But it is not difficult to suggest some general criteria. The most important is that they should be as nearly invulnerable as possible, so as to offer an adversary no advantage in striking first. Although they certainly need not be particularly rapid in their delivery time (indeed, a force capable of slow reaction would be desirable), they should also be highly reliable and difficult to defend against and thus offer an adversary no ground for unrealistic expectations of minimizing damage. Their quantity should be verifiable, so as not to arouse fears of a sudden "breakout" of clandestinely produced weapons. They should be sufficiently few in number so as not to arouse suspicion that their possessor harbors hidden plans for nuclear war fighting, yet numerous enough so that the bilateral (or, indeed, multilateral) nuclear weapons balance would not be decisively affected by a power's sudden deployment of hitherto concealed forces. Probably they should not number more than 2,000 deliverable warheads, a quantity large enough to prevent an adversary from gaining much from "breakout," yet small enough so as to discourage any recidivist inclinations toward nuclear war fighting. Such forces might be created from components of present-day U.S. and Soviet forces. Or they could be made up of new systems constructed under a mutually agreed departure from the freeze regime, such as small, single-warhead, land- or submarine-based missiles.

DENUCLEARIZATION AS THE GOAL OF ARMS CONTROL

There will undoubtedly be objections to the argument thus far. Ethicists may object to what may seem my overly complacent attitude toward what can only be described as the relentless armaments race between the United States and the Soviet Union—complacent in the sense that I think that the result of a continuing buildup will be a monstrous waste of resources and an inversion of societal priorities, but probably not a nuclear war. Ethicists may also regard it as something of a cop-out that I have suggested no set of arrangements that offers the promise of departing fundamentally from the mutual hostage relationship in which the two superpowers find themselves—nor any real change in the international hierarchy that finds the two at the top of the heap. (That hierarchy depends heavily on nonnuclear military capabilities; it would remain much the same even if drastic nuclear arms reductions on the part of

24. Rhodes, chap. 6, app. 2.

the United States and the Soviet Union were not accompanied by reductions in British, French, and Chinese forces.)

Strategists may object that I have cast my discussion of arms control in terms of one particular objective, minimizing the role of nuclear weapons in international politics. Many strategists would reject that goal and would contend that the best way to deter the outbreak of large-scale war, and therefore the risk of escalation to nuclear war, is for the United States to retain large and diverse nuclear forces capable of attacking a wide range of potential targets. They would agree with four distinguished Germans who, replying to a recent proposal for no first use of nuclear weapons, proclaimed: "The longest period of peace in European history is inconceivable without the war-preventing effect of nuclear weapons."[25]

These are not inconsiderable objections. Nor are they easy to answer. I would begin a reply by stating that while I do not think that nuclear war is very likely even if the arms race continues, two considerations make me far from complacent. The first is that even very small risks of very great disasters should be taken very seriously. Although conventional war between East and West—anywhere, but especially in Europe—would be a very great disaster, a nuclear war, with its ever-present possibilities of escalation to a civilization-destroying all-out exchange, would pose the possibility of a catastrophe of incomparably greater magnitude. The various measures subsumed above under the heading "denuclearization" would undoubtedly raise by some degree the probability of conventional war. But my judgment—obviously only one analyst's judgment—is that the added risk would be slight. In Europe, the lines dividing East from West are now so deeply etched, and the likely gains to any party from risking war to disturb them so small compared to the likely costs, that the probability of conventional war even without the shadow of the overhanging nuclear sword is tolerably low.

Outside Europe, in regions like the Persian Gulf or Southeast Asia, the risks are perhaps greater but, surely, not much greater. That is not only because the two superpowers have a healthy respect for each other's conventional military capabilities but also because even in a world of shrunken and sheathed nuclear forces the risk of escalation to nuclear war could never be entirely absent. And that risk would continue to exert a deterrent effect: so long as nuclear weapons exist they will inspire caution and not merely in the nuclear realm. "Denuclearization" cannot eliminate together the possibility of nuclear war. But the kinds of nuclear force deployments and the other limitations suggested in this paper would be likely substantially to reduce the probability that any state would (or profitably could) resort to nuclear war fighting. By contrast, if current

25. Karl Kaiser, Georg Leber, Alois Mertes, and Franz-Josef Schulze, "Nuclear Weapons and the Preservation of Peace," *Foreign Affairs* 60 (1982): 1157–70, p. 1159. The proposal to which they objected was in McGeorge Bundy, George F. Kennan, Robert S. McNamara, and Gerard Smith, "Nuclear Weapons and the Atlantic Alliance," *Foreign Affairs* 60 (1982): 753–68.

developments in nuclear warheads and delivery systems are unchecked, they will have the effect of making nuclear war fighting seem much more feasible.

The second consideration I would raise is of quite a different nature. It is that nuclear weapons (all nuclear weapons, but particularly those perceived to be useful for first strike counterforce attacks and not merely for retaliation) are fundamentally incompatible with democratic government. They place the most awesome decision an organized society could ever face in the hands of a very small number of persons who at the moment of decision would almost certainly be totally isolated from, and thus unable to consult, the publics in whose name they would presume to act. In a centralized modern state the decision to make war of any sort, even in response to an act of war by another state, will always raise troubling issues of responsibility and accountability. But when the possibility exists of using nuclear weapons, the issues raised are very much more troubling. War with even the most lethal conventional weapons (the category "conventional" here excludes not only nuclear weapons but others—e.g., chemical and biological—of mass destruction) is likely to occur over a time span sufficiently long so as to allow for some measure of interaction between leaders and led; as the American experience in Vietnam showed, a polity can force its leaders to end a conventional war if the costs it imposes begin to seem incommensurate with any possible benefits. But a nuclear war would impose its very much greater costs so rapidly and so completely as to allow no opportunity for public opinion to make itself felt.

It is paradoxical indeed that millions of Americans so vocal in their opposition to the lengthening reach of the federal government's authority and so anxious to return decision making to local governments or (better still) to private hands are so evidently unconcerned over the fact that they have delegated to the President the authority to launch weapons whose use might result in the nearly instantaneous devastation of their society. Yet such a delegation is a necessary concomitant of the process of organizing a nation to fight a nuclear war. The denuclearization proposed in this paper would not eliminate this condition because it would leave open the possibility of nuclear retaliation in response to a nuclear attack, and leaders would be unlikely (or unable) to consult the led in making the decision whether to retaliate. However, because it would so diminish the incentives (indeed, the possibilities) for nuclear war fighting, it would nevertheless diminish some of the most profoundly antidemocratic aspects of a national nuclear capability.

The same sort of considerations apply, it should be noted, to the Soviet Union as well as to the United States. The two political systems are scarcely comparable. But in each case preparing for nuclear war strengthens those political forces that are most centralizing, antidemocratic, and potentially or actually repressive. In our own country that means giving more weight to the national security establishment and to the apparatus of presidential power. The effect on Soviet society, already so immensely centralized and antidemocratic, may be even more pernicious.

Moreover, the ever-present possibility of nuclear war has made the relationship between the United States and the Soviet Union like that of no other dyad in history. Never previously have two states coexisted with the continuing knowledge that each could almost instantly be destroyed by the other. That possibility, and the separate measures each has taken to forestall it, necessarily exacerbates a distrust that ultimately colors every aspect of the dyadic relationship, magnifying conflicts over other issues and giving rise at moments of tension to an upwardly spiraling hostility.[26] So long as nuclear weapons exist, that distrust is unlikely altogether to vanish. But the knowledge that neither possesses nuclear forces configured or deployed so as to facilitate an attack on the other might well have a transforming effect on other aspects of their bilateral relationship. In particular, it might defuse the processes that cause nearly any incident or dispute to ratchet up the overall level of tension between Washington and Moscow. Thus it might facilitate negotiations to build the foundations of a more satisfactory modus vivendi.

This second consideration would be the basis, also, of my reply to the strategists' objection. To them I would emphasize what I consider to be the possibility of substantial change in the bilateral U.S.-Soviet relationship. And I would repeat a point made earlier in this essay—that because what I have termed "denuclearization" might by some degree raise the risks of nonnuclear war, particularly in Europe, I would make the satisfactory conclusion of negotiations for achieving parity in European conventional forces, preferably at lower than existing levels, a precondition for agreeing to deep reductions in nuclear weapons and perhaps even for maintaining indefinitely a policy of nuclear no first use. That, of course, is a topic for a paper in itself.

Not to fix what is not broken is always good advice. So is the admonition not to rock a boat. There is a danger, however, that one may fail to detect in time that a structure on which one has grown used to relying is in fact broken or to perceive that a boat will rock through no action of one's own. There are good reasons for thinking that technological changes now occurring will make "the nuclear future" (as Michael Mandelbaum has called it)[27] not simply a linear extrapolation of the past and that the weapons systems that both superpowers are in the process of deploying will in a crisis impel one or the other to strike first lest it be struck. That is why denuclearizing international politics should be the primary long-term goal on the arms control agenda.

26. For the theoretical construct on which this generalization is based, see Robert Jervis, *Perception and Misperception in International Politics* (Princeton, N.J.: Princeton University Press, 1976), pp. 62–113.

27. Michael Mandelbaum, *The Nuclear Future* (Ithaca, N.Y.: Cornell University Press, 1983). It should be noted that Mandelbaum has a somewhat more complacent view of the nuclear future than I do.

Getting on the Road to Peace:
A Modest Proposal*

Jan Narveson

INTRODUCTION: SECURITY, MISTRUST, AND INSECURITY

The world's superpowers and their allies currently maintain military establishments of utterly unprecedented destructive power and costliness; and, notoriously, they add daily to their armaments. If we were to ask either of them what the purpose of all this activity is, we would be sure to get the same reply, Defense, or, Security. If we were further to ask, Security from what? each would unhesitatingly cite as the overwhelmingly major object of concern the other party. Neither has much to fear from anyone else, especially if the other possible threateners are taken individually. Even Russian concern about China seems scarcely of a kind to call for the assembling of thousands of megatons of nuclear warheads to secure the situation. And certainly both the United States and the Soviet Union would strongly disclaim any aggressive intentions. The whole thing is for defense, both would insist. It's the other party's fault! Thus, for example, what was once known as the War Department in the United States has for decades been called the Department of Defense.

On the face of it, this situation is anomalous, if not downright absurd. How could two states each go to enormous trouble and expense to arm themselves to the teeth against each other if each really believed that the sole reason the other was taking up arms was for defense against itself and no one else? Evidently there is some serious misunderstanding or mistrust on the part of at least one. But of both, actually—it can hardly be asymmetric. Imagine that Jones seriously mistrusts Smith, to the point where he equips himself with a revolver, but that Smith does not mistrust Jones at all, feeling in fact perfectly confident that Jones will never use the weapon in question. In that case, Smith will not arm himself in response, one would suppose; and one would further suppose that his

* This paper will appear in *Nuclear War: Philosophical Perspectives*, ed. Michael Allen Fox and Leo Groarke (New York: Peter Lang, 1985). I wish to thank the University of Chicago's Nuclear Study Group for giving me the opportunity to present what turned out to be the first, informal version of this paper and for the useful criticisms presented at that meeting (June 6, 1983). I am also grateful to Leo Groarke and Bob Goodin for helpful criticisms. I hope that this is a better paper as a result.

refraining from doing so would eventually lead Jones to dismantle his revolver or at least to leave it at home when a likely encounter with Smith was in the offing. It would be surprising, in the absence of mistrust or misunderstanding, if they did not soon resume normal civil relations.

Mistrust can be a potent source of misunderstanding, as we know. Othello's readiness to believe that Desdemona is unfaithful betrays a strong streak of fear or mistrust: if he loved her in the right way, we take it, his standards of evidence for assessing charges of infidelity would be much more rigorous than the ones he actually employed. In the nuclear age, such attitudes bring with them perils of the worst kind. For a superb illustration, consider the notorious incident which occurred about the time this essay was first being written (autumn 1983). Pilots of the Soviet Air Force, acting on explicit orders from higher up, shot down an airliner with some hundreds of civilians on board. That unfortunate plane had strayed far from its route and deep into Soviet air space, overflying some major Soviet military installations. On being duly accused of murder in the Western press, the Russians replied that their pilots had warned the airliner, as required, but that their attempts had elicited no response.

Why did he not respond? Two hypotheses came to public attention. (*a*) He was asleep, or else the attempts were insufficient to get his attention. (*b*) Although he did see the warnings, he was actually engaged on a spying mission of such a level of duplicity that he was constrained to fake response *a* in hopes that the Russian pilots would let him blunder onward. As between these two, the second was manifestly incredible. For one thing, the Russians knew that the Americans operate spy satellites over the site routinely. And they knew that the Americans know that they are quite capable of shooting down stray airliners if it comes to that. Above all, they must surely have known that no plane on a spying mission could conceivably fail to be aware of the presence of Soviet fighter planes in the vicinity and that any pilot attempting to fake it in the way called for by hypothesis *b* would have to be literally insane. In short, the first hypothesis was overwhelmingly more reasonable than the second was. Nevertheless, the Soviets professed to believe the second, and so persistently that one began to wonder if they did not really believe it. In their minds, it seems, intruders on Russian air space are to be assumed guilty unless proven innocent beyond the shadow of not only a reasonable doubt but even a wildly unreasonable one.

Behavior of the kind illustrated by the Russians in this incident sends a chill through Western spines, and for good reason. Contemporary weapons systems are enormously complicated but are still operated, in the end, by mere fallible humans. Error is possible. But the consequences of misinterpreted error are unfathomable. Thus the need to make allowance for the possibility of such errors, to anticipate them and build in safeguards against rash response, is urgent. If the Soviet response in the airliner case is indicative of their standard frame of mind, then how is any sort of "security" to be possible in present technological circumstances?

What are we to think of those who exemplify, or worse yet instill, such sets of mind? One's first impulse is to write them off with a modishly clinical adjective: "paranoid." And no doubt the history of Russia provides support for that description. But doing so seriously has two disadvantages. In the first place, the label is widely taken to be pejorative, and rightly so; and it can hardly help to promote the cause of peace to go around attaching such labels to one's putative enemy. And in the second place, paranoia is a pathological condition. These are conditions one "treats" rather than inviting a rational response. And among the things that do not help any is taking a patronizing attitude toward one's putative enemy. It is obviously dangerous. Moreover, I suggest, it is unjust.

It is unjust to assume that someone is evil who cannot prove innocence beyond the shadow of an unreasonable doubt. It is also unjust to assume, without very good evidence, that he is irrational. Reason requires us to presume that those we deal with are neither malevolent nor irrational. It does not require that we love them or share their ends; it does require that we refrain from hatred, or at least the actions that flow therefrom. And it requires that we respect their right to pursue their ends so long as such pursuit is compatible with our pursuit of our own; and where it is not, to be willing to negotiate on terms of moral equality regarding trade-offs from our maximally preferred courses of action.

Why does reason require this? Because we will all be worse off if we act on contrary assumptions. If I assume that you are out to get me by whatever methods you can as soon as you can, my obvious move is preemptive attack. If you assume that I have made this assumption, your obvious move will be pre-preemptive attack. If I distrust you to the point where, even when we do make a treaty, I do my best to fudge it in my favor, I invite a similar response from you. And so on.

Of course the presumption that the other party is rational and non-malevolent is rebuttable. Reason certainly does not require an absolute faith in one's enemy, even in these rudimentary respects. The question is, rebuttable how? Military thinking generally proceeds on what has come to be called "worst-case reasoning": assume the worst the enemy could do, and prepare for that. But military thinking concerns our dealings with known enemies, people who are known to be intent on killing us because they have already tried to do so or have otherwise made their intentions exceedingly clear. However, when we are dealing not with known enemies but only with those with whom we have differences of ideology or perceived interest, the worst-case assumption is not obviously appropriate. In the worst case, my dear and good friend Bill would suddenly turn into a homicidal maniac, or it would suddenly become clear that he has for all these years been intent on my ruin, pursuing this with surpassing ingenuity that has deceived us all. Should I, then, shoot him now, just in case? Should I be on guard every moment, lest the dire issue of this worst case come about? After all, I cannot claim to know, beyond the aforementioned unreasonable shadow of a doubt, that this hypothesis is untrue. The situation is merely that I have not the slightest reason to believe it.

But that is not all there is to it. Mere lack of any basis for making this outrageous assumption is not all that prevents me from doing so. For there is also the fact that if I were really to take up this strange stance—say, a slight stiffening when Bill comes into view, a tendency to edge toward the nearest escape or to hide the cutlery when he is about— then I would be behaving in a way that invites Bill's suspicion, doubt, and fear. This is not how one behaves toward a friend—nor indeed toward any civilized stranger. Behavior of the kind motivated by the belief that he is about to kill me, in addition to being positively idiotic under the circumstances, is also poisonous, insidious, and intolerable. Who would want to live the sort of life called for by continuous application of worst-case reasoning to all and sundry?

Reason does not require, of course, that we be "friends" with the Soviet Union. But there is an idea of good relations among states that does not involve anything quite so committal, and it is not unreasonable to assume that decent relations in that sense ought to be the norm in international dealings. We should not get hung up on niceties. Whatever the minimal norms of international relations should be thought to be, it is surely clear that pointing large numbers of thermonuclear-tipped missiles at nation X is not compatible with having such relations with X. That behavior invites fear, suspicion, and response in kind; and the invitation has, not surprisingly, been accepted. There is ample reason to think that NATO policy in the years since the Second World War has been dominated by worse-case reasoning. And we surely ought to ask whether that kind of reasoning is really justified in the circumstances that have prevailed since then.

If we were engaged in what has come to be called a zero-sum game with the Soviet Union, worst-case reasoning would, of course, be appropriate; it is, indeed, the sine qua non of rational action in such cases. But the idea that we are in the midst of such a game is misguided. Doubtless there are competitions of various kinds—ideological, especially (competition for the "hearts and minds" of people). But the zero-sum format does not apply there. If my enemy "loses" in an ideological competition with me, he has surely, in my view, won: for now he has the truth (at least in my view), which he did not before. And in any case, if the Russians were to vaporize us all, it is hard to see how that would do anything for a program of ultimate world communism. Economic competition is likewise benign, or at least there is no reason in principle why it should not be; for the "winners" are merely those who sell more and better goods than the "losers," and consumers in the "losing" country benefit as well as those in the "winning" one.

Of course, the stakes in the nuclear era are very high, and with such stakes, aversion to risk is indicated. The consequences of wrongly assuming that there is no threat are indeed catastrophic. Were there no comparable consequences for wrongly assuming that there is a threat, it would obviously make sense to assume this. But there are such consequences. Western overreaction to a presumed Russian threat is certain, given this century's track record, to stimulate similar reactions on their part. Thus the arms race continues. Yet such a race is both extremely expensive and quite dangerous. With many thousands of nuclear weapons already deployed, the world we live in is not a terribly safe place; and assuming that the risk of accident increases as the number of weapons increases, we are surely making the world a less safe place with each passing week. Not to mention that so long as the weapons are there, ready for use by sovereign states, there is a risk not only of accidental or mistaken use but also of irrational intentional use. Really irresponsible leaders are hardly unknown in the history of mankind; but they have never been in a position to do as much damage as they could now. If the arms race is due to worst-case reasoning, then worst-case reasoning can make things worse. It can help to bring the worst case about. The possibility that it has done so, with proposed correctives, is the subject of this essay.

The question we need to raise is why there is a threat, insofar as there is one. The standard assumption has been that the threat is all one-way: the Soviet Union is out to get us, or everybody. But what if the threat is due to their perception that we are the threat? What if our assumption that there is a terrible threat against which we must defend ourselves has prompted "defensive" moves on our part which do not look defensive to them and which have in turn prompted them to increase their armaments as defensive measures against us? What, in short, if we are the "bad guys"?

TWO VIEWS OF SOVIET ACTIONS

Clearly, a rational defense depends on a rational appraisal of the sort of threat that exists. And that depends, in turn, on the assumption that the presumed enemy is rationally motivated, unless one has very good evidence that he is irrational. There is, certainly, an alternative on the borderline between those two possibilities, for conceivably an enemy might simply prefer war to peace. That is a preference which most of us do not very well understand. Considering the risks and discomforts of conventional war, only an extremely dull or miserable civilian life could be reasonably thought inferior to life—an expectedly short life at that—on the battlefield. But in any case, the nature of nuclear war is such as to make any such preference totally irrational. Indeed, nuclear war of the kind we mainly think of, with exchanges of hundreds of warheads in the megaton class, is not exactly "war" in the usual sense of the term. Such virtues as conventional wars have enabled people to display in the past can hardly find any scope for operation when the pressing of a few buttons by a very few people, none of them in any sort of direct contact with the enemy, will result in the impersonal extermination of millions, nearly all of them noncombatants with literally no possibility of defense against the aggressor. Only profound ignorance or total lack of imagination, one supposes, could permit the thirst for war as we have known it in the past to motivate this new kind of war.

And of course the publicly professed motivations of the superpowers are entirely contrary to any such bellicose motivations. Both have loudly proclaimed the virtues of peace, and not just peace on their own preferred terms but peace in the sense of coexistence with their rival. No doubt we should not simply take their word for it, but can we seriously think that either has any interests that would conceivably be promoted by resort to full-scale war, nuclear or conventional, between the superpowers? In the case of nuclear war, there is, for one thing, the question how you go about "building socialism" or "building democracy" in an area rendered uninhabitable, as well as uninhabited, by a surfeit of H-bombs, even supposing one had anything left to do the building with. But conventional war makes no sense either. Just the stupefying costs involved, even if one were on the winning side, would render it a bad bargain for either, quite apart from the cost in lives. And it is very questionable whether it is in the Soviet Union's interest to "conquer" Western Europe. Would it be happy to have nations enormously stronger than, say, Poland or Hungary as supposed members of the Soviet team? Germany, for in-stance—and of course it would have to be a reunified Germany at that— would be an extremely formidable tail for the Soviet dog to try to wag. And on the economic front, it is surely reasonable to suggest that the Soviets have more to gain from peaceful trade than from attempts at conquest. Western powers, perhaps, have more to gain from a Soviet block at last practicing democracy. But really, this is an altruistic gain in the main. We would "gain" mainly the satisfaction of knowing that those oppressed peoples are at last free from the burdens of communism. This is important, but it is hardly a reason for military conquest, especially one that kills off a large fraction of the people we would be supposedly liberating.

Well, if there is no good reason for war on the part of either side, and there are only two sides, then why is there not peace? Or rather, why is there not a much more secure and satisfying peace than the present tension-ridden situation? It must be that neither side really believes the other's professed interest in such a peace since otherwise their military behavior over the past forty years would make no sense. So the question is, why do they not believe them? Perhaps it is naive to believe that, if the causes of the current uneasy situation can be found, then a less dangerous and expensive peace would be possible. But it is difficult to see what else there is to do but hope that it is not naive and press on.

We must, then, seriously address ourselves to those causes, with a view to asking ourselves what we can do that offers a reasonable prospect of improvement. We need, to start with, answers to two major questions. (*a*) Which Soviet actions have constituted reasonable grounds for Western mistrust? (*b*) Which Western actions have constituted reasonable grounds for Soviet mistrust? In both cases we want to know whether some other interpretation of those actions is reasonable, one that would provide the basis for a less dangerous policy vis-à-vis the other.

In general, the answer to *a* is, a few details apart, fairly easy. First, since the Second World War, the Soviet Union has acted to establish a ring of "buffer" states around its borders, insofar as possible, seeing to it, by force of arms or threat of such force when necessary, that only regimes "friendly" (as they put it) to the Soviet Union ruled in those states. We may take it that Afghanistan is another case in point. And second, it has maintained a very large military establishment, both in conventional and, later, in nuclear terms. The first of these facts has led Western leaders to believe that the Russians were embarked on a program of world domination. The second backed up this conclusion, which was also reinforced by traditional Russian secretiveness and (as it appeared to us, at least) diplomatic belligerence and intransigence. In short, the Soviet Union was perceived as a militaristic, imperialist power whose evil designs called for the reestablishment of American and European military power to counter it.

Was this American construction of the postwar situation borne out by the facts? Possibly not. For there was, and is, a rival hypothesis: that these Soviet actions can be construed as genuinely defensive in nature rather than essentially offensive. The United States enjoys excellent relations with its immediate neighbors and has (a few overenthusiastic critics to the contrary notwithstanding) shown no tendency (in recent times, anyway) to try to tamper with the internal politics of either of them; nor has it deployed significant military forces near its continental borders with a view to shoring up its security against them. These facts undoubtedly contribute to American inability to contemplate the tamer hypothesis concerning Soviet intentions. We interpret moves to subvert neighbors as threats to world peace; but perhaps the Soviets see them as entirely reasonable means of securing their own borders against potential aggressors, of which, goodness knows, Russia has seen plenty in its history. It has also engaged in a good deal of its own, to be sure, and this is a fact not to be ignored. But it requires no stretching of the facts to take it that Soviet movements in relation to its own border states have been motivated by essentially defensive concerns. And the "American" hypothesis, that the Soviet Union is instead out for world conquest, does encounter serious problems, such as the cases of Finland and Austria. In both those cases, the Soviet Union actually had armies within their borders and could easily have left them there and created puppet governments. It voluntarily chose not to do so, and neither of those countries has been under threat of Russian military conquest since the late 1940s. Why should they leave such defenseless countries alone if their aim is what it is claimed to be on the harsher hypothesis?

Obviously we should not accept the idea that one may secure one's borders by militarily subverting the governments of neighboring states when the latter themselves show no evident sign of hostile designs. But a critic on the other side will have no difficulty trotting out cases of American military action against weak neighbors with the very same evident purposes—Americans will not soon be allowed to forget Grenada, for instance, or Nicaragua. The point is that Russian actions may be viewed in a way that makes sense in the light of relevant facts and presents us with a much different and distinctly less uncomfortable picture (for the world, if not for Soviet neighbors). If Soviet intentions are basically defensive, even if their view of what constitutes "defense" is rather strong stuff by our standards, that fact would have enormous implications for world security at the nuclear level.

But first let us turn to question *b*: what Western behavior is occasion for reasonable mistrust on the part of the Soviets? In part, they point to the past, citing especially such things as the sending of armies to aid the White Russians following the Revolution.[1] As against such facts, the West can reasonably respond by pointing out, first, that America contributed substantially to the Russian war effort against the Nazis and, second (with a *tu quoque*), that Russian military assistance, including personnel as well as arms, has been frequently invoked in the recent past to shore up governments believed friendly to the Soviet Union or to assist revolutionary activity of types they approve.[2] More seriously, the Soviets can point to the fact that the Americans have consistently been in the lead in the development of nuclear arms and delivery systems. The United States was the first to build an atomic bomb, the first and still the only party to have used one in wartime, first with the H-bomb, first to develop the MIRV, and in the early stages of the nuclear arms race its stockpile of weapons was, as is now publicly known, enormously much greater than that of the Soviet Union.[3]

Of these, the second is much the more important from the present point of view. On the hypothesis that Russian intentions are fundamentally aggressive, Western (especially American) military activities in the nuclear sphere make a certain amount of sense. But on the lesser hypothesis, they decidedly do not. Let us try to frame a reasonably accurate global

1. For a synopsis of the Russian situation, see Ground Zero's *What about the Russians— and Nuclear War?* (New York: Pocket Books, 1983). More general background on American attitudes following the war is to be found in Greg Herkin, *The Winning Weapon* (New York: Alfred A. Knopf, Inc., 1980). For the development of such attitudes during the war, see Martin J. Sherwin, *A World Destroyed* (New York: Alfred A. Knopf, Inc., 1975).

2. See Thomas Powers, *Thinking about the Next War* (New York: Alfred A. Knopf, Inc., 1982), chap. 15 ("The Moral Fallacy," pp. 105–21), in which there is a splendid series of "What about . . . ?" questions, such as "What about Afghanistan?" "What about Vietnam?" etc.; see pp. 118–19 esp.

3. I assume I am speaking from common knowledge here, but a useful storehouse of relevant information for all these claims may be found in G. Prins, ed., *Defended to Death* (New York: Penguin Books, 1983), chaps. 2–4 in particular.

picture. For perhaps two decades after World War II, Russian conventional military forces were of a size that conceivably might, with some plausibility, be thought to have been capable of supporting an invasion of Western Europe—the prospect that has always been invoked to justify NATO military expenditures, especially the development of battlefield nuclear weapons. In fact, even its strategic nuclear force was justified by that prospect, at least indirectly, since the assumption was that Soviet bombing would be in support of such an attack.[4] But in the recent past it has been argued, convincingly in my view, that the supposed immense superiority of Russian conventional forces required by this picture simply does not exist.[5] (It has also been argued that it never did exist, for that matter, though this is not so relevant here.)[6] What does matter is that Russian conventional strength has been exaggerated, and Western weakness likewise overdrawn, so as to justify Western arms increments.

And yet, it is also commonly accepted that, in order to mount a conventional invasion with any prospect of success, the attacking army must have great superiority in numbers and equipment. Mere parity will not do. Yet this is at most what currently obtains, according to most estimates.[7] But this means that the Russian army is capable only of resisting

4. See Herkin.

5. See Prins, ed., pp. 178–79. But more impressive still is Andrew Cockburn, *The Threat* (New York: Random House, 1983). Chapter 6 in particular analyzes numerical strengths. The book as a whole gives a most interesting picture of the Soviet military machine, one which overwhelmingly disconfirms any idea that the Soviet army could overrun Western Europe in a matter of days, for instance, as has often been claimed. Cockburn suggests that it would have a hard time "overrunning" it in a matter of months, even against absolutely no opposition whatever!

6. See Cockburn, p. 101.

7. Edward N. Luttwak, who is a senior fellow at the Center for Strategic and International Studies at Georgetown University and the author of many books, dissents from my previous claims and those supported by Cockburn in particular. According to Luttwak, in "How to Think about Nuclear War," *Commentary*, vol. 79 (1982), "If nuclear weapons were now disinvented . . . the Soviet Union would automatically emerge as the dominant power on the continent, fully capable of invading and conquering Western Europe and beyond if its political domination were resisted" (p. 21). Luttwak agrees that there is, on paper, a rough overall parity between NATO and Soviet forces. But he argues that many of the ground forces are untrained for the relevant kind of fighting—one wonders what he would say about Cockburn's reports, got from first-person accounts by people who had been in the Soviet draftee army, about the level of Soviet personnel preparedness! And he claims that NATO, far from being able to rest with less than or even equal forces, needs more of certain forces, especially tanks (of which it has about one-third the number of its Soviet counterpart, or so he claims). This in turn rests on the claim that the Soviets could "be concentrated during an offensive against a few narrow segments of the front, while NATO's divisions must defend all along a 600-kilometer border" (p. 23). Why NATO could not anticipate where the Soviets would be attacking with a concentrated force of heavy armor is an interesting question. If we assumed utterly legendary powers of organization and mobility, of course, something of the sort might conceivably be brought off. But unless we assume that NATO commanders are crackbrained, instead of being highly competent Germans, Americans, and Englishmen, this hypothesis is simply silly. It would take the Russians months of hard work to assemble such a force, during which time every movement

invasion from Europe by NATO forces and not of mounting an invasion of Western Europe from the East. If this is so, however, then it is difficult to see how the hypothesis that Soviet actions are motivated by aggressive desires for conquest and the like squares with the military facts. For whatever the facts may be concerning strategic-size nuclear weapons — and only the very hawkish estimate the situation there as at all advantageous to the Soviet Union—the fact is that strategic nuclear weapons are not what one could use for invasions. The milder hypothesis, therefore, squares much better with current facts, indisputably, and perhaps past facts, if more disputably, than the stronger one. Under the circumstances, such things as the American refusal to embrace a no-first-use policy, as well as its relentless pursuit of technologically more advanced weapons, would certainly appear to constitute prima facie evidence of aggressive intent on the part of the West in the eyes of the Russians. The trouble is, it would also seem to be such evidence. This ought to worry us, if peace is our concern.

How do we choose between these rival hypotheses? I have already inveighed against worst-case reasoning, both as a general strategy and in reference to the present situation. In light of the above considerations, "worst case" would seem to be indefinable: what is the upper limit if irrational actions are envisaged? But trying to fix the worst rational case, the worst thing our presumed enemies could do to us insofar as they are rational agents, depends on our assessment of their goals. It cannot sensibly be attempted independently of such appraisals since doing the absolutely worst possible thing with what they have would be utterly insane and thus not worth contemplating as a possible course of action for a rational agent.

What we need is to select the appropriate response to actions lying within a spectrum that can reasonably be thought to include Soviet intentions, given purely defensive intentions on the part of the West. Or at any rate, this is what is needed if that is the correct description of Western intentions. One may be forgiven for sometimes suspecting that something more lurks in the backs of the minds of Western leaders. Perhaps some think that maybe we just could liberate all those unfortunate people in Eastern Europe, break up the Soviet "evil empire," and so forth. It should hardly be necessary to dismiss such ambitions as dangerous fantasies, and I do not suppose that the people who sometimes appear to be harboring such thoughts would for a moment come right out and give public voice to them. But if some are entertaining such ideas, then it will surely be salutary for them to appreciate what is required by genuine commitment to defense only, leaving anything further to the evolution of internal politics in the relevant states. Such is the purpose of the present essay.

---

would be carefully monitored by satellite. And if Americans are good at anything, it is logistics. Luttwak's article beautifully illustrates the kind of worst-case reasoning needed to frame any sort of case for beefed-up defenses, in my judgment.

The problem of finding an appropriate stance in relation to current Soviet actions, given the history of the past few decades especially, is of course compounded when one does not really know what their intentions are, and compounded further when one does not know how one's actions will be taken by them. But my suggestion is that two guiding principles ought to be followed. (1) One should have a defensive capability that would be sufficient for protection against any likely aggression; and (2) one's actions should be such as (*a*) to make it clear to the putative enemy that they are purely defensive and (*b*) to make it possible for him to respond to one's actions in such a way as to confirm a hypothesis that his actions are likewise defensive if they are—and conversely, to be clearly identifiable as aggressive if that is what they are.

Of course, in adumbrating such principles I am assuming that there is a distinction between defense and aggression. And it must be agreed that the distinction is not always easy to make out. That is why I formulate 2*b* as I do; for it may be that some possible actions would be ambiguous and others clear and that some among the clear ones would be clearly defensive. In those cases, 2*b* is intended to require the agent to choose the latter rather than the former. Clarity is to be preferred because it enables the opposing party to show by his responses what he is up to. If there are countermoves on his part that are the obvious ones to make if his intentions are peaceful, then if he does make them, that is encouraging, and if he does not, then we have justification for the less benign further moves we would then be inclined to make. Thus my point is that my position does not presuppose that the distinction is clear; it requires, instead, that clarity is one of the variables that we can, to a degree, control and our management of which has a crucial bearing on the outcome. Thus a refined notion is not, I think, necessary for immediate purposes.[8]

OPTIONS

It has become customary to distinguish four general nuclear strategies, as follows.

> 1. *Superiority or first strike capability.*—Enough nuclear weapons to destroy the other side's nuclear capability while retaining further strategic capability.
> 2. *Parity.*—Roughly match the other side's nuclear capability.
> 3. *Minimum deterrence.*—Enough strategic nuclear capability to inflict unacceptable damage on the enemy, but not more.
> 4. *Unilateral nuclear disarmament.*—Dismantle all nuclear weapons, retaining only conventional capability (possibly, at an enhanced level).

The proposal to be advanced in this essay differs from all these, however, lying somewhere between 2 and 3. By way of arguing for it, let us begin with a brief review of each of the four as characterized above.

8. One can hardly do better than consult Michael Walzer, *Just and Unjust Wars* (New York: Basic Books, 1977), for a start on this matter; see esp. pt. 2, pp. 56–126.

1. Little needs be said about superiority. It is, for one thing, generally thought to be impossible, given the known ability of the Soviet Union to tag closely along behind every American technological advance. And it is obviously unstable and obviously stimulates the arms race to the maximum possible degree. For if A is known to be working on a system capable of achieving that level by time t, then there is a motivation on the part of B to launch a preemptive strike at $t - x$, where the degree of nervousness generated among all parties approaches infinity as x approaches 0. And obviously it is logically impossible for both sides to pursue this strategy successfully. So an arms race with no possible upper limit is in store for us if either side pursues it; and there being no such upper limit, it is difficult to see how it could ultimately end in any way short of war. It is depressing that American policy has looked, and continues to look, disconcertingly as though it is committed to a superiority strategy.

2. The official stance of each superpower today, no doubt, is parity. But just what is the rationale of parity today? As has repeatedly been pointed out, a credible threat of retaliation against a strategic nuclear attack does not require a similar number of weapons. Perhaps the leaders attach intrinsic significance to parity: if A has more nuclear weapons than B, then A is a Greater Power than B, and being a Great Power is a Good Thing. So the compromise is for both to have an equal number and thus be, at any rate, equally Great Powers.

Neither of the propositions cited commends itself to the sober intellect, especially if we delete the upper case letters. Taken in and of itself, being a Great Power, at least in the military sense, is not a good thing. It is, instead, expensive, dangerous, and in extremely questionable taste at the very least. And having more nuclear weapons than the other fellow, if it means anything, means only that you can kill more people (it probably does not even mean that, considering that each side can kill virtually everybody anyway). Surely, if one proposes to employ that as a criterion of being a Great Power in the first place, one's criteria of greatness are due for a rethink.

In any case, there is a serious problem about embracing parity. To begin with, nobody knows what it is. There are many measures of nuclear strength, and by different measures, different superpowers are stronger.[9] One could in principle, no doubt, negotiate an agreement about what is to constitute parity, but it would be arbitrary. Worse, however, is that it is unstable. The history of arms negotiations in the recent past makes it eminently clear that an agreement specifying levels of this and that type of hardware is treated by each side as an invitation to redouble one's energies at increasing the items not covered and to fudge on every imprecise variable that is agreed on. To aim at parity is, for all practical purposes, to aim at continuing the arms race.

9. See the Harvard Nuclear Study Group's *Living with Nuclear Weapons* (New York: Bantam Books, 1983), chap. 6, pp. 115–32, for a thorough explanation.

3. Minimum deterrence has its advocates and is perhaps the most popular stance today among intellectuals. One main problem is that it is impossible to identify it. One thought is that, when you can wreck the other party's country totally, then that is enough if anything is. But perhaps only 25 percent of his country would be enough? Or 10 percent? How do you find out—ask?

Besides this, there is the difficulty that what thus deters would evidently have to be the threat to destroy centers of population, that is, to go in for mass killing. Without a lot of weapons, one could hardly threaten to destroy all the relevant military targets (notably missiles—but if they are cruise missiles, one will not be able to locate them for such purposes—then what?); but apart from people and their property, what else is there? A handful of government buildings, perhaps; but presumably their normal occupants would be exceedingly well protected, notably by being somewhere else at the time.[10]

4. Unilateral nuclear disarmament (UND) also has its attractions. Very intelligent people have come out in favor of it, and it can hardly be laughed off. Nevertheless, it must be admitted that it is politically impractical to the point of fantasy; any politicians running on a UND platform are in for quick and decisive defeat at the polls. And there are the usual questions about nuclear blackmail and the like. Of course there are also the usual questions about the conceivable moral permissibility of nuclear weapons, as well. In the main, however, I wish simply to table this one, especially on the ground that whistling in the dark is not a very profitable activity on this matter.

It should be noted that all the policies I have listed, and the one I shall advocate, are unilateral. Now, obviously one cannot simply object to multilateral arrangements in themselves. It is just that they require at least two parties, and the other party is unlikely to be about to agree to anything we might have to say to him. Or at least, it is so at present. What we need are unilateral initiatives that will stimulate the right kind of response, including perhaps a willingness to come to the bargaining table for a joint solution. The option I propose is a unilateral one, but among its main virtues is that it would set the stage for stable mutual disarmament.

A MODEST PROPOSAL

What would the military establishment of a state really concerned only about defense look like? The answer, I suggest, is fairly simple in general outline: *the offensively usable part of it would look distinctly less formidable than that of its opponents.* If B, the "enemy," has various amounts of various kinds of military hardware and personnel of a type suitable for offensive

---

10. I am indebted to Terry Tomkow for bringing this home to me, in his paper "Three Cheers for the Arms Race," presented at the Waterloo Conference on Philosophy and Nuclear Arms, Waterloo, September 29, 1984.

warfare, then A ought in general to have clearly less in each relevantly corresponding category, barring special conditions. (Thus, geography might make it easy for state A to attack B in a way that would require B to have an unusually large complement of weapon X against which A would have to defend itself.) It should be emphasized that this principle applies to offensive weapons only. Items not usable for offense, if there are any such, would not come under this restriction since no danger of war originating with the state so armed could be traced to its possession of those particular weapons. For instance, antitank wire-guided missiles are of no evident use except for destroying tanks, which are offensive weapons par excellence. A's tank force, on the other hand, should be sufficiently less numerically impressive than B's so as to make it clear that no invasion led by tanks would be possible from A's side. (This criterion is presumably met by NATO in Western Europe.)

Against nuclear missiles there is as yet no defense, though perhaps this will soon change. In the meantime, deterrence is the only option. Thus a state bent only on defense cannot but equip itself with weapons usable for offensive purposes. My proposal, in effect, is that it make clear its defensive stance by limiting itself to a force that could not plausibly be employed to serve basically aggressive purposes. My proposal calls for A opposing B with a force that is clearly quantitatively inferior to that of B by any reasonable measure. In particular, it would use the measures that B has proposed, so long as they are not plainly outrageous. Further, I do not take "quality" into account in general. This is partly because that consideration could become imponderable, which would make application unworkable, and also because presumably no state is going to admit that its weapons are technically inferior, even if they are. The world is not going to take quality into account when A says, But I've got to have more because B's are better! A nuclear-armed state that would attempt a nuclear attack with an inferior force would be committing suicide even more obviously than would one attempting it with a superior force—though it is admittedly questionable why one form of suicide should be intrinsically preferable to another. The point, however, is that quantities of various kinds of arms is a publicizable variable, one that is obviously strongly relevant even if not the only relevant variable and thus suitable for entering into a principle of the present kind, whereas one can hardly require a state to manufacture inferior equipment when it could instead make superior equipment, in its view.[11]

What is the rationale for the present proposal? Two different considerations converge to support it. In the first place, it is assumed that nothing is really lost in the way of defensive security by inferiority as compared with parity or even superiority. Thus the state following my

11. The factor of personnel quality, for instance, is of decisive importance—who would attack the Israeli army with anything short of overwhelming superiority? But obviously this factor cannot enter into the formulation of a principle of the kind I am proposing.

policy will not expose itself to greater risk than is faced by anyone exposed to attack by nuclear missiles. And in the second, this stance offers a clear inducement to the opponent to reduce, and certainly not to increase, his arms establishment. In the eyes of the onlooking world, there would be no doubt as to which superpower is the aggressive one, which is to blame for those of the world's tensions that are due to the possibility of superpower conflict, if one of them is plainly keeping his military forces in a condition which could not permit aggression against the other. And if that other seriously means it in proclaiming—as both presently do, remember—to be concerned only with defense, then the onus would certainly be on the one with the greater force to reduce it under the circumstances. The deescalation ball would be in that one's court. Up until very recently, at least, it has in general been in the court of the West, and we have not picked it up.

Undoubtedly the most disputable of these two assumptions is the first. Hawkish thinkers will contend that one does lose security if one settles for a smaller force than the other side has. The common view is certainly the one I take here, and I can hardly go into this important but technical question here. It will have to stand as an assumption, criticisms of which would need to be refuted. But not here.

Were my policy to be adopted by both sides, then we should be in for a spiral of the opposite kind from what we are presently witnessing. Just as mutual pursuit of superiority tends toward infinity, so, of course, mutual pursuit of inferiority must tend toward zero. I do not offer a detailed proposal about the end point of this process. International inspection procedures and so forth are presumably to be expected since my unilateral initiatives would presumably eventuate in multilateral agreements. And we in the West will expect that at some point the Soviet Union is likely to withdraw from my proposed contest, for it will insist on retaining what is in fact a rather large army for the control of its own captive populace. The political value of this from the Western point of view is evident; and in any case, a force just sufficient for that purpose is not sufficient for mounting an invasion against Western Europe. Thus the primary objective of my proposal would have been achieved.

Whether other nations would retain sizable armies just for show is doubtful. But given the political state of the rest of the world, it must be admitted that there is little basis for expecting a general reduction in arms to insignificant levels. And it must also be admitted that there is little basis for expecting a reduction in the number of wars between various pairs of states. The possession of nuclear weapons by the superpowers, as we know, has done nothing whatever to prevent such wars. It may even have promoted them, as the lesser states can be confident that more than one superpower would never directly intervene in one of its "small" wars for fear of escalation to the nuclear level. Even where one member of the pair is a superpower, if the small state, say B, is small enough, a superpower military establishment much too small for aggressive use against another superpower might well be large enough for intervention in a war where B is a principal (or in a situation of internal strife in B). At some point, leaders will find war preferable to peace from the point of view of their vision of their state's national interest. When defense is no longer the only consideration, my argument will plainly have no purchase. For these other cases, what is needed is a satisfactory theory of justice between states—satisfactory, that is, not only to the theorists who think it up but also to the leaders of states involved in conflicts of interest of a level that can lead to war, including wars in which one or both superpowers have intervened in one way or another into Third World conflicts. Producing a principle or principles sufficiently sensitive to handle the range of disputes underlying present small-state conflicts is no easy matter. The present essay makes no claim to have done that.[12] But the superpowers do claim to be motivated by defensive consideration alone, just as they also claim to agree that only such considerations are permissible for nuclear arms. So my argument should have application to this largest and, from the global perspective, most threatening of arms races.

The major question, surely, is whether defense is the only relevant consideration. It almost certainly is not, de facto. But both powers, as I say, do profess this, and the underlying value judgment, that defense is the only consideration that can justify resort to nuclear arms—if indeed any can—is surely overwhelmingly plausible.[13] Mutual nuclear devastation must surely be worse, from the long-run point of view of each superpower, than the mutual nonattainment of domination, revolution, or whatever might otherwise be aimed at in any possible war between today's great powers. Since that is scarcely deniable, it behooves us to do whatever is necessary to avoid that eventuality. That requires renunciation of any ambitions beyond those of defense, and it requires them of all parties. But the implementation of peace in circumstances of international mistrust requires a careful gauging of others' intentions rather than a cavalier attribution to them of aggressive aims; and it requires that we give others no good reason for attributing such aims to us. The principle, and the proposal, suggested here is the only one I can think of that does not involve extravagent idealism, or at least the appearance of it, and yet offers a clear way to the relaxation of tensions. Any other nonidealistic alternative will leave us where we are now: with an arms race whose dangers increase with each successive wave of "improvements," ending who knows where?[14] Operation on my proposed principle would match

12. Again, Walzer's book has much to offer on these subtle matters.

13. The basic argument is, of course, Hobbesian. For one attempt at a reasonably applicable contemporary formulation, see Jan Narveson, "In Defense of Peace," in *Moral Issues* (New York: Oxford University Press, 1983), pp. 59–71.

14. This may be over hasty. I now think, e.g., that the cruise missile is a major improvement over the ballistic missile. It is too slow to use as a first-strike weapon and at the same time invulnerable because portable, so that the enemy could never target them

our military deeds to our oft-reiterated words: namely, by being demonstrably confined to legitimately defensive ends. This would seem to be both the most and the least that can reasonably be asked in a difficult world.

---

stably even if it could find them in the first place. To start a nuclear war with cruise missiles, therefore, would be sheerest folly; to retaliate with them, on the other hand, will always be possible. One might almost classify the cruise missile—in its current form—as a "purely defensive weapon." Yet its development will undoubtedly stimulate further developments on the offensive side, in which case my dictum will again apply. Meanwhile, the principle proposed in this essay would at least call for the drastic reduction, or perhaps even elimination, of ballistic missiles as the stock of cruise missiles increases.

Nuclear Weapons, No First Use, and European Order*

Josef Joffe

Among those who approach the nuclear dilemmas of our age in moral terms, there is almost universal agreement that nuclear weapons must never be unleashed first. One common prescription calls on the Atlantic Alliance, whose strategy has always included a first-use option, to adopt a no-first-use policy. The aim of this essay is to examine the feasibility of such a proposal.

No first use (NFU) is a strategic principle that would enjoin the Western Alliance not to launch nuclear strikes under any circumstances but one: the first use of nuclear weapons by the Warsaw Pact. To put it more strongly, NATO ought to accept defeat in a conventional war rather than resort to nuclear weapons in order to reverse the fortunes of battle. Yet while the argument is cast in military terms, it is only ostensibly about strategy. Like all nuclear debates within the alliance and between the two blocs, NFU is at root an argument about the fundamentals of interstate politics in Europe—about the nature of Europe's order.

That order is based on three premises. First, Western Europe is not strong enough to counterbalance the Soviets. Second, Western Europe therefore depends on a permanent security guarantee by the United States. Third, the essence of that guarantee is expressed in the language of the atom. Specifically, the guarantee assumes that, in the moment of truth, the United States will use nuclear weapons on behalf of its allies and will use them first if other means of dissuasion fail.

The third premise is crucial. Although the threat to unsheathe America's nuclear sword has been blunted by mutual vulnerability and parity (meaning that the United States might court suicide in the process of defending its allies) the Europeans continue to regard it as the core of the transatlantic security bargain struck in the late 1940s. So do the Soviets, for otherwise they would not have mounted a massive, four-year campaign against the reaffirmation of the United States' pledge through the deployment of cruise and Pershing II missiles. (And that campaign

* This essay builds in part on arguments developed in my "Can Europe Live with Its Defense?" in *The Troubled Alliance*, ed. Lawrence Freedman (London: St. Martin's Press, 1983).

merely echoed their historical efforts against *all* alliance arrangements that foresaw the deployment of American nuclear weapons in or for Europe.) In view of the great stakes, the removal or even the muting of the nuclear threat must have great political consequences with respect to the two girders of the European order—the European-American alliance and the balance of power on the Continent.

NUCLEAR WEAPONS AND STABILITY

Even the most casual glance at postwar Europe reveals an order of astounding stability. Modern Europe has witnessed only one period of peace as long as the postwar era: the four decades between the end of the Napoleonic Wars (1815) and the outbreak of the Crimean War (1854). For a state system that almost consumed itself in the second Thirty Years War between 1914 and 1945, this is a remarkable achievement. It looms even larger if one recalls Europe's past propensity for murderous violence as well as the myriad unresolved conflicts left in the aftermath of World War II.

Certainly, Europe's unprecedented stability does not flow from satisfaction with the status quo. The continent is divided between two hostile blocs. Their perimeters touch in the heart of Germany, a nation saddled with a built-in revisionist legacy and not renowned for pacific behavior in periods past. Rivals for power, the two blocs are also governed by antithetical ideologies and politicoeconomic regimes. While the nation-states of Western Europe are no longer aspiring to territorial change, there is hardly a country in Eastern Europe whose borders remained unaffected by the cataclysm of World War II. And most of them are still contending with nationality problems inside and outside their frontiers.

And yet there is peace which has jelled into ultrastability during the past four decades. Given the paradoxical coexistence of so many smoldering challenges and the actual durability of the postwar order, attention is inevitably drawn to the powerful ligaments of the status quo. And then the paradox is not hard to resolve.

The first factor is the projection of the two superpowers into the heart of the Continent. Order, although not always in harmony with the aspirations of the lesser powers, has become the counterpart of partition. By extending its rule as far as its armies could march, the Soviet Union built an imperial (and pontifical) domain that has suppressed both revisionist instincts and repeated national revolt. By protecting Western Europe against itself and the hegemonic ambitions of the Soviet Union, the United States has fashioned the voluntary equivalent of an empire: a security community where old rivalries persist but where force is no longer the continuation of politics with other means.

The second pillar of stability is the unprecedented concentration of peacetime military power on either side of the divide. By fielding about a million troops each in central Europe, the two alliances have not just raised the price of conquest. More important, huge and well-equipped forces-in-being perpetually evoke the certainty of vast damage in the mind of the would-be aggressor. In 1914, the German general staff could still believe in the merits of a lightning strike that would reap victory before the cumbersome Russian mobilization machinery had gathered steam. In 1939, Hitler could sweep across much of Europe because none of his enemies was prepared for war. Today, however, a latter-day Schlieffen, even a Hitler, would be intimidated because the costs of miscalculation loom so predictably large.

Third, and most important, there is the presence of nuclear weapons — a bottomless reservoir of destruction that has virtually eradicated the distinction between aggression and suicide. Raising the specter of instantaneous megadeath in the United States and the Soviet Union as well as in Europe, nuclear weapons have not only exponentially raised the costs of war, they have also cast a terrorizing taboo over the use of any force. During the Berlin crisis, especially during the tense weeks of confrontation after the erection of the Wall in August 1961, not a single shot was fired, even though battle-ready Soviet and American combat formations stood almost literally eyeball to eyeball. In this, as in other confrontations, nuclear weapons have imposed a degree of caution on the United States and the USSR that is not normally a distinguished trait of great powers.

Logically, of course, we can never prove why something—for example, a war—did not happen. Yet it stands to reason that nuclear weapons are an inextricable element of Europe's unprecedented stability. It stands to reason that thousands of so-called tactical nuclear weapons in the European theater, backed up by the vast strategic arsenals of the United States and the Soviet Union, have imposed unprecedented caution on their possessors. It was not the sudden gift of wisdom but pure fear that has kept the alliances on their best behavior in Europe. And it stands to reason that the awesome might of nuclear weapons has played a central role in keeping Europe a solitary island of peace while the rest of the world (outside the relationship of major tension between the two superpowers) was racked by some 150 violent conflicts and wars since 1945.

NO FIRST USE OR NO USE AT ALL?

If nuclear weapons represent one, if not the key, pillar of Europe's stability, NFU will detract from stability rather than contribute to it. To begin with, mere declarations of intent mean little. The Soviet Union pledged adherence to NFU in 1982.[1] Or, in the words of Soviet Defense Minister Dimitri F. Ustinov: "Only extraordinary circumstances—a direct nuclear aggression against the Soviet state or its allies—can compel us to resort to a retaliatory strike as a last means of self-defense."[2] Yet the

1. John Goshko, "Soviet Chief Renounces First Use of A-Weapons," *Washington Post* (June 16, 1982).

2. D. F. Ustinov, *Sluzhim rodine i delu kommunizma* [Serving the motherland and the communist cause] (Moscow: Izdatelstvo Ministerstva Oborony SSR, 1982), p. 72.

proclamation has not been followed by the appropriate doctrinal, tactical, and practical reforms. Soviet officials and strategists continue to "emphasize the need for massive conventional and nuclear strikes against the enemy's forces. . . . These doctrinal writings are reinforced by Soviet military exercises, which almost always include massive nuclear operations on virtually all levels of conflict, and by the number and character of Soviet theater and tactical nuclear weapons."[3] Nor have the Soviets recently diminished their nuclear arsenals in the central European theater; they have in fact added to them with the introduction of a new generation of shorter-range missiles (SS-21, SS-23).

The point is not hypocrisy (on which the Soviets have no monopoly) but the vacuity of verbal pledges, no matter how solemnly uttered. Nations plan for war not by listening to their rivals' commitments but by looking at their capabilities. As long as NATO has nuclear weapons in the field, they might be used. As long as they might be used, they must be destroyed—by conventional means if possible, by nuclear means if necessary. Thus an NFU declaration on the part of NATO could not change the basic objective of Soviet planners, which is to eliminate their opponent's nuclear weapons before they are used.

A NATO NFU declaration, however, could conceivably change their risk assessments. The key prescription of those four former American officials, whose article in *Foreign Affairs* has given rise to the current debate,[4] is that the alliance must accept defeat in a conventional war rather than resort to the ultima ratio of nuclear weapons. This prescription is clad in absolute terms. "Even the most responsible choice of even the most limited nuclear actions to prevent even the most imminent conventional disaster should be left out of authorized policy. What the Alliance needs most today is . . . a clear-cut decision to avoid [nuclear actions] as long as others do."[5]

Such an injunction is more than a mere variation of NATO's prevailing doctrine. It is in effect, though not in intent, a prescription for unilateral nuclear disarmament in the European theater. If the alliance will not resort to nuclear weapons to avert conventional defeat, it will not even use these weapons to defend them—their bases, stockpiles, and launch vehicles—against conventional aggression. To propose such a policy is to issue a standing invitation to the Soviets to turn the pledge into a certainty by launching a preemptive conventional attack against Western nuclear assets in Europe. And if they do so, the distinction between no first use and no use at all simply vanishes along with the weapons held in reserve for "second use." With the weapons either obliterated or captured

3. Barry M. Blechman, "Is There a Conventional Defense Option?" *Washington Quarterly* (Summer 1982), pp. 59–66, p. 64.

4. McGeorge Bundy, George F. Kennan, Robert S. McNamara, and Gerard Smith, "Nuclear Weapons and the Atlantic Alliance," *Foreign Affairs* 60 (1982): 753–68.

5. Ibid., p. 762.

through a reduced-risk conventional foray, there will be no first, but also no second or nth, strike.

No first use—possession for the sake of retaliation and retaliation only—is thus a principle that collapses on itself. It is meaningless in terms of its own objectives, which are to preclude first use but to allow for second use. It changes neither Soviet objectives (which are to remove Western weapons from the battlefield) nor Soviet strategy (which is to accomplish that task, if possible, with conventional means alone). To offer one's weapons for preemption by renouncing the threat of escalation cannot strengthen deterrence in Europe.

Indeed, the NFU proposal of the four American *Foreign Affairs* authors makes little sense unless it is seen for what it is: a halfway house toward a strictly conventional posture. Hence the apocalyptic language of statements such as: "Any use of nuclear weapons in Europe, by the Alliance or against it, carries with it a high and inescapable risk of escalation into a general nuclear war which would bring ruin to all and victory to none."[6] Hence also the "son of no first use" sequel by Robert S. McNamara one year later, which makes the point in all its baldness: "Nuclear weapons serve no military purpose whatsoever. They are totally useless—except only to deter one's own opponent from using them."[7]

CONVENTIONAL VERSUS NUCLEAR DETERRENCE

To be meaningful, the NFU principle must transcend itself; to change reality, the principle must be taken to its ultimate conclusion, which is NUN: no use—never! To do so requires concrete and visible steps that mark the difference between declaration and demonstration. Most of NATO's battlefield weapons are concentrated close to the inter-German border. Since the Soviets cannot dismiss them as long as they are in place, they would have to be pulled back or pulled out completely. A prominent instance of the pullback idea is contained in the so-called Palme Commission Report.[8] The commission proposes the establishment of a nuclear-free zone in central Europe, meaning an area void of nuclear munitions and storage sites and extending for 150 kilometers in either direction from the inter-German border. (A complete ban on nuclear weapons in Europe is again quite meaningless because it would force the British and French to dismantle their independent deterrents.)

No first use plus a nuclear-free zone would evidently demonstrate to the Soviets that the West planned to practice what it preached. Yet such a move would not contribute to the stability of the European order. Stability is often confused with one of its conditions, namely, a rough

6. Ibid., p. 757.

7. Robert S. McNamara, "The Military Role of Nuclear Weapons," *Foreign Affairs* 62 (1983): 59–80, p. 79 (original italics).

8. *Common Security*, Report of the Independent Commission on Disarmament and Security Issues (London: Pan Books, 1982).

equality of power between contenders. But there must be more. Even ultimate defensive superiority does not necessarily discourage aggression. If it did, Sadat would not have attacked Israel in 1973; nor would Hitler and Hirohito have launched a war against the Soviet Union and the United States, respectively, in 1941. Especially where the safety of allies is at stake, at least two additional conditions must obtain: the clarity and certainty of commitments. If guarantees are ambiguous and riddled with qualifications, would-be aggressors will be tempted to test or ignore them (as did Austria when it moved against Russian-sheltered Serbia in 1914). Yet even clear commitments may fall short of deterrence, as the German attack against Poland in 1939 demonstrated. Hitler moved in spite of formal obligations that bound England and France to treat aggression against Poland as casus belli. Hence the crucial requirement of certainty that enjoins patron powers to limit their freedom of choice—including the freedom to abandon an ally during the moment of truth.

A classic implementation of the certainty principle is a hostage posture. The United States has tied its hands in Europe by inserting some 200,000 troops and several thousand nuclear weapons close to the potential point of confrontation, that is, the inter-German border. These dispositions embody a three-part message. First, the United States will be involved ab initio. Second, nuclear weapons may be launched as soon as the conventional tide turns against the West. These two messages add up to a third, which is the essence of deterrence—the threat of vast damage that exceeds the value of the aggressor's objectives.

Now assume that one element of this equation is physically removed—by withdrawing nuclear weapons to a more distant periphery. At first sight, this is an attractive notion. Would it not help the cause of peace if adversaries put some distance between themselves and the brink of conflagration? The perverse logic of nuclear weapons yields a different answer. Because nuclear weapons spell swift and massive devastation, favoring the offense over the defense, they deliver a crucial advantage to the side that moves first. Because this is so, both sides will labor under the burden of pernicious expectations. In crisis, each side may fear that the other may rush to fill the vacuum, tempting both to act first. Yet mere physical movement, though intended to deter, may signal the intent to use, triggering preemption and war.

Alternatively, the Soviets might actually believe in an NFU pledge once it was married to a nuclear-free zone. That faith will evidently change their cost calculations as they contemplate conventional aggression. As the Egyptian thrust across the Suez Canal in 1973 showed, nations do not necessarily go to war to defeat or occupy their enemies. They may aim for minor military objectives in order to score a major political gain, for example, to dislodge an opponent, to transform the political constellation, or to acquire a commanding position in future negotiations. In Sadat's case, only six kilometers beyond the canal sufficed to overturn a Middle Eastern status quo seemingly frozen in perpetuity.

Now assume, as the Palme Commission suggested, a nuclear-free zone stretching westward from the Elbe river for 150 kilometers. At its narrowest, the Federal Republic is only 225 kilometers wide. A third of West Germany's population and a quarter of its industrial potential are located within a 100-kilometer strip west of the inter-German border. Hamburg is but one tank hour (forty kilometers) from the Lauenburg checkpoint, and the Rhine-Ruhr industrial heartland begins but 160 kilometers from the line of demarcation. With nuclear weapons dispatched along with the risk of immediate escalation, a conventional lunge, stopping well short of the new nuclear perimeter in the West, will look visibly less irrational than under current circumstances. And if victorious, the Soviets would pocket a momentous political and strategic asset, while shifting the onus of nuclear escalation to the West.

The point here is not to invoke scenarios of doom and to elevate worst-case analyses into a theory but to dissect some paradoxes of nuclear strategy. In a deterrence setting, forces in situ are better than the threat of Armageddon at one or several steps removed. It is better to be safely ensconced at the brink than to rush back in a moment of crisis and to provoke its degeneration into actual conflict. Low nuclear thresholds, embodied in the sheer presence of nuclear weapons, are better than high nuclear thresholds or none at all. If the former inhibits adventurism by imposing an exorbitant price on miscalculation, the latter may precisely invite such folly and then confront us with the worst of all possible worlds: "a failure of conventional deterrence *and* nuclear war"[9] because we might rebel at the verdict of conventional defeat and go nuclear to reverse it. In short, if nuclear weapons are the queens of deterrence, then their removal from the board will liberate the conventional pawns from the restraints of the game.[10]

The problem is not that the Warsaw Pact may have more pawns (which it does). The problem flows from the notion of "conventional deterrence" that has recently come to fascinate those who believe that nuclear weapons are not only dangerous but also unnecessary. The key assumption behind that concept is that the West could muster enough conventional power to deny victory to the aggressor and thus to deter him from ever launching a war. The practical difficulties of accumulating overwhelming defensive strength are legion (NATO has tried and failed since 1952); yet the real flaw rests in the concept itself because it ignores a fundamental element of nuclear deterrence: the threat of unacceptable punishment.

Deterrence through conventional defense signals: "You will not get what you want because we will repulse you." Deterrence through pun-

---

9. Henry A. Kissinger, "Arms Control and the Peace Movement," *Washington Quarterly* (Summer 1982), pp. 31–39, p. 35.

10. I have borrowed this simile from R. A. Mason, "Military Strategy," in *Soviet Strategy toward Western Europe*, ed. Edwina Moreton and Gerald Segal (London: Allen & Unwin, 1984), p. 193.

ishment signals: "If you try, you (and your society) might be destroyed."
At which point a conventionalist replies: "It is true that the second threat
is more effective, but the first threat is more credible. You will not impress
your opponent if you threaten mutual suicide, especially since the United
States has to threaten suicide on behalf of nations other than its own."

This argument is persuasive as far as it goes. But there is more to
deterrence than credibility. Deterrence flows from the size of the threat
and the probability of its execution. (It is, if you will, the mathematical
product of both factors.) A very low probability multiplied by potentially
infinite damage still yields a deterrence product of potentially infinite
value. While it is true that the West might be self-deterred from launching
nuclear strikes, which is the more effective threat: denial through conventional defense or incalculable punishment through nuclear retaliation?
Even the small probability of losing one's head (nuclear war) seems more
awe-inspiring than the more certain prospect of losing a hand (conventional
defeat). It is the difference between mutilation and death. And so the
gains of aggression must inevitably pale in the fact of the existential costs
that lurk down the road. The West will not be better off if it merely keeps
the conventional stumbling blocks in place while renouncing the threat
to trigger the nuclear avalanche when the situation so demands.

Finally, nuclear deterrence has a track record, and conventional
deterrence has at best only a very dubious one. After surveying twelve
instances of conventional deterrence between 1938 and 1979, John J.
Mearsheimer concluded that it worked in two and failed in ten cases.[11]
"This 83.3 percent failure rate for deterrence by conventional defense
after 1938," notes Samuel Huntington, "contrasts rather markedly with
the zero failure rate for deterrence by nuclear retaliation for a quarter
century after 1945."[12]

ALLIES, ANGST, AND NO FIRST USE

When McGeorge Bundy et al. published their NFU proposal in the spring
of 1982, the swiftest and most massive counterattack came from West
Germany, the country that stands to lose most from any doctrinal shift
that would loosen the link between conventional aggression and the
threat of general war.[13] The German *Foreign Affairs* foursome devoted
their most painstaking efforts to reading between the lines of the American

11. John J. Mearsheimer, *Conventional Deterrence* (Ithaca, N.Y.: Cornell University Press, 1983).

12. Samuel Huntington, "Conventional Deterrence and Conventional Retaliation in Europe," *International Security* 8, no. 3 (1983–84): 32–56, p. 38.

13. Karl Kaiser, Georg Leber, Alois Mertes, and Franz-Josef Schulze, "Nuclear Weapons and the Preservation of Peace," *Foreign Affairs* 60 (1982): 1157–70. The authors represent a "grand coalition" in the German political context. Karl Kaiser, a professor of political science, is a member of the Social Democratic Party (SPD). Georg Leber is a former SPD Minister of Defense. Alois Mertes is a Christian Democrat and currently a state secretary (equivalent of an American undersecretary) in the foreign office. General Franz-Josef Schulze (ret.) was deputy chief of staff, Allied Command Europe, from 1973 to 1976.

proposal, and the exercise left them rattled. Predictably, they fastened on the American authors' "redefinition" of the United States' "extraordinary [security] guarantee" and read it as implied "withdrawal from present commitments of the United States."[14] Moreover, "if the ideas of the authors were to be followed, conventional conflicts in Europe would no longer involve any existential risk for the territory of the Soviet Union and . . . *would be without risk for the territory of the United States as well*" (emphasis added).[15] No wonder, then, that the Germans perceived the *Foreign Affairs* foray as fuel for the worst of their trauma: as a prod to greater conventional efforts which, at last, would permit the United States to retreat safely behind its nuclear umbrella on the opposite shore of the Atlantic.

Whatever the reality of these fears—and they were reinforced one year later by Robert McNamara's one-man sequel, in which he admitted that he had counseled Presidents Kennedy and Johnson that "they never initiate, under any circumstances, the use of nuclear weapons"[16]—one political lesson stands out in dramatic detail. In their NFU plea, the four Americans were inspired by NATO's "disarray" and its "divisive debates" on matters nuclear. To address oneself to the "internal health of the Western alliance," that is, to the domestic revulsion against nuclear weapons, was a laudable and timely effort. Yet what use is an idea like no first use if it fails to pacify the militant pacifists (who resent the very existence of nuclear weapons on their soil) while it profoundly unnerves those who represent the political establishment of Western Europe (and strongly oppose NFU). If the issue is reassurance and the reinvigoration of public support for defense, then the real question in a divided society is, Reassurance for *whom?*

The Federal Republic's established political elites have never been reassured by American attempts to marginalize nuclear weapons, and hence the NFU proposal struck the rawest of nerves. According to the four German critics, the NFU article of McGeorge Bundy et al. "makes completely clear that a withdrawal of the United States from its previous guarantee is at stake. . . . The proposed no-first-use policy would destroy the confidence of the Europeans and especially of Germans in the European-American Alliance as a community of risk."[17]

Why did the NFU proposal trigger such an obsessive reaction in Europe and especially in West Germany? It did so because it went squarely against the first commandment of extended deterrence under conditions of parity: there shall be no sanctuaries. To pose the issue in the form of a paradox, nonnuclear allies feel least vulnerable when their protector is most vulnerable. Nonnuclear allies are haunted by the nightmare of a war that might start *and* end in Europe, by a conflict that would spare the homelands of the superpowers while turning Europe into the venue

14. Ibid., p. 1162.
15. Ibid.
16. McNamara, p. 79.
17. Kaiser et al., p. 1162.

and victim of limited war. Hence the relentless European search for "coupling" (tying America's nuclear fate to their own) which is just another word for the homogenization of risks and the extension of vulnerability across the Atlantic divide (and the Soviet border).

Nor is it so strange that the weak should seek safety through the exposure of the strong. Precisely because the suicidal character of nuclear weapons threatens to render all vows and obligations null and void during the existential crunch, the Europeans have perennially pressed for strategies that chain the possessors and the protected to a common nuclear fate and that guarantee that an attack on Europe is an attack against the United States. If a client can increase the exposure of his patron, he reaps a triple gain. He limits his guarantor's choices, he forces him to accept all threats as indivisible, and as a result of both, he can signal to their common adversary: "If you attack me, you unleash global war."

Nuclear weapons in a forward position offer a perfect coupling device. As long as they are in place, they might be used, and once even the smallest weapon explodes, there may be no firebreak short of Armageddon (total vertical escalation) and Moscow (total horizontal escalation). The ultimate logic of nuclear weapons close to the point of potential confrontation is the destruction of sanctuaries. If a war in Europe threatens to engulf the United States, it will deter the Soviet Union. If all are equally vulnerable, all will be equally safe. Poised to carry nuclear destruction into the territories of both superpowers, nuclear weapons in Europe promise to leap any barriers between "small" and "big" wars, and that is the murderous foundation on which the safety of lesser allies thrives.

The German critics reacted so harshly against the NFU proposal because they read its implications correctly. A strategic policy that would deliberately accept conventional defeat in Europe is the very opposite of coupling. It would increase American options rather than constrain them. It would strengthen the distinction between regional and global war. It would deliver the United States from imprisonment as hostage to European security, and it would reaffirm Europe's role as hostage to Soviet might. In short, a meaningful NFU posture would strike at the core of the transatlantic security bargain (which is based on the fusion of risks), and while the compact might still endure, it would not be the kind of alliance that has guaranteed Europe's stability for forty years.

NO FIRST USE AND THE SOVIET UNION: SOME PRACTICAL PROBLEMS

Assume a meaningful NFU posture. With nuclear weapons no longer carrying the weight they once did, some compensation would have to be provided in the form of conventional improvements. According to the words of somebody who understands such matters: "The acceptance of such an [NFU] obligation objectively presents rigorous demands for improving the combat readiness of our army, their technical equipment, for perfecting command, control and communication, and strengthening the moral-political conditioning of the troops. This is essential so that the aggressor will not be tempted to use nuclear weapons first with impunity."[18]

These words were written by the Soviet defense minister but they might have been authored by one of his Western counterparts. Indeed, this would put it too mildly from a Western perspective. For the West, the problem has always been an asymmetry of Eastern and Western capabilities that required an asymmetrical response. From the early days of the Alliance, nuclear weapons were to compensate for some evident geostrategic advantages of the Warsaw Pact. The Pact has more forces and more equipment (notably tanks) in central Europe, and the Soviet Union can accentuate that advantage more quickly because its reserves are massed close to the heart of Europe, whereas the United States must ferry its reinforcements across 3,000 miles of ocean. That asymmetry presumably prompted the four American authors to note: "It is obvious that any such policy would require a strengthened confidence in the adequacy of conventional forces of the Alliance, above all the forces in place on the central front and those available for prompt reinforcement."[19]

There are three theoretical solutions to the problem of asymmetry. As one possibility, the Soviet Union would honor a meaningful Western NFU posture with a substantial reduction of its forward forces, most importantly by diminishing the three-to-one tank superiority the Warsaw Pact enjoys in central Europe. A second solution is compensation by the West, meaning a substantial increase in manpower and equipment— especially in tanks, self-propelled artillery, frontal aviation, and precision-guided munitions that can strike beyond the line of battle. The third solution is a change in Western doctrine. In order to threaten unacceptable punishment in the absence of nuclear weapons, NATO would abandon its strictly defensive posture and adopt a "conventional retaliation" doctrine as suggested by Samuel Huntington. The key element is an immediate counteroffensive that would strike deep into Eastern Europe immediately after the pact had initiated hostilities.[20]

None of these solutions stands a realistic chance of implementation. Solutions 1 and 2 are predicated on a fundamental change in the balance of conventional power in favor of the West. The logic of international politics—which is the logic of reciprocity—does not countenance free gifts and neither do the Soviets. While the Soviet Union, as elucidated by Marshall Ustinov, would claim for itself the right to enhance its conventional might in parallel with an NFU posture, it would deny such compensation to the West. Or as a Hungarian official familiar with these matters puts it: "A no-first-use policy, even if jointly adhered to, would not be of much help in alleviating the risks and burdens of military

18. D. F. Ustinov, "To Remove the Threat of Nuclear War," *Pravda* (July 12, 1982).
19. Bundy et al., p. 759.
20. Huntington.

confrontation in Europe if the price set by the West is such a heavy investment in conventional arms that it triggers further Soviet/WTO [Warsaw Treaty Organization] investment. The Western claim for an improved balance can hardly be endorsed. . . . The crucial issue . . . is that an increase in NATO's conventional offensive capabilities as planned in Airland Battle 2000 will clearly be seen as provocative and part of the broader U.S. effort to attain military superiority."[21]

Nor does the idea of conventional retaliation stand a chance of acceptance in Western Europe, no matter how enticing it may be in terms of pure strategy. Essentially, Huntington proposes that the West respond to a Soviet attack with an immediate NATO counterthrust that would strike into Czechoslovakia and the German Democratic Republic. The theoretical attraction of such a doctrine is fourfold. It would liberate NATO from the debilitating constraints of passivity, which, under prevailing doctrine, allows the Soviet Union to determine the place of engagement. Second, it would shift at least one focus of battle into the enemy's territory and conceivably protect the West German population against a replay of World War II. Third, by drastically increasing the price of war to the East Europeans, a counterthrust would correspondingly reduce their enthusiasm in support of Soviet aggression. Fourth, and most important, conventional retaliation would return the indispensable element of punishment to the idea of conventional deterrence by threatening an asset the Soviets presumably value even more dearly than dominance over Western Europe: their political and pontifical empire in Eastern Europe.

While the logic is sound, the politics are disastrous, as serious American moves toward a conventional retaliation stance would undoubtedly trigger the swift demise of the Atlantic Alliance. No West European government will associate itself with a strategy that poses an existential threat to the Soviet empire in Western Europe. The Allies expect the United States to come to their rescue, and with nuclear weapons if need be, in case of a Soviet attack. Given the Soviet Union's often demonstrated stake in preserving its East European *cordon Stalinaire,* the West Europeans expect no less from Moscow. They will not, therefore, accept a conventional-retaliatory posture that exponentially increases the risk of Soviet nuclear strikes. Nor will they want to punish the East Europeans—tacit partners rather than actual enemies—for the sins of the Soviets.

CONCLUSION

What do Bundy et al., Kaiser et al., and Ustinov have in common? Their proposals, pledges, and critiques, though expressed in the vernacular of nuclear strategy, address themselves to the nature of Europe's order. Each is reacting to the larger implications of nuclear parity in terms of national interests that are informed by geography, power, and dependence.

21. Istvan Kormendy, "No-First-Use: A Window of Opportunity?" (Institute for East-West Security Studies, New York, 1984, photocopy), p. 16.

For Americans concerned merely about the nation's physical security, it is only logical to loosen the nuclear tie that binds the United States to Western Europe. As the television film "The Day After" (1983) suggested in the language of popular fantasy, a nuclear war is not likely to start with the proverbial "bolt from the blue" but in the aftermath of escalation elsewhere—in Europe (as depicted in the film), in the Middle East, or in the Persian Gulf. In centuries past, great powers have regularly fought wars on the periphery that spilled over into the center; in a nuclear setting, where the survival of the center itself is at stake, peripheral risks must be carefully hedged. In terms of sheer physical security (the protection of the American homeland), it makes sense to cut into the link between regional and global war that is forged by American nuclear weapons in faraway theaters. Indeed, the American foursome was too timid in advocating an NFU posture only. Given the great existential risks the United States has shouldered, the nuclear battlefield should be withdrawn from the locus of potential conflict, while long-range weapons (like the Pershing II and cruise missile) should never have been installed. That the United States has assumed this extra risk suggests that both the Carter and Reagan administrations continue to define American interests in larger terms than mere "core" security—and rightly so. The United States has fought two world wars in this century to prevent Europe's domination by a hostile power. It is better to deter World War III than to fight it.

In terms of Russian interests, it is similarly advantageous to have the West adopt a posture of meaningful no first use, that is, nonuse. In the absence of countervailing conventional measures (which, if implemented, the Soviets will not let go unanswered) the Soviets will gain twice. Militarily, the withdrawal (or devaluation) of the nuclear queen will strengthen the advantage of the more numerous Soviet pawns. Politically, an American NFU pledge—whether meaningful or not—will undoubtedly weaken European, and especially German, faith in the solidity of America's commitment, and hence the very foundation of the European-American alliance. Such a constellation—a Europe not strong enough to defend itself, yet dependent on a devalued American guarantee—spells a diplomatic advantage that need not be belabored.

It is American and Soviet interests that explain the rattled reaction of the Germans. In the American and Russian perspective, central Europe is a theater and glacis; for the Germans the glacis is home—all there is. For them, it is just as logical to insist on weapons that point both ways, so to speak, that extend wars and destroy sanctuaries, as it is logical for Americans and Soviets to widen the firebreak between regional and worldwide conflict.

No first use, then, poses a larger issue than strategic reform. At stake is the nature of the postwar order, more precisely, the distribution of risks and the solidity of guarantees. All alliances are built on a bargain that strikes a balance of risks between members; no alliance has ever flourished when the strong attempt to shift that burden toward the weak.

Substituting Conventional for Nuclear Weapons: Some Problems and Some Possibilities

George H. Quester

Most of the ethical theorists who contemplate the issues of modern warfare conclude that nuclear weapons are more immoral than conventional weapons. Even if all war is evil, a limited war, entailing the use of only nonnuclear weapons, is still somehow deemed a little less evil. If nuclear weapons could be eliminated entirely, such theorists would thus generally be happy. And when the mere threat of nuclear warfare is held over the world, allegedly contributing to peace by deterring someone else's use of nuclear or conventional weapons, such moral theorists will tend to be unhappy.

Yet, if clarity of logic is to be an important feature in any application of ethical theory, the role of the nuclear/conventional firebreak in the limiting of war is not always so very straightforward; and even the moral value of limiting war (rather than deterring all outbreaks of war by the prospect that such outbreaks cannot be kept limited) will not always be so obvious.

In the ensuing discussion, I will thus first sort out some complexities of the relationship of this firebreak to limiting war. I shall then turn to some of the moral dilemmas inherent in whether we would indeed want to limit war. After this, I shall speculate about some developments of technology which are making the nuclear arsenal look more attractive, allegedly because this arsenal can now be used within limits. Finally, I shall ponder whether the same technological developments do not instead suggest even more the replacement of nuclear warheads with conventional warheads.

As long as nuclear weapons are thought of as aimed at cities and their populations, it is fairly easy to see a close linkage between the conventional/nuclear distinction and any limiting of war. Yet one could quickly cite some examples to upset the logic here. Compare the use of nuclear depth charges in the hunt for an enemy submarine with the use of conventional explosives against a land target inhabited by civilians. Or compare the use of a small nuclear warhead to intercept some enemy bomber squadron, which could not otherwise be shot down, as it approaches a target very valuable to the civilian life of some country.

Anyone hoping that the use of nuclear weapons could be limited, as some other firebreak would be observed once the nuclear one had been crossed, is of course burdened by having absolutely no practical experience on his side. Since much of the continuation of limits in warfare is based on carrying forward our experience (the experience we have accumulated in the wars which gave us some practice), it may be all the wiser to stay below this conventional/nuclear firebreak.

Yet, before we enshrine this particular firebreak so totally, we ought first to consider what the core logics of limited warfare might be. If the greatest advantage of the conventional/nuclear distinction stems from its simple salience and recognizability, this salient visibility may not be as important for one logic of limitation as for another.

WHY LIMITS?

Broadly one can think of at least six distinct reasons for the sides to a war to avoid hitting certain targets, thus imposing a limited amount of damage on their adversaries even while a war is under way. Four of these arguments existed before the invention of nuclear weapons, thus supporting the traditionalist military strategist who scoffs about whether "limited war" is such a new idea. But two very central arguments are indeed quite new here.

A first traditional argument for limits is straightforwardly that of morality. The laws of war discourage and forbid the deliberate or unnecessary destruction of civilian targets. Realists about international politics will scoff at the strength of this argument in light of the depredations of World War II. Yet those who believe in an afterlife will feel some trepidation about unnecessary escalations of violence, as will those who fear the reactions of the neutral bystanders here on earth. It was such reactions, of course, which brought the United States in on the side of the British and French in World War I, sealing the defeat of imperial Germany.

If one's submarines sink merchant ships, the Americans become angry. If one's troops shell a cathedral, other neutrals become angry. If one destroys a cathedral, moreover, God may become angry.

A second traditional reason for avoiding hitting cathedrals and aiming instead at military targets was that the hitting of cathedrals would be a waste of ammunition. If the central aim of our side in a war comes to be to disarm the enemy as quickly and effectively as possible (this will not always be the aim, of course), then the application of accuracy might indeed entail the sparing of some culturally valuable targets on the other side. The purest form of counterforce *can* involve an avoidance of countervalue.

A third traditional argument simply reflected the fact that wars were being fought over territorial spoils, so that it would be folly to destroy the prize in the process of winning it. We might thus spare a cathedral simply because we looked forward to being crowned emperor in it or because we intended to add the cathedral, and the province in which it was located, to our territory. Frederick the Great's Prussian army, in being sent in to seize Silesia from the Austrian Empire and Maria Theresa, was surely instructed to be careful not to inflict unnecessary damage on what would become an important new portion of the Prussian kingdom.[1]

Related to this, a fourth traditional argument for care in aiming one's fire stemmed from the fact that many of the people around a battlefield might be friendly to our side. Perhaps we were simply in the process of recovering territories that had been temporarily occupied by a foreign invader. Perhaps we rather had the support of some dissident minorities within the territories of our enemy or even the support of a majority of the population in his country. It would have been foolish for American bombers to kill too many Frenchmen or Czechs in the process of air attacks on German military forces in World War II, for this would only have been to disable the people we loved, the soldiers we were about to recruit.[2]

All of such arguments are thus sufficient to support the traditionalist who questions whether limited war is a totally new concept or phenomenon. Yet these arguments are now outweighed by some very new considerations, as a result of the tremendous destruction that can be inflicted by the biggest of nuclear weapons, and of the vertical dimension means of delivery which can carry such destruction back to the enemy's targets, even when he has been defeating us on the immediate battlefield. Two distinctly new arguments for limiting one's attack, for aiming carefully, emerge from this combination of nuclear warheads with bombers, missiles, and submarines.

First and foremost, we will avoid destroying an enemy's cathedrals and his cities now because he can always so totally devastate ours. His cities must remain intact as the hostage by which we persuade him to leave ours intact, and vice versa.[3] If any thermonuclear attack should befall our cities, it is not obvious what would keep his from being attacked, and vice versa. This is a mutual bargaining exchange, by which each side deliberately and consciously forgoes a fair amount of countervalue destruction, even the destruction that would not have been ruled out by any of the four traditional reasons for restraint noted above, simply because the other side is practicing similar restraint. Even if the destruction of a city or a cathedral would have made sense in terms of defeating the enemy (perhaps not being looked forward to as some prize to be acquired),

1. For comparisons with the earlier logic of limited war, see Henry A. Kissinger, *Nuclear Weapons and Foreign Policy* (New York: Harper Brothers, 1957).

2. For the analogous argument, within the context of nuclear war, see Bernard S. Albert, "Constructive Counterpower," *Orbis* 19 (1976): 343–66.

3. Wolfgang Panofsky ("The Mutual Hostage Relationship between America and Russia," *Foreign Affairs* 52 [1973]: 109–18) presents a telling rendition of this argument.

it may well now be spared. These limits here depend very much on being *seen* as an exchange by both sides. Each side must know that it is getting something in the exchange, that there is a firebreak or a line behind which the other side is staying.

Second, as a crucial ingredient to this kind of limitation process, it is important for each side that the other retain command and control over its forces. To keep our cities secure, we must keep the other government not only desirous of maintaining but also able to maintain restraints. An attack which crippled the ability of the opposing ruler to communicate with his missile commanders might thus be counterproductive to this goal of limitation.

ADVANTAGES OF A CONVENTIONAL STRATEGY

Since nuclear weapons are normally greater in destructive impact than conventional explosives, one might offhandedly conclude that avoiding their use serves each and every one of the six discrete arguments for limited war that we have listed. Yet there will be instances, as the labors of Los Alamos or Livermore bear fruit, where a nuclear warhead would be just as free of collateral damage, perhaps even freer. How many civilians would have been killed if a British nuclear weapon had been used to destroy an Argentine submarine off the Falklands?

If the importance of the distinction is instead to stem from its qualitative salience, its visibility to both the parties to an exchange, then this aspect of the conventional/nuclear firebreak may be the most relevant only to our fifth argument on the list.

With regard to not wasting ammunition (the second argument on our list) or avoiding the destruction of valuable prizes and the destruction of cherished friends and allies (the third and fourth), or preserving the enemy's command and control (the sixth), what we actually do is considerably more important than the appearance of what we do. If someone could make the case that a nuclear attack would stand a better chance of avoiding the collateral damage we seek to avoid, then it would be largely counterproductive, for these parts of the war-limitation process, to use conventional warheads instead.

Even with regard to morality (the first argument on our list), what we actually do should be more important than what we are seen to be doing. God and history will discover the truth, in any event, about whether we needlessly exposed innocent civilians to suffering. Of course, the neutral gallery of Swedes, Indians, and Zambians may be more affected by the visible appearances of what is happening, such that the substitution of nuclear warheads for conventional, even if it had genuinely saved lives in some elegant and esoteric approach to military targeting, would probably draw their condemnation, perhaps thus directing their moral and material support to our adversaries.

We thus see the interaction of two distinct considerations about restraint on weapons used or targets aimed at. One is the assessment of greater versus lesser damage. And the other is simply the consideration of finding some visible line of distinction.

These two considerations may for the moment still blend together very well for the conventional/nuclear distinction. Yet technology marches along. As very high accuracies are now predicted for delivery systems, and as the weapons laboratories offer nuclear weapons of very small yields, the proponent of an introduction of such weapons into future wars may make the moral case that unintended targets can be more reliably spared even while intended targets are more effectively hit. Such a prospect might seem attractive enough for the engineers; but for the manager of a limited war, this can produce some new disarray, as our two considerations supporting the conventional/nuclear firebreak would no longer be so strongly reinforcing to each other.

One already can note a noncongruence here on many of the other lines of restraint which have been observed in the limited wars fought since 1945. Bombing was kept south of the Yalu in the Korean War. This was important to Beijing, Moscow, and Washington as an observable distinction of restraint, but would the total destructiveness in the war really have been greater if the U.S. air force had been allowed to use its conventional bombs on both sides of the Yalu? Most of the weapons banned for war may be more destructive and horrible than the ones allowed, but this is hardly an ironclad rule.

Tear gas is forbidden for use in armed combat, while napalm is not forbidden. Surely a reversal of the line of distinction here would seem more humane.[4] Vietnamese and Cambodians are allowed to fight against each other with backing from the United States and the Soviet Union, just as these two sides use leftists and rightists in El Salvador. Would the local population suffer more, or suffer less, if these local wars were fought instead by Soviet and American paratroops flown in for the purpose, with the Asians and Central Americans being held in reserve, as "weapons imposing too much collateral damage." Most of the wars fought since World War II have been fought on or over dry land, with very little warfare (the South Atlantic War for the Falklands/Malvinas being the great exception) being fought on or over the high seas. Yet the damage to civilian life in such wars might have been less if exactly the reverse had been the rule. (A war fought "all at sea" might spare us civilian losses even if nuclear weapons were used.)

Any limit is better than no limit where the object is to see to it that the final escalation to all-out thermonuclear war does not occur.[5] Yet the "any limits" that we use are often only those that we have stumbled into

4. On the relative damage potential of different kinds of chemical weapons, see Carnegie Endowment for International Peace, *The Control of Chemical and Biological Weapons* (New York: Carnegie Endowment, 1971).

5. This was outlined early and well in Thomas C. Schelling, *The Strategy of Conflict* (Cambridge, Mass.: Harvard University Press, 1960), pp. 53–80.

in the past and then retained and reused as a matter of recognizable custom. We sometimes thus forbid categories of weapons, or draw boundaries around battlefields, in ways which do not seem to relate very well to any moral calculations of collateral civilian suffering, and this stems from the larger considerations of grasping for any stopping point whatsoever.

As noted, this tension between the considerations underpinning a limitation process have to date been minimal on the nuclear/conventional distinction. Yet, extrapolating from the logic of the other firebreaks observed in war (and then crossed from time to time, as in the sinking of ships in the Falklands war or the Iraqi use of poison gas against Iran), we must bear the possibilities of such a tension in mind for the nuclear firebreak as well, lest a technology that offers interesting new options suddenly spring some nasty surprises on us.

LOSSES IN A CONVENTIONAL STRATEGY

If it made sense to forgo using nuclear weapons as long as our adversary did so as well, even when both sides are fighting an active war with conventional weapons, we would thus have what is also often described as a "no-first-use" policy.[6] Whether or not such a policy has been declared, it has been accepted in practice for all the wars fought since Nagasaki. One central topic of our discussion here would be whether such a policy should also cover all the wars we could conceivably fight. If we accepted no first use for Vietnam, and are accepting it for Central America, should we accept it as well for any wars in Europe, staying below the nuclear/ conventional firebreak if fighting were to erupt there, just as we would in other corners of the world?

It is thus always debatable whether the possibility of limited war is good news or bad news.[7] For the person who in 1945 thought that all wars would be avoided now because of the damage that was possible when such wars went to the absolute, limited wars are bad news, and the Korean, Vietnam, and other wars have come as an unpleasant surprise. For another person who expected that wars would still occur but feared that the next such outbreak of fighting would mean the end of mankind, limited war has been good news, as armed conflicts do not have to mean the termination of all communication and cooperation with one's adversary.

In the abstract, this is how the limited-war phenomenon might have pleased or disappointed two different Americans in 1945. The same question can be posed as a retrospective exercise for an American student

6. On the arguments for a no-first-use policy, see Richard Ullman, "No First Use of Nuclear Weapons," *Foreign Affairs* 50 (1972): 669–83; McGeorge Bundy, George F. Kennan, Robert S. McNamara, and Gerard Smith, "Nuclear Weapons and the Atlantic Alliance," *Foreign Affairs* 60 (1982): 753–68; Robert S. McNamara, "The Military Role of Nuclear Weapons," *Foreign Affairs* 62 (1983): 59–80.

7. For a very clear analysis of the limited war phenomenon, see Morton H. Halperin, *Limited War in the Nuclear Age* (New York: John Wiley & Sons, 1963).

today. Should we lament the existence of nuclear weapons, or should we be glad of these weapons' existence? And should we then lament, or be glad of, the possibility of limited war? Compared to what was normal as a volume of warfare for earlier decades of our international system, the years since 1945 have probably seen less of such warfare, as the ominous possibilities of a thermonuclear war have worked to deter some wars that otherwise might have occurred, for example, along the NATO central front. Compared to the possibility that all war would be deterred, however, the limited wars fought elsewhere around the globe have then been a disappointment.

The choice is much more real and immediate, of course, for West Germans and West Europeans. Would they not have been exposed to a replay of World War II by now if thermonuclear weapons had not existed? Would not a limited war in Europe, if it could be kept from escalating (perhaps through the adoption of some no-first-use policy and the withdrawal of nuclear weapons from the potential battlefield area), not basically amount to such a replay of World War II?[8] A replay of World War II would surely be preferable, even for these Europeans, to a first run of World War III. But peace is surely preferable to any such limited-war replay.

Anyone proposing an explicit no-first-use policy for the United States is indeed normally addressing himself quite specifically to South Korea, the Persian Gulf, and the NATO central front. Other corners of the globe already are governed by a de facto U.S. inclination to avoid the use of nuclear weapons, even if we were threatened with a military defeat in the conventional exchange.

Yet what, then, about the territorial integrity of the United States itself? Would Robert McNamara and his associates favor the nonuse of nuclear warheads, even if the home areas of this country were being invaded by Communist ground forces? It is easy for an advocate of no first use to scoff away the question as a pointless academic abstraction. As things stand, the national guard of each of the states could indeed probably repulse any invasion by the Soviet marine corps, so that "deterrence by denial," the preservation of peace by traditional approaches to military operations, takes care of itself.

The question is not quite as abstract and unworldly as this. Much can happen in the next two decades, as conventional military balances will remain unpredictable. What is happening in Central America is not totally guaranteed against happening in Mexico as well. People like Robert McNamara could thus answer our hypothetical question in either of two ways, each of which is troublesome. Very simply, in terms of the logic: (1) they could declare that we would never use nuclear weapons first under any circumstances, a morally consistent position; or (2) they could

8. An articulate statement of West German concerns here can be found in Karl Kaiser, Georg Leber, Alois Mertes, and Franz-Josef Schulze, "Nuclear Weapons and the Preservation of Peace," *Foreign Affairs* 60 (1982): 1157–70.

declare that we should never use nuclear weapons first outside our own borders, a position more consistent with what has been normally imputed to states pursuing their selfish national interests.

Perhaps we would never use nuclear weapons first, even if we were about to be totally defeated and occupied by any enemy, with all our cities falling under enemy control. But this would be an answer that runs counter to all of what analysts have presumed about the role of nuclear weapons in international politics since 1945, and it is an answer that has thus far been proffered by only one of the world's nuclear powers, by the Chinese.

Beijing's official policy on the use of the nuclear weapons acquired after 1964 took a new and interesting form, in a categorical and explicit endorsement of no first use.[9] Again and again, the Chinese statements over these two decades have been that China will never use nuclear weapons unless another country uses them first, even if the contingency posed was an American invasion or, later, a Soviet invasion.

But other possessors of nuclear weapons have not exactly followed suit. Moscow has very recently issued an endorsement of no first use, but it is hardly as categorically or repeatedly put forward as the Chinese statement. France, in the clearest contrast, makes it very explicit that French nuclear weapons would certainly come into use, even if no one else had used such weapons, whenever any conventional invasion were penetrating the boundaries of France itself. If forced to answer the hypothetical question, McNamara and his coauthors might well thus have to admit that, yes, they would use nuclear weapons if the United States itself was about to be overrun.

This hypothetical ultimate policy of the United States, and the less-hypothetical policy of France, thus pose serious problems for convincing countries like West Germany to accept a shift to a totally conventional defense of Western Europe. Unless McNamara and like-minded people were prepared to go as far as the Chinese, categorically rejecting a use of nuclear weapons even in the direct defense of the United States itself, they will not substantially deflect the feelings of those West Europeans who regard a conventional occupation by the Soviets as comparably as bad as a nuclear war. And unless the French opt for withholding the use of their own nuclear arsenal, as long as the Soviets have not yet used theirs, any American policy of no first use would be undercut by the independent nuclear decisions of one of our allies.

The goals of sound military strategy in the nuclear era are always the same as the goals of sound arms control: to reduce the likelihood of war, to reduce the costs of war if it happens, to reduce the burdens of a preparation for war in peacetime. Substituting nuclear warheads for

9. A good discussion of Chinese declaratory and actual policy on nuclear weapons can be found in Jonathan D. Pollack, "China as a Nuclear Power," in *Asia's Nuclear Future,* ed. William H. Overholt (Boulder, Colo.: Westview Press, 1977), pp. 35–66.

conventional weaponry has surely been a means of furthering the third goal. The tough question for strategic policy has all along been how to relate this choice to the first two goals.

The hard fact now for all strategy and arms-control analysis is that such goals tend to conflict with each other. The prospect of nuclear escalation surely increases the damage of war if war occurs, but as a deterrent it may work to reduce the likelihood of war.[10] How then do we choose? Do we now want to work to reduce the damage in war by opting for the conventional deterrent?

The United States has certainly made such a decision for some corners of the globe, for Thailand, Lebanon, and perhaps Central America. It has just as surely not yet made this choice for Western Europe or for South Korea. Sorting out this apparent inconsistency, it might be argued that the following rule of thumb has been applied: where the risk of war is low (in part because of the risks of nuclear escalation) our policy has been to keep the risks low by retaining American nuclear weapons and American troops in place. Where the risks of war are higher, our policy has rather been to reduce the costs of war by getting nuclear weapons away from the potential battlefield, perhaps even by getting American troops away.

What we will be discussing here might thus amount to a substantial undermining of the logic of extended nuclear deterrence. If we invest in substantial efforts to provide for a conventional defense, this may be a very humane move, but it also telegraphs to the world that we are more afraid of nuclear war now, more reluctant to use the prospect of a global disaster to head off aggressions against our allies.

All is well and good if a reliable conventional defense is developed in the process or if we find sufficient means of punishing aggressions by conventional attack.[11] A surefire tank killer may render it impossible for Soviet tank forces to gain any part of West Germany. Knocking down every bridge in Poland may make it equally impossible for Soviet tank columns to advance. Hitting valued civilian targets inside the USSR might make the Soviets reluctant to continue a conventional advance.

Yet the patterns of effectiveness in conventional warfare since 1945 have seemed considerably less predictable and stable than the patterns of what would be all-out nuclear war. Thermonuclear weapons look "new" and "revolutionary," but they are now reliably blunt and destructive, as assured destruction continues to be assured. By contrast, the outcomes of tank-versus-tank battles, or contests pitting precision-guided missiles

10. This is the argument that Henry A. Kissinger came to in his third book, *The Troubled Partnership* (New York: McGraw-Hill Book Co., 1965). See also Bernard Brodie, *Escalation and the Nuclear Option* (Princeton, N.J.: Princeton University Press, 1966).

11. The possibilities of a conventional defense at the tactical level are discussed in John J. Mearsheimer, *Conventional Deterrence* (Ithaca, N.Y.: Cornell University Press, 1983); Johan J. Holst and Uwe Nerlich, eds., *Beyond Nuclear Deterrence* (New York: Crane Russak, 1977).

(PGMs) against tanks, or PGMs against any important military or civilian targets, are highly unpredictable, with each new round of warfare in the Middle East seemingly disproving the conclusions obtained from the previous round.[12]

What if we therefore develop an airtight defense for the NATO central front for 1990, allowing us once and for all to rely on "deterrence by denial" rather than on "deterrence by punishment,"[13] allowing us to move all the nuclear warheads out of the prospective combat area, thus markedly reducing the likelihoods of escalation if war breaks out? Would we not then face the prospect that such defenses would be circumventable again by 1995, as new technology was brought to bear to favor the Warsaw Pact once more over NATO or to favor the offense over the defense? What if we uncover very elegant ways to use conventional warheads against targets inside the USSR, and the Soviets then augment their defenses enough to blunt any attack depending on such warheads?

SOVIET RESPONSES TO A CONVENTIONAL LIMIT

One objection to a shift toward conventional weaponry, as part of a no-first-use and nuclear-free-zone arrangement, might be less powerful than many people believe. An issue of verification is often raised. If we withdraw our own nuclear weapons from South Korea or from the NATO area, how can we be certain, in the absence of extensive on-site inspection, that our Communist adversary has done the same?

The answer can never be airtight; there might be some occasions (as we shall discuss below) where the Soviets would wish to escalate to the use of nuclear weapons, perhaps if they were doing very badly in the conventional war.

Yet it is all too plausible that the Soviets would not want to conquer a radioactive Western Europe but would be interested in capturing this prize because of its future value to their economy (i.e., that they would feel about Western Europe in the same way as Frederick the Great felt about Silesia). If we are indeed correct about the analogy to Silesia, the Soviets would welcome our own decision to shift from nuclear to conventional weapons on the battlefield and would also (without any verification or inspection to assure this) find it very much in their own interest to follow suit.[14] The logic of escalation is that the presence of *either* side's nuclear weapons in the battlefield area amounts to a tripwire, making it likely that the nuclear/conventional threshold will be crossed simply in the heat and confusion of battle. Having seen NATO pull its own nuclear

12. Paul F. Walker, "Precision-guided Weapons," *Scientific American*, no. 245 (August 1981), pp. 37–45.

13. Glenn Snyder, *Deterrence and Defense* (Princeton, N.J.: Princeton University Press, 1961).

14. For an interesting argument that the Soviets are not planning for earlier use of nuclear weapons in a European War, see Philip A. Petersen and John G. Hines, "The Conventional Offensive in Soviet Theater Strategy," *Orbis* 27 (1983): 695–739.

weapons back to rear areas, to avoid the risks of escalation to all-out war, the Soviets would be very foolhardy to replace NATO tripwire nuclear warheads with their own.

The more serious fear regarding the nuclear/conventional decision has all along been that a denuclearized NATO central front would be too inviting to a Soviet conventional aggression, offering the prospect of an invasion simply to seize a valuable prize. If conventional weaponry does not offer some new approaches to effective defense, to a "deterrence by denial" in Glenn Snyder's phrase rather than a "deterrence by punishment," then this will remain a serious fear. But the prospect of Soviet cheating, in failing to match the Western performance in some shift to a nuclear-free-zone arrangement, does not play so very much of a role here at all.

Under what circumstances would the Soviets nonetheless want to escalate to the use of nuclear weapons, if the war has thus far been fought only conventionally? Under what circumstances would the Soviets wish to pose the prospect of such escalation? As with U.S. decisions, these are two distinct questions, easily blurred and confused with each other but requiring very separate answers.

To begin with the first question, the Soviets are sometimes conjectured to have devised some very elegant uses of nuclear weapons, speeding their advance to the English channel, preempting the use of whatever nuclear weapons are based in the NATO area, while still avoiding most of the collateral damage that would make Western Europe worthless as a prize and, presumably, also avoiding the risks of escalation to all-out nuclear war that would make every prize worthless.[15] If American nuclear weapons had been withdrawn from the NATO area, this preemption mission would presumably be vitiated, but some of the other applications might still apply.

All of such reasoning is very much subject to doubt, however, precisely because of the extreme difficulties all parties have encountered in trying to predict and encompass the damage that nuclear warheads will inflict, and because the first use of nuclear warheads by anyone, anywhere, has such unpredictable consequences for human communication and calculation of the war-limitation process. If the Soviets have any good chance of scoring a victory in Western Europe by the use only of conventional weapons, they would surely be foolish to poison the winds and risk much greater escalation by the introduction of nuclear weapons merely to speed up this victory.

But what if the Soviets were unable to break through NATO's defenses, having been given a bloody nose in the first rounds of conventional warfare? Having failed to break through, the Soviet forces might be in

---

15. An example of the argument that the Soviets have standardized on planning for early nuclear escalation can be found in Joseph D. Douglass, Jr., "The Theater Nuclear Threat," *Defense Science 2001 +* (December 1983), pp. 23–37.

a stalemated situation or might be facing the prospect of being pushed back into Eastern Europe as NATO suddenly became intent on liberating some territories from Communist rule.

Here our two questions become interestingly separated. If merely denied the conquest of Hamburg or Frankfurt, would the Soviets feel driven to escalate to nuclear warfare, amid all its possible consequences, rather than suffering a defeat? Most probably not, by all we know and have seen of Soviet behavior. Might the USSR wish the West to feel it plausible that such Soviet nuclear escalation could occur, perhaps in the hope of intimidating the West into not mounting an effective conventional resistance? Perhaps yes, although the price of this kind of "extended nuclear deterrence" would be great if it stampeded the NATO command into bringing its nuclear forces back into the theater or committing them to use.

If, for any reason, the Soviets were facing the loss of East Germany, Hungary, or Poland, would they want to escalate to nuclear warfare? More possibly the answer here is yes; yet all the same doubts have to be voiced here that have been aired so often about the credibility of an American nuclear escalation, when only Western Europe was being lost. Would the Soviets like the West to sense the prospect of such nuclear escalation in such an event? Almost surely they would.

If Eastern Europe boils over on the model of Hungary in 1956, Czechoslovakia in 1968, the current Solidarity movement in Poland, or the East German uprisings of 1953, with the *Bundeswehr* or other Western military forces being tempted to come to the aid of anti-Communists across the Elbe, would the deployment of "tactical nuclear weapons" not then turn out to be a decided embarrassment for the West (and would not the threat of escalation to nuclear war suddenly look like a trump card for the hard-pressed status-quo-oriented Soviet side, rather than for the West?)

The central hope to be explored in this article is that new Western applications of conventional warheads might amount to an effective military instrument, substituting for the threat of nuclear escalation, literally substituting for nuclear warheads on the front of some delivery systems. No one can deny the importance of the counterquestion of whether the Soviets would sit still for this, would match this shift from nuclear to conventional preparations. Yet the question hardly hinges on verification or on commitments to the sanctity of treaties. Rather the willingness of the Soviets to sit still for a conventional war will be a matter of particular scenarios and will also be a matter of reality versus bluff or actual practices versus the prospect of practice.

We have been considering at least four kinds of situations or possibilities here, capable of being outlined by the matrix below. Will the United States and NATO keep nuclear weapons in the potential combat zone, yes or no? Will the Soviets utilize nuclear warheads in any aggression against West Germany, yes or no?

Soviet nuclear use

		Yes	No
NATO nuclear deployment	Yes	A	C
	No	B	D

It is often assumed that the Soviets would have to use nuclear weapons in any war if American and other NATO nuclear weapons remain deployed near the combat zone, on the presumption that such nuclear weapons would come into use willy-nilly in any event (this is outcome *A* in the matrix). And the hope of those who favor a withdrawal of NATO nuclear weapons, as part of a shift to conventional options, is that the Soviets would find it to their own interest to follow suit, on the arguments just stated (outcome *D*).

Skeptics about the advantages of NATO's denuclearizing the battlefield contend that the Soviets might use nuclear weapons (outcome *B* above) even if all U.S. and NATO warheads had been put out to sea or held back in Britain, Spain, and the continental United States. Here is where the issue of verification is raised so often.

The counterargument here is that this is indeed unlikely, unless NATO has defended itself so well against the first round of a Soviet conventional attack that the defenders are suddenly advancing into the Ukraine (a very unlikely working out of this contingency, perhaps, but never impossible, given the wide ranges of unpredictability in the outcomes of land warfare and the unpredictable loyalties of all the East European armies allied with the USSR).[16]

Considerably more likely, ahead of this insertion of Soviet nuclear warheads into conventional war might be a Soviet all-conventional attack even when American nuclear warheads remained in place in West Germany (outcome *C*), an attempt by Moscow to disarm and disable American nuclear weaponry without using any of its own such weapons, that is, to win without crossing the nuclear threshold.

THE ULTIMATE SUBSTITUTION

The debate outlined above about whether wars should be limited, at the cost that they may thereby be less deterred, is sure to persist into the future. Intertwined with this, as also noted above, is a possibly growing debate about whether the nuclear/conventional distinction is so crucial to limiting war.

16. Samuel Huntington, in his own chapters of the book he edited, *The Strategic Imperative* (Cambridge, Mass.: Ballinger Publishing Co., 1982), presents an argument that the United States should welcome a capability for plunging into Eastern Europe if the Soviets have attacked Western Europe.

If escalation to all-out war is to be prearranged, as part of deterring a Soviet attack, then planning for the use of tactical nuclear weapons may be a direct way to accomplish this. Advocates of such uses of nuclear weapons might indeed be kidding themselves when they argue that a limited nuclear war can be fought; yet this self-delusion would serve the purposes of deterrence and peace.

A more serious difficulty will arise, however, if we instead conclude that such escalation to all-out war should not be wired into place. If the managers of new missile systems and the developers of smaller nuclear warheads sincerely convince themselves and others that the nuclear threshold could be crossed without total escalation, we must ask ourselves whether this prospect is so sure or so real. And, in this section, we can also ask ourselves whether the very enhancements of missile accuracy on which such prospects depend might not also be put to better use if they were mated with conventional warheads.

We are certainly not unaccustomed to balancing conventional weapons more generally as alternatives to strategic nuclear weapons. Additional antitank weapons thus might make additional ICBMs unnecessary. A very reliable conventional defense of NATO would eliminate the need for threats of nuclear escalation. But the remainder of this essay will carry this logic over into possibilities of something discussed a little less often, the direct substitution of conventional warheads for nuclear, a substitution on the very same delivery systems, missile or bomber, perhaps aimed at geographically very much the same targets.

I will begin by slicing into the early 1980s debate about new options for strategic nuclear war, often portrayed as "limited nuclear war," and into the technological developments thought to be nourishing the excitement about these options. I will then have a try at translating these into conventional options.

The many possible uses of strategic nuclear weapons have indeed become a lively topic again[17] in ways which disturb those who regard any liveliness here as a threat to peace and in ways which may also bemuse closer students of the history of the strategic planning for such weapons, as some old wheels get reinvented, again and again.

What are the various technological changes that might explain such a rekindling of interest now? More than the addition of multiple warheads, more than the introduction of penetration means to bypass the defenses contemplated on either side, more than any new development of nuclear warheads, it is the achievement of extreme accuracies for ballistic and cruise missiles that has gotten the nuclear strategic targeting discussion going again. It is this accuracy which has led a James Schlesinger, a Colin Gray, or a Leon Sloss[18] to argue that nuclear weapons can be used to do

17. For a much quoted illustration of this kind of thinking, see Colin Gray, "Nuclear Strategy: The Case for a Theory of Victory," *International Security* 4 (1979): 54–87.

18. Leon Sloss and Marc Dean Millot, "U.S. Nuclear Strategy in Evolution," *Strategic Review* 12 (1984): 19–28.

more than deter by threatening mass destruction; other options need to be considered concerning the use of our nuclear arsenal and the targeting debate needs to be reopened. The possibility for surgical strikes, and for very effective strikes against difficult-to-hit targets, is enlivened much more by the diminution of CEPs (circular error probable) than by any increasing or decreasing of likely yields on nuclear warheads.

Enhanced accuracies are thus now widely viewed as lifting the nuclear taboo, a taboo which made us plan only for the use of conventional weapons in limited wars, holding nuclear weapons in reserve as a deterrent. Yet there is an interesting paradox about this discussion, which will grip us for the remainder of this essay. If such accuracies are now great enough to encourage finely tuned nuclear escalation, they may also offer very attractive options for accurately attacking targets with conventional warheads as well, rendering the possibility of nuclear escalation (with all its pitfalls, risks, and costs) unnecessary.

The creative targeter may have been frustrated until now by the inaccuracy of missiles, an inaccuracy which would have made any nuclear strike a very destructive and massive countervalue exercise. Yet, if freed to apply his creative ingenuity now to the application of mini-nuclear weapons delivered by high-accuracy missiles, he might find even more of an outlet for creativity in planning strikes with conventional warheads.

If the accuracies of ballistic missiles and cruise missiles are now as great as advertised, we must thus surely assign some more thought and speculation to possible uses of such delivery systems with conventional warheads. The advantages of maintaining the nuclear/nonnuclear firebreak remain very great indeed. If we were capable of destroying a key power generator in the USSR by an ordinary dynamite warhead hitting directly on target, would this not be a far more valuable option to cultivate for some of the scenarios of Soviet aggression we fear than to use nuclear warheads (which after all are still always held in reserve to be brought to bear later)?

Just as on the battle lines itself, where high-quality conventional antitank munitions would substitute for so-called tactical nuclear weapons, such a conventional-for-nuclear substitution might be workable for various kinds of counterforce strikes at Soviet military capability. And the substitution could work also for countervalue strikes, for various kinds of carefully graduated retaliation. Limiting a war has not meant sparing the other side all punishment. It has rather meant imposing some punishment, to put him into the mood to terminate the war, while sparing him a robust list of intact hostages, to keep in the mood to forgo all-out escalation.[19]

19. For some early speculation about such scenarios, see Klaus Knorr and Thorton Read, eds., *Limited Strategic War* (New York: Praeger Publishers, 1962).

NEW OPTIONS TO EXPLORE

If the accuracies of the newer cruise missiles are as good as anticipated, this might thus provide a substantial augmentation of NATO defenses in a manner not nearly so likely to escalate into World War III. As Soviet armored forces rolled forward, the array of Western cruise missiles would be fired to attack the railway and highway bridges, airports, fuel dumps, and other logistical targets on which the Soviet advance depended. The mathematics would be very different from those of an attack on the strategic missile siloes back in the USSR. If some large fraction of such tactical targets could be destroyed, it would not help the Soviets very much to know that 30 percent of such targets had survived. A Western attack which destroyed 70 percent of the tactically relevant targets in Poland would be a great success, forcing the Russians themselves to escalate into the nuclear war which might lead to World War III or forcing them instead to retreat. Bridges are not so easily rebuilt once they have been destroyed, nor are tunnels. The gauge-change points between the Soviet and East European railways have always looked like inviting targets, and they might indeed be vulnerable to conventional attack as well, if only the CEP is brought down enough.[20]

There is absolutely no denying that conventional warheads here would be somewhat less effective than nuclear. A conventional warhead might destroy a railroad bridge, but only a nuclear warhead could destroy an entire railway marshaling yard in a single shot. A tunnel on the Trans-Siberian railway might with good luck be blocked by a conventional warhead, but could more surely be blocked using the nuclear. Yet there is equally no denying that a reliance on conventional warheads would be far less escalatory, avoiding crossing the most important firebreak of limited war, avoiding the opening of calculations of radioactive fallout, et cetera.

Given the likely increase in cost of cruise missiles and the likely erection of defensive barriers against them, it might strike many analysts as wildly unrealistic that they should be squandered in the delivery of conventional warheads. Before this all is written off as the idle speculative exercise of professors inclined to abstraction, however, we might simply remember the use of the B-52s in the Vietnam War. Who would ever have predicted in 1961 that this splendid vehicle for delivering the H-bomb to the Soviet Union over ranges of 10,000 miles would become consigned instead to delivering "iron bombs" of TNT over the short range from Thailand to North and South Vietnam?

Such a utilization of the B-52 indeed made sense, as part of an effort to avoid escalation to more general war and as part of an unsuccessful effort to cripple the Communist advances in the south by attacking the logistical lines from the north which supported them. (Incidentally, such

20. See Edward J. Ohlert, "Strategic Deterrence and the Cruise Missile," *Naval War College Review* 21 (1978): 21–32.

a use made mockery of the program budgeting Secretary McNamara had introduced in 1961, by which budgetary items were labeled not by the type of weapon purchased but by the end purpose it was to serve. The B-52 was clearly in the strategic warfare package in any 1961 budget, but its use "in anger" in the end was to come instead in tactical war.)

Like the B-52, the cruise missile in the future might thus be used at shorter range and with conventional warheads. Also like the B-52, however, it will be impossible to offer our adversary any assurance that such weapons could be used only in these modes. Any cruise missile can be stretched in range by readjusting the balance of warhead weight and fuel weight (as well as by adding some auxiliary fuel tanks). One way to reduce warhead weight is, of course, to go to nuclear warheads, with tremendous increase in explosive power as well as tremendous strain on the limits to any war. The straightforward arms controller would thus worry about what is to verify the inclination to limited use here and what is to assure the other side of a less escalatory targeting approach.

The reassurance here is not so impossible to find. Each side in any limited war must be relying not just on predetermined limits of its adversary's weapons and military capacity but also somewhat on the adversary's good sense. Limited war does not entail being disarmed so much as holding back the use of the various weapons one indeed has ready. Such mutual recognitions of the opponents' good sense are of course reinforced by what Thomas Schelling identified as the core of tacit communication, the ongoing day-by-day pattern of restraint which implicitly signals an intention to continue restraint.[21] If the first cruise missiles fired in a European war steer for railway bridges in Poland and impact with conventional rather than nuclear detonations, the Soviet leadership will be getting a signal that the West has for the moment chosen to try to keep the war nonnuclear. (This of course assumes that the Soviet attackers have also elected to hold back their nuclear weapons, which would be a signal to the West that the Communists as well preferred to remain at the conventional level.) The pattern of where the cruise missiles landed would similarly be a Western signal of what the geographical limits to the exchange were slated to be.

In selling the Soviets, during the SALT II negotiations, on the counting rule for the MIRVing of strategic missiles (the rule by which any missile tested with multiple warheads is assumed to have such warheads), American negotiators may have generated a major logical problem for the future strategic situations in which the direction of the imperative is reversed. The Soviets, with a great deal of justice, can contend that every American cruise missile capable of carrying a nuclear warhead must be assumed to be so armed, since the United States, in the absence of verification to the contrary, might obviously find it to its advantage to sneak in the more potent nuclear weaponry. But what if a nation in the future could

21. Schelling.

achieve greater strategic leverage by equipping a dual capable weapon with a conventional warhead? How does the counting rule function then? Could we even envisage clandestine removals of nuclear warheads from American missiles and installations of TNT warheads instead?[22]

CONVENTIONAL TARGETS INSIDE THE SOVIET UNION

Much of the current excitement about new and different uses of nuclear warheads is spurred by alleged Soviet inclinations toward war-fighting attitudes, toward the seeking of victory and political power in any future war, and by alleged Soviet preparations for the civil defense sheltering of Communist party leadership and key workers, or even the evacuation of Soviet cities.[23]

Many of the proposals for Western nuclear responses to such Soviet options then founder on the fact that nuclear destruction will be much more difficult to contain and channel than the needs of any careful "surgical strike" would require.[24] The argument here is that all this American thinking about careful and effective responses to Soviet civil defense and war-fighting techniques might have much more of a payoff if it were shifted again to the application of conventional warheads.

Two very unrelated developments are now likely to expand our ability to differentiate among kinds of destruction, the improvement in U.S. missile accuracies and this Soviet investment in additional civil defense preparations.

The general point about civil defense here is thus two-edged. A Soviet capacity for evacuation of cities is clearly worrisome, in that it might one day embolden the Politburo to undertake an aggression, thinking that less of its population and work force would suffer as a consequence. Yet such an evacuation capability also offers us a much longer list of alternative targets and opportunities for leverage in trying to dissuade the Soviets from beginning or from continuing such an aggression. It simultaneously makes our strategic problem more difficult and more interesting. Hanoi's civil defense system, in a paradoxical way, was co-operating in 1972 with the U.S. Air Force in holding down the casualties from the B-52 air strikes, thereby making such strikes more possible; similarly, the USSR's investment in civil defense preparations not only makes Soviet toughness more worrisome, it also allows us to undertake forms of attack which we might otherwise have felt were too escalatory.

22. For a discussion of some of the verification problems with cruise missiles, see Thomas K. Longstreth, "Cruise Missiles: The Arms Control Challenge," *Arms Control Today* 13 (1983): 1, 7–10.

23. An example that attracted a great deal of attention can be found in Richard Pipes, "Why the Soviet Union Thinks It Could Fight and Win a Nuclear War," *Commentary* 64 (1977): 21–34.

24. For some very well researched skepticism about our capabilities for limiting damage in a war that has become nuclear, see Desmond Ball, *Can Nuclear War Be Controlled?* Adelphi Papers, no. 169 (London: International Institute for Strategic Studies, 1981).

If we were thus to limit ourselves to conventional explosives, as part of keeping a cap on escalation, would we also still, for the same reasons, have to confine our attacks to targets outside the Soviet Union? Perhaps. Perhaps not. Of the two thresholds to be crossed, the nuclear/conventional line may be considerably more sensitive than the line of the formal boundaries of the USSR.

Firing anything whatsoever into Soviet airspace would of course be the crossing of an important threshold, one which has not really been violated before (the U-2 doesn't count). If not handled properly, it might still stampede the Russians into an unwanted response. Yet we might be talking here about the firing of a single missile, or just a few, so that the risk of the incoming salvo being mistaken for a full nuclear strike would be substantially reduced. Public declarations could also be made in advance that the United States in some situations reserves the right to strike at the USSR itself, with conventional arms delivered by missile.

If one felt very much constrained to assist the People's Republic of China in a military engagement with the USSR, for example, an engagement which had not yet gone nuclear, would there not thus be great payoffs in a conventional warhead missile strike against the tunnels of the Trans-Siberian railway? If we could then destroy a bridge, a dam, or a Soviet government building by conventional means, we would have shown substantial punch without yet crossing the nuclear firebreak, without throwing away the most important lid we have on escalation.

The day will probably never come when a nonnuclear warhead will be powerful enough, whatever its accuracy, to destroy an ICBM missile silo, or a hardened command post. The more we thus get in the habit of assigning conventional warheads to any strikes inside the Soviet Union, the more we will reassure the Soviets that we will be limiting ourselves to what could be called "good counterforce," to attacks on their ground force strength, their ability to project power into other territories and out to sea, that is, their conventional forces, and the less we shall be causing any apprehensions about "bad counterforce," attacks on Soviet missile siloes, or Soviet command-and-control, or the shelters of the Soviet leadership; the latter are the kinds of targets we should try to avoid, for fear of putting the Soviet leadership into a position of "use them or lose them" with regard to their own nuclear missiles.

All of these are targeting options which have captured attention inside the U.S. government since the third year of the Carter administration, with PD-59 demonstrating some of this interest,[25] with the options being part of the sales pitch for cruise missiles and the MX. And all of such options have been easy to debunk where a nuclear warhead would be required.

25. A discussion of PD-59 can be found in Louis Rene Beres, "Presidential Directive 59: A Critical Assessment," *Parameters* 11 (1981): 19–27; Colin S. Gray, "Presidential Directive 59: Flawed but Useful," *Parameters* 11 (1981): 30–37.

Yet, without the tremendous and often unpredictable collateral damage of a nuclear warhead, some of such scenarios would be a little less easy to debunk. The problem of keeping the Soviets out of the mood for aggression against Western Europe remains real for many of us, moreover, and is not just the product of febrile imaginations in the Reagan or Carter administrations.

SERVICE IN DETERRENCE VERSUS USE IN COMBAT

The closest that an ethical theorist usually comes to defending the role of nuclear weapons is that their very threat may preclude their coming into use. Deterrence might be morally acceptable, as long as deterrence works, as long as nuclear weapons do not actually get fired against population centers. Yet the same moral comparison can apply to conventional weapons. The best thing to be said about the Swiss army is that it has discouraged other countries from ever invading Switzerland, that is, has kept the Swiss army from getting any combat experience and has kept Swiss young men and other Swiss from being killed.

The idea of conventional strikes at targets in Eastern Europe or inside the Soviet Union is shocking, even if it is less shocking than the idea of an escalation to nuclear warfare anywhere on this globe. Yet the moral shock would again be thinned somewhat, if the mere prospect of such new conventional uses of cruise missiles and ballistic missiles was sufficient to deter the outbreaks of the very wars for which they were designed.

If a deterrent force works well, it never gets demonstrated in use. We are hardly arguing here that Americans should look forward to directing conventional warhead cruise missiles or ballistic missiles at targets in Eastern Europe or within the Soviet Union itself. The suggestion instead is that it might be healthier and wiser to regard such conventional responses, rather than nuclear responses, as the bounty offered by missile accuracy; this would be in response to the argument, now so often heard in Washington, that the best deterrent is a military response which the United States could actually bring itself to undertake without committing suicide.

One should stress other reinforcements for NATO defenses, also moving away from a reliance on nuclear escalation, including extensive deployments of new PGM antitank weapons, the "smaller brothers" of the accurate cruise missiles and ballistic missiles we have been discussing here. If many Soviet tanks are destroyed as they advance by antitank guided missiles (ATGM), while their reinforcements have difficulty getting through Poland because too many bridges have been destroyed by cruise missiles, the prospect of all of this may be sufficient to deter Moscow from ever launching an aggression into West Germany in the first place.

Will we ever see cruise or ballistic missiles striking at bridges in Poland, at tunnels of the Trans-Siberian railway, or in a demonstration shot at some shelters for the Soviet leadership? One hopes that it will never have to come to this, as the prospect once again replaces the reality.

As an aside, will we indeed see cruise missiles ever come into use with conventional warheads anywhere, once and for all showing what they can do? The possibilities here, somewhat more removed from Soviet-American military actions, are perhaps a little more real, just as the B-52s never came into use inside the USSR but saw previously unimaginable service in Vietnam.

One can imagine such a truly "surgical" (no radioactive fallout, little collateral damage) use of conventional warhead missiles for at least one important and serious situation. Turning to the nuclear proliferation front, suppose that we had strong evidence that a regime like Colonel Khaddafy's in Libya were embarking on a diversion of fissionable materials to nuclear warheads. The world consensus might indeed be supportive of a move to head this off, as long as it was not too messy, as long as it did not itself entail the use of nuclear weapons in battle. The destruction of the reactor or plutonium separation plant in question, by a direct hit with one or two conventional warhead missiles, might be exactly what the world would applaud.

SUMMARY

In summary, we have argued that the logical or ethical arguments for avoiding the use of nuclear weapons are fairly closely related to those for limiting war in general. Yet they are not perfectly related, so that the prospect of more accurate delivery systems and smaller nuclear warheads could challenge our assumptions here.

This challenge should probably be refuted. In the end, even if all of this technology works as well as promised, a case could be made for marrying the accuracy of new missiles instead to conventional warheads, since this is still the more likely to keep a war limited.

The second of our questions may be harder to answer, however. Substituting conventional for nuclear weapons makes wars easier to limit, almost beyond a doubt. Yet making wars easier to limit can make them more likely to happen. I am hardly yet convinced that the United States should reassure the Soviets that we will never use nuclear weapons if Western Europe is invaded. Leaving tactical nuclear weapons deployed in West Germany and leaving nuclear warheads on the front of ballistic missiles and cruise missiles may be the best way of preserving peace in Europe.

The primary task of U.S. strategic procurements remains to see to it that the United States will always be able to retaliate if the Soviets use nuclear weapons. As a consequence, we will also always be able to escalate to the use of nuclear weapons, even if the other side had not used them in battle but is merely advancing by the use of conventional weaponry. Cultivating additional conventional options does not change what is possible here; but it may change what the Soviets expect the United States to do. If we show too much interest in conventional weapons options, do we thereby betray an unwillingness to use nuclear weapons first?

The credibility of an American willingness to escalate to nuclear war is now continually questioned, in Washington as well as in Europe. Even if these questionings are badly premised, they may take their toll and limit our choices for the future. If analysts within the U.S. government itself continue to insist that the United States cannot be counted on to escalate merely because of our pledged word and treaty commitment but would do so only if we acquired new nuclear war-fighting options, then the choices will have changed.

For the nuclear war-fighting options may have too many collateral effects to give us any of this "rational" deterrent leverage which is allegedly so needed; and something like conventional options may then have to be substituted, whether we like it or not.

Nuclear Disarmament as a Moral Certainty*

Robert E. Goodin

One of the most biting comments on postwar American history comes from the pen of Arthur Schlesinger, Jr. It goes like this: "As the traumatic experience of the Great Depression led to the resolution to make the economy depression-proof, so the traumatic experience of Pearl Harbor led to the resolution to make the nation war-proof." Laudable though those goals might be, Schlesinger's advice is simply, "Let's not get carried away" seeking certainties where none are available.[1]

According to the now-conventional wisdom, American foreign policymakers in particular must "accept the fact of uncertainty and learn to live with it. Since no magic will provide certainty, our plans must work without it."[2] Modern deterrence theory is especially deeply imbued with this renunciation of the quest for certainties. There is no such thing as a perfect deterrent, we are firmly told. There is no absolute guarantee of perpetual peace. The Harvard Nuclear Study Group advises, "Any form of atomic escapism is a dead end. Living with nuclear weapons is our only hope. It requires that we persevere in reducing the likelihood of war even though we cannot remove the possibility altogether." Or in the immortal words of John Foster Dulles, "You have to take chances for peace, just as you must take chances in war."[3]

* This essay has benefited from the comments and criticisms of audiences at the Australian National University, the California Institute of Technology, the University of Maryland, and the Aspen Conference on the Ethics of Nuclear Deterrence and Disarmament, September 1–4, 1984, Aspen, Colorado. I am particularly indebted to Brian Barry, Stanley Benn, Dave Bobrow, Arthur Burns, Bruce Cain, Frank Cowell, John Dryzek, George Eads, Steve Elkin, Bob Fullinwider, Sam Gorovitz, Will Jones, Greg Kavka, Dan Kevles, Morgan Kousser, Doug Lackey, Andy Mack, Peter Menzies, Jan Narveson, Toby Page, John Passmore, Huw Price, George Quester, Richard Routley, Norman Schofield, Henry Shue, Jack Smart, Jack Snyder, and Marc Trachtenberg. Needless to say, final responsibility remains mine alone.

1. Arthur Schlesinger, Jr., "Unlearning the Lessons of Pearl Harbor," *Washington Post* (December 6, 1981), pp. C1, C3.

2. Roberta Wohlstetter, *Pearl Harbor: Warning and Decision* (Stanford, Calif.: Stanford University Press, 1962), p. 401.

3. Harvard Nuclear Study Group (Scott D. Sagan et al.), *Living with Nuclear Weapons* (Cambridge, Mass.: Harvard University Press, 1983), pp. 254–55. John Foster Dulles quoted

At this point, however, I can only echo Schlesinger's admonition. Let's not get carried away, renouncing the quest for certainties even where they can reasonably be sought. Even if we are not able to tie down everything, we can still hope to tie down some of the most important things. That, as I understand it, is what the movement for nuclear disarmament is all about. Its aim is to produce modal changes in the possibility of a large-scale nuclear war rather than just marginal changes in its probability. That limited quest for certainties is, I shall argue, eminently defensible.

I

To understand what I am arguing for, it might help to know what I am arguing against. That is nothing less than nuclear deterrence itself. Its basic idea is that each side can, by emphasizing the risks of nuclear war, deter the other from steps that might turn that risk into a reality. But this is very much a gamble since for the deterrent to be credible the risk must be real. So in essence deterrence is a scheme for making nuclear war less probable by making it more probable.[4]

That the logic of nuclear deterrence is incorrigibly probabilistic is widely acknowledged. Strategists and social scientists describe as its "fundamental premise" the proposition that "nuclear weapons make *probable* the rejection [by one's opponents] of armed aggression as a potential policy alternative" (emphasis added). Moral philosophers also fully acknowledge the nature of the gamble. In the words of Bernard Williams, "The morality of deterrence is, I think, legitimately one in which you think principally about those steps which make it *less likely* that the weapons get used" (emphasis added).[5]

My argument is that all such notions of probability and likelihood are simply inappropriate in these circumstances. Maybe such concepts are not even meaningful at all when applied to situations involving reflective

---

in Daniel Ellsberg, "The Theory and Practice of Blackmail," Rand Paper P-3883 (Rand Corp., Santa Monica, Calif., July 1968, mimeographed), p. 38.

4. Literally this is of course a non sequitur. But the phrase captures something of the spirit of deterrence. The Harvard Nuclear Study Group, e.g., advocates "taking a *small risk* of nuclear war" in hopes of "preventing an even *larger risk* of nuclear war" (p. 15; emphasis added). Notice, too, that the "threat to lose control" is an often used deterrent threat; see Barrie M. Blechman and Douglas M. Hart, "The Political Utility of Nuclear Weapons: The 1973 Middle East Crisis," *International Security* 7 (1982): 132–56. On balance, it seems that Barrie Paskins and Michael Dockrill, *The Ethics of War* (London: Gerald Duckworth & Co., 1979), pp. 64–77, 239, are quite right to conclude that "deterrence makes trusting to luck the foundation of security."

5. Richard A. Brody, "Deterrence," *International Encyclopedia of the Social Sciences,* ed. David L. Sills (New York: Collier-Macmillan Publishers, 1968), vol. 4, pp. 130–33, p. 130. Bernard Williams, "How to Think Skeptically about the Bomb," *New Society* (November 18, 1982), pp. 288–90, pp. 189–90. See, similarly, David Gauthier, "Deterrence, Maximization, and Rationality," *Ethics* 94 (1984): 474–95.

human agents rather than mere random processes.[6] But in any case it is clear that, where probabilities of nuclear war are concerned, we just do not know enough about the shape of the underlying distribution to justify employing any of the standard techniques for estimating probabilities. That we can have no reliable probability estimates is in itself quite enough to render probabilistic reasoning about such affairs wildly inappropriate.

Certainly we have no solid objective statistics, based on frequency counts or such like. The balance of terror has kept the peace for the past thirty-five years, to be sure. But thirty-five years is just too short a run on which to base our probability judgments, given the unacceptability of even very small probabilities of such a very great horror. Besides, nuclear war is just not the sort of thing whose probabilities we dare to estimate by trial-and-error procedures—the first error may well mark the learner's own end.[7]

Nor do we have any well-validated scientific theories (about, e.g., the genesis and escalation of international conflicts) from which we might hope to derive reliable estimates of the probability of a breakdown in deterrence which would lead to a large-scale nuclear war. We suffer not from a lack of such theories but rather from a surfeit of them; and none can prove itself decisively superior to all the others.[8]

Nor, finally, do we have any particularly good reason to place any great faith in subjective probability estimates. Of course, we can always bully people into stating their "best guess" as to the chances of anything occurring; we can even bully them into rendering those probability estimates consistent. But when such estimates are as groundless as those concerning the chances of nuclear deterrence collapsing into nuclear war are, we should not set any great store by them. Ellsberg says, "It's no use bullying me into taking action . . . by flattering my 'best judgment.' *I* know how little that's based on."[9] Alas, most people do not. Psychological evidence suggests not only that "individuals are poor probability assessors" but also, "and perhaps more important, that they underestimate their

6. This is a particular theme of Arthur Lee Burns, *Ethics and Deterrence*, Adelphi Papers, no. 96 (London: International Institute for Strategic Studies, 1970).

7. All the standard arguments about nuclear reactor safety apply here; see Robert E. Goodin, *Political Theory and Public Policy* (Chicago: University of Chicago Press, 1982), esp. chap. 10.

8. "Where we have several competing theories which give different predictions, all these theories should be regarded with suspicion, and we should be prepared for a risk that is higher than what is predicted by any of the theories," as Dagfin Føllesdal argues in "Some Ethical Aspects of Recombinant DNA Research," *Social Science Information* 18 (1979): 401–19, p. 405. For a critical survey of competing theories, see Francis W. Hoole and Dina A. Zinnes, eds., *Quantitative International Politics: An Analysis* (New York: Praeger Publishers, 1976).

9. Daniel Ellsberg, "Risk, Ambiguity and the Savage Axioms," *Quarterly Journal of Economics* 75 (1961): 643–69, p. 663. See, similarly, R. Duncan Luce and Howard Raiffa, *Games and Decisions* (New York: John Wiley & Sons, 1957), p. 304.

poorness by assessing probabilities too tightly."[10] Knowing this—and knowing all the severe distortions to which judgments under uncertainty are prone[11]—it would be sheer folly for us to predicate any profoundly important policy choices on such fallible subjective probability estimates.

The upshot is that it is altogether inappropriate to engage in probabilistic reasoning about the chances of a breakdown in the balance of terror that leads to a large-scale nuclear war. Objective statistics are unavailable; theories are too numerous and too divergent; subjective estimates are known to be too unreliable.[12] The problem is not just that we cannot estimate point probabilities with any great precision—that we cannot say whether the probability of nuclear war this century is 10 percent or 15 percent. Nor is it even just that we cannot make the sorts of order-of-magnitude judgments that would allow us to make ordinal judgments about relative probabilities. We are in a worse situation still. We cannot even say with confidence in what direction any particular strategic innovation pushes the probability of all-out nuclear war. Some theories maintain that that risk is increased by cruise missiles or space-based defenses or nuclear proliferation. Others hold the opposite.[13] Neither logic nor experience enables us to choose confidently between these theories, and only a fool would trust unaided hunches with so much at stake.

The most that can be claimed for deterrence is that it will probably work to prevent war. So if probabilistic reasoning is inappropriate in these circumstances, deterrence is too. In short, my complaint against nuclear deterrence is that it amounts to playing the odds without knowing the odds. That constitutes recklessness par excellence. It would be the height of irresponsibility for anyone to wager the family home on rolls of such radically unpredictable dice. Where millions of lives are at stake, that judgment must surely apply even more harshly.

The conventional wisdom holds that the only responsible response to such radical uncertainty would be to adopt a diversified defense portfolio,

10. Richard Zeckhauser, "Procedures for Valuing Lives," *Public Policy* 23 (1975): 419–64, p. 445. For evidence, see Daniel Kahneman, Paul Slovic, and Amos Tversky, eds., *Judgment under Uncertainty* (New York: Cambridge University Press, 1982), pp. 287–354.

11. See, in general, Kahneman, Slovic, and Tversky, eds.; and, more particularly, Baruch Fischhoff, "Strategic Policy Preferences," *Journal of Social Issues* 39 (1983): 133–60.

12. See, similarly, Jon Elster, "Risk, Uncertainty and Nuclear Power," *Social Science Information* 18 (1979): 371–400; Talbot Page, "A Generic View of Toxic Chemicals and Similar Risks," *Ecology Law Quarterly* 7 (1978): 207–44, esp. pp. 225–29; Gregory S. Kavka, "Deterrence, Utility and Rational Choice," *Theory and Decision* 12 (1980): 41–60; and S. I. Benn, "Deterrence or Appeasement?" *Journal of Applied Philosophy* 1 (1983): 5–19.

13. See, e.g., the debate between Keith B. Payne and Colin S. Gray, "Nuclear Policy and the Defensive Transition," and William E. Burrows, "Ballistic Missile Defense: The Illusion of Security," *Foreign Affairs* 62 (1984): 820–42, 843–56. For a novel argument that nuclear proliferation might reduce the chances of nuclear war by making all of us more careful, see Aaron Wildavsky, "Nuclear Clubs or Nuclear Wars?" *Yale Review* 51 (1962): 345–62.

hedging against all the conceivable risks. But of course it is in the nature of such things that, in the course of spreading ourselves to secure some protection against all possibilities, we leave ourselves less than fully protected against any of them. And, furthermore, some of the things that diversifying our defense portfolio might dictate (e.g., damage-limitation or postwar-reconstruction planning) could be seen as provocative by our opponents, thereby increasing the risk of the very worst eventualities we are hoping to protect against. Risk hedging is not a bad strategy if it is the best we can do. Often it is. Sometimes, however, another strategy is available, and when it is, it proves decidedly superior. It is to this new strategy that I now turn.

II

Here I shall offer a method of approaching such problems that deals in possibilistic rather than probabilistic terms. In possibilistic reasoning, there are only three categories to concern us: (1) the impossible, (2) the possible, and (3) the certain.[14] And there are only four logically distinct ways of changing possibilities:

a) something previously impossible can be made possible;
b) something previously merely possible can be made certain;

or moving in the opposite direction:

c) something previously certain can be made merely possible; or
d) something previously possible can be made impossible.[15]

Some special significance of a logical sort clearly attaches to movements across the boundaries that define these modal categories. Where the outcomes in question are themselves matters of moral concern, that special significance is moral as well. If an outcome would be morally desirable, then (other things being equal) it is morally desirable for that outcome to be made not just more probable but certain or for that outcome to be rendered possible if before it was not. Conversely, if an outcome would be morally undesirable, then (other things being equal) it is morally desirable for that outcome to be made not just less probable but impossible or for it to be reduced to a mere possibility if before it was a certainty.

14. All can be analyzed in terms of the others: to say that "it is impossible that *x*" is merely to say that "it is not possible that *x*"; and "it is certain that *x*" is equivalent to "it is not possible that not *x*." On the use of modal logic for social analysis more generally, see Jon Elster, *Logic and Society* (London: John Wiley & Sons, 1978). All talk of "degrees of possibility" (e.g., ranging from "just barely possible" outcomes through "remotely possible" ones to "well and truly possible" ones) can be shown to reduce to an ordinary probability calculus; see Charles Hamblin, "The Modal 'Probably,'" *Mind* 68 (1959): 234–40.

15. Just for the sake of completeness, we might add two further composite categories: (*e*) something previously impossible can be made certain (combining *a* and *b*); or (*f*) something previously certain can be made impossible (combining *c* and *d*).

For those steeped in modern Bayesian decision theory, replacing probabilistic with possibilistic reasoning might seem queer indeed. For a wide variety of people in a wide variety of practical circumstances, however, it seems to come very naturally. Of course, that does not prove that there are good reasons for their so acting—arguments to that effect will come later. But as an important preliminary to those arguments, let me first respond to the "argument from queerness" by illustrating the role of possibilistic reasoning in everyday affairs. Consider first the evidence of a wide variety of psychological experiments showing that there is something like a "certainty effect" governing people's responses to choice situations. However they choose between ordinary gambles, people seem disproportionately sensitive to outcomes that are certain: even by the standards set by their own previous choices among gambles, people will pay considerably more than they should (in terms of probabilistically expected costs) to avoid a loss that is certain or (in terms of probabilistically expected gains forgone) to secure a gain that is certain.[16]

The same sort of logic seems to pervade the White House in crisis decision making. There, too, the emphasis seems to fall heavily on certainties and impossibilities rather than on fine-grained probability estimates. Notice that, during the Cuban missile crisis, President Kennedy justified taking a risk of nuclear war on the grounds that it was necessary "to avoid *certain* war later." Robert Kennedy added that American actions did not cross any modal boundaries on the other side either, saying that "we all agreed in the end that if the Russians were ready to go to nuclear war over Cuba, they were ready to go to nuclear war, and that was that. So we might as well have the showdown then as six months later."[17] Whether or not any of this was true—or whether or not it was even genuinely thought to be true, at the time—it is nonetheless revealing that the rationalizations (if that is what they are) are phrased in terms of modalities, the certainty of war, and such like.

The same emphasis on possibilistic reasoning is also reflected in the special importance traditionally attached, both legally and morally, to the "first intervening agent" and the "last intervening agent" in any causal chain. Both make essentially possibilistic contributions to the outcome: the intervention of the first makes it possible, that of the last inevitable. It is hard to say precisely how to apportion responsibility between these

16. Amos Tversky, "A Critique of Expected Utility Theory," *Erkenntnis* 9 (1975): 163–73. Daniel Kahneman and Amos Tversky, "Prospect Theory: An Analysis of Decision under Risk," *Econometrica* 47 (1979): 163–91. This grows out of work on the Allais Paradox, summarized in Luce and Raiffa, sec. 13.5; Ellsberg, "Risk, Ambiguity and the Savage Axioms"; and Maurice Allais and Ole Hagen, eds., *Expected Utility Hypotheses and the Allais Paradox* (Dordrecht: D. Reidel Publishing Co., 1979).

17. Jack Snyder, "Rationality at the Brink," *World Politics* 30 (1978): 345–65, pp. 357, 345. See also Robert Jervis, "Deterrence Theory Revisited," *World Politics* 31 (1979): 289–324, pp. 310–11.

two agents.[18] Between them, however, the first and last intervening agents were traditionally thought to bear the bulk of the responsibility for the outcome. Recently we have come to appreciate the importance of other agents along the way—those who could have put an end to the causal chain but who failed to do so. In law, the increasingly popular doctrine of "comparative negligence" shares out some of the blame among them, also.[19] What is significant in the present context, however, is this: first, last, and intermediate agents are all blamed for their possibilistic contributions to the causal chain. Just as the first is blamed for making the harmful outcome possible and the last for allowing it to become inevitable, intermediate agents are blamed for failing to take opportunities when they had them to make the harmful outcome impossible.

All this is merely by way of refuting the "queerness" objection. Be the intuitions of Bayesians as they may, possibilistic considerations certainly do seem to loom large in many areas of ordinary decision making. Now I want to turn to argue that there is a class of extraordinary decision situations in which possibilistic considerations deserve special and, indeed, exclusive emphasis. In standard applications, possibilistic notions rightly operate in conjunction with probabilistic ones. Whether and how much we praise or blame people for their actions ordinarily depends at least in part on how probable it was (or is) that the possibilities they opened up would be actualized.[20]

Under certain circumstances, however, those probabilistic elements drop out of the calculations, leaving us with a purely possibilistic analysis of moral responsibility. Here I shall concentrate on two such conditions. These are not necessarily mutually exclusive; indeed, both arguably obtain in the case of nuclear weapons decision making. Nor are they necessarily exhaustive of all the circumstances that force us to rely on purely possibilistic

18. A. N. Prior, "Symposium on the Consequences of Actions, I," and D. D. Raphael, "Symposium on the Consequences of Actions, II," *Proceedings of the Aristotelian Society* 30, suppl. (1956): 91–99, 100–119. H. L. A. Hart and A. M. Honore, *Causation in the Law* (Oxford: Clarendon Press, 1959). William Prosser, *Handbook of the Law of Torts*, 3d ed. (St. Paul, Minn.: West Publishing Co., 1971), chap. 12.

19. Forceful pleas for "comparative negligence" are found in Prosser, chap. 12. Notice that the older and harsher doctrine of "contributory negligence" only makes sense if the plaintiff could have done something to prevent the harm from befalling himself; likewise, "vicarious liability" only makes sense on the assumption that masters/parents/owners could have done something to prevent their servants/children/dogs from inflicting the harm. Unless they could have done something to make the harmful outcome impossible—i.e., unless their negligence was a necessary condition of that outcome—it makes no sense to assign them liability for it.

20. In tort law, e.g., people are not held responsible for unforeseeable "freak" accidents. Some, such as Oliver Wendell Holmes, *The Common Law* (Boston: Little, Brown & Co., 1881), might analyze that as "anything . . . which [the actor] could not fairly have been expected to contemplate as possible, and therefore to avoid" (p. 94). But the more standard analysis—of, e.g., Hart and Honore, chap. 9—would analyze that notion in terms of what could be foreseen as both "possible and probable."

reasoning. Still, they seem to be the most important ones for the present application at least.

One relatively familiar factor that forces us to shy away from probabilistic reasoning is the magnitude of the possible payoffs. Where there is any risk of something infinitely awful happening, then probabilities simply do not matter. Just so long as that outcome is possible—so long as there is some nonzero probability of its happening—we must do whatever we can to avoid it.[21] Infinite costs, discounted by any probability larger than zero, are still infinite.[22] And while few payoffs are literally infinite, the same sort of argument might still work where possible payoffs are virtually infinite. For all intents and purposes, probabilities might still drop out of our reckonings for much the same reason as before.[23]

All that is, I think, both true and important. But it is also pretty standard. My more novel suggestion is that there is a second condition, completely independent of the first, which might also force us to fall back on possibilistic rather than probabilistic standards of moral responsibility. That condition is as follows:

i)   the agent's choice among alternative courses of action might make a morally significant difference in the outcome;
ii) the agent's judgment about the probability that any particular outcome will result from any particular action is (and is or should be known by the agent to be) highly unreliable; and
iii) the agent's judgment about what outcomes his various actions would make possible or impossible is (and is or should be known by the agent to be) highly reliable.[24]

The emphasis in this second argument is on the differential reliability of possibilistic judgments over probabilistic ones. Often there will be no

21. The most plausible way anything could have infinite disutility would be by foreclosing an otherwise potentially infinite stream of future payoffs; see John Dryzek, "Present Choices, Future Consequences," *World Futures* 19 (1983): 1–19. In the limiting case, there is Page's "zero-infinity dilemma," i.e., "a virtually zero probability of a virtually infinite catastrophe" (see pp. 208–12).

22. The same should, in principle, be true of infinitely large benefits: so long as there is any possibility of them accruing, we should pursue them; infinite benefits, discounted by any nonzero probability, are still infinitely large. But in practice we are much more reluctant to accept the argument in that case. The reason, I suspect, has to do with the fact that we think that some harms can indeed carry a virtually infinite disutility, whereas we do not believe that any benefit, however large, can be infinitely (or even virtually infinitely) great.

23. Notice that this bears a striking resemblance to the way in which tort law assigns anyone engaged in "ultrahazardous activities" (or "abnormally dangerous activities," as they are now called) strict liability for any harms that might result, blatantly ignoring the probabilistic calculus that characterizes ordinary standards of negligence; see William Prosser, *Second Restatement of the Law of Torts* (St. Paul, Minn.: American Law Institute, 1965), chap. 21.

24. How "reliable" "reliable enough" is (and, for that matter, how "certain" "certain enough" is) for the purposes at hand is a function of potential costs and benefits. It is presumably permissible to play unreliable odds for small stakes, in a way it is not for large ones. See Ellsberg, "Risk, Ambiguity and the Savage Axioms," p. 663; and Luce and Raiffa, p. 27.

such differential: whatever makes us uncertain of probabilities also makes us uncertain about possibilities. But at least occasionally we will have good grounds—which almost inevitably have to be good theoretical grounds rather than experiential ones—for supposing that some courses of action will make an outcome impossible, whereas other courses of action merely alter its probability in ways we cannot reliably predict.

Under this perhaps peculiar constellation of circumstances identified by my second argument for possibilistic reasoning, the only way an agent can confidently exert effective control over morally important consequences is by manipulating possibilities. And if the consequences really do matter morally, then clearly he should do so. This means that, ceteris paribus, a moral agent should make morally desirable outcomes possible or certain (and morally undesirable ones impossible or uncertain) wherever he can; that a moral agent should open up as many possible paths to good outcomes (and close off as many possible paths to bad ones) as he can; et cetera.

Under either of these two sets of circumstances, the morally responsible course of behavior is to pursue policies producing modal changes in the desired direction. The first argument tells us that we should aim, above all else, to remove the certainty or to guarantee the impossibility of outcomes that are really heinous. The second tells us that, even where the payoffs are less dramatic, we should nonetheless concentrate on pos-sibilities if probability judgments are deemed grossly unreliable: then all that is left is for us to choose between alternative courses of action on the basis of the possibilities they open up or close off for good or bad outcomes. Either of these conditions alone would force us to shift from probabilistic to possibilistic reasoning. Where both conditions are operative, as I shall shortly argue they are in the case of nuclear armaments, they can be powerfully reinforcing.

This approach contrasts sharply both with the standard ethical practice of assessing policies in terms of their probable consequences and with the standard deontological alternative to that approach. Unlike the former, I shun probabilities; unlike the latter, I still want to embrace consequences.[25] My approach also contrasts sharply with all the standard decision-theoretic rules that would allow us to dispense with reckonings of probabilities.[26] Maximin, maximax, minimax regret, and Arrow-Hurwicz rules all choose between options on the basis of possible payoffs, without asking how probable they might be. But all these rules are preoccupied with limiting cases—with the best or worst or most regrettable possible outcome. Thus

25. Benn leaps from the observation that probabilities are unreliable where nuclear strategies are concerned to the conclusion that consequentialistic reasoning is therefore precluded. That argument ignores the option for which I am here arguing, i.e., possibilistic consequentialism.

26. See Luce and Raiffa, chap. 13, for a survey; and for a fuller discussion of how some (but not all) of these decision rules might apply to nuclear strategy, Douglas P. Lackey, "Morals and Missiles: A Utilitarian Look at Nuclear Deterrence," *Philosophy & Public Affairs* 11 (1982): 189–231.

they ignore the existence of a great many other possibilities that might be almost as bad or as good; they likewise ignore how many or how few possible paths might be open to each of these outcomes. In short, decision theorists, in their zeal to break loose of the influence of probabilistic reasoning, have come to neglect important changes even in the set of possibilities facing us. Remedying that neglect is one of the major tasks of this essay.

III

This focus on the moral importance of modal shifts can be shown to have important implications for nuclear weapons policy. The preconditions for applying my argument surely all exist. Little need be said to justify the claim that the consequences in view matter morally. Maybe consequentialistic considerations are not the only ones that should guide our choices, of military policies or any others; but where the consequences in view are so momentous as those involved in an all-out nuclear war, it would be sheer lunacy to deny such considerations any role at all.[27]

For present purposes, there is no need to specify what makes the consequences of a large-scale detonation of nuclear weapons so morally heinous. We can leave open the question of whether it is the dead bodies (or cities or civilizations) that should offend us or whether it is the violations of moral rights and duties that would inevitably be entailed by a full-blown nuclear war. The question here is merely how to allocate responsibility for avoiding outcomes that can be seen to be morally heinous from any number of perspectives.

Nor is there much doubt about the existence of both conditions independently driving us from probabilistic principles to possibilistic ones. As for the first, the potential costs of an all-out nuclear war surely are enormous and surely must count as "virtually infinite" if any do. As for the second, my introductory argument has already shown that, where risks of nuclear war are concerned, probabilistic reasoning is inappropriate.

What crucially remains to be shown is that there is any action which we can confidently predict *will* make a modal change in the desired direction. Often it seems we know no more about possibilities than about probabilities, or that opening up some bad possibilities is the necessary price of closing off others equally bad, or that opening up some bad possibilities is the necessary price of opening up some others that are equally good. This sort of indeterminacy, at least, seems absent in the case of nuclear weapons policy.

27. "It is thoroughly unreasonable to suppose that the goodness or badness of an action is entirely independent of its probable consequences, and no one but a moralist riding a theory to death would maintain this view for an instant," in the judgment of C. D. Broad, "On the Function of False Hypotheses in Ethics," *International Journal of Ethics* 26 (1916): 277–97, p. 278. See the strikingly similar passage in Bernard Williams, "A Critique of Utilitarianism," in *Utilitarianism: For & Against* (Cambridge: Cambridge University Press, 1973), p. 90.

Consider first the responsibilities involved in moving up the ladder of possibility, from impossibility to possibility to certainty. According to the above analysis, there would be two classes of prime candidates. One would be those who were responsible for creating (inventing, funding, and building) the nuclear weapons in the first place—for making nuclear war a possibility. The other would be those who would be responsible for taking the last step that makes all-out nuclear war inevitable. One of the great troubles with this as with all great "accidents" is that it is often not clear, either in retrospect or, much less, in prospect, what the "last step" is before some inexorable chain of events is set in motion. But in the case of nuclear war, this much at least is certain: the first superpower to launch nuclear weapons directed at the other's homeland has thereby made all-out nuclear war inevitable.

Some might say that nothing is "inevitable," in any morally important sense, so long as other people retain some subsequent choice in the matter. Thus when you refuse a blackmailer's demands, knowing full well that he *will* kill the child, that does not burden you with the responsibility for the child's death.[28] Nor on this account would the agent launching the first nuclear strike be responsible for the ensuing exchange of weapons—assuming the other side could, in some meaningful sense, choose whether to launch a second strike. But there is an equally persuasive argument in the opposite direction. If you could have foreseen the other's reaction, then you should have taken account of it in making your own decision; if you have failed to do so and the injury occurs, then both of you are liable for it.[29]

Besides, in the case of nuclear war there are powerful reasons for doubting that the other side really could "choose" in any meaningful sense whether or not to launch a retaliatory strike. One reason is purely psychological—turning the other cheek after an unprovoked nuclear attack may well be beyond the psychological capacities of most people. Another even more important reason is technological. Most strategists now seem to agree that a first strike would try (probably successfully) to knock out some important components of the other side's command-control-communications systems.[30] That means that the counterstrike would be fired by a headless automaton. The official line, and the fond hope, is that no one cut off from the commander-in-chief will have

28. Nancy Davis, "Utilitarianism and Responsibility," *Ratio* 22 (1980): 15–35, esp. pp. 31–34, and "The Priority of Avoiding Harm," in *Killing and Letting Die*, ed. B. Steinbock (Englewood Cliffs, N.J.: Prentice-Hall, Inc., 1980), pp. 172–214, esp. pp. 201–10.

29. See J. H. Beale, Jr., "Recovery for the Consequences of an Act," *Harvard Law Review* 9 (1895): 80–89, p. 87.

30. Desmond Ball, *Can Nuclear War Be Controlled?* Adelphi Papers, no. 169 (London: International Institute for Strategic Studies, 1981). Spurgeon M. Keeny, Jr., and Wolfgang K. H. Panofsky, "MAD versus NUTS," *Foreign Affairs* 60 (1981–82): 287–304. Paul Bracken, *The Command and Control of Nuclear Forces* (New Haven, Conn.: Yale University Press, 1983).

authority to launch a nuclear counterstrike. The great danger is that no one, in those circumstances, will have the effective authority to stop it.

At this point, nuclear weapons have been discovered, built, and deployed. Those who did so may have a lot to answer for. But from the perspective of present policymaking, all that is history. The question before us is what, given that history, we are now to do. To present policymakers therefore falls a peculiarly strong responsibility to make sure that, now that nuclear war is possible, they do nothing to make it inevitable. That, as I have just argued, means that each side should abstain from any first nuclear strike on the other superpower's homeland.

Next let us consider the responsibilities involved in moving down the ladder of possibility, from certainty to possibility to impossibility. Again, there are two classes of prime candidates for responsibility. One would be those who were responsible for averting an otherwise certain nuclear exchange—for transforming the certainty of nuclear war into the mere possibility of one. The other would be those who were responsible for making an all-out nuclear war impossible.

It is difficult to imagine what desperate circumstances might be described by the first category (an all-out nuclear war being inevitable in the absence of the agent's intervention). But suppose, for example, that the troops in the silos (theirs or ours) had standing orders to launch a nuclear attack under certain narrowly specified conditions, unless instructed otherwise by their commander-in-chief.[31] Then an all-out nuclear war would be inevitable unless the commander-in-chief gives the order for them to hold their fire. He would, therefore, have a peculiarly strong responsibility to do so. Much the same can be said for everyone along the chain of command that would be responsible for transmitting the commander-in-chief's order to launch a nuclear attack or counterattack. All-out nuclear war would be inevitable unless one or some group of them acts so as to prevent that message from getting through. Consequently each of them would have a peculiarly strong responsibility so to act.

The second category is, however, of more immediate relevance. Whoever has an opportunity to make all-out nuclear war impossible would, on this argument, have a peculiarly strong responsibility to seize that opportunity. Herein lies the case for nuclear disarmament. Of course, if all sides were to undertake such a policy, nuclear war between them would be quite literally impossible. Universal nuclear disarmament is

---

31. These circumstances are, alas, not so fanciful as they might seem. It is widely reported that North American Air Defense (NORAD) commanders used to have authority, in certain circumstances, to launch a nuclear attack on their own authority; and there are now increasingly frequent demands for "preplanning" of surgical nuclear strikes by NATO field commanders, incorporating the description of circumstances in which they are authorized in the Single Integrated Operational Plan. See Daniel Frei, *The Risks of Unintentional Nuclear War* (London: Croom Helm for the U.N. Institute for Disarmament Research, 1983); and Peter Pringle and William Arkin, *SIOP* (London: Sphere Books, 1983).

most strongly to be commended on these grounds, therefore. But under certain circumstances—circumstances which arguably obtain in the present world—unilateral nuclear disarmament by one of the two superpowers, combined with a reorientation of its conventional force posture, would produce the same effect. There is simply no credible scenario by which a nuclear-armed superpower—provided it is at once minimally rational and governed by the standard goals guiding world politics—would, either by accident or by design, be led to launch a full-scale nuclear assault on an opponent armed only with conventional weapons of a merely defensive sort.[32] In a war of conquest, no aggressor strives to destroy its spoils.[33]

This case for unilateral nuclear disarmament is hedged in various respects. Let me elaborate a little. Notice, first, that I am assuming a world in which there are only two nuclear superpowers. Only in that case would unilateral nuclear disarmament by one party preclude an all-out nuclear war. Mine is an argument for reducing the number of nuclear-armed superpowers *to* one, not just *by* one. Were there more than two vast nuclear arsenals in the world, the same sort of argument I have

32. In his commentary on an earlier version of this essay presented at the Aspen conference, Marc Trachtenberg argued that history belies this point: "Consider the example of the United States in its period of atomic monopoly. If war had broken out around 1950, this country, which thought of itself as liberal, civilized and humane, would almost certainly have dropped every bomb in its arsenal on the Soviet Union, and especially Soviet 'urban industrial' targets. If America would have behaved in this way, are we certain that the Soviets, given similar circumstances, would not?" See, similarly, Lawrence Freedman, *The Evolution of Nuclear Strategy* (London: Macmillan Publishers, 1981), chap. 4. My reply is that circumstances would not be similar. The American nuclear attack was contemplated only in the event of an overwhelming conventional assault by Soviet forces on America's European allies. Were a superpower to undertake both unilateral nuclear disarmament and the reorientation of conventional forces in a purely defensive posture, then neither history nor strategic doctrine more generally yields any credible scenario by which it would be subject to an all-out nuclear assault. "No credible scenario" is indeed the proper standard of impossibility. Possible worlds, recall, must be constructed out of possible steps from the actual world; and what is "incredible" is inconceivable and hence impossible, at least from our present perspective. There are of course "degrees of credibility," akin to the degrees of possibility discussed in n. 14; these degrees, like those, are resolvable into an ordinary probability calculus. Here I am focusing instead on the limiting case of impossibility, i.e., the situation in which there is no scenario with any credibility at all leading to the outcome in question.

33. In his Aspen commentary on an earlier version of this essay, Doug Lackey offered the reductio that, following this logic, we would be obliged to remove all potentially lethal objects from our homes and thereby render ourselves incapable of committing murder. Although I certainly think it would be a good idea for Americans to remove some of the lethal weapons from their homes (e.g., handguns), I am happy enough for them to hang onto others (e.g., kitchen knives and frozen legs of lamb). The reason, as Lackey intimates, has to do with the relative probabilities that they will in fact be used to commit murders. Our long experience with guns, knives, and legs of lamb lying around the house allows us to form reasonable estimates of the probabilities they will be used as murder weapons; our all-too-brief experience with nuclear weapons, alas, offers no such basis for reliable probability estimates.

been offering would lead to a call for multilateral nuclear disarmament, ideally by all nuclear superpowers but at the very least by all but one.[34]

Notice, second, that I merely claim that unilateral nuclear disarmament would avert "full-scale" or "all-out" nuclear war. Nuclear weapons might still be used in anger: there are still the lesser nuclear powers who might make some little mischief; and if one superpower retains nuclear weapons, it might occasionally detonate some of them, either to back up its blackmail or to prevent the other from rearming. Naturally, no nuclear blast is to be welcomed. Nonetheless, I assume that there are scale effects and that, for a variety of reasons, an all-out nuclear war would be far, far worse than the detonation of just a few nuclear devices. Where this threshold lies depends, of course, on what precisely it is that makes an all-out nuclear war so much worse than a limited one. If it is the prospect of a "nuclear winter," and if (as some suggest) detonating even as few nuclear weapons as France will soon possess might trigger it, then once again we would need concerted action aimed at more widespread nuclear disarmament in order to guarantee that the threshold would never be crossed.[35] I ignore that possibility here not because I think it unimportant but merely because if true it constitutes an even more powerful argument for the suicidal superfluousness of nuclear weapons than my own.

Third, notice that unilateral nuclear disarmament renders all-out nuclear war impossible only if the remaining nuclear superpower is at once "minimally rational" and in pursuit of "the standard goals guiding world politics." These caveats are necessary because a grossly irrational power might launch an all-out nuclear assault on a nuclear-disarmed opponent, however counterproductive that might be.[36] And a nation bent on the pursuit not of wealth, status, and power but rather of genocide

34. Strategic thinking inevitably leads each nation to hold out, each wanting to be that one nuclear superpower in a nuclear-disarmed world. The dangers attending such an Unequal Coordination Game constitute the best argument for unilateral nuclear disarmament not only in the two-nation but also in the *n*-nation case. Russell Hardin, "Unilateral versus Mutual Disarmament," *Philosophy & Public Affairs* 12 (1983): 236–54, pp. 249–50, shows this to be true and concedes that this is a plausible model of the world; he shrinks from its implications not for any moral reasons but merely because they are "politically ruled out" (p. 254). The limits of the excuse of political impossibility are discussed, however, in Goodin, chap. 7. There is a persuasive argument for believing that, as one superpower divests itself of nuclear weapons, those lesser powers that formerly lived under its nuclear umbrella will be driven to acquire or increase nuclear arsenals of their own. But so long as those arsenals remain below some threshold, discussed in the following paragraph, all-out nuclear war still would be impossible.

35. Carl Sagan, "Nuclear War and Climatic Catastrophe: Some Policy Implications," *Foreign Affairs* 62 (1983–84): 257–92, p. 286.

36. Jan Narveson teases me with the paradox that, if I am presupposing really rational actors, then the best way to guarantee nuclear peace is through deterrence, for really rational actors would never (under certain favorable circumstances we could specify, and perhaps even institutionalize) fall into an all-out nuclear war. But that argument presupposes much more rationality—"superrationality," if you will—than my argument requires. There is a substantial body of evidence (e.g., in Snyder; and Jervis) that superpowers, facing the

would not regard it as counterproductive at all—the complete destruction of the loathed group, its artifacts and culture, is precisely the end in view. The only way of rendering all-out nuclear war impossible, when a mad/genocidal power is involved, is for that power to be deprived of a nuclear arsenal of any size itself. Certainly there can be no guarantee that we (assuming we are the ones who are neither mad nor genocidal) will not be subjected to a full-scale nuclear attack by such a power, even if we undertake unilateral nuclear disarmament ourselves. In the terms of my argument, that means that we would be morally at liberty to retain a nuclear arsenal ourselves. That, however, is not to say that so doing is morally obligatory or even necessarily advisable. (There is even less reason to believe that mad/genocidal opponents will be deterred by our nuclear arsenal or be induced by it to bargain with us for mutual arms reductions than there is to believe that ordinary opponents will respond in these ways; and, as I argued at the outset, that is not enough to bank on even in the ordinary case.) It is merely to say that the moral case for us engaging unilaterally in nuclear disarmament loses much of its force under such circumstances.

Thus, my case for unilateral nuclear disarmament depends on various empirical assumptions. I assume that there is only one other superpower besides the United States with a nuclear arsenal sufficiently large to produce whatever effects we fear from an all-out nuclear war and that that would remain true even after an American nuclear disarmament. Furthermore, I assume that, for now and the foreseeable future, none of the world's nuclear superpowers are either mad or genocidal. Granted these assumptions, unilateral nuclear disarmament combined with a strictly defensive conventional force posture on our part would render all-out nuclear war impossible; and such a policy is, therefore, morally mandatory on the argument I have here been discussing. Anyone wishing to reject this conclusion must find good grounds for rejecting either that moral theory or one of those empirical assumptions—and these must be grounds that do not lead to an even stronger indictment of nuclear weapons than my own.

Some might seize on my last pair of caveats for an excuse for maintaining a nuclear arsenal as a kind of hedge against the eventuality that a mad or genocidal opponent might someday emerge. That is, after all, a possibility—just the sort of possibility that has been plaguing me elsewhere in this essay. The difference, however, is this: we have long and sad experience of mad and genocidal rulers; and based on this experience, we have a pretty good basis for predicting them before they emerge or

---

perceived threat of imminent nuclear destruction, behave quite irrationally. No doubt it is asking too much for superpowers not to be "irrational" in those ways. But all my condition of "minimal rationality" requires is that a nuclear-armed superpower, facing no real threat to its strategic interests (and specifically no nuclear threat), should refrain from gratuitously destroying some other nation. That sort of rationality is, presumably, far more common.

at the very least for picking them out long before they have a chance to make any real trouble for us. In short, I am inclined to assume that we can see mad/genocidal leaders coming and rearm in time to deal with them, if nuclear arms or offensive conventional forces are indeed the right way to deal with them at all.[37]

IV

So far I have been discussing the problem of how best to pursue a single goal. Nuclear deterrence, remember, was defended by the Harvard Nuclear Study Group as a matter of taking a smaller risk of nuclear war to avoid a larger risk of nuclear war.[38] My conclusion has been that, owing to certain peculiar features of the problem (which may in fact be common to a wide range of other problems), the only justifiable strategy for pursuing that goal is to seek changes in the possibility of nuclear war occurring rather than merely changes in its probability.

However, avoiding nuclear war is not the only goal that nuclear deterrence is meant to serve. Among other things, it is also meant to prevent a nation from being conquered by tyrants; and that goal is not extensionally equivalent to the first. (The rule of tyrants might be avoided by going to nuclear war, after all.) It is typical for a policy to impinge on a multiplicity of independent goals in this way. Therefore, the prescriptions for possibilistic evaluation of policy options, couched above in ceteris paribus terms for the analysis of impacts on goals one by one, must be broadened so as to address situations in which one goal must be traded off for another.

I have little novel to say on the broader questions of how, whether, and when we should make trade-offs between moral goals. Here I shall confine myself merely to emphasizing that, even in a world of moral trade-offs, shifting from probabilistic to possibilistic reasoning still does make some practical difference.

Talk of trade-offs conjures up various images that fit comfortably with the probabilistic model. We ordinarily—and ordinarily rightly—think in terms of swapping a little more of this for a little less of that or a little greater risk of one evil for a little less of another. But if probabilistic reasoning has been deemed inappropriate where one of the goals (e.g., avoiding all-out nuclear war) is concerned, then there can be no question

37. Colin Gray, in commenting on this essay at the Aspen conference, replied that (a) we have not been very good at predicting crazy leaders very far in advance, judging from our recent experience with Iran and the Russian succession, and (b) it may take a decade or more to reorient our defense posture completely. I take the latter to be the more serious point: no leader, however mad or however well armed the nation, is in a position to initiate the holocaust on the first day in office. Certainly it is true that there are some defense plans it would take a decade to implement, but it is not at all clear that those are the only (or even the most likely) to deter a mad/genocidal opponent. Notice that, my possibilistic guarantee of no all-out nuclear war having failed in the face of a mad/genocidal opponent, we are back in the realm of deterrence and its concomitant probabilities now.

38. Harvard Nuclear Study Group, p. 15.

of swapping a little more risk of that for a little less of any other evil. In the context of that goal, "more" and "less" risk are meaningless terms. We are obliged to think instead in possibilistic terms and trade off that goal (if we do so at all) only in very large modal lumps. We can only ask how much it is worth (in terms of some other goal, such as avoiding tyranny) to have nuclear war made possible where it might have been made impossible or how much it is worth to have it made certain where it might have been merely possible. We cannot talk meaningfully in terms of incremental trades within those large modal lumps.

Of course, none of that is to deny that we should trade large lumps of one goal for some quantity (large or small) of some other goal. It all depends on the relative importance of each goal. We rightly trade away large lumps of relatively unimportant goals all the time. But the more important the goal, the more inclined we are to opt for the "all" branch of the "all-or-nothing" choice that such lumpiness forces on us.

This has some new and important implications for nuclear policy debates. Traditionally, ban-the-bombers have felt obliged to argue the immorality of making any trade-off at all between the goal of avoiding all-out nuclear war and any other goals, such as (merely) avoiding tyranny. Or, at the very least, they felt obliged to argue that the former was morally so terribly much more important that, even if trade-offs were allowed in principle, the latter goals would never have any real chance of trumping the former.

Both those propositions seem to me to be defensible, and from a surprising range of moral perspectives.[39] If the above arguments are correct, however, both claims are far stronger than strictly necessary in order for the goal of avoiding all-out nuclear war to prevail in this trade-off. All that is strictly necessary is that that goal be at least as important, morally, as all the countervailing moral considerations taken together. Then, given the peculiarities of the possibilities facing us, the goal of avoiding all-out nuclear war will automatically prevail.

The argument goes like this. The modal lumpiness inherent in the goal of preventing all-out nuclear war means that we must pursue that goal in an all-or-nothing fashion. If we opt for an all-out pursuit of that goal, then we can have that and more since there would still be some things we could do to promote—to some extent or another—those other goals. (Conventional deterrents or passive defenses may be more-or-less effective ways of avoiding rule by tyrants, even if we dismantle unilaterally our nuclear arsenal.)[40] If we opt instead not to pursue the goal of avoiding

39. Both consequentialistic and deontological arguments arguably converge on this result; see Robert E. Goodin, "Disarming Nuclear Apologists," *Inquiry*, vol. 28 (1985), in press.

40. Lackey, p. 205, rightly criticizes Kavka for equating unilateral nuclear disarmament with unilateral disarmament *tout court*. On the potential of nonnuclear defenses, see the Alternative Defence Commission, *Defence without the Bomb* (London: Taylor & Francis, 1983).

all-out nuclear war at all, then the most we could possibly hope to accomplish would be complete satisfaction of a set of goals which, taken together, are no more important than that goal we have forsaken. Assuming that goal is at least as important as all the others that might be competing with it, then the policy that offers us that much and more is clearly preferable to one that offers us that much or less. The upshot is that we would be obliged to strive, above all else, to avoid all-out nuclear war in the ways I have outlined.

No doubt some will deny that these circumstances do in fact obtain. But my argument requires far less than advocates of nuclear pacifism ordinarily assert and are ordinarily thought to need to assert if their case is to prevail. So even if my argument does not win over everybody, there is some reason to hope that it might attract a fair few who find the larger claims of nuclear pacifists to be just too implausible.

V

I conclude that the best thing that can be said on behalf of various pacifist proposals—unilateral nuclear disarmament and not being the first to launch a nuclear attack on the other's homeland, especially—is that they produce "moral certainties." This does not constitute an unconditional argument for either of those policies. Both are contingent on certain empirical assumptions. Neither does this quite constitute a conclusive case for such policies, given the need to make moral trade-offs. But it is hard to imagine what trades might tempt us if "the fate of the earth"— or any appreciable chunk of it—really did hang in the balance.

Strategic Defense, Deterrence, and the Prospects for Peace

Colin Gray

THE MORAL DIMENSION

Since President Reagan announced on March 23, 1983, that he intended to direct America's weapon scientists to explore the technical feasibility of providing defense against nuclear-armed ballistic missiles,[1] controversy has raged over what the President meant or should have meant. The President's speech and the subsequent implementing organization of a Strategic Defense Initiative (SDI)[2] does, of course, have major implications for foreign policy, for strategy, for the direction of military research and development, for budgetary allocation among possibly rival military functions, and eventually for force posture, but in essence the President outlined a moral vision. Indeed, in a speech on September 4, 1984, President Reagan termed his SDI a "moral obligation."[3]

The President appeared, at least, to envisage a path of military technological development that would enable the United States and its allies to transcend nuclear deterrence. One of the President's closest aides, science advisor George Keyworth, has explained Mr. Reagan's "ultimate goal" in the following words: "It's to reduce the military effectiveness of nuclear weapons *so dramatically* that they become *unreliable* for modern warfare" (emphasis in the original).[4]

1. "President's Speech on Military Spending and a New Defense," *New York Times* (March 23, 1983).
2. A Strategic Defense Initiative Office, with General James Abrahamson as director, was created in the spring of 1984. For unclassified summaries of the initial studies conducted in 1983, after the President's announcement, see Fred S. Hoffman, *Ballistic Missile Defenses and U.S. National Security, Summary Report,* prepared for the future Security Strategy Study (Washington, D.C.: Department of Defense, October 1983); Richard D. DeLauer (Undersecretary of Defense for Research and Engineering), *The Strategic Defense Initiative: Defensive Technologies Study* (Washington, D.C.: Department of Defense, 1984); Caspar W. Weinberger (Secretary of Defense), *Defense against Ballistic Missiles: An Assessment of Technologies and Policy Implications* (Washington, D.C.: Department of Defense, 1984).
3. Lou Cannon, "Reagan Defends 'Star Wars' Proposal," *Washington Post* (September 5, 1984).
4. George A. Keyworth, "Strategic Defense: A Catalyst for Arms Reductions," remarks to the Third Annual Seminar of the Center for Law and National Security (Charlottesville: University of Virginia, June 23, 1983), p. 1.

There is no reason to doubt that, although there are many strategic rationales that may be advanced in support of the SDI,[5] there is a set of moral issues that should not be neglected. What are these?

First, strategic arguments to one side for the moment, the SDI is intended, in President Reagan's words, "to save lives [rather] than to avenge them."[6] It can be argued that the U.S. government has a moral obligation to make what provision it is able to for the saving of American life—as an absolute value. The SDI could save millions, and possibly tens of millions, of American (and American-allied) lives and kill no Russians in the process. Considered in isolation from strategic offensive forces, strategic defense would constitute an inoffensive deterrent.

Second, supporters of the SDI argue that strategic defense offers the only promising path to nuclear disarmament on a very major scale.[7] To the uncertain degree to which nuclear weapons are, or should be, judged to be uniquely morally troublesome, the SDI offers a program of action to address such concerns. Nuclear disarmament will be politically and strategically feasible for the first time, so the argument proceeds, both because nuclear delivery vehicles simply will not "work" in the face of a complex architecture of layered defense—meaning that states will choose not to waste scarce resources on such obsolete systems—and because the risks of disarmament will be either removed or very substantially alleviated, given that strategic defenses would be able to negate the value of any nuclear weapons that had been stockpiled covertly.

Third, the point is made that strategic defenses, even of less than a "reliable and thoroughly effective" character, to employ Secretary of Defense Weinberger's ambitious phrase,[8] should greatly reduce the risk of nuclear war occurring. If the prospects for nuclear war are affected by calculations of net military advantage—that is to say, if strategic stability, technically defined, is important to discourage attack—then the deployment of only modestly competent active defenses has to threaten the assurance an attacker requires before deciding to begin a nuclear war.

Finally, the SDI offers a possible way out of the moral dilemma that saps and threatens the very legitimacy of Western security policy. The dilemma is that the West has a moral duty to defend humane values as well as a political duty to protect its citizens and their means of livelihood, but in a nuclear-armed world that moral duty to defend humane values reposes, in extremis, on the sustaining of a credible threat to trigger a

5. See Leon Sloss, "The Strategist's Perspective," in *Ballistic Missile Defense*, ed. Ashton B. Carter and David N. Schwartz (Washington, D.C.: Brookings Institution, 1984), pp. 24–48; and my contribution to chap. 11 of the same volume, "Reactions and Perspectives," pp. 400–409.

6. "President's Speech on Military Spending and a New Defense."

7. See Keyworth; and Colin S. Gray, "In Defense of Disarmament," *Bulletin of the Atomic Scientists* 40 (1984): 46–47.

8. Caspar W. Weinberger, *Annual Report to the Congress, Fiscal Year 1984* (Washington, D.C.: Government Printing Office, February 1, 1984), p. 30.

nuclear holocaust. A technologically mature SDI would enable the United States and its allies to defend their values against nuclear intimidation or even actual nuclear assault without, in the process, negating everything that they stand for.

Needless to say, perhaps, the claims and arguments introduced above form only one window on the SDI. To date, criticism of the SDI has focused heavily on technological and strategic theoretical matters and has tended to sidestep the ethical themes raised here. This is unfortunate because these ethical themes deserve both to be treated on their own terms and to be integrated into strategic debate. The ability of a democracy to sustain an adequate military posture year after year (for decades and even longer) is not unrelated to the popularly perceived compatibility of moral values with defense policy.

It is essential that readers be apprised of my attitude toward the moral issues outlined here and of my view of the interface between moral and strategic matters. The dominant moral argument of a consequentialist kind for the President's SDI is that strategic defenses may, indeed should, make a very positive and useful contribution to reducing the risks of war. Issues in this realm, relating to the somewhat general concept of stability, are examined through the bulk of the analysis that follows.

In deontological perspective, I agree with President Reagan that there is a firm moral obligation to explore the technical possibility of nonnuclear defensive weapons that might render offensive nuclear arms "impotent and obsolete," in the President's words. The prospects for success in this venture admittedly are uncertain, but they are certainly not wholly trivial. In short, the moral arguments of different kinds are, to my mind, mutually reinforcing. However, I am a professional defense analyst and not a moral philosopher: the discussion that follows addresses the consequentialist case for and against strategic defense.

STRATEGIC DEFENSE: HOW COULD IT WORK?

It is not the task of this essay to review the candidate technologies for the defensive mission. But because the policy debate over the SDI is interdicted at every turn by attitudes and judgments toward the promise of the technology, a brief treatment of the technical concept is essential.

For the purposes of this discussion, a ballistic missile may be considered as having five flight regimes: boost phase, postboost, mid-course, early terminal, and late terminal (immediately prior to detonation). The United States' SDI is exploring a wide, indeed a very wide, range of technologies that might be able to function in a layered fashion in each of the five flight regimes just cited. A complex, sequentially applied defense should work synergistically for enhanced effectiveness. A layered defense would function by cumulative attrition. If each layer of a five-tiered defensive architecture could impose 50 percent attrition on a Soviet attack of 10,000 nuclear warheads, 312 warheads should survive to detonate. The important point from the perspective of deterrence is that Soviet defense planners could not possibly know which 312 warheads would constitute this (statistical) "assured arrival" force.

There are, and can be, no authorities today on the subject of precisely what will be technically feasible, at what dollar cost, by any particular date in the future. However, provided one does not insist on perfection in defense, the technological prospects look distinctly promising. Terminal defense of hardened military assets with nuclear-armed interceptors could be implemented within this decade and with nonnuclear interceptors probably early in the 1990s.

The SDI would have strategic value at every stage of its construction. Ideally, one would like five layers of different defensive technologies deployed. But initial deployment of only one or two layers, in and of themselves, would introduce healthy new uncertainties for Soviet attack planners and thereby would help protect the strategic offensive forces that would be guarding the defensive transition. An evolving SDI should promote growing concern in Moscow, but that concern would be matched and, it is hoped, overmatched by the growing burden of difficulties that would be posed to Soviet target planners. The incentive to ambush the SDI should be thwarted by the diminishing prospects of success in such a desperate venture.

How well, or otherwise, the defense would be judged to function must depend on the scale of the burden it is allotted. A defensive architecture that, overall, could impose only 50 percent attrition would be very unattractive indeed were its job the defense of cities. In that event the defense probably would have little or no merit because it would have taken many billions of scarce dollars that could have been applied to funding more robust general purpose or strategic offensive forces. However, a 50 percent effective defense of military targets would be deemed very valuable for deterrence and even for defense if deterrence were to fail.

It is not very controversial to claim, for a prospective fact, that the strategic nuclear war-fighting assets of the United States—that is to say, the forces and their means of command, control, communications, and intelligence (C^3I)—could be accorded effective protection by ballistic missile defense (BMD) well before the end of the century. Terminal phase(s) defenses, perhaps with some assistance from mid-course intercept systems, could effect a drastic reduction in the strategic benefit of a surprise first strike.

Whether the United States could secure and maintain a technological advantage over Soviet strategic defense with an evolving and maturing SDI is problematical and, ultimately, a matter of secondary significance. The matter of primary importance is the relationship of net advantage between U.S. defense and Soviet offense, and between U.S. offense and Soviet defense.

The U.S. government has not sought to discourage the idea that the superpowers might negotiate partially cooperative defense transitions. However, although one can design arms control regimes that would prompt the early effectiveness of the SDI, the case for strategic defense cannot rest on such a fragile prospect. The SDI is a major move in the strategic arms competition, certainly is defined as such by the Soviet Union, and will be subject to hostile attention by every instrument of discouragement available to Soviet statecraft. Indeed, the Soviet campaign to abort the U.S. SDI already has begun—in the guise of repeated calls for the United States to enter a process of negotiation formally assigned the mission of "preventing the militarization of space," with the banning or restriction of antisatellite (ASAT) weapons as the first order of business. The strategic, tactical, and technological overlap between ASAT and BMD using space-deployed assets is such that only the most innocuous of agreements in the realm of "space arms control" would be compatible with an SDI that was moving beyond development into test activity. Satellites, as contrasted with missile warhead "buses" or ballistic reentry vehicles, are inherently very soft targets. A U.S. defensive transition relying heavily on space platforms for surveillance and target tracking, as well as for BMD weapon deployment, would have to have very robust defensive capability against Soviet satellites functioning as ASAT devices.

A cooperative defensive transition could, and should, be offered to the Soviet Union. It seems unduly fanciful to imagine such cooperation extending as far as technology sharing, but it certainly could take the form of a negotiated drawdown in strategic offensive force levels, keyed to agreed new defensive deployments. Given that the U.S. SDI would be designed to negate as much of the strategic value of Soviet missile forces as might prove technically feasible, it is reasonable to suppose that Soviet leaders will discern very compelling reasons to withhold any measure of cooperation that would have the net effect of assisting the putative war-fighting effectiveness of U.S. strategic defenses.

There is only one avenue of hope for Soviet cooperation with a United States determined to effect a transition to a defense-dominant (or at least, more substantially defended) world, and that lies in the admittedly distant prospect of the Soviet Union's calculating that it faces a future of major military disadvantage in the event that the offense-defense competition proceeds without formal regulation. In other words, Soviet defense planners would have to believe that, without an arms control regime, they confront, plausibly, a strategic condition wherein U.S. defenses could keep most Soviet offensive missiles out but wherein Soviet defenses could not keep many U.S. offensive missiles out. The point cannot be overstressed that the SDI, if it is to "work" vis-à-vis any of its possible strategic missions—the defense of hardened military and C^3I targets, the "light" area defense of urban America, or the "thick" defense of the American people—will have to work in most severe competition with a Soviet Union that will have strong incentives to seek the SDI's actual political and prospective military defeat.

THE ARGUMENT ABOUT STABILITY

By far the most frequent objection raised to the SDI thus far on policy grounds is that it—though "it," as emphasized throughout this discussion, is only a program of technology exploration for the next five years— will prove to be destabilizing. Stability, a notoriously elusive concept in strategic analysis, is understood, ultimately, to bear on the likelihood of war occurring. The moral consequentialist case for strategic defense rests on the validity of the proposition that defense, on balance, will strengthen the stability of deterrence. Before discussing the merits, or otherwise, of the instability charge against the SDI, it is useful to offer some brief illustrative points on the difficulties inherent in an analysis of stability.

First, there is no transnational, culture-independent science of strategy. Soviet military science does not address the various ramifications of the concept of strategic stability that pervade Western literature on arms control. Soviet military writings unequivocally equate (Soviet) war-fighting prowess with the strength of deterrence and, hence, with the prospects for peace.

Second, a backdrop to the strategic defense debate in the United States is the belief on the part of many senior policymakers that there is a growing mismatch between the foreign policy supportive burdens placed on U.S. strategic offensive forces and the capabilities, and hence the deterrence clout, of those forces. In other words there is an emerging instability in the largely offense-offense competition. An important motive behind the SDI is the hope that through the development of strategic defensive technology the United States may be able to achieve what would amount to a "knight's move" in the arms competition and escape from what is perceived (correctly or otherwise) as a losing tail chase on the offensive side. Very few among the people who debate strategic policy questions have drawn attention to the crisis in U.S. nuclear strategy that reposes in the fact that, technically, U.S. offensive forces cannot accomplish what high-level policy guidance, by and large reflecting a "denial of (Soviet) victory" theory of deterrence, requires of them.[9]

Third, it is worth noting that the dangers to peace that lurk, allegedly, in strategic instability are more than a little bereft of firm historical evidence in their support. Decisions for war tend to be supremely political in motivation and character. Moreover, even on the occasions when one can discern military considerations that argue for "war now"—as in 1914 for Austria-Hungary and Germany, and in 1939 for Germany again— the character of the state and the structure of its foreign policy problems,

---

9. The countervailing, or denial of victory, theory of deterrence, was developed in detail during the Carter administration. See Walter Slocombe, "The Countervailing Strategy," *International Security* 5 (1981): 18–27.

as it perceived them, were of more basic importance than were the technical details of believed military advantage (and impending disadvantage). No less significant was the fact that in both these cases the proponents of war had plausible, though obviously incorrect, theories of prompt victory.[10] It does matter which country enjoys a military advantage. A Soviet lead in the deployment of strategic defenses against ballistic-missile attack on a nationwide scale would have very different implications for international order from an American lead.

Among the many issues pertaining to stability that may be affected for good or ill by an evolving SDI, four in particular are isolated here for discussion. These issues are (1) the safe management of a defensive transition, (2) crisis instability, (3) arms race instability and arms control, and (4) alliance cohesion.

1. *Managing the transition: The danger of nuclear ambush.*—The argument is advanced that no matter how benign are U.S. policy intentions in terms of Western stability theory, the Soviet Union cannot but perceive the U.S. SDI as a threat to effect the functional disarmament of their offensive missile force and, thereby, to reclaim a meaningful strategic advantage. It follows, or may be held to follow, that the Soviet Union will not acquiesce pacifically in the reemergence of a condition of profound disadvantage. This argument comes in weaker and stronger variants. The weaker variant says that the Soviet Union will not permit U.S. deployment in space of platforms essential to the SDI mission. Soviet ground or space-based ASAT weapons will attack the space-deployed architecture of U.S. strategic defense.[11] The stronger variant of this argument holds that it would be stylistically uncharacteristic for the Soviet Union to take very limited measures against U.S. space assets because such action would, legally speaking, be acts of war, would lead promptly to the alerting of U.S. strategic forces, and could trigger a general war under conditions where surprise would have been forfeited. In other words, the prudent Soviet military planner, designing the Soviet reply to the emergence of space-based layers of U.S. strategic defense, will plan to go to war, not to go to war only in space.

Aside from the point that such action would elevate military-technical calculation to a level of policy determinism that would be culturally highly uncharacteristic, three replies are appropriate to the "ambush" charge. First, it will be essential that the United States guards its defensive transition with a modernized strategic offensive force posture always capable of denying the Soviet Union victory today. Even if the future looks sufficiently bleak to Soviet planners that they are driven to consider desperate remedies,

10. It should be recalled that in 1914 Germany had a plan for the defeat of France in forty days. See Steven Van Evera, "The Cult of the Offensive and the Origins of the First World War," *International Security* 9 (1984): 58–107.

11. See Charles Krauthammer, "The Illusion of Star Wars," *New Republic* 190 (May 14, 1984), pp. 13–17, p. 16.

the prospects of military success today must never be other than severely discouraging.

Second, SDI space assets must not be vulnerable to surprise attack. Soviet strategic culture may not find selective attacks on U.S. space platforms to be attractive, but it would be wise for the United States to minimize the technical feasibility of such an option. Proponents of the SDI concede readily that the potential vulnerability of space platforms is a problem area of the first order of magnitude.

Third, the uncertain rhythm of U.S. defense preparation would yield the Soviet Union several potentially attractive alternatives to war for the political interdiction of the SDI. Courtesy of legal and illegal technology transfer, of an arms control regime that could buy time for a high-technology catch-up, and of some tailoring of force posture evolution so as to stress U.S. defenses maximally, Soviet defense planners may conclude that a nominally awesome U.S. technological threat can at worst be alleviated and at best be deflected almost entirely.

Given the range of alternatives to war that the Soviet Union certainly would have and given the uncertainties that are inseparable from military action, the danger of a Soviet military reaction to U.S. deployment of space-based defenses would seem to me to be of trivial dimensions.

It should be understood that proponents and opponents of the SDI do not necessarily disagree on the causes of war in general or even on the estimated likelihood of an acute crisis developing over the next several decades. The SDI should contribute to reducing usefully candidate-attacker confidence in military success and certainly should provide an alternative to some offensive nuclear capabilities that otherwise might need to be provided to meet the performance requirements of U.S. strategy. Without opening the subject of the wisdom in current U.S. nuclear strategy, it is not difficult to appreciate that the scale of new U.S. ICBM deployments (MX and the small missile) could differ very markedly, depending on whether they were defended. To what degree the U.S. should design its offensive-force deployments to offset Soviet defensive developments is a complex issue. This essay envisages any such tailored design more as a bid to secure leverage for a negotiated offensive-force disarmament regime than as a determined endeavor to achieve a military advantage.

2. *Crisis instability: The SDI will increase perception of a "first strike bonus" and hence will encourage reciprocal fears of surprise attack.*—Strategic defenses that would be swamped by a massive coordinated first strike—say, on the order of 8,000–9,000 warheads—should perform very much better against the disorganized and heavily depleted remnant of forces that could be mustered and launched for second strike retaliation (perhaps 2,000–3,000 warheads). The crisis instability case against the SDI holds that, notwithstanding the new uncertainties introduced by the presence of ballistic missile defenses, both sides would know for certain that those defenses would function with the least effectiveness if they are assaulted by surprise and on a very large scale. Each side would calculate that the

other feared a first strike based on the expectation, or hope, that alerted defenses could hold the damage inflicted in a ragged strike-back down to a level compatible with victory (embracing the achievement of offensive and defensive [e.g., recovery] goals). This reciprocal fear of surprise attack would place the possibility of central war on a hair trigger, or so the argument alleges.[12]

This charge has some limited merit as abstract strategic logic. But it needs to be offset by the same generic point advanced under 1 above. Why would superpower decision makers be sufficiently confident in the military, and hence political, advantages of preemption against a heavily defended adversary as to decide to fight? It should be true that a first strike fares better against defenses than does a second strike, but so what?

Lightly deployed strategic defenses minimize the prospective scale of the first strike bonus, while heavy, multilayered defenses must raise the specter of defeat of the offensive in the minds of target-planning staffs and their policy masters. Logically, U.S. strategic defense deployment on a scale sufficient to provide the Soviet Union with an incentive to strike first (for fear of inability to penetrate if they strike second), should be on, or close to, a scale of estimated effectiveness where they would threaten the war-fighting missions of that putative first strike.

On balance, the crisis instability charge is not very persuasive. In a world of "leaky" but more than notional superpower defenses, no American President is going to unleash a central "exchange" because his military advisers are confident (how confident?) that the ragged Soviet strike-back would inflict "only" several tens of millions of casualties, prompt and delayed (what if those advisers were wrong and U.S. defenses failed catastrophically?). Soviet defense planners may be confident that they could "defeat" U.S. defenses, but they would know that even very "leaky" U.S. defenses must deny them anything other than a strictly statistical "assured arrival" force (as noted earlier). The logic of the first strike bonus would not prosper as military reality if, before they were over-whelmed, U.S. defenses had (1) bought time for the National Command Authorities to assess the Soviet attack and issue emergency action messages; (2) prevented or broken early pin-down attacks by Soviet submarine-launched ballistic missiles (SLBMs) against the ICBM fields; and (3) pur-chased vital minutes of escape time for strategic air command (SAC) bombers and tankers.

3. *Arms race instability and arms control: The SDI will overtake and overwhelm the extant framework of arms control.*—This charge holds that U.S. persistence with the SDI must stimulate Soviet incentives to augment and improve its offensive forces—thereby altering fatally the balance of incentives

---

12. See Union of Concerned Scientists, *Space-based Missile Defense* (Cambridge, Mass.: Union of Concerned Scientists, March 1984), pp. 79–84. The classic analysis of the strategic logic of "the reciprocal fear of surprise attack" is Thomas C. Schelling, *The Strategy of Conflict* (Cambridge, Mass.: Harvard University Press, 1960), chap. 9.

that render SALT/START negotiated restraints even a distant possibility—and, both in and of itself and by way of what it will encourage and license the Soviet Union to do with its very active BMD research and development programs, the SDI will ring the death knell for the ABM Treaty regime.

There is considerable merit in this charge, but it does not follow, necessarily, that damage to U.S. national security and to international order would be the consequence. For reasons that far transcend the limited mandate of this essay, the 1970s-style arms control process manifestly has failed. Whether or not one sees net merit in the U.S. weaponizing of the SDI and moving into a period of defensive transition in the 1990s, there is no doubt that the United States does not confront a simple choice between the SDI and negotiated arms control. In the interest of fairness in debate, one should acknowledge that the failure, or crisis, of arms control long predated President Reagan's resurrection of the idea of direct homeland defense in 1983.[13]

If arms race instability is understood to refer to a fairly rapid succession of weapon generations and to a context wherein the incentives for rapid change in the quality and perhaps quantity of weapons are fairly high, it is plain to see that the competition already is unstable and that the driving engine of this instability is the scope and momentum of Soviet offensive-force modernization. A principal motive for the U.S. SDI is the determination to restore stability in the deterrence relationship by exploring defensive technologies that might offset a Soviet strategic offensive modernization program that has been generally unaffected by the on-off arms control process of the past fifteen years.

The Soviet Union will, of course, seek to negate the strategic value of whatever the SDI might become. However, Soviet arms competitive effort cannot usefully be comprehended solely, or even very substantially, within the framework of (external threat perception/anticipation) stimulus-response models. Leaving aside the possibility that the Soviet Union may wish to break out of the ABM Treaty regime before the end of the century, critics of the SDI do their cause no good if they neglect to speculate over the probable future course of the offense-offense competition.

It is true to claim that a weaponized SDI would be inimical to the arms control negotiating process as it has been organized since the early 1970s. Nevertheless, to record that prospective fact is not to acknowledge that the SDI and arms control are incompatible. On the contrary, an impending defensive transition will compel the United States to rebuild its arms control theory and policy so that firm linkage between offense and defense is reestablished. It should be recalled that such linkage was firmly intended by U.S. policymakers during the course of the SALT I

---

13. See Richard Burt, "A Glass Half Empty," *Foreign Policy* 36 (1979): 33–48; Barry Blechman, "Does Negotiated Arms Control Have a Future?" *Foreign Affairs* 59 (1980): 102–25.

negotiations but that it withered on the vine as a consequence of U.S. unwillingness in the 1970s to face up to the strategic implications of the Soviet modernization programs that postdated SALT I ratification.

If arms control considerations—for example, retaining the ABM Treaty as *virgo intacta*—should preclude the United States from defending its retaliatory forces and their essential C^3I and from moving out to develop space-based, or deployable, defenses that might save tens of millions of lives, that would constitute a perversion of the goals of arms control, as they have long been understood.[14] In consequentialist perspective, there is nothing necessarily immoral about an arms race instability fueled in part by the introduction of new defensive weapons—particularly when the arms race is unstable today because the superpowers compete to prevent military disadvantage overwhelmingly in the realm of offensive arms.

4. *Alliance cohesion: The SDI is a threat to the political stability of the Western Alliance.*—NATO-Europeans are disturbed by the SDI for a mix of the following reasons, which readily translate into charges: (1) the SDI is (in the first instance) symbolic of a latent isolationist impulse in the American body politic and, if pursued, will encourage "decoupling"; (2) the SDI affronts the principle of equality of risk that is central to the political cohesion of NATO; (3) the SDI, as it matures, may encourage an American President to behave recklessly, in the (false?) belief that the U.S. homeland is very substantially defended; (4) the SDI threatens the very structure of the East-West arms control process and hence must serve to place yet another major obstacle in the path to better East-West relations; and (5) the SDI, in its Soviet analogue, will imperil the credibility of the national nuclear deterrents of France and Britain. This itemization by no means exhausts the litany of objections. Almost needless to say, European analysts have discovered the same alleged perils to crisis and arms race stability as have some American analysts, and they share the doubts popular, or fashionable perhaps, in the United States over technical feasibility and affordability.

The rush to fairly negative judgment that was characteristic, in general, of the initial NATO-European reaction to the President's speech of March 23, 1983, has been superseded by a more balanced appraisal—in good part as a consequence of the Reagan administration's proceeding beyond bare presentation of the moral vision and beginning to assemble a coherent consequentialist policy story for the near as well as the far term. From the perspective of strategic analysis, which, admittedly, is a perspective only of limited relevance to the defense politics of the alliance, the SDI should be found innocent of the charge of alliance disruption.

14. See Donald G. Brennan, "Setting and Goals of Arms Control," in *Arms Control, Disarmament, and National Security,* ed. Donald G. Brennan (New York: George Braziller, Inc., 1961), pp. 19–42; Thomas C. Schelling and Morton H. Halperin, *Strategy and Arms Control* (New York: Twentieth Century Fund, 1961).

Technically, the SDI will embrace exploration of strategic defense weaponry that could offer protection to the friends and allies of the United States. Just as the defense of selected military targets in the United States should reduce very usefully the calculability of the outcome of a central war campaign and must weaken candidate-attacker's confidence in success, so antitactical ballistic missile (ATBM) defense of critical military assets in Western Europe should strengthen deterrence in the theater.

Far from serving to "decouple" the United States from NATO-Europe, a U.S. defensive transition would, in the relatively near term, provide enhanced survivability for those U.S. strategic force assets that are Europe's last line of deterrence. With respect to the longer term, one need not be a strategic logician to appreciate that a United States capable of limiting damage to itself would be a United States that should be perceived by Soviet leaders as far more willing (than may be presumed to be the case today) to take extreme risks on behalf of allies. The only theory of damage limitation present in U.S. nuclear strategy today is the hope that the Soviet Union would choose to exercise self-restraint in its targeting. American policymakers are well aware of the strong probability that the Soviet Union, should it make the decision to go to war, will not recognize any of the "thresholds," and other refinements for escalation control, that have pervaded U.S. nuclear targeting doctrine since the issuance of National Security Decision Memorandum (NSDM) 242 in 1974.[15]

With respect to equality of risk, there is no doubt that the U.S. government will be very willing, indeed eager, to take its European (and Asian) allies into partnership to provide active defense for the Western world. However, even if BMD were not technically feasible for the NATO allies, which is not at all likely to be the case, that is no good reason why the American people should forgo whatever degree of direct defense they can achieve. Any European politician who sought to assert that because Western Europe could not be protected, North America should not be defended either, aside from the leap of logic in the assertion, would not and should not meet with a sympathetic hearing in the United States.

The charges that the SDI will encourage American recklessness is a familiar theme—Europeans want reassurance against nuclear war as well as deterrence of the Soviet Union.[16] All that one can say is that it is

---

15. See Benjamin S. Lambeth, "On Thresholds in Soviet Military Thought," *Washington Quarterly* 7 (1984): 69–76. On U.S. nuclear targeting policy, see Desmond Ball, *Targeting for Strategic Deterrence,* Adelphi Papers, no. 185 (London: IISS, Summer 1983); Jeffrey Richelson, "PD-59, NSDD-13 and the Reagan Strategic Modernization Program," *Journal of Strategic Studies* 6 (1983): 125–46; Leon Sloss and Marc Dean Millot, "U.S. Nuclear Strategy in Evolution," *Strategic Review* 12 (1984): 19–28.

16. A powerful statement of this thesis is Michael Howard, "Reassurance and Deterrence: Western Defense in the 1980s," *Foreign Affairs* 61 (1982/83): 309–24. The reassurance of nervous allies could, of course, entail the forgoing of taking military measures necessary for high-confidence deterrence of the Soviet Union.

exceedingly unlikely that any American President would overvalue the denial worth of strategic defenses that everyone will acknowledge to be "leaky." The argument that the SDI will damage the prospects for arms control and, ergo, for better East-West relations, has little merit. The formal process of East-West arms control is in deep crisis for reasons that have nothing to do with the newfound American interest in strategic defense. If the political will to improve political relations is present, then emerging strategic defense possibilities, far from fracturing settled "rules of the road" in the arms competition, will be appreciated as they should be, as providing long overdue opportunities for an actual nuclear disarmament regime.

The claim that a U.S. (and therefore Soviet) defensive transition, or addition, will threaten the credibility of the French and British national deterrents should be viewed as being largely disingenuous. Pending the genuine Europeanization of Western European defense, the last line of protection for security in Europe is the strength and character of the unilateral U.S. nuclear guarantee—a guarantee that can be robust only so long as Americans are content with the balance of associated risks and benefits.

CONCLUSIONS: DEVELOPING THE POLICY BASE

The cases for and against strategic defense admittedly are complex. The stridency with which affirmations of faith in American technological prowess are recorded is matched fully by the stridency of assertions alleging that strategic defense will never work—save in performance of relatively undemanding tasks. It is prudent to observe that the jury is still out on the subject of how well unbuilt defensive weapons will perform in the face of equally unbuilt countermeasures.

In ethical dimension, the SDI is intended to, and should, help save lives through strengthening deterrence for the prevention of war; it may provide, for the first time in the nuclear age, a suitable base of strategic security on which the superpowers could, should they so choose, construct an edifice of nuclear disarmament on a truly radical scale; and, in extremis, the SDI could save tens of millions of lives in the event of a war that neither a defense-heavy nor any other character of strategic posture and policy could deter. Among other possibilities, strategic nonnuclear defenses could be the deciding factor in whether or not "nuclear winter" effects were triggered.[17]

---

17. "Nuclear winter" is a hypothesis, no more and no less. Scientific enquiry, to date, has not, while further research almost certainly cannot, prove that detonation of 500–2,000 nuclear warheads for certain would catalyze nuclear winter effects. The nuclear winter danger is argued in Carl Sagan, "Nuclear War and Climatic Catastrophe," *Foreign Affairs* 62 (1983/84): 257–92; Richard P. Turco et al., "The Climatic Effects of Nuclear War," *Scientific American* 251 (1984): 33–43. The burden of proof, to be prudent, should rest on those who would argue that a nuclear war would not trigger a nuclear winter.

In the near term, certainly before the end of the century, strategic defense of retaliatory forces and their directing and supporting command and control should be able to strengthen the stability of the nuclear deterrence system. Given that no prudent, radical alternative to the deterrence system has emerged, the moral consequentialist case for strategic defense is virtually self-evident. In the medium-term future, perhaps early in the next century, it is distinctly possible that the superpowers may be driven by the strategic logic of increasingly effective defenses to agree to reductions on a large scale in offensive missile forces. Over the much longer term, as a distant possibility, thickly deployed and multilayered defenses might render offensive nuclear armaments functionally obsolete— they simply would not work. I am agnostic as to the likely reality of this distinct possibility, but I am respectful of, and sympathetic toward, an American president who affirms the quest for such defensive technology to be a "moral obligation."

There should be no confusion over the enduring fact that the causes of war, and hence the conditions for peace, lie in the political character of states and the nature of the political relations among states (and possibly in the nature of humankind itself), and only secondarily in the technical details of weaponry. Strategic defense, presuming that a defensive transition is prudently managed, cannot deliver "peace" and will not constitute anything even approximating a final move in the arms competition. But, on balance, it has great promise for contributing to the vital negative goal of the absence of war through its prospective aid to the deterrence system. That modest objective will be no mean achievement given the structure of political antagonism that divides East from West.

Space War Ethics*

Gregory S. Kavka

Throughout human history, advances in science and technology have transformed the means by which people are able to kill one another. Most notoriously, in fueling the long and gradual transition from thrown stone to nuclear-tipped missile, scientific knowledge has vastly increased the destructive power of weapons. In the last century, however, science has also produced a revolution in the basing of weapons. While weapons once had to be launched from (or just above) the ground or from ships on the surface of the sea, today's most advanced weapons are designed to be launched from planes high in the air, hardened silos under the ground, or submarines beneath the surface of the oceans. In fact, the capability to launch strategic nuclear weapons from any or all of these three locations is the heart of the "triad" posture, on which the defense systems of both modern superpowers—the United States and the Soviet Union—are based.[1]

It is now, or soon will be, technically feasible to turn the triad into a "quadrad" by placing offensive or defensive weapons in orbit in space. The possibility of doing so is being researched by the U.S. (and doubtless the Soviet) military and was mentioned in President Reagan's so-called star wars speech of Spring 1983.[2] Here I shall consider the question whether the development and deployment of such space-weapons systems are desirable from a moral point of view. In doing so, I shall discuss three sorts of space-based weapons systems: space-launched nuclear weapons, space-based antiballistic-missile (ABM) systems, and antisatellite weapons. Somewhat different issues are raised by the three systems, though similar conclusions will emerge in each case.

* I am grateful to John Ahrens, Robert Goodin, Russell Hardin, Karl Hufbauer, Carey Joynt, and Edward Regis, Jr., for helpful comments on earlier drafts of this paper and to the participants in and staff of the University of California Institute on Global Conflict and Cooperation summer seminar, June 1983, for stimulating my thoughts on this subject. An earlier version of the paper was presented at the Aspen Conference on the Ethics of Nuclear Deterrence and Disarmament, Aspen, Colorado, September 1984.

1. The U.S. triad has substantially more balance among the three elements than does that of the Soviets, who rely mainly on land-based missiles.

2. Ronald Reagan, speech of March 23, 1983, reprinted in *Department of State Bulletin* 83, no. 2073 (April 1983): 8–14.

To focus our attention on the special questions raised by space-based weapons, I shall for the most part assume that it is morally permissible for each superpower to practice some form of nuclear deterrence.[3] The question at issue is whether it would be morally desirable for some space-based weapons systems to replace, or be added to, one or more of the existing legs of the strategic triad. In posing this question, my main concern will be whether the United States should pursue rapid development and deployment of such systems instead of seeking to achieve or sustain treaties with the Soviets mutually banning them. My primary attention is on U.S. policy because it is our country and because it appears that the United States has, or soon will have, a substantial technological lead in developing space weapons.[4] (Most of what I say will, however, apply also to Soviet development and deployment of space weapons.) Mutual treaties banning such weapons seem the appropriate practical alternatives to consider since such treaties already exist for two of the weapons systems under consideration—ABMs and space-launched nuclear weapons—and negotiations have occurred between the superpowers concerning the third sort of system, antisatellite weapons.[5] Finally, I will largely limit my analysis to the foreseeable future, say, the next twenty years. For beyond that, the technical and political factors on which the current moral assessment is based may well have changed so much as to vitiate my reasoning and conclusions.

What moral principles or goals should be employed in evaluating space-based weapons? I propose three primary goals, of obvious moral importance, ordered in terms of their priority, as follows.

1. Nuclear war prevention.
2. Minimizing the damage suffered by humankind in a nuclear war, should one occur.
3. Preservation of economic resources for nonmilitary use.

Goals 1 and 2 are to be given priority over goal 3 because of the unprecedented amount of human death, suffering, and social disruption

3. For discussion of this assumption, see my "Some Paradoxes of Deterrence," *Journal of Philosophy* 75 (1978): 285–302, "Deterrence, Utility, and Rational Choice," *Theory and Decision* 12 (1980): 41–60, and "Nuclear Deterrence: Some Moral Perplexities," in *The Security Gamble: Deterrence Dilemmas in the Nuclear Age,* ed. Douglas MacLean (Totowa, N.J.: Rowman & Allanheld, 1984), pp. 123–40.

4. See Thomas Karas, *The New High Ground: Strategies and Weapons of Space-Age War* (New York: Simon & Schuster, 1983), chap. 6 (on antisatellite weapons) and chap. 3 (on military uses of the space shuttle). See also Union of Concerned Scientists, *Anti-Satellite Weapons: Arms Control or Arms Race?* (Cambridge, Mass.: Union of Concerned Scientists, June 30, 1983), sec. 2.

5. For texts of outer space and ABM treaties, see Jozef Goldblat, *Agreements for Arms Control: A Critical Survey,* Stockholm International Peace Research Institute (London: Taylor & Francis, 1982), pp. 159–62, 197–201. On antisatellite negotiations, see Karas, pp. 172–77; and Union of Concerned Scientists, pp. 1, 38, where the Soviet Draft ASAT (Antisatellite) Treaty presented to the United Nations in 1981 is discussed. It may be noted that as of

likely to result from any sort of nuclear war involving one or more superpowers.[6] This does not mean, however, that 3 is a trivial moral consideration. Given the likely enormous costs of building space-weapons systems, we have very good reason not to build them unless they really contribute to the attainment of goals 1 or 2. Goal 1, nuclear war prevention, is given priority over goal 2, damage limitation in the event of nuclear war, based on the plausible assumptions that nuclear war is not very highly probable (in the time period under consideration) if appropriate steps are taken to prevent it and that a nuclear war even with damage-limiting technology would likely cause many millions of casualties.[7] If nuclear war can be avoided, and would be a moral and human catastrophe if it occurred, our first moral priority must be the prevention of such a war.

An analysis of space-weapons development in terms of our three goals will be prudential as well as moral. For any risks of war engendered by a nation's pursuit of such weapons, and their economic costs, will be borne, in substantial part, by the citizens of that nation. The crux of my argument will be that for the United States to develop and deploy space weapons in the foreseeable future would be unwise because of the likely effects on ourselves as well as immoral because of the likely effects on all humanity. In developing this consequentialist argument against space weapons, I leave aside another sort of argument that might be raised. Such an argument contends that it would be somehow obscene or shameful for mankind to clutter the peace and serenity of outer space with weapons of war to settle our merely earthly conflicts. Such misuse and spoilage of the beauty of outer space might be seen as an evil in itself, independent of the suffering it might cause to human beings, and parallel to the evil of polluting and destroying the earthly environment in which we live. Now there may well be something to this argument, but I do not see how to develop it in any systematic way. Hence I shall limit my attention to the human risks and benefits engendered by space-weapons development.

---

this writing neither side has ever officially charged the other with violation of a U.S.-Soviet arms control treaty. See Ground Zero, *What about the Russians—and Nuclear War?* (New York: Pocket Books, 1983), pp. 199–200.

6. On the likely effects of one thermonuclear bomb exploding over a major urban area, see Office of Technology Assessment, *The Effects of Nuclear War* (London: Croom Helm, 1980), chap. 2. The limited effectiveness of damage-limiting technologies is discussed in Sec. II below. A general rationale for giving priority to war prevention over damage limitation is provided in my "Deterrence, Utility, and Rational Choice"; see esp. pp. 55–56.

7. In principle, attaining goals 2 and 3 to a very high degree (i.e., assuring, by inexpensive means, that there would be little loss of life and property in a nuclear war) would vastly reduce the importance of goal 1. But since such attainment of goals 2 and 3 is not possible in practice, goal 1 should be given highest (though not absolute) priority.

I. SPACE-BASED NUCLEAR MISSILES

One decision that the leaders of nuclear nations must make is how close to major population centers to base their strategic nuclear forces. The closer these weapons are based to cities, the more "collateral" damage the civilian population is going to suffer if an enemy makes a nuclear counterforce strike against one's strategic assets. On the other hand, awareness of this fact by a nation's potential adversaries may strengthen deterrence against such a counterforce strike by increasing the credibility of the threat to retaliate against the attacker. For while an adversary's leaders may dream that no retaliation might be forthcoming after a largely successful counterforce strike without massive civilian casualties, they know that the destruction of cities will produce a retaliatory response. Thus, in principle at least, there is a trade-off between minimizing collateral damage in a counterforce strike and most effectively deterring such a strike.

If leaders gave deterrence complete priority over damage limitation (and did not mind constantly reminding their citizens of the nuclear danger), they would locate their strategic missile and bomber bases in major cities. For the most part, they do not do this. Feeling that their threats of retaliation are sufficiently credible in any case, they seek to minimize potential civilian destruction in nuclear war (and domestic political problems in the present) by basing such weapons in relatively remote and unpopulated areas. The strategic missile–launching submarines carry this trend further: if they were attacked while at sea, there would be few if any civilian casualties (save for those resulting from the fighting spreading to other locations).[8] When we imagine nuclear missiles based in space (e.g., launched from orbiting platforms), we reach a virtual end to this range of possible basing modes designed to minimize collateral civilian damage in case of an attack on strategic systems.

This fact forms the basis of the main moral argument for space basing our strategic nuclear missiles: this would minimize civilian damage in the case of nuclear counterforce war, thus accomplishing goal 2. In the extreme case, if both sides space based their missiles, we could even imagine a full counterforce strategic war without a single human casualty!

A second argument for developing and deploying space-launched nuclear weapons is that strategic stability and deterrence would be strengthened by expanding from a strategic triad to a quadrad. The idea behind the triad is that deployment of more kinds of strategic systems makes one's deterrent less vulnerable to a technical counterforce break-through by the other side. Other nations' scientists might suddenly discover a means to neutralize one part of the triad, but it is much less likely that they would score such breakthroughs with respect to all three parts before we would have a chance to develop countermeasures. In addition, having

---

8. Since submarines, once located precisely, can be destroyed with conventional weapons, attacks on them would not necessarily spread nuclear fallout.

differently based weapons systems enormously complicates an adversary's planning for a possible surprise first strike; in particular, it may be nearly impossible to strike one sort of strategic system without thereby giving sufficient warning for another to be put to use. But both these considerations, as well as giving reasons for preferring a strategic triad to a system with only one or two legs, also give reasons for preferring a quadrad to a triad. Adding space-based missiles as a fourth leg of our strategic arsenal would further complicate the surprise-attack problem and provide greater protection against technological breakthroughs by the other side. If it thus increases strategic stability, is it not morally desirable?

The first point to notice about the case for space-based missiles is that the two arguments concern different options for the introduction of space-based nuclear weapons. The first argument involving counterforce nuclear wars without civilian casualties is plausible only if we suppose that space-based weapons would replace one or more legs of the current triad,[9] while the second argument stressing stability assumes that space-based nuclear weapons would be added to the current triad. Let us consider each possibility in turn, beginning with the more realistic one — addition of space-launched nuclear systems to the present U.S. triad.

There are two good reasons not to transform the current strategic triad into a quadrad by adding space-based missiles. It would doubtless be very costly. And it would have very little, if any, positive net effect on strategic stability. This is because, in the first place, the current triad is extremely stable already. Our missile-launching submarines alone carry more than enough weapons to devastate Soviet society many times over, and, according to knowledgable experts, they are very likely to remain invulnerable to attack over the next decades.[10] In addition, there is no way for the Soviets to attack our land-based missiles without giving enough warning for our strategic bombers to take off, while the bombers cannot be attacked without giving sufficient warning for the missiles to be launched.[11] Second, adding space-based missiles to our arsenal would

9. The possibility that a nuclear counterforce war in space would not spread to earth, given that both sides retain their relatively vulnerable land-based missiles, seems remote.

10. The Scowcroft Commission (Brent Scowcroft et al., *Report of the President's Commission on Strategic Forces* [Washington, D.C.: Government Printing Office, April 6, 1983], p. 9) writes: "Ballistic missile submarine forces will have a high degree of survivability for a long time." See also Harold Brown, "Strategic Forces and Deterrence," Arms Control and International Security (ACIS) Working Paper, no. 42 (Los Angeles: Center for International and Strategic Affairs, August 1983), pp. 19–21; and Kosta Tsipis, Anne Cahn, and Bernard Feld, eds., *The Future of the Sea-based Deterrent* (Cambridge, Mass.: MIT Press, 1973).

11. The most plausible surprise attack on bomber bases and missile silos has the former attacked by submarine-launched ballistic missiles from off the coast and the latter by ICBMs. But if the two sorts of missiles are launched simultaneously, there will still be time to fire the land-based missiles after the bomber bases are hit (since the ICBMs take much longer to arrive than the submarine missiles do). On the other hand, suppose the launches are timed so that both sorts of missiles arrive at the same time. Then satellite warnings of the

have some negative effect on stability since these weapons would likely possess two features that generally characterize "first strike" weapons— short delivery times and vulnerability. The delivery times would be short (compared to those of ICBMs and bombers) because the weapons would only have to travel down on their targets from overhead. And short delivery times are generally thought to provide one's adversaries with some incentive to adopt dangerous launch-on-warning procedures (at least for extreme crisis situations). Space-launched weapons systems would also likely be vulnerable since it would be costly or impossible to hide or harden them in the open space environment. (Indeed, as will be noted in Sec. III below, the United States and the Soviet Union have already begun to develop potentially effective antisatellite weapons.) But vulnerable weapons can destabilize a crisis situation since the enemy may try to strike them before they can be used and their possessor may try to use them before they can be struck. Thus, the marginal stability gains that adding space-based missiles to the triad might provide by decreasing the adversaries' technological breakthrough and surprise-attack capabilities must be weighed against the potential instabilities due to the first strike characteristics of such missiles. Given the stability and reliability of the present triad over the foreseeable future, it is very doubtful that the net stability effects of adding a space leg to the nuclear triad would be worth the great economic costs of doing so. In fact, should the Soviets make the mistake of introducing space-based nuclear missiles, we should probably not follow their lead but respond in a more stabilizing and less costly fashion by increasing the number of weapons in our current triad.

What about replacing one or more of the existing legs of the strategic triad with space-based nuclear missiles? If this were done, presumably the system most likely to be replaced would be land-based missiles since they are thought to be vulnerable because of their current lack of mobility and the increased accuracy of Soviet missiles. This replacement would have the morally relevant advantage of moving a substantial part of our arsenal further from population centers, so that people would not be destroyed along with the weapons if those weapons were attacked. But there are disadvantages to this replacement as well. It would probably be cheaper to decrease missile vulnerability by making our land-based missiles mobile than by moving them (or suitable replacements) to outer space.[12] Further, the civilian-protection advantage of such replacement

---

missile launches will allow the recallable bombers to take off before they are destroyed on the ground. Thus assurance of retaliation by one system or the other is obtained without resorting to launch on warning of unrecallable strategic weapons. This point is made in Scowcroft et al., pp. 7–8.

12. According to the *New York Times* (July 10, 1983, sec. 1), the Air Force has estimated the cost of the Midgetman mobile missile system at seventy billion over ten years. I have heard that experts at the Rand Corp. expect that any space-based system would be much more expensive than this, but apparently the idea has not been taken seriously enough for detailed cost studies to be undertaken.

seems uncertain for two reasons. A strategic war in space would be highly likely to escalate back to earth, with strategic bombers and submarine-launched missiles being used. And even if somehow confined to space, such a war could—for all we know—have substantial detrimental environmental and ecological consequences for human populations. Finally, and most important, if we deployed space-based nuclear missile systems, we would be violating the obligations our country undertook in signing and ratifying the 1967 treaty banning nuclear weapons in outer space. Unilateral violation or abrogation of an important arms control treaty such as this would have a variety of negative political effects that would likely increase the long-run probability of nuclear war between the superpowers. It would increase distrust, would bring other existing arms control measures into question, and would make future arms control agreements much more difficult to reach than they otherwise would be. For these reasons, any unilateral move into outer space strategic weapons would probably be more dangerous than the status quo is, even if these weapons replaced a vulnerable existing leg of our triad.

But what of a negotiated bilateral move into space-based nuclear weapons? This would be very hard to achieve if the systems to be replaced by space-based weapons were land-based missiles, for the Soviets rely on their land-based missiles as the heart of their strategic forces and are unlikely to agree on their replacement. What instead of a more balanced proposal to replace the entire triads on both sides with space-based missiles, so that a counterforce missile war would not directly endanger populations? Neither side would conceivably agree to this, for bureaucratic and political factors aside, it would open to each side the possibility of striking first against the other's vulnerable space missiles and using remaining forces for nuclear blackmail. Further, the prime advantage of space-based weapons—remoteness from civilian populations—is already shared in large degree by another strategic system, the nuclear submarines, which are nonvulnerable and already in operation (hence less costly to put into operation). If the superpowers were to agree to rely on one type of strategic system, submarines rather than space-based missiles would be the one to choose.

This brings us to a final possibility. There are, as we have noted, reasons involving strategic stability for not relying on only one type of strategic system. So it might be that a mutually negotiated "dyad" of submarine and spaced-based missile systems, with bombers and land-based missiles eliminated, would be preferable to each side's retaining only submarine systems. Such a dyad might provide both adequate protection against surprise attack and against technological breakthroughs and substantially reduced population losses in the event of counterforce warfare, compared to the present triad postures. Whether the space-sea dyad would be more desirable overall than the present arrangement is depends on whether the population protection the former might provide is enough to outweigh its economic costs and the increased risk of counterforce war (and subsequent escalation to city strikes) that might follow from leaders believing that the new basing modes make a winning counterforce war possible. The uncertainties surrounding this particular comparison are too great, I think, to allow us to draw any definite conclusion. But the considerations advanced above strongly suggest that this is the only use of space-based nuclear weapons that might make moral or prudential sense. It may be wise, and permissible, for the superpowers at some time in the future to negotiate to replace bombers and land-based missiles with space-launched missiles, thereby replacing our current triads with space-sea dyads. All other plans for nuclear missile deployment in space seem to increase either the risks of war or the costs of defense, or both (without producing sufficient compensating benefits), so as to render such deployments imprudent and immoral.

II. SPACE-BASED ABM SYSTEMS

Scientists are currently researching strategic defense systems that would be able to destroy enemy ballistic missiles in flight.[13] Orbital space lasers are key components in such systems. As indicated by President Reagan's star wars speech, the development of ABM systems is being given consideration at the highest political levels. There are a number of arguments one might give for developing and deploying ABM systems using space lasers. These defensive systems might protect us against nuclear attack by the Soviet Union and would likely be very effective protection against nuclear strikes from a third power or accidental Soviet launches of a small number of missiles. If the Soviets did not develop their own ABM system, our system—even if imperfect—would improve our "destruction inflicted/destruction suffered" ratio enough so that we would be more likely to prevail in a nuclear war if deterrence failed. And it would enhance deterrence by increasing Soviet uncertainties about the effectiveness of any nuclear attack they might contemplate launching.[14] If, on the other hand, both superpowers developed such systems, they would no longer have to rely on the prospect of "mutual assured destruction" (MAD) for defense. This would be desirable because MAD seems unlikely to deter war forever and because it involves each side in the morally dubious practice of threatening (and risking the lives of) the civilian population

13. See Karas, chap. 8; and Kosta Tsipis, "Laser Weapons," *Scientific American* 245 (December 1981): 51–57. See also the series of articles in *Aviation Week and Space Technology* (Clarence A. Robinson, Jr., "Panel Urges Defense Technology" [October 17, 1983], pp. 16–18, and "Study Urges Exploiting of Technology" [October 24, 1983], pp. 50–51, 55–57; Michael Feazel, "Europeans Support U.S. Space-based Systems" [October 24, 1983], p. 59; Clarence A. Robinson, "Panel Urges Boost-Phase Intercepts" [December 5, 1983], pp. 50–61) which purports to summarize the contents of the report of the Reagan administration's Defensive Technologies Study Team (Fletcher Committee) in which development of a multicomponent ABM system is recommended.

14. See Colin Gray, "Strategic Defense, Deterrence, and the Prospects for Peace," in this volume.

of the other side. In addition to these familiar considerations, there is a game-theoretic argument in favor of ABM systems which I shall now present.

Antiballistic-missile systems, to the extent that they work, prevent enemy missiles from reaching their targets. Hence an ABM system with a certain percentage of effectiveness is equivalent to a like percentage reduction in the other side's missile force, in terms of its effect on one's own vulnerability.[15] From this perspective, it seems that, rather than reducing their mutual vulnerability a certain degree by building ABM systems, the superpowers could achieve the same effect more cheaply and reliably by mutual reductions in offensive missile systems. This is true, but it requires cooperation and (at least tacit) agreement between the two sides because the incentives for unilateral action in an arms competition inhibit arms reductions. But when it comes to defensive systems, such as ABMs, incentives for unilateral action favor steps that will decrease vulnerability. Hence in a situation in which arms agreements are hard to come by, building ABMs might be the only feasible way of reducing mutual vulnerability.

Game matrices may be used to illustrate the substance of this argument. Matrix A represents the choices each superpower faces in deciding whether to maintain its status quo arsenal (S.Q.) or disarm by dismantling a certain percentage of its missiles (Disarm). In each quadrant, left-hand numbers represent U.S. payoffs (in terms of preference order), and right-hand numbers represent Soviet Union payoffs. In the standard way, it is assumed that each side's ordering of outcomes from most to least preferred is: other's unilateral disarmament, mutual disarmament, mutual status quo, one's own unilateral disarmament.[16]

The result is a familiar Prisoner's Dilemma matrix with S.Q. being the dominant move for each side, so that if each acts rationally and independently, the mutually preferred mutual disarmament outcome is not achieved. Matrix B represents the choice of each superpower between maintaining its status quo and defending itself by deploying an ABM system in addition to its current arsenal (Defend). It is assumed that each

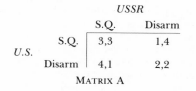

		USSR	
		S.Q.	Disarm
U.S.	S.Q.	3,3	1,4
	Disarm	4,1	2,2

MATRIX A

15. For present purposes, I ignore the real possibility that deploying an ABM system will influence the other side's targeting policy. For discussion, see my "Nuclear Deterrence," sec. 4.

16. I here ignore the possibility that mutual disarmament beyond a certain level may be dispreferred because it is less stable, since the same applies to mutual defense.

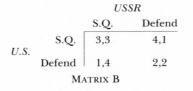

USSR

		S.Q.	Defend
	S.Q.	3,3	4,1
U.S.			
	Defend	1,4	2,2

MATRIX B

side most prefers being the only side defended[17] and least prefers only its adversary being defended. Each, however, prefers mutual defense to the mutual status quo because of the reduced vulnerability entailed by the former. In matrix B, Defend is the dominant move for each. Comparing the two matrices, we see that of two outcomes that may equivalently reduce mutual vulnerability—mutual ABM building and mutual disarmament—one may be achievable by rational unilateral action while the other is not. This is the most powerful theoretical argument I know which favors development of ABM systems, of which space lasers are among the currently most promising types.

Arguments against U.S. development of space-laser ABM systems differ according to whether one considers unilateral development or cooperative development with the Soviets. Let us first discuss unilateral development. A major objection to space-laser ABM systems is that they would not work very well. A number of major technical problems confront such systems: having enough laser weapons in orbit to have Soviet missiles always in target range, being able to destroy large numbers of fast-moving missiles in a very short time span, having very large energy sources to power the lasers, having large accurate mirrors in orbit to focus the laser beams, and having sufficient surveillance and computing capacity to identify and target missiles and to identify and retarget missiles that survive the first laser salvo.[18] In addition, such systems would be quite vulnerable to countermeasures such as coating of missiles to deflect laser energy, physical attacks on the components of the system, or overloading the system's capacity by building more offensive missiles.[19] In addition, a different system with different capabilities would probably be needed to protect

17. Even a superpower with purely defensive motives would prefer being the only side defended to having its opponent defended as well. For the absence of defense on the other side ensures the effectiveness of one's own deterrent and may also increase one's political bargaining power.

18. See Tsipis; and Richard L. Garwin, "Weapons in Space: Are We on the Verge of a New Arms Race?" IBM Research Report (February 25, 1981), pp. 9–12. The Fletcher Committee Report apparently acknowledges these difficulties but thinks they are ultimately solveable. See, e.g., Robinson, "Study Urges Exploiting of Technology," pp. 51–52.

19. See Tsipis, pp. 56–57. The Fletcher Committee Report deals with hardening (see Robinson, "Study Urges Exploiting of Technology," pp. 51, 56) but does not appear to have solved the problem of overloading, as its proposals are "predicated on providing the capability to defend the U.S. effectively against a near simultaneous launch of 1,000 ballistic missiles by the USSR" (Robinson, "Study Urges Exploiting of Technology," p. 56). The game-theoretic argument sketched below suggests that development of such a defensive capability would lead to the Soviets possessing forces capable of making a larger strike.

against bombers or cruise missiles carrying nuclear weapons. And even if technological advances were able to solve the specific problems currently at hand, ABM systems with (or without) substantial space-based components are unlikely to provide adequate defense of the United States for two reasons: very nearly 100 percent interception rates are needed for adequate defense (because of the enormous destructive power of nuclear weapons) and the Soviets are likely to find partly effective countermeasures to each advance we make.[20]

If, despite these considerations, the United States proceeded to develop and deploy space-based ABMs, it would be enormously expensive. Published estimates of the cost range from around one hundred billion to half a trillion dollars, and it does not appear that these estimates take account of needed replies to all likely Soviet countermeasures.[21] There would also be the political cost of unilateral abrogation of the 1972 ABM treaty, which would include worsened relations with the Soviets that might well increase the risks of war. Nor, if we maintained our strategic deterrent as a backup (which would be both likely and prudent, given that the ABM system would be untested in combat and unlikely to work perfectly), would we be escaping whatever moral opprobrium might attach to our threatening Soviet civilians with nuclear destruction. Finally, even if a space ABM system were unlikely to be fully effective, it might seem to be effective enough to place its unilateral possessor in a position to neutralize his adversary's nuclear arsenal and practice nuclear blackmail. Fear of this situation might lead the other side to race to deploy its own ABM system first, to increase its nuclear forces massively, to issue an ultimatum against deployment of the system, or even to make a preemptive strike before the system is able to go into operation.[22]

But what of the game-theoretic argument that ABM systems are desirable precisely because they allow reductions of mutual vulnerability by rational unilateral actions? We are now in a position to see what was wrong with that argument—it considered too few options on each side, either doing nothing, building ABMs, or disarming. But even putting

20. For an argument along these general lines, see Herbert York, *Race to Oblivion* (New York: Simon & Schuster, 1970), pp. 190–91, 205–6. To achieve a high kill rate, the Fletcher Committee envisions a multilayered ABM system that can attack ballistic missiles in their boost phase, postboost phase, midcourse phase, and terminal (target-approaching) phase. Still, according to Robinson, "Study Urges Exploiting of Technology," its report acknowledges that "it is not technically credible to provide a ballistic missile defense that is 99.9% leak proof" (p. 51).

21. Robinson, "Study Urges Exploiting of Technology," p. 59; and Karas, p. 186. After reading the description of the proposed multilayered system, it is easy to believe that the actual cost might reach (or exceed) the higher figure.

22. Concern about the dangers involved in a superpower race to complete an effective ABM system has been expressed by such diverse sources as a former National Security Council staff member whom I heard speak and a writer in a booklet produced by an antinuclear protest group (see Jim Heaphy, "Militarization of Space," in *International Day of Nuclear Disarmament* [Berkeley: Livermore Action Group, 1983], p. 67).

aside the drastic alternatives of making a strike or an ultimatum, there is still the option of building more offensive nuclear systems and/or taking countermeasures against the other side's actual or potential ABM systems. This new option is represented by the strategy choice "Arm" in matrix C.

This matrix was constructed on the basis of certain plausible technical-strategic and motivational assumptions. The technical assumptions are that:

T1. The status quo, both Defending, and both Arming are all conditions of strategic equality.
T2. If one side Defends (builds ABMs) and the other Arms (spends an equivalent amount on offensive systems and countermeasures), the latter gains a relative advantage.[23]
T3. If one side remains at the status quo, the other gains a greater relative advantage by Defending (building ABMs) than by Arming.
T4. If one side Arms, it gains a greater relative advantage if the other remains at the status quo rather than Defending.

Assumption T2 is plausible because of the great expense of ABM systems compared to the expense of building more offensive systems and taking countermeasures (e.g., coating missiles). Assumption T3 is plausible because the prospect of preventing your opponent from being able to retaliate effectively yields a greater strategic advantage than does an extra margin of offensive overkill capacity.[24]

The three motivational assumptions are:

M1. Each side prefers relative strategic advantage, equality, and relative disadvantage, in that order.
M2. Each side prefers a greater relative advantage to a lesser one and a lesser relative disadvantage to a greater one.
M3. Among equal outcomes, each side prefers lesser mutual vulnerability to greater.

		USSR		
		S.Q.	Defend	Arm
U.S.	S.Q.	5,5	9,1	8,2
	Defend	1,9	4,4	7,3
	Arm	2,8	3,7	6,6

MATRIX C

23. This relative advantage may not be worth very much in war-fighting terms if both sides retain an overkill capacity. Nonetheless, both superpowers act as though strategic advantages are worth having, even when there is overkill on both sides, and such strategic advantages may in some cases yield political benefits.

24. Note that if we assume the opposite of the third assumption, that Arming yields a greater relative advantage in this case as well, Arming is then a dominant strategy. We would thereby reach more directly the conclusion offered below: that Arming is the rational strategy for each to follow.

Combining all seven assumptions leads to matrix C.[25] There is no dominant strategy in this matrix, in contrast to matrices A and B. (Arming is not dominant because, if the other side remains at the status quo, one would prefer to Defend.) But the Arm-Arm outcome is the only equilibrium— that is, the only outcome such that neither party would prefer to depart from it unilaterally. Therefore if we think of the parties to the situation monitoring one another's behavior over time and switching their moves to obtain more preferred positions, then (in the absence of explicit or implicit cooperation) the long-run tendency will be for them to move from the other sections of the matrix to the bottom right-hand corner. (For example, if each initially plans to Defend and perceives that the other so plans, either can gain [i.e., move from a fourth preference to a third] by switching to Arm. But the other then gains [i.e., moves from a seventh preference to a sixth] by Arming as well.) And they would remain there in the bottom right corner at the point of maximum mutual vulnerability, despite the outcome being merely the sixth preference of each.

Lest it be thought that this game-theoretic reasoning is only of theoretical interest, it is worth noting that it accurately reflects the outcome of an earlier stage of the nuclear arms race. In the 1960s and early 1970s, the superpowers faced an essentially similar choice between the status quo, building ABM systems (Defending), and proceeding with the development of newer and more effective offensive weapons, especially multiple-warhead missiles (Arming). The result was mutual abandonment of the more expensive and less reliable defensive systems and continuation of the race in offensive arms—or, in terms of matrix C, a move to the lower right-hand corner.[26]

That the Soviets, at least, are aware of the possibility of moving toward the lower right-hand corner again, in the present context, is suggested by this comment on space ABM systems by the director of

25. Let '1' through '9' represent, for a given party, the outcome in matrix C which corresponds to that number (in preference order) for that party. (For example, for the United States, '7' stands for U.S. Defends and USSR Arms.) That the outcomes are preferred in the order indicated in matrix C may be seen as follows: T3 and M2 imply that 1 is preferred to 2 and 8 to 9; T4 and M2 imply that 2 is preferred to 3 and 7 to 8; T1, T2, and M1 imply that 3 is preferred to 4 and 6 to 7; and T1 and M3 imply that 4 is preferred to 5 and 5 to 6.

26. I am not claiming that the decision makers saw the alternatives in precisely these terms or that they explicitly reasoned in game-theoretic terms. My contention is that the underlying structure of that situation was like that of the present situation and can roughly be represented by matrix C. The extent to which multiple-warhead missiles were designed as countermeasures to actual or possible ABM systems is a matter of some controversy. See Graham Allison, "Questions about the Arms Race: Who's Racing Whom? A Bureaucratic Perspective," in *Contrasting Approaches to Strategic Arms Control*, ed. Robert Pfatzgraff, Jr. (Lexington, Mass.: D. C. Heath & Co., 1974), pp. 31–72; Herbert York, "Multiple Warhead Missiles," *Scientific American* 229 (November 1973): 18–27; and Ted Greenwood, *Making the MIRV: A Study of Defense Decision Making* (Cambridge, Mass.: Ballinger Publishing Co., 1975).

Moscow's Institute of Space Research: "It will always be possible to create less expensive countermeasures for such a system or to increase the number of attackers."[27] This comment also reveals the fatal flaw in the argument—mentioned earlier—that unilateral ABM development would improve our destruction capacities, relative to our opponent, in the event of nuclear war. Once we take into account likely Soviet countermeasures, it is doubtful that even unilateral development of an ABM system would significantly improve our chances of prevailing (in any meaningful sense) in a nuclear war. What might happen, however, is that unilateral development of an ABM system would make its possessors mistakenly feel invulnerable. And this could lead to a nuclear war in which neither side prevails, or survives.

Admittedly, the possibility of overloading, or building countermeasures to, an ABM system does not refute the argument that such a system would enhance deterrence by introducing additional uncertainties into Soviet strategic plans and calculations. For the Soviets would not know, ahead of time, how well their extra missiles and countermeasures would fare against a U.S. ABM system. But given the high survivability of U.S. strategic forces at present and in the forseeable future (as noted in Sec. I), it is doubtful that we need these extra uncertainties to deter Soviet strategic attack. Thus any marginal increase in effective deterrence by uncertainty, which an ABM system might provide, would likely be outweighed by the increased dangers of war which it would engender: possible Soviet preemption against the defense system or its possessors, war emerging from increased political tensions created by an accelerated arms race, and so on.

In summary then, there are numerous dangers inherent in the United States's attempting unilaterally to develop and deploy space-based ABM systems. One possibility is a highly dangerous and costly race between the United States and the Soviet Union to assemble the first such system. Another possibility is that unilateral development will produce a false sense of invulnerability which could result in war. Perhaps the most likely outcome of all is that pursuit of such systems will never result in deployment of effective ABM systems but will instead stir the development of yet greater and more sophisticated offensive arsenals on both sides, thus wasting valuable resources while actually increasing mutual vulnerability to nuclear destruction. It seems highly unlikely that protection against improbable third-power or small accidental attacks is sufficiently important to outweigh these great costs and dangers.

What of the possibility of U.S.-Soviet cooperation in developing space-based ABM systems, as hinted at by President Reagan in an interview with reporters soon after his star wars speech? This would seem to avoid the political and competitive problems associated with unilateral devel-

27. Robert B. Cullen and John J. Lindsay, "A Shield or a Sieve?" *Newsweek* (June 25, 1984), p. 36.

opment while promising to result in decreased mutual vulnerability and protection against third-party and accidental attacks. And surely it would be a much less objectionable approach than is unilateral development and its attendant risks. But even bilateral cooperative development of space-based ABMs has its disadvantages. There is always the danger of cooperation breaking down partway through the process and resulting in a highly dangerous race with each side attempting to finish and deploy its own ABM system first. Also, for the bilateral approach to work effectively, each side must expect that the other will not engage in secret parallel research to develop counters to the system or to enable a unilateral "breakout" leading to first deployment of an effective system. These expectations may be based either on a belief in the other side's reliability and trustworthiness or on a belief that the other side is farsighted and rational enough to see that seeking short-run unilateral advantage in this manner is likely to yield bad consequences (e.g., a fiercer and more dangerous arms race) for both sides in the long run. But if the two sides have, or can develop, this much faith in each other's reliability or rational farsightedness, they can probably decrease mutual danger and vulnerability more cheaply by mutual reductions in offensive systems and improved political relations.

Supporters of cooperative bilateral ABM development might reply in two ways. They could claim that offensive reductions beyond a certain point may decrease strategic stability by leaving each side without an "assured destruction" second strike capacity.[28] Also, successful bilateral ABM development would provide protection against third-party and accidental launches that would not be provided by offensive reductions. But the point about strategic stability applies to ABM systems as well. A first strike on one's ABM system and offensive strategic systems might well leave one without sufficient assets to penetrate significantly the striker's own intact ABM system. So each side possessing an ABM system that was highly effective but vulnerable to attack could actually increase strategic instability. The point about third-party and accidental launches is well taken. But given the massive costs of space-based ABM systems, it seems likely that equal or greater protection against these contingencies could be attained by spending these funds instead on improving warning and command and control systems to prevent accidents and on nonproliferation

28. Assuming a fixed percentage of effective missile "kills" by a first-striker, a second-striker's retaliatory capacity will be a fixed percentage of his original arsenal. But with small enough arsenals, this may not be enough to impose "unacceptable damage" on the first-striker. (See Thomas Schelling, *The Strategy of Conflict* [London: Oxford University Press, 1963], pp. 235–37.) A variant on the argument in the text is presented in Gray, where it is suggested that ABM systems reduce the risks of mutual disarmament by protecting each side against the negative effects of covert stockpiling of weapons by the other side. But at high levels of nuclear armament, such stockpiling represents little threat. At very low levels of nuclear weapons possession, the argument may make sense. But then the rational course of action is to reduce offensive arms to such levels and then cooperatively build (smaller and cheaper) ABM systems.

and Third World aid measures to decrease the likelihood of third-party attacks.

All things considered then, it seems best in the real world to stick by the ABM treaty for the foreseeable future and to pursue cooperation with the Soviets in the direction of reducing mutual vulnerability by reducing offensive arms. If such reductions are obtained and political relations are improved enough to make a cooperative ABM development program feasible, then it might be permissible to proceed with such a program, for example, if the third-party attack danger has grown more serious or if domestic politics make mutual ABM development—but not further offensive reductions—achievable. What we must be extremely wary of, however, is that the vague prospect of bilateral ABM development will function, in public debate, to justify unilateral pursuit of space-based ABM systems "in the meantime." Given the severe dangers of attempted unilateral ABM development discussed above, it would be neither prudent nor moral to proceed with such an attempt, either as a means of gaining a unilateral strategic advantage or as a means of encouraging Soviet participation in a cooperative development program.

III. ANTISATELLITE WEAPONS

Each superpower currently maintains a number of military satellites in orbit around the earth which gather and send back data on the other side's military deployments and programs. Each is also in the process of developing antisatellite (ASAT) weapons designed to destroy the other's space assets. The Soviets are generally believed to have tested a crude ASAT weapon capable of destroying low-orbit satellites.[29] And the United States is developing a more sophisticated system that should be able to destroy high-orbit satellites as well.[30] Thus, in the near future, the prospect of space wars may not be confined to science fiction movies.

Antisatellite weapons are war-fighting machines, designed to destroy enemy intelligence and communications equipment in orbit around the earth. In view of this, I can imagine only three morally respectable arguments for their development. The first is that they could perform a damage-limiting role during a nuclear war by depriving an attacker of the information he would need to employ his remaining strategic weapons most effectively (e.g., by depriving him of confirmation of targets being hit, it might force him to hit them again rather than go after new intact targets). Second, should the Soviets suddenly abrogate the space or ABM treaty and place nuclear weapons or defensive laser systems in orbit, we would be able to neutralize their potentially dangerous unilateral advantage with an ASAT capability. Finally, since there is no ASAT treaty between the United States and the Soviet Union, it might be claimed that we need our own ASATs as bargaining chips to get the Soviets to agree on a

29. See Karas, pp. 149–50.
30. Karas, pp. 151–57.

mutual ban or as defensive weapons able to destroy Soviet ASATs that might threaten our satellites.

In response to the first argument, it may be noted that once a superpower nuclear war has started, if it ever does, by far our best hope for survival will be a quick termination of the war by political decision after an initial limited exchange.[31] Given the sizes of the current nuclear arsenals and the destructive power of the individual weapons, any attempt to protect ourselves by destroying the enemy's ability to retaliate or its capacity to monitor our own activities would invite a spasm attack of all its remaining weapons and would be virtually suicidal. Leaving the other side's surveillance capacities intact so that its leaders will be able to observe our very limited response and leaving its communications facilities (including satellites) intact so that leaders could communicate "stop" or "hold" messages to their strategic commanders would be a much more prudent course of action. (This is not to say that I am optimistic that nuclear war could be controlled in this way; it is rather that the other damage-limitation options seem even less likely to succeed.)

The second argument for ASATs concerns insurance against a Soviet breakout in space-based nuclear weapons or ABM systems. But a Soviet breakout to a quadrad with a space leg would be no immediate danger, in any case. And both offensive nuclear weapons and ABM systems in space are currently controlled by treaties which both sides are generally thought to have adhered to quite well in the past. Yet deployment of an ASAT system could threaten future adherence to the ABM treaty, as the other side might not be able to distinguish antisatellite weapons from space weapons with an ABM capacity. Suppose, however, that this possibility worries us less than does the possibility that, in the absence of further control and verification mechanisms, the Soviets will make a space-laser breakout. Then we should first seek to negoitate such further mechanisms rather than embarking on a full-scale race in ASAT weapons. For such weapons, in addition to their likely great cost, would have a negative effect on strategic stability because of their capacity to destroy the other side's early warning satellites. In virtue of this capacity they constitute a kind of first strike weapon, and their deployment would introduce at least two new potential sources of nuclear war—escalation of orbital weapons warfare or war initiation resulting from misinterpretation of satellite breakdown as being the result of enemy ASAT attack which is part of a strategic first strike.

If ASAT weapons are destabilizing, expensive, and likely to make early nuclear war termination even harder than it is at present, everyone would be better off if neither side deployed them. The third argument above accepts this judgment but contends that U.S. ASAT development is necessary to counter or hedge against Soviet development and to provide

---

31. See Thomas Schelling, *Arms and Influence* (New Haven, Conn.: Yale University Press, 1966), pp. 128–29, 204–20.

us with bargaining chips in ASAT negotiations. But surely the most promising way of protecting our space assets would be not to build our own ASAT or anti-ASAT weapons but rather to restart with the Soviets the ASAT treaty negotiations that died during the Carter administration. Successful negotiation of a treaty, along the general lines of the twelve-article draft currently being circulated by the Union of Concerned Scientists,[32] would likely provide much more reliable protection for our early warning and intelligence-gathering space systems than would an all-out ASAT race with the Soviets. Nor should we delay such negotiations to allow ourselves to achieve a clearly superior ASAT system to use as a bargaining chip. For the past history of arms-control negotiations suggests that situations of inequality in development of a kind of weapons system are not propitious for achieving mutual superpower bans on such systems. Most notably (and most regrettably), a ban on MIRVs was not achieved in SALT I partly because some on the U.S. side did not want to give up the advantage we then held in MIRV development and testing and because the Soviets were reluctant to accept being frozen into a permanent inferiority in MIRV technology.[33] But SALT I negotiators did limit ABM systems, where there was rough equality—in the form of small Soviet deployments conjoined with prospects of a much more advanced system being deployed by the United States in the rather near future. This is roughly analogous to the current situation regarding ASAT weapons, suggesting that good-faith efforts to negotiate a mutual ban on ASATs might well succeed at the present stage of technological development.

Though the details of the arguments are different in all three cases, we have reached similar conclusions about the development and deployment of space-based nuclear missiles, ABM systems with substantial space-based components, and ASAT weapons. A race with the Soviets to develop any of these systems is likely to be very expensive and to increase significantly the risks of nuclear war without providing a realistic prospect of limiting destruction to an acceptable level should such a war occur. Thus in terms of the goals set out at the beginning of this article and from both moral and prudential perspectives, it would be much preferable, for the foreseeable future, to sustain the treaties banning nuclear weapons and ABM systems in space and to try to conclude a treaty banning ASAT weapons. (At the same time, it would be wise to monitor Soviet development and testing closely and to continue limited research ourselves on ABM systems and especially the protection of

32. Union of Concerned Scientists, app. 1, pp. 33–34. The Union of Concerned Scientists favors an immediate ban on ASAT tests, followed by negotiation of a treaty banning the weapons themselves.

33. On U.S. decision making on MIRV, see Seymour Hersh, *The Price of Power* (New York: Summit Books, 1983), chaps. 12, 13. On the Soviets, John Newhouse, *Cold Dawn: The Story of SALT* (New York: Holt, Rinehart & Winston, 1973), writes: "Moscow wondered whether Washington would seek by some such means [i.e., a MIRV ban or moratorium] to monopolize this technology after having mastered it" (p. 167).

missiles against them so as to minimize the prospects of a dangerous and destabilizing Soviet breakout on such systems. We must take care, however, not to allow such programs to become so large as to generate uncontrollable institutional and political pressures for ABM deployment.) In the longer run, as noted above, negotiated mutual replacement of land-based missiles and bombers by space missiles (to reduce civilian vulnerability) or co-operative mutual development of spaced-based ABM systems (to guard against accidents and third-party attacks) might be permissible.

There is a general theme lying behind these conclusions. The problems posed by the existence of nuclear weapons in a world of political conflict will not be solved by purely technical means. In Genesis we are told that God created the heavens and the earth. Expanding our arsenals into the heavens will not safeguard the earth or human civilization. We must seek earthly solutions to earthly problems.

Controlling Military Technology*

Karl Lautenschläger

The specter of a general nuclear war destroying entire societies and possibly most of humanity has led to the search for ways to prevent such a war. The magnitude of the disaster that would come with a global nuclear war clearly justifies not only concern but also continued efforts to further reduce the chances for its happening. Regardless of the intensity of the current debate over the role of nuclear weapons in national security, all sides agree that the prevention of nuclear war is a first priority. It can be said that there is general agreement about the moral responsibility of national leaders, their military leaders, and their advisers from all parts of society to prevent nuclear war. The disagreement, of course, is over how best to meet this responsibility.

Moral commitment to a goal, however strong, does not automatically bring solutions or guarantee that considerable effort will not be wasted or even counterproductive. Some approaches may turn out to be more useful than realized, while others may be impractical or even undesirable. Although the prevention of nuclear war is clearly a goal of paramount importance, it cannot by itself justify every expenditure of effort. Therefore, examining the prospects and problems of pursuing a particular avenue to help prevent nuclear war is a logical prerequisite to committing ourselves to intensive effort in that direction.

This essay examines the control of technology as just one of many approaches to reducing the danger and chances of nuclear war. The control of military technology can be considered as a process alone, without assuming causal relationships between technological momentum and the chances of nuclear war, a proposition probably impossible to prove either way. This process can also be considered without assuming that the nations involved can be induced to institute essential measures of control, which is another set of problems altogether. The central questions are: What is meant by the control of technology? Is it possible to control technology, to channel research and development away from ends determined to be undesirable? What would be involved in controlling technology? How do we identify what technology is undesirable? And

* The views expressed in this paper are mine and do not represent the official positions of the Los Alamos National Laboratory, the University of California, or the U.S. Department of Energy.

finally, what are some of the broader implications of attempting to impose controls on technology?

REQUIREMENTS FOR CONTROL

Control of technology in the sense used here is more specific than what is generally considered to be arms control. It means directing or restraining technological developments before they are transformed into a military capability. It deals with a general area of human endeavor, as opposed to numbers and characteristics of government-controlled hardware. In this sense it is unlike traditional forms of arms control and should be considered as something altogether different. Control of technology involves the solution of at least five kinds of problems. One is understanding the process of technical change in order to provide a basis for establishing controls. Another is identification of undesirable military capabilities and correlation of technologies critical to those capabilities. A third is isolation of negative from positive effects of new and developing technology. Fourth is the temporal problem: preemption of technological developments before they are tranformed into an unwanted military capability. And fifth is the implementation of workable controls on an international basis. Each of these five problems can be summarized briefly before proceeding to more detailed discussion of the issues.

Understanding the process of technological change is knowing what we are trying to control. Controlling military technology involves affecting the process in which many individual discoveries and developments are brought together to produce a new type of weapon system. Too often, technology is referred to as a single entity, perpetuating the erroneous conception of some kind of organism that can be locked up, put away, or stamped out. "Technology" is in fact a very slippery term, defining no single object, set of concepts, or sequence of developments. Simple cause and effect, that is, a one-on-one correlation of specific technical innovations with particular weapon developments, is common in arguments for the control of technology, but this approach is clearly inadequate for exploring the feasibility of controls, let alone devising effective controls. The prerequisite to addressing the problem is understanding the complex and difficult-to-define process of technical change.

Control of technology also assumes identification of its undesirable results and correlation of specific technical knowledge and particular experimental devices with those results. It may seem obvious that all technological progress cannot be stopped, but if only selected developments are brought to a halt, some means of identifying and measuring undesirability comes into play. This involves judgment about beneficial and negative applications of given techniques and apparatus. It is a part of the broader issue of value judgments about how technology affects the quality of human life. Equally important is the problem of identifying specific research work and techniques critical to a given new weapon, a major problem, given the complexity of technological change.

Once an undesirable application of technology has been identified, it will be necessary to isolate that application from other potential and existing positive applications of the same technical concept. This problem will invariably arise with any attempt to control technological developments, given that, historically, there has been controversy over benefits versus liabilities of most new technology. Isolation also involves the attempt to reconcile immediate gains in arms control efforts produced by the control of a type of technology with long-term progress in international security and stability that could result from the pursuit of that technology.

Preempting a series of developments before they become a military capability determines whether the problem will be about the control of military technology or a completely different set of issues. This points to the distinction between what has traditionally been considered the realm of arms control and a substantially different set of problems intrinsic to the control of technology. From the perspective of negotiating and implementing international agreements, the problem is substantively different, depending on whether we seek to control research or the advanced development, production, or deployment of weapons. The transformation of scientific principles and rudimentary inventions into military capability may be conceived of in four stages. For convenience, these can be called (1) research and development, (2) design and testing, (3) production, and (4) deployment. The first involves knowledge, experiment, and innovation. The second is the design, testing, evaluation, and refinement of a specific system. The third has mainly to do with industrial capacity, flexibility in the economic structure of a country, and the willingness and ability of a government to impose quotas on production. The fourth is the problem of limiting the size and makeup of military force structure. The stage at which controls intervene determines what kind of controls are necessary and the kinds of problems that are to be overcome in doing so. Only intervention at the first stage and in the transition from the first stage to the second can be considered the actual control of technology.

The implementation of workable controls on an international basis is the final critical step in channeling technological developments. If controls on technology are to be more than symbolic and cosmetic, then they require agreement and adherence by all nations that are important sources of the technology to be limited. Otherwise, alternative national sources of technology will remain to breed the very apprehension and instability that we seek to avoid. The prospect of one country, not a party to such a treaty, developing technology into the capability to be controlled threatens the countries that have agreed to exercise restraint. The controls must be applied in areas of research that are limited in scope, observable, and enforceable under domestic laws. In order to sustain confidence in such an agreement, there must be provisions and means for verifying compliance by the signatory governments. While as significant as the other requirements for the control of military technology, the implementation of workable controls is more a political and diplomatic problem and does not fall within the scope of this short survey.

DYNAMICS OF CHANGE

Control of technology depends first on what one calls "technology" and how the process of technological change is conceived. In considering controls on specifically military technology, a first requirement is to understand the dynamics of technological change in general. The four stages suggested above actually come in multiple phases, all overlapping and many running concurrently. The early benchmarks of this process are conception of a scientific principle and then demonstration or validation of that principle through experiment. The next steps transform principles into applications, moving from what is by convention called science to applied science to engineering. Design and engineering development for a particular practical application bring many other technological concepts together, and a prototype is usually built. Testing in this stage is no longer the demonstration of concepts but verification that a complex of engineered components will function as a system. To this point, the dynamics of change are common to both military and civilian, lethal and nonlethal, technology.

Beyond the prototype or initial engineering phase, the control of technology as such is no longer at issue because the technology must be available to be incorporated into the final design. Military service trials precede advanced engineering development and more trials. Service adoption, production engineering, series production, operator training, and deployment complete the evolutionary process from conception of a scientific principle to an operational military capability. If international controls are to be applied in these latter phases, they will impose limits on testing or production of hardware, or on the makeup and deployment of forces. By then, the technology is essentially mature and its development at least temporarily static.

A major characteristic of technological change is its complexity. The intrinsic complexity of technological development, like that of any human endeavor, makes organized conception of it only symbolic and a gross simplification. We tend to think, write, and talk about technology in the singular, as if it somehow appears fortuitously in discrete packages, produced by direct lines of evolution. This stems in part from the very human desire to identify a single inventor with an important technological development, allowing association of national identity with important milestones of progress and providing the convenience of single dates for traditional history. The singular conception of technology also stems from an inclination to see direct cause and effect. Although common, these perceptions are unrealistic.

The actual history of every package of inventions that we usually call "a technology" is the product of uncountable variables. The benchmarks given above can only be a simple framework for describing the process in which they are brought together. They are no more than a shorthand that reflects the limits of language to describe briefly the complex process under consideration here, limits that are immediately felt in any discussion of technological change. If technological developments are to be conceived at all as single units, the smallest entity that bears any relationship to reality is an ensemble of essential components. These components are invariably discovered or invented in isolation from one another, over a period that commonly spans decades. Many essential components come into being by serendipity alone, as was the case with the microwave oven and the artificial sweetener saccharin. Thus, technological developments, as usually conceived, represent a mere shadow of the myriad human activities that contributed, intentionally or incidentally, to an invention, and many of these inventions are necessary for what we today call a technology.

In chronicling the development of manned flight, for example, the works of Charles H. Gibbs-Smith show that there were scores of major and minor contributions between George Cayley's first conception in 1799 of what would become a practical flying machine and the Wright brothers' demonstration of it in 1903.[1] Problems to be solved were more complicated than providing lift and power, although these offered formidable obstacles in themselves. Control and stability, also essential for sustained flight, were ignored by most of those who experimented before the twentieth century. Even with birds as working models, and partly because of them, there were many more diversions and digressions than contributions to the thread of developments toward practical flight by humans. Furthermore, inventions that would prove essential to powered flight, such as the internal combustion engine, had origins unrelated to the quest for flight.

Another striking characteristic of the process of technological change is how long it takes. We are accustomed to hearing about how technology is affecting our daily lives in these rapidly changing times. Some of the effects of technology are as new and radical as they are far-reaching, but the technology that makes these changes possible is for the most part very old. This applies in particular to the development and application of technology for military purposes. Radar, for example, was demonstrated and patented in 1904, but it was not refined sufficiently for military use for more than three decades.[2] Most of today's seemingly new technologies are also actually quite old. The hydrofoil boat was demonstrated in 1908. Tilt-rotor aircraft, receiving so much attention in the current JVX program, first flew as prototypes in 1958, and the laser was demonstrated a quarter of a century ago, in 1960.

1. Charles Harvard Gibbs-Smith, *The Invention of the Aeroplane, 1799–1909*, Science Museum, London, Publication (New York: Taplinger Publishing Co., 1966). Two complementary books by the same author are *The Aeroplane: An Historical Survey*, 2d ed. (London: Her Majesty's Stationery Office, 1966), and *A Directory and Nomenclature of the First Aeroplanes, 1809–1909* (London: Her Majesty's Stationery Office, 1965).

2. Arthur Hezlet, *Electronics and Sea Power* (New York: Stein & Day, 1975), pp. 168–74; Fritz Trenkle, *Die deutschen Funkmessverfahren bis 1945* (Stuttgart: Motorbuch Verlag, 1979), pp. 14–17.

The length of this process can be measured using two of the bench-marks suggested above. These measure the time span from lab experiment to fighting unit, from demonstration of a physical principle to the operational deployment of the system that uses this principle. An example is the introduction of military jet aircraft. Leonard and Albert Euler and John Smeaton used experiments and models to demonstrate the principles of turbine machinery from about 1750. An efficient gas turbine engine was demonstrated in 1936, and the first experimental jet aircraft flew in Germany in 1939.[3] A reasonably successful jet fighter was operational with the Luftwaffe in late 1944, but in order to become a central element of aerial warfare, jets had to become efficient ordnance carriers.[4] They could not match the range/payload capabilities of propeller planes until 1956, when the B-52 Stratofortress joined land-based squadrons, and the A3D Skywarrior went aboard operational aircraft carriers.[5] Among small tactical aircraft the transition took even longer. The first jets to surpass the range/ordnance-lifting capabilities of piston-engine planes were the Royal Navy's Buccaneer S.1 and the U.S. Navy's A-6 Intruder, which entered service in 1963 and 1965, respectively.[6] The application of turbine technology to military aircraft thus took no less than two decades and as much as a century, depending on which events one chooses for dating the salient benchmarks of this development.

If there are universal characteristics of technological change, they are complexity, diversity, randomness, and gradual progress. Any earnest attempt to control technology must take these characteristics into account.

3. David Gordon Wilson, "Turbomachinery—from Paddle Wheels to Turbojets," *Mechanical Engineering* 104 (October 1982): 28–40; Wilhelm Gundermann, "Germany: By a Short Nose," *Air Enthusiast* 3 (August 1972): 78–81; Edward W. Constant II, *The Origins of the Turbojet Revolution* (Baltimore: Johns Hopkins University Press, 1980).
4. Woldemar Voigt, "Gestation of the Swallow," *Air International* 10 (1978): 135–43; William Green, *The Warplanes of the Third Reich* (Garden City, N.Y.: Doubleday & Co., 1970), pp. 361–65, 619–38.
5. The Soviet Tu 20 "Bear" turboprop intercontinental bomber also entered squadron service in 1956. Performance data and operational dates are taken from a number of unpublished official sources. Published sources that give useful but less detailed information are Ray Wagner, *American Combat Planes*, rev. ed. (Garden City, N.Y.: Doubleday & Co., 1968), pp. 134–54, 352–58; U.S. Air Force, Strategic Air Command, *Development of the Strategic Air Command, 1946–1976* (Offut Air Force Base, Nebr.: SAC, Office of the Historian, 1976), pp. 49, 52–53; Owen Thetford, *Aircraft of the Royal Air Force, 1918–58* (London: Putnam & Co., 1958); Philip Moyes, *Bomber Squadrons of the RAF and Their Aircraft*, rev. ed. (London: Macdonald & Jane's, 1976); Bill Gunston, *Aircraft of the Soviet Union* (London: Osprey Publishing, 1983); William Green, "The Billion Dollar Bomber," *Air Enthusiast* 1 (1971): 265.
6. The U.S. Navy's AD Skyraider was a single-engine, single-seat, piston-engine aircraft that could carry 6,500 pounds of ordnance over 500 statute miles and return. It remained in first-line service until 1968. Rosario Rausa, *Skyraider: The Douglas A-1 "Flying Dump Truck"* (Annapolis, Md.: Nautical & Aviation Publishing Co. of America, 1982); A. J. Jackson, *Blackburn Aircraft since 1909* (London: Putnam & Co., 1968), pp. 480–95; Mike Byrne, "Buccaneer: The 15-Year Stop-Gap," *Air International* 23 (1982): 59–67, 93–98; David W.

IDENTIFICATION

If control of military technology is to have any chance of working, identification of technology critical to specific military capabilities is necessary to designate the research efforts to be isolated and curtailed. Control of military technology does not of course mean the curtailment of all research and development. This would not only be impractical, it would be undesirable because technology has been and will be essential for improving the human condition. Neither all technology nor all military technology is undesirable. At least some technology that is essentially destructive is necessary for national security. Methodical identification is essential to make these types of distinctions.

The identification problem can be broken into two components: value judgments about undesirable applications of technology and correlation of specific research with those applications. The standards for making these types of value judgments, that is, distinctions between "desirable" and "undesirable" applications of technology, constitute more than theoretical and philosophical problems. These standards determine the validity and utility of the value judgments used in bounding and focusing the problem of control. Sound analysis of the many potential effects of particular applications of technology brings in a broad range of considerations. It is not a matter of setting the moral dimension against political incentives. It is the old problem of attempting to judge what will be beneficial to society, the nation, and humanity in the long term. No simplistic standard of values will provide useful answers.

The development of MIRV (multiple independently targetable reentry vehicle) provides a dramatic example of how specific applications of technology can turn out to be undesirable and, at the same time, how a broad range of considerations comes into play in making the decision to develop those applications. The MIRV was deployed by the United States with the intention of enhancing its strategic deterrent in part by countering ballistic missile defenses of the Soviet Union and by increasing the number of targets that each missile could strike. The MIRV was soon developed by the Soviets to carry high-yield warheads that armed ICBMs (intercontinental ballistic missiles) in the Soviet arsenal. With improved accuracies, the combination became the key to vulnerability of U.S. land-based ICBMs.[7]

This application of technology was intended to enhance strategic stability and thus reduce the chances for nuclear war, but instead it turned out to be potentially destabilizing. The high yield and increased accuracy of Soviet warheads made them more lethal against protective silos of

H. Godfrey, "The All-Weather Tacticians," *Air International* 10 (1976): 7–14, 29–32; David A. Brown, "A-6A Fills Interdiction Mission in Vietnam," *Aviation Week and Space Technology* 83 (December 27, 1965): 18–20.

7. Herbert F. York, "Multiple-Warhead Missiles," *Scientific American* 229 (November 1973): 18–27; Ted Greenwood, *Making the MIRV: A Study of Defense Decision Making* (Cambridge, Mass.: Ballinger Publishing Co., 1975).

U.S. missiles. With MIRV, each large-payload Soviet missile could carry many more high-yield warheads than its American counterpart, increasing the chances that the U.S. ICBM force could be destroyed or crippled in one massive blow. Since the lower yield and fewer warheads carried by each U.S. missile could not threaten a large part of the Soviet missile force in its silos, and since the Soviet ballistic missile defense system turned out to be much less extensive and less capable than anticipated, Western strategists have since wondered aloud if MIRV wasn't much more of a technological curse than a blessing. The broad range of political, strategic, and economic problems to be considered before proceeding to develop and field any major weapon system is beyond the scope of this brief survey. However, this topic is covered nicely by Richard K. Betts in an essay on another controversial weapon system, the latest generation of cruise missiles.[8]

Identification of technologies to be controlled also involves correlating research and development with results. A major difficulty in accomplishing this derives from the complex relationships, and in many cases the lack of direct relationships, between intended goals of research and its actual results. The motivations for demonstrating and refining new technological concepts change as new discoveries are made, and the most significant effects of new technology, be they generally constructive or destructive, are seldom perceived in advance.

At the forefront of technology, in the area of very advanced research, the problem of correlating the direction of research with particular ends or results is especially difficult. Sources of funding for this type of work often complain of how they can't observe sufficient progress or direction in the research they fund to justify further spending. Researchers counter that they cannot simply sit down and invent a solution to a problem, that research seldom proceeds according to anyone's schedule or desires. Research, they say, often leads in its own directions, as new discoveries are made and new approaches to a problem are conceived. If a scientist cannot be told what to discover and an inventor cannot know how he will solve technical problems, it is hardly plausible that they can be told what not to discover or invent.

Part of the complexity in correlating the direction of research and development with intended goals and then with actual results is the diversity of motivations for first developing and later refining or modifying new technology. Radar had its first significant applications in the military sphere. When first invented, however, it was conceived as a foul weather navigation aid for ships. Indeed, eight years after the patent for this new device was filed, the *Titanic* sank after striking an iceberg, and a few commentators bemoaned the fact that this type of navigation aid was

---

8. Richard K. Betts, "Complexities, Uncertainties, and Dilemmas," in *Cruise Missiles: Technology, Strategy, Politics*, ed. Richard K. Betts (Washington, D.C.: Brookings Institution, 1981), pp. 511–61.

not in general use. There were in fact one or two others who already saw radar as developing into some kind of death ray. Although important in military applications, radar never came close to being developed as a weapon. Among the many technological developments during World War II, radar is one of the two or three considered most significant in deciding the outcome of the war. Yet today it affects our daily lives most as the instrument of air traffic controllers and highway patrolmen. This simple summary of the history of radar hardly does justice to the many technical concepts that went into its development, but it illustrates how the correlation of technology with its effects varies considerably with changing perceptions of its roles.

A current example of the correlation problem is nuclear weapon research. Greater lethality of nuclear delivery systems is commonly assumed to derive from nuclear research and testing, and a direct connection is made between nuclear testing and the destabilizing effects of arms competition between the superpowers. The reality is far more confused than this. It is not nuclear warhead technology that endows the latest land-based ICBMs and submarine-launched ballistic missiles with the potentially destabilizing capability to destroy hardened missile silos. It is in fact increased accuracy of the delivery systems. Exact computations of lethality are complex, with many variables introduced by changing conditions. A general rule of thumb, however, is that an eightfold increase in yield is required to produce the same increase in lethality that comes with only twice the accuracy (that is half the circular error probable).[9] It is hardly sensible to build higher-yield weapons when commensurate improvements in accuracy are less difficult to achieve and decrease collateral damage rather than increase it geometrically as higher yields would. In fact, the trend in the modernization programs of both superpowers has been toward greater numbers of smaller and more accurate warheads on each missile.[10] There are potential developments in nuclear technology that might enhance the lethality of strategic systems to some extent. However, the curtailment of nuclear research and development would not affect the current trend toward significantly greater lethality against hardened targets such as missile silos. This trend is made possible by developments in computers, inertial guidance and navigation, vernier rockets, and satellite navigation systems. These are only some of the many technological en-

9. Albert Legault and George Lindsey, *The Dynamics of the Nuclear Balance*, rev. ed. (Ithaca, N.Y.: Cornell University Press, 1976), pp. 48–50; Alton H. Quanbeck and Barry M. Blechmann, *Strategic Forces: Issues for the Mid-Seventies* (Washington, D.C.: Brookings Institution, 1973), pp. 72–73, 75–77. For a much more detailed discussion of lethality measurement, see Lynn E. Davis and Warner R. Schilling, "All You Ever Wanted to Know about MIRV and ICBM Calculations but Were Not Cleared to Ask," *Journal of Conflict Resolution* 17 (1973): 207–42.

10. International Institute for Strategic Studies, *The Military Balance* (London: International Institute for Strategic Studies, 1972, 1979, 1983), *1972–73*, p. 65; *1979–80*, pp. 86–87; *1983–84*, pp. 118–19.

sembles related to improvements in accuracy, emphasizing the diversity of technical sources to be correlated with this particular military capability.

Another facet of the identification problem is the difficulty in obtaining agreement of a simple majority, let alone consensus, on the desirability of particular weapons. The issue of desirable versus undesirable technology is certainly not clear in the case of one of the most controversial of weapon technologies: enhanced radiation warheads. The so-called neutron bomb is really a reduced blast weapon in which not only collateral blast injuries and material damage but all collateral effects against humans are greatly reduced. It was proposed as a means of reducing collateral effects of battlefield nuclear weapons, while retaining lethality against armored troop formations. The notion that it was lethal against people while harmless to property became a central part of the public debate over whether to deploy enhanced radiation weapons, but this is a fallacious idea that ignores the laws of physics. The neutrons of an enhanced radiation weapon, or of any nuclear weapon, easily penetrate the steel armor of tanks. They are easily stopped, however, by earth and concrete, the materials that are most likely to shelter a civilian population.

The whole point of the weapon was not to use it anyway, even against Soviet soldiers. Its deployment, if undertaken, was intended to convince the Soviets that an invasion of Western Europe would be futile. If the enhanced radiation weapon reduced the chances of devastating Europe by its deterrent effect, one could call the technology desirable. If it reduced the danger to civilians living in close proximity to potential battlefields, should deterrence fail, this would be another argument for calling the technology desirable.

However, there were compelling arguments against the deployment of enhanced radiation warheads as well. It was possible that they could make nuclear war more likely instead of less. The deployment of neutron weapons could lower the threshold of nuclear war by making it less devastating and therefore more thinkable. Others argued that the presence of such weapons would in effect eliminate all conventional war-fighting options and strengthen the links to general nuclear war in case the Soviets were not deterred from invading Western Europe. Still others suggested that the defensive advantage to be gained with such weapons would soon be neutralized when the Soviets inevitably developed and deployed them, resulting not in enhanced security and stability, but in another round of competitive modernization.[11] Here, then, were three arguments for labeling the technology undesirable. Furthermore, it should be stressed that this debate took place among informed professionals and not just in the public at large.

11. Samuel T. Cohen, *The Neutron Bomb: Political, Technological and Military Issues* (Cambridge, Mass.: Institute for Foreign Policy Analysis, 1978); Fred M. Kaplan, "Enhanced Radiation Weapons," *Scientific American* 238 (May 1978): 44–51.

ISOLATION

Once the technology to be controlled has been identified, specific requisite research must be somehow isolated from the many research activities related to it. In many cases, this would mean inhibiting the negative effects of a given line of research, while attempting to still exploit its beneficial products.

One type of isolation and control might be to eliminate specific tools of research. Taking one type of research installation will serve to highlight the problem. Linear accelerators serve as research tools in the development of nuclear weapon designs. They are also essential to research in theoretical physics and continue to be used in making some of the more significant contributions in the field. The implications of this type of research extend beyond the already substantial importance of an entire field of pure science. The direction of subatomic research points to new interpretations of the origins and makeup of the universe in what may become the kind of scientific revolution described by Thomas Kuhn.[12] A third application of the linear accelerator shows promise in the treatment of specific types of inoperable cancer. An accelerator is necessary to separate subatomic particles, called pi-mesons or pions. Limited research has shown that pi-mesons may be an effective way to treat certain types of brain tumors, whose victims usually die within a few months. The same accelerator used in designing the most devastating of weapons is also at the center of research that is now altering the laws of physics and may produce a new conception of the universe, and it has brought some progress in the effort to find cures for one of man's most horrible diseases.[13] Dismantling linear accelerators would affect both the constructive and potentially destructive results of their use.

Considering later stages of research and development, isolation is also a difficult problem. Aircraft technology brought a devastating means for warfare to be waged directly on civilian populations. The great strides in aircraft technology that brought this capability were made during the 1920s and 1930s. However, they were not made in military programs, which had been severely curtailed due to financial exigencies. The significant advances came in the private sector. Improved power-to-weight ratios in engines, monocoque airframe construction, the variable pitch propeller, and other essential contributions were first made in commercial aircraft. These developments mainly improved range, payload, and speed

---

12. Thomas S. Kuhn, *The Structure of Scientific Revolutions,* International Encyclopedia of Unified Science, vol. 2, no. 2, 2d ed. (Chicago: University of Chicago Press, 1970).

13. *The Clinton P. Anderson, Los Alamos Meson Physics Facility* (Los Alamos, N.Mex.: Los Alamos Scientific Laboratory, [1979]); Sandi Doughton-Davis, "Scuttled Pion-Therapy Program Left Questions," *Los Alamos Monitor* (August 3, 1984); Carl F. von Essen, "Report on a Long Term Follow Up of Patients and Records of the Los Alamos Pion Therapy Program," *SIN Jahrbericht 1983* 2800, no. 3 (1984): 19–24.

of aircraft, characteristics that are essential to profitable commercial aviation, but which also produced an effective bomber force.[14]

Taking the example of MIRV again, we see random development of essential components, many originally for nonmilitary purposes. One such component was a main propulsion rocket engine that could be shut down and restarted in flight. Others included an accelerometer, guidance and restart controls, and a computer of small size and mass that could be programmed for each mission. Although all would be required for MIRV, none was developed specifically for it. These features were first combined in the Able-Star second stage booster rocket for multiple satellite launches. Tested in 1960, the system put a Transit II-A navigation satellite, a solar radiation measurement satellite, and a Canadian cosmic noise detection array into similar orbits the same year. Atlas-Agena boosters, also with restart capability, were used to put satellites into completely different orbits. In 1963, this system put two Vela satellites into orbits 180 degrees apart at 62,000 and 72,000 miles, respectively, in order to verify compliance with the atmospheric test ban treaty. The Transtage postboost control system represented the next major step in placing eight defense communication satellites in more radically different and more precise orbits. This precision was made possible in large part by the development and refinement of vernier rockets to control the pitch and yaw of the last stage of the booster which carried the payload, a capability that was seen later as essential for MIRV.

All of the components of the MIRV postboost vehicle were thus demonstrated by 1966. The decision to develop MIRV was made in 1964, long after its technical components were demonstrated individually and well along in their refinement. The initial incentive for combining them into a multiple delivery system was economic: the high cost of launching individual satellites. These satellite payloads had scientific, commercial, arms control, and military support functions, but the technology for the multiple delivery system was developed quite independently of any weapon delivery program.[15]

The isolation problem is also confounded when a single area of research both enhances and undermines national security. An example is antisubmarine warfare (ASW) technology, a critical element of survival for any maritime nation, but at the same time a means of undermining strategic nuclear stability. Both superpowers are currently expending considerable resources and effort to develop advanced technology for ASW applications. This can undermine strategic stability by threatening the sea-based deterrent forces of the superpowers. Ballistic missile sub-

14. Ronald E. Miller and David Sowers, *The Technical Development of Modern Aviation* (London: Routledge & Kegan Paul, 1968).

15. Greenwood, pp. 2–3, 167–69; Edmund L. Castillo, "Navigating by Man-made Stars," *U.S. Naval Institute Proceedings* 86 (1960): 74–81, pp. 79–80.

marines of both sides are more secure against attack or neutralization than land-based ICBMs or intercontinental bomber forces. They are said to be the most stable instruments of deterrence because they do not invite preemptive attack. There are good arguments to show that advanced ASW technology could not undermine this stability for a long time.[16] Nonetheless, curbing developments in this sphere of research would extend the period of security for ballistic missile submarine forces and thus help to insure continuing strategic stability.

On the other hand, not to continue advances in ASW technology would undermine the security of the many maritime nations that depend on their sea lines of communication for their economic vitality and their national survival. Fierce struggles in the Atlantic in two world wars and annihilation of the Japanese merchant marine in the Second World War show the vulnerability of these ocean arteries in conventional conflict. Today, ocean commerce could be threatened by conventionally armed, torpedo-carrying submarines of nonaligned nations as well as those of the major alliances. Advanced, diesel-electric submarines with sophisticated sensors and weapons (soon to include submarine-launched, antiship cruise missiles) are currently available to essentially any country able to pay for them. This fact and the lack of inhibitions about attacking merchant shipping in recent air and mine assaults in the Persian Gulf and the Red Sea show that sea lane security in conventional war is no trivial problem.

Segregating positive from negative, even in the development of nuclear weapons (warheads as opposed to weapon systems), is not as clear-cut as it might seem. Since nuclear weapons are instruments of destruction, the later, less theoretical research contributing to their development could be designated as technology to be controlled. However, in the American case at least, halting all nuclear weapon development would have detrimental effects from the humanitarian point of view as well. A great deal of the current U.S. development effort goes into enhancing safety and security. If a nuclear freeze went into effect today and all weapon development were stopped, thousands of weapons would remain deployed around the world. Negotiations for the reduction of force levels could take years, even assuming relatively cordial political relations. In the meantime, safety and security would remain of paramount concern. Continuing to enhance the safety and security features of these weapons would thus be a positive endeavor, notwithstanding the most dramatic progress in arms control.

Safety features reduce the chances of an accidental ignition of the high explosive in a weapon that might scatter radioactive materials. There are already so many safety mechanisms in our nuclear weapons that an

---

16. Joel S. Witt, "Advances in Antisubmarine Warfare," *Scientific American* 244 (February 1981): 31–41, pp. 40–41; Richard L. Garwin, "Will Strategic Submarines Be Vulnerable?" *International Security* 8 (1983): 52–67; B. W. Lythall, "The Future of Submarine Detection," *Naval Forces* 2, no. 2 (1981): 41–49.

accidental nuclear detonation (as opposed to a conventional explosive detonation) is close to impossible. Nonetheless, there is continued effort to enhance both types of safety features in U.S. nuclear weapons. Security features are particularly important in enhancing the already elaborate locks and safeguards against tampering and against use by terrorists in the unlikely event that security forces were overwhelmed or evaded and a nuclear weapon was taken. One relatively recent refinement in U.S. nuclear weapons that enhances both safety and security against terrorist activity is insensitive high explosive. Invented in the 1880s and refined in the 1970s for use in nuclear weapons, this explosive substance can be dropped from hundreds of feet, smashed into a concrete wall at considerable speed, heated to hundreds of degrees, and even penetrated by a high-powered rifle bullet without detonating.[17] Its advantages in preventing an aircraft crash or fire from becoming a worse disaster are obvious. It is also one of the dozens of features in current U.S. nuclear weapons that make them unattractive as instruments of terrorism. No important change in nuclear weapon design, such as the substitution of insensitive high explosive for conventional high explosive, can take place without considerable modification and testing to insure that the new package will function properly and be safe.

This example shows that there can be significant humanitarian advantages as well as disadvantages to continuing research on nuclear weapon designs. These are not conclusive arguments for further nuclear weapon research. However, they do show that isolation is not necessarily just a question of segregating nuclear from nonnuclear technology. Isolation can also involve separating what is deemed to be beneficial from that which is considered undesirable within the field of nuclear weapon research.

A final aspect of isolation problems in technology control arises when given lines of research and development both benefit and impair the more traditional types of arms control. Curtailing research might contribute to one goal of arms control, while pursuing that line of research could contribute to another. An example is the case of heavy gun technology and its relation to the British government's efforts to limit battleships, the most powerful and expensive of naval weapon systems in the 1920s and 1930s. The battleship represented the epitome of offensive capability, and with its heavy ordnance, intricate optical gunnery control, and ballistic computers, it embodied a highly developed state of naval technology. The Washington Naval Treaty of 1922 limited battleships to 35,000 tons displacement and sixteen-inch guns, but British policy, advocated by the cabinet and admiralty as an economy measure, was to push for lower limits of 25,000 tons and twelve-inch ordnance. An economy measure already implemented had reduced the Royal Navy's ordnance research and design establishment.

17. "PBX-9502 Insensitive High Explosive," Film Y-343 (Los Alamos National Laboratory, March 1979, 7 minutes, unclassified).

Because of curtailed research and development capabilities, Britain had to choose between risking her security and undermining her arms control policy. As foreign navies pushed for larger ships and heavier guns, the British found themselves in a dilemma. Once committed to designing one caliber of heavy gun, they could not change to a larger or smaller caliber without several years delay in construction, because of the limited numbers of qualified personnel in their gun design establishment. If the British Admiralty chose twelve-inch guns and the foreign powers did not exercise the restraint called for in British policy, the Royal Navy would be left either with new capital ships of inferior power or with no modern capital ships at all while larger guns were developed and new construction was delayed. On the other hand, if the Royal Navy went immediately for larger guns, the British would be contributing to resumption of the very arms race they sought to avoid.[18]

This historical example shows that control of technology can detract from the other, more usual, forms of arms control. In this case, technological constraints were the result of economic problems, but the effect would have been the same if the naval gun establishment has been reduced under international controls. The issue of British battleship armament may seem trivial in the context of today's nuclear world. But it should be recalled that Britain's national survival depended on the protection of her overseas trade, and the fleet that protected that trade was built around battleships. The capability to develop several types of naval guns simultaneously would seem like a technology to control in the interest of reducing naval arms competition. However, the lack of that capability put security objectives in conflict with the objectives of arms control. Curtailment of technology in this case eliminated options that otherwise would have been available, again emphasizing the difficulties in isolating negative and positive results of technology.

PREEMPTION

A fourth set of problems associated with the control of technology is preemption of research before it leads to a usable set of technologies for a particular military application. The essence of the preemption problem is a paradox of exclusivity. If a given technology is clearly identified with a military capability, it is a mature technology and no longer offers the problem of controlling technology. If research is to be stopped while it is in its early evolutionary stage, before it is developed and available for practical applications, it is usually not yet refined sufficiently to be identified with a particular capability. To ignore some kind of direct connections such as these is to invite random control of scientific research in the hope that something undesirable will be stopped from development.

18. Stephen W. Roskill, *Naval Policy between the Wars*, 2 vols. (Annapolis, Md.: Naval Institute Press, 1968, 1976), vol. 1, pp. 428, 500; vol. 2, pp. 45, 135, 286–89; Oscar Parkes, *British Battleships*, 2d ed. (London: Seeley Service & Co., 1966), pp. 661, 663; Alan Raven and John Roberts, *British Battleships of World War Two* (Annapolis, Md.: Naval Institute Press, 1976), pp. 273, 280.

334   *Karl Lautenschläger*

The paradigm suggested here for the evolution and introduction of military technology identifies multiple phases in the process that transforms the conception of scientific principles into a military capability. Combining these into the four general stages suggested in the introduction, we have (1) research and development, (2) design and testing, (3) production, and (4) deployment. In considering the institution of controls on military technology, the phase in the process is critical to determining the type of control. If the goal is to channel or curtail technological developments as such, controls are necessary at the first phase, during research and development. Controls imposed at later phases of the process, on advanced development and testing, on production capacity or schedules, or on force structure, do not represent problems in the control of technology. They are the traditional problems of arms control. A system under advanced testing uses technology that is already fully demonstrated and well along toward maturity. At this stage, understanding how to utilize the technological concept is probably also widely available in the private sector, easily in more than one country. A system in the third or fourth stage, having reached production or deployment, is fully developed and long past its technological evolution. Since we cannot turn the clock back, preemption is clearly an essential part of technology control.

The widespread assumption that a comprehensive ban on nuclear testing will have an important effect on nuclear arms competition between the superpowers indicates that distinctions between stages of technological evolution are not usually made. As emphasized in the discussion of lethality in strategic systems, today's advances in technology affect nuclear delivery systems significantly and the warheads hardly at all. Nuclear weapon concepts were demonstrated four decades ago, and thermonuclear concepts three decades ago. They have long since developed into mature technology. The atmospheric test ban treaty of 1963 does not actually control technology. Neither is it really an arms control agreement, except in the very broadest sense of the term. The central purpose and effect of the treaty is to protect the environment. Given the maturity of the technology and the environmental controls already in effect, a comprehensive ban on nuclear testing between the superpowers would be largely cosmetic.

Preemption to control technology must inevitably involve prediction. With consistently long lead times between demonstration of a technical principle and its military application, the problem is how to predict accurately the military employment of a newly demonstrated technology as well as predicting the context and consequences of that employment. As emphasized in the discussion of the dynamics of technological change, a great many variables affect the transformation from concepts to hardware. It is for this reason that historians find it very difficult to trace the evolution of particular technologies. It is extremely difficult to identify the essential components of a technological ensemble because there are so many and their origins are usually diverse and redundant. Pointing to where in the process that development could have been halted with the desired effect is equally difficult because the development of ideas is ill-defined and sporadically documented. People still argue over the origins and sequence of developments that led to MIRV, for example.[19] If historians have the benefit of considerable data, documents, and hindsight but encounter these difficulties, predicting future developments would seem to be a far bigger problem. This suggests that by the time we identify what technology we want to control, it will already be developed and available, making it far beyond the point of preventive technological control.

Not only does the complexity of technological change make prediction difficult, perceptions of its roles change over time. For example, the idea of bombing thousands of civilians concentrated in cities or of holding defenseless citizens hostage to the vicissitudes of international power politics is abhorrent to us today as a callous blurring of military and civilian affairs. But to have projected today's situation from the perceptions of aviation technology between 1914 and 1945 would have been a superhuman accomplishment indeed.

The idea of bombing cities grew up in an entirely different context, and it went through several transformations. During the wars of the French Revolution and Empire, the distinction between military and civilian became obscured with the mobilization of entire populations to contribute to the war effort, giving rise to the concept of the nation at war.[20] In the early part of World War I, there were suggestions that the new capability brought by zeppelins and airplanes might allow strikes at the sources of the enemy's manpower and industrial base as a logical extention of the nation-at-war concept. Later in the war, the long and bloody stalemate on the western front stimulated a search for a way to end the war with a quick, decisive stroke. In a struggle that at times killed more soldiers in a day than the United States lost in its ten-year combat involvement in Indochina, thinkable alternatives could be wide ranging. With this goal in mind, civilian as well as military leaders in Germany, Italy, Great Britain, and finally the United States advocated the use of air forces for industrial and population bombing.[21] By this time, it was

19. Contrast, e.g., George W. Rathjens, "The Dynamics of the Arms Race," *Scientific American* 220 (April 1969): 15–25, with Graham T. Allison, "Questions about the Arms Race: Who's Racing Whom? A Bureaucratic Perspective," in *Contrasting Approaches to Strategic Arms Control*, ed. Robert L. Pfaltzgraff, Jr. (Lexington, Mass.: D. C. Heath & Co., 1974), pp. 31–72.

20. Basil H. Liddell Hart, *The Revolution in Warfare* (New Haven, Conn.: Yale University Press, 1947).

21. Nino Salvaneschi, *Let Us Kill the War; Let Us Aim at the Heart of the Enemy* (Milan: Bianco & Nero, 1917); J. L. Boone Atkinson, "Italian Influence on the Origins of the American Concept of Strategic Bombardment," *Air Power Historian* 4 (1957): 141–49; Memo from Commander Peter Strasser, Commander of the German Naval Airship Division, to Vice Admiral Reinhard Scheer, Commander in Chief of the High Seas Fleet, August 10, 1916, trans. and reprinted in full in *The Zeppelin in Combat*, by Douglas H. Robinson (London: G. T. Foulis, 1962), p. xv; Raymond H. Fredette, *The Sky on Fire: The First Battle of Britain, 1917–1918, and the Birth of the Royal Air Force* (New York: Holt, Rinehart & Winston, 1966).

not a mere extension of general war but a desperate attempt to save lives. The air assaults made by German forces on British cities had little effect on the outcome of the war, and the conflict ended before the Allies could retaliate in kind.

After the First World War, however, industrial and population bombing were still promoted as a way to avoid the carnage of trench warfare in the next conflict, should it break out. A significant point is that in modern times before the advent of nuclear weapons, the killing and devastation wrought by massive land campaigns was the most destructive situation conceivable. During World War II, strategic bombardment, as it was called by then, was seen as the only way for Britain and the United States to strike at Germany while their forces were marshaled for invasion and liberation of the continent. However, a central argument for the bombing continued to be that it would shorten the war and save lives that would otherwise be lost in stalemate warfare between massed armies.[22] This is also what led the United States to firebomb sixty-five Japanese cities and drop two nuclear bombs on two other Japanese cities in 1945. The objective was to induce Japan to surrender before the United States would have to invade the Japanese home islands and suffer an estimated 500,000 casualties.[23] As horrifying as the killing and destruction was, the perception at the time was that an extended land campaign in either the European or Pacific theaters would be much worse for both sides. The bomber force represented the substitution of technology for cost in human lives. It was seen as a devastatingly effective but relatively more humanitarian instrument of war: the lesser of two necessary evils.

There is a further problem with preemption. The application of controls at early stages of research raises issues of government interference in people's creative thinking and in economic enterprise. Controls at the conception stage amount to restraint on intellectual freedoms. Hindering technology at early phases of its development, when it could have several potential applications, would easily impinge on economic vitality, since innovation is a key to economic competition. Even assuming sound forecasting and accurate identification of connections between technological ensembles and undesirable military technology, who decides what is to be controlled, what values form the basis of the decision, and how is control to be administered and enforced? The essence of open societies

22. Wesley Frank Craven and James Lea Cate, *The Army Air Forces in World War II,* 7 vols. (Chicago: University of Chicago Press, 1948), vol. 1, pp. 558–661; Charles Webster and Noble Franklin, *The Strategic Air Offensive against Germany, 1939–1945,* 4 vols., History of the Second World War, United Kingdom Military Series (London: Her Majesty's Stationery Office, 1961), vol. 1, pp. 72, 82–83, 93–98, 103–4; vol. 4, pp. 88–95; Haywood S. Hansell, Jr., *The Air Plan that Defeated Hitler* (Atlanta: Higgins-McArthur/Longino & Porter, 1972).

23. United States, Strategic Bombing Survey, *Pacific War,* 108 reports (Washington, D.C.: Government Printing Office, 1946); report no. 1: *Summary Report (Pacific War),* pp. 9–30; report no. 66: *The Strategic Air Operations of Very Heavy Bombardment in the War against Japan;* Craven and Cate, vol. 5, pp. 92–175, 614–58.

is that they embrace lack of agreement among their citizens about values. The implementation of effective controls could easily bring with it abuse of power and threats to what open societies consider basic freedoms. This is a fundamental issue of social and political philosophy.

In order to overcome many of these problems, preemption should come at the point that technology is refined for a specific military application. This would be just before the beginning of stage 2: design and testing of a weapon system. It assumes agreement about the undesirability of developing the weapon system and reasonable prediction of salient effects of deploying such a system. The isolation problem is ameliorated by imposing controls at the very end of the research and development stage. However, controls at this point act little on the availability of technological concepts. They bear more on the application of those concepts, bringing us out of technology control and back into the realm of traditional arms control.

CONCLUSIONS

Technological developments are randomly scattered throughout human activities of thought, creation, and innovation. Many are conceived as having weapon applications that never come to fruition. Others are undertaken for nonlethal purposes and only become identifiable as weapon technologies after development of techniques and equipment is essentially complete. Most evolve from conceptions that have no ulterior motive except inquiry, and most never have a military application.

The complexity of technological developments makes it extremely difficult even to identify what should be controlled in a program to curtail the development of lethal or destabilizing weapons. The diversity of applications for given scientific concepts makes isolation of desirable from undesirable technology another major obstacle to effective controls. Finally, predicting the outcome of scientific and technical research in time to affect the direction of that research comprises both the general problem of prediction and one of changing conceptions of what is on balance desirable and what is not.

The desire to control technology should not be dismissed lightly. It has been argued persuasively that human beings find machines to be inherently ominous.[24] It is therefore fully understandable that the products of technology can be as horrifying as they are awesome. Given the nature of the problem and the magnitude of the task, efforts to control technology are probably not worthwhile, however. This kind of control is an elusive goal and an approach to problems that is more often advocated than understood. Efforts to reduce the likelihood of nuclear war are better made in much more promising directions than attempting to control what is hardly definable let alone controllable.

24. For two views on this phenomenon, see John Naisbitt, *Megatrends*, 2d ed. (New York: Warner Books, 1984), pp. 35–52; Robert M. Pirsig, *Zen and the Art of Motorcycle Maintenance: An Inquiry into Values* (New York: Bantam Books, 1974).

The more traditional method of arms control, with its focus on deployed forces, remains the most promising approach. It is neither new nor without problems, but it bears on some of the more tangible entities: those which can be counted, measured, and photographed and are thus subject to straightforward methods of verification. A constructive progression might be to start with the fourth stage of technological evolution, instituting controls on deployment according to current practice. Then proceed backward through stage 3 to stage 2, systematically working out treaties on the production and then the testing and advanced development of weapon systems that the parties to the treaty agree are destabilizing. In these cases we are not concerned about the control of technology but with political control of what is to be done with it.

Whether these particular conclusions are accepted is not as important as the recognition that the issues raised in this survey of the problem must be addressed if one insists on pursuing the control of technology. Recognition of these issues in place of empty advocacy would represent a minimum of progress toward practical solutions. It is hoped that, if nothing else has been accomplished by this survey, at least the problem has been framed more clearly.

One of the secrets of success is to direct vigorous effort into areas where there are prospects for producing results. A good cause does not by itself insure that even a vast expenditure of effort will bring results. If we are to have success in preventing nuclear war, we must exploit opportunities to reduce the chances of such a war. Attempting to control the intangibles of technological innovation is a diversion of effort from this goal and against the flow of human inclination to inquire and innovate.

Distrust, Secrecy, and the Arms Race*

Sissela Bok

I

Distrust among nations undermines joint action to reduce the danger of nuclear war. Keeping pace with the escalating forces of destruction, distrust also spurs them on while blocking all moves to curb them. Out of a degree of mutual distrust that would once have seemed pathological, nuclear powers now compete with one another in perfecting the means to global catastrophe. But paradoxically, in so doing they are often forced to rely on an equally unrealistic degree of trust: trust in the rationality and competence of all who are in control of the weapons.

All trust and distrust between human beings arises from some connection between them, however indirect. I may take an interest in persons who cannot now act in ways that affect my life—say, in members of medieval guilds—but my interest won't be one of trust or distrust. Only when I take the activities of others to be capable of affecting my life can questions of trust arise, influencing my expectations and responses.

Both trust and distrust are therefore needed for human interaction. People tend to exaggerate the need for trust and the dangers of distrust without seeing the delicate balancing of each that is necessary for the functioning of any relationship. Were it not for questioning, doubts, and challenges to preconceived ideas there would be few pressures for change, few checks on those who would abuse trust, whether in families, among colleagues, in professional relationships, or in politics.[1]

Between governments as between individuals, different forms of trust and of distrust arise as soon as they can influence, and especially when they can endanger, one another. In contractual relationships between nations, trust or distrust for a government reflects the level of confidence others have that it will live up to its commitments and to its declared

* This essay draws on a paper prepared for the International Conference on Common Security organized by Stockholm International Peace Research Institute (SIPRI) in Stockholm, September 2–4, 1983, and to be reprinted under the title "Common Insecurity" in a volume reporting on the conference.
1. Bernard Barber, in *The Logic and Limits of Trust* (New Brunswick, N.J.: Rutgers University Press, 1983), discusses the role of trust and distrust in societies, pointing out that they are combined with forms of social control such as laws, auditing arrangements, and insurance against malfeasance. These forms of social control are far weaker in the international community; as a result, greater strain is placed on trust and distrust.

intentions and standards of conduct. Other forms of trust are indirect. However weak our trust in, or claim on, any government's fidelity to commitments or standards of conduct, we may assume that it will not risk its own survival—an assumption that matters to us whenever, as in the nuclear predicament, its survival is tied to our own. We may then trust that we shall escape destruction, if not because of that government's sense of responsibility toward us, at least indirectly as a side effect of its acting in its own best interest.

All such judgments are subjective and open to criticism. We make them differently for different governments on the basis of past experience, present arrangements, consistency and credibility, the possibility of verification, and the presence or absence of provocation; and without adequate reasons for trust in any one of these respects, increased distrust is often appropriate.

To be sure, blind trust is occasionally justified; so, at times, is all-consuming distrust. But most often, and surely in the relationship between citizens and governments or between states, there is need for a subtler blend: for trust that is not blind, for distrust that is founded on experience, and for the sensitivity and power to shift from one to the other as circumstances require. In all such relationships, however, every effort should be made to cut back on the capriciousness and duplicity that heighten distrust and block the chances for cooperation.

What hampers joint efforts to reduce the risk of war is therefore not that governments harbor a blend of trust and distrust toward one another. Those who long for a world without any distrust are as sure to be disappointed as those who imagine that nations can coexist without any trust whatsoever. The difficulties arise, rather, from the extent and the intensity of existing distrust, from the way in which it calls forth distorted forms of trust, and from the links of both trust and distrust to manufactured or shaky evidence.

A

The mutual distrust between nuclear powers has become self-perpetuating: it creates the very evidence which reinforces it. This distrust promotes the construction of "worst-case scenarios" wherein each nation imagines the enemy's most ingenious and devastating schemes and then prepares to be capable of retaliating with enough severity to deter anyone from putting such schemes into action.

Worst-case scenarios have a long history and have gone under many names.[2] Traditionally, they form part of any prudent defense policy. It makes sense to calculate the worst possible outcomes in order to be able

2. For recent discussions of such scenarios, see Jerome B. Wiesner, "Comprehensive Arms Limitation Systems," in *Where Science and Politics Meet* (New York: McGraw-Hill Book Co., 1965), pp. 209–46, p. 234; and Michael Howard, *The Causes of War* (Cambridge, Mass.: Harvard University Press, 1983), pp. 5–6.

to meet them. Such calculations represent a reasoned response to the need for both trust and distrust between adversaries. They may trust one another up to a point and in certain matters but will not mortgage their survival on the basis of such trust. Rather, they imagine possible circumstances under which their trust might turn out to have been unwarranted and consider how to meet such eventualities.

By now, however, worst-case scenarios no longer serve the function of prudent defense planning that Clausewitz and others envisaged for them in the past. Modern technology and forms of warfare have pushed back the limits to what one can imagine an adversary planning; and the resources available for armaments have made these scenarios dwarf anything evisaged in the past. The sky is the limit now when it comes to resources that might be expended on military preparations. And since there is no adequate defense against many of today's most lethal weapons, worst-case scenarios have come to call for ever grimmer plans for retaliatory or preventive offensive war. Because the precautions are limitless in scope and frequently offensive in nature, they generate ever more sinister scenarios on the part of adversaries. And because the process is reciprocal between the superpowers, it risks turning the arms race into a mutually self-fulfilling prophecy. As Jerome Frank has written, enemies then "finally become what they imagined each other to be, whether they started out that way or not; some enemies are warlike and treacherous to begin with, but all become so in time."[3]

Superpowers that see one another as thus "warlike and treacherous" find their beliefs verified by the response each makes in the face of such threats. Each witnesses the other's relentless military buildup, aggressive propaganda, efforts at subversion, massive arms donations and sales abroad, and violations—surreptitious or flagrant—of international law. Given the secrecy surrounding weapons development, moreover, it is reasonable for each to suspect the other of far more than can be detected. The resulting mutual distrust is rational as it counsels caution in the face of unprecedented danger; but it is also irrational in that it adds to the danger and heightens the risk of precisely the annihilation against which it guards. Both sides recognize that no war carrying out such plans could achieve the benefits for which nations in the past have been prepared to fight. The citizens of a state, its lands, its very form of government— all that the scenarios are meant to defend—would be destroyed if they were ever carried out.

B

Under such paradoxical circumstances, any trust that governments will honor commitments or standards of humane conduct is severely strained. Peoples in nations not aligned on either side in the arms race see their survival threatened by a conflict not of their making; the spirals of ar-

---

3. Jerome Frank, *Sanity and Survival* (New York: Random House, 1967), p. 146.

maments and distrust only underscore their plight. And the superpowers themselves can hardly base trust on judgments about the accountability or goodwill of their opponents.

Three grounds for confidence are nevertheless often advanced to encourage a level of indirect trust that would ordinarily seem excessive, considering the danger now facing mankind. Many who decry as alarmist the warnings raised by scientists and peace advocates around the world tell us to have trust, if not in the altruism of government leaders or in their concern for long-range global safety, at least in their urge to self-preservation—their refusal to act suicidally—and in their rationality. We are told to bank on the hope that the heads of nuclear powers will not be insane enough to trigger the destruction in which they may well perish along with a large proportion of their fellow citizens. To buttress such confidence, advocates of high-voltage deterrence point out that the world has, after all, survived for forty years without nuclear war: that indeed the many predictions of such war within five, ten, fifteen years have thus far proved incorrect. Why should that not continue to be the case?

In view of the vastness of the risks involved, neither the arguments about self-preservation and rationality nor the one about precedent offer a convincing foundation for such indirect trust. The superficial plausibility of the first two arguments does not withstand scrutiny. It is true that there is often more reason to place trust in the urge to self-preservation on the part of human beings than in their respect for commitments or their standards of conduct; but suicide statistics remind us that this urge is not equally dominant in everyone. Heads of state have surely been known to risk, even invite, self-destruction and to bring countless others with them in death. And we have reason to be concerned over any defense policy that has to rely on the continued rationality of all who are in control over nuclear weapons—friends and foes alike. For if our confidence in their capacity to ward off disaster is not to be monumentally misplaced, they must not only be immune to self-destructive impulses and to fantasies of personal invulnerability but also know how to avoid misjudgment about risks, even under extraordinary international pressures or when domestic opinion approaches the boiling point. No matter what the circumstances, they must somehow all remain rational enough and competent enough to avert any malevolent, erroneous, or accidental response that might trigger ruin for all.

It is hardly reasonable to place so much confidence in human competence and rationality, considering what one commentator has termed "the historical record of human folly and accident which led us into the international catastrophes in the past."[4] But even if all individuals in charge of the growing number of weapons were somehow immune to

4. Freeman Dyson, "Bombs and Poetry," in *The Tanner Lectures on Human Values,* vol. 4, ed. Sterling M. McMurrin (Salt Lake City: Utah University Press, 1983), pp. 81–145, p. 109.

the incompetence, the miscalculations, the obsessions, and the despair that can beset others, why should we have further confidence that all technological controls will avoid massive malfunctioning year in and year out?

True, the risks of any one of these difficulties in any one period is low. But the fact is that, for the avoidance of a nuclear exchange, there must not be a single instance of any one of them. Ever. And while hotlines and other safeguards may in principle prevent such an exchange, once initiated, from unleashing an all-out war, no one can know in advance whether they will suffice in an actual emergency.

This is why the third argument—that, after all, nuclear war has been held off for four decades in spite of predictions to the contrary—presents such a fragile basis for trust. It would be one thing if nuclear weapons had never been used and if they were, in some sense, "unthinkable." But they have already been used on two occasions against large populations. They are at the disposal of more nations now than they were in 1945; still others stand ready to manufacture them. And the fact that erroneous predictions have been made in the past proves nothing about the future. It is clearly unwise for anyone to assume that war is bound to come within a specified number of years. But it is equally unwise to argue that, because some have made erroneous forecasts, all who warn of war in the near future are thereby proved wrong: that the diagnosis can be set aside because some have made too rash a prognosis. And to conclude, with the help of such reasoning, that nuclear weapons will not be used in the foreseeable future requires a vast leap of inductive faith.

It is becoming increasingly difficult to muster the requisite faith. We might, to be sure, be willing to place a modest wager on the basis of some such reassuring extrapolation from past experience. But we would hardly agree to bet our lives on it, if given a choice, much less wager the lives of a large portion of humanity.

The current blend of trust and distrust does not serve us well. It obstructs efforts to negotiate and to keep the peace. The trust in enduring human rationality and in cool competence under stress hardly squares with experience. The consuming mutual distrust between nations generates ever more convincing evidence with which to justify still greater vigilance. Worst-case scenarios, prudent when limited, become potentially suicidal when governments can draw on ever greater resources and scientific expertise for military purposes.

The spiral of distrust, and its counterpart of unwarranted indirect trust, intertwines with that of the arms race, each boosting the other. In turn, they both reinforce and draw strength from practices of secrecy. Rarely has this interaction been so clearly visible as in the aftermath of the shooting down of the South Korean airliner KAL 007. It demonstrated the speed with which an act of armed violence, itself born out of vaulting distrust and pervasive secrecy, triggered shock, heightened distrust, and helped spur the rush to escalate the arms race still further; and it showed the febrile acrobatics world leaders need to juggle both the growing distrust and the ever more improbable confidence in cool rationality that the arms race continues to require.[5]

II

Between states, secrecy and the deception that it allows are hardly new. Every state requires a measure of secrecy in order not to be entirely predictable, entirely open to attack; and the weaker the state, the more indispensable its reliance on surprise and strategems. But in recent decades practices of secrecy and deception have, like modern armaments, taken on new and far more debilitating forms because of technological innovations. Encodement, clandestine action, secret wiretapping and scrambling of messages, censorship, and espionage now use methods of unprecedented power. They play an immense role in escalating distrust; throughout the world, they are used as weapons in cold and hot wars alike and as aids in schemes of corruption and oppression; and in every such conflict, each side suspects more treachery and hostility than meets the eye, once again for understandable reasons having to do with rational and ordinarily prudent worst-case scenarios.

Secrecy is equally dangerous domestically. To be sure, states require certain practices of secrecy for administrative and diplomatic purposes.[6] Yet most governments resort to far more secrecy than is needed for such purposes. Whenever secrecy shuts out criticism and feedback, it debilitates judgment; and like all exercises of power, it risks corrupting those who use it. The domestic dangers of secrecy are clear from a look at secretive states around the world. Insofar as governments manage to impose secrecy and censorship beyond the required minimum they undermine the most fundamental freedoms. Their control reaches not only what concerns national security but all that would present a challenge to their power or that would expose failures and abuses.

And since military secrets have to be kept from a state's own citizens in order not to reach its enemies, citizens lose ordinary democratic checks on precisely those matters that can affect them most strongly. Consider, for example, the decisions by different governments to develop atomic weapons. The United States government made this decision under conditions of strict wartime secrecy. But even after the war was over, leaders in the Soviet Union, Britain, France, and China moved to develop such weapons without any public knowledge, much less debate. From the point of view of what citizens knew or whether they could influence the decision,

5. A few days after the incident, West Germany's assistant foreign minister Alois Mertes could still echo this confidence: he stressed his full confidence in the rationality of the Soviet leadership, adding that Europe was one of the safest regions on earth (address to the SIPRI International Conference on Common Security, Stockholm, September 3, 1983).

6. In the pages that follow, I draw on the more detailed discussion of secrecy and openness in my *Secrets: On the Ethics of Concealment and Revelation* (New York: Pantheon Books, 1982).

there was no difference in this respect between democratic states and others so long as the decision was made in secrecy. (By contrast, states such as Sweden, in which citizens took part from the beginning in thorough public debates on whether to develop such weapons, have so far decided against such a step.)[7] In Western nations with a nuclear capacity, public debate now has access to much more information about existing and planned strategies and weapons; as a result, citizens have a greater opportunity to participate in decisions. But secrecy helped shut them out from the original choice—perhaps the most fateful decision that ever confronted their nations.

When it comes to most practices of secrecy, however, the disparity between superpowers is great, unlike the approximate parity with respect to armaments and levels of distrust. The pervasive control over what is spoken and said that the Soviet government exercises has deep roots in Russian history. It contrasts sharply with the relative openness of the major Western democracies. But both the arms competition and the present degree of distrust put pressure on Western nations to emulate their adversaries with respect to secrecy as well. In the United States, the 1980s have seen intensified government efforts to impose censorship on public servants and scientists, to curtail trade and supervise research in the interest of national security, to control and sometimes prohibit visits by foreign scientists, students, and writers, and to extend the scope of what can be classified and of clandestine paramilitary activities. Such emulation carries great risks. As Carl Friedrich has written, the apparatus of modern police states has forced other nations to respond by increasing security measures, making it difficult for them to keep both secrecy and propaganda within functional limits. Friedrich warned that these forms of official manipulation "represent at present perhaps the most serious pathology for free democratic systems."[8]

In such rivalries, nations are tempted to settle for the lowest common denominator when it comes to kinds of means of secrecy. Debates over such activities often remain on a superficial cost-benefit level and rarely raise moral questions about their justifiability. Actions that would be condemned on the part of individuals are routinely justified on behalf of states as necessary for national security: defenders of such actions argue that even if governments could be held to ordinary moral standards (something many reject as not feasible, given the impossibility of enforcing such standards) the emergency conditions of the Cold War warrant responding in kind.[9] They point out, further, that their opponents, who

7. See Alastair Buchan, ed., *A World of Nuclear Powers?* (Englewood Cliffs, N.J.: Prentice-Hall, Inc., 1966), pp. 39–87. It is far from inconceivable, however, that a process of public debate could issue in a decision to go ahead with nuclear weapons. Certain forms of nationalism and of hostility toward outsiders could facilitate such a choice.

8. Carl Friedrich, *The Pathology of Politics: Violence, Betrayal, Corruption, Secrecy, Propaganda* (New York: Harper & Row, 1972), p. 231.

9. For a discussion of arguments concerning morality in international relations, see Stanley Hoffmann, *Duties beyond Borders* (Syracuse, N.Y.: Syracuse University Press, 1981).

already resort to such actions, cannot complain if others play by the same rules. In self-defense and in retaliation, "dirty tricks" under the shield of secrecy then come to seem more acceptable.

But the claim that such acts are indispensable to national security is rarely scrutinized; nor is the legitimacy of stooping to every shady practice employed by adversaries self-evident.[10] A form of worst-case analysis sometimes operates here, too: whatever secret misconduct one imputes to the enemy then seems more legitimate as a means of retaliation. Policymakers rarely stop to ask what such dirty tricks do, not only to adversaries, but also to those who carry them out and to innocent by-standers—or to what extent reciprocal practices of such a nature increase or decrease international tension and the attendant risks of war.

It is especially important to reexamine the justifiability of each practice carried on in secrecy now because the role of secrecy among nations is changing. The advent of such techniques as signal intelligence, radar, and infrared photography on board spy planes and satellites, along with the sheer amount of information that is now openly available, has unsettled the standards for keeping and probing secrets, already precarious in the present international climate of heightened distrust. Adversaries now have access to much information about one another once cloaked in secrecy, in such matters as weapons deployment and test explosions. Many state secrets have become less safe, and few are permanently safe.

Some analysts have argued that secrecy between nations is therefore receding. They have suggested that as the new technologies of surveillance and data processing make concealment harder, secrecy will play a diminished role internationally. One has gone so far as to claim that there "is no *privacy* from a well-financed, technically adept person or agency determined to gain personal information about an individual, group, or country."[11]

Are nations becoming ever more transparent to one another in this way? The answer depends on how we interpret the word "transparent" that is now so frequently used in this context. If we take it to mean that governments now know more about one another's weapons systems and military capacity, surely the answer must be yes; and wherever such knowledge is available and reliable, the scope for irrational distrust or blind trust is greatly reduced. This is why verification is so important in

---

10. To the extent that moral principles in international relations are thought to be contractual, it may be argued that they are less binding if seen as not reciprocated. A habitually deceptive government official, according to such a view, forfeits the right to be told the truth in return. But I have argued, in *Lying: Moral Choice in Public and Private Life* (New York: Pantheon Books, 1978), chap. 9, that this argument does not give sufficient grounds for justifying lying to liars. One still has to consider what reciprocating in such ways does to oneself, to others, and to general trust, whether in individual or in international relations. The same considerations hold for other breaches of acknowledged principles such as those ruling out torture.

11. Robert K. Holz, introduction to "Social Implications of Remote Sensing," in *The Surveillant Science: Remote Sensing of the Environment*, ed. Robert K. Holz (Boston: Houghton Mifflin Co., 1973), pp. 360–90, p. 361.

arms negotiations; where successful, it has brought about greater openness between nations in specific contexts than had previously been possible.

But if we take the word "transparent" to indicate, rather, that governments are in some sense easier to interpret, more understandable to one another, the answer must, rather, be no. Governments now dispose of powerful methods that combine the manipulation of information already in the public domain with extensive practices of secrecy. In many states the new technologies of information and the increased distrust have brought a heightened sense of vulnerability and provoked stronger efforts at manipulation through such means as disinformation, propaganda, increased censorship, the ever more elaborate coding of transmitted messages, and tightened trade and scientific secrecy.

At the same time, the secrecy that newer weapons permit makes them increasingly resistant to verification. It is one thing for nations to keep one another's large immobile land-based missiles under surveillance and quite another to pinpoint the whereabouts of hidden or highly mobile smaller ones or to keep track of every nuclear-armed submarine. Preparations for chemical and biological warfare are perhaps least verifiable of all.

Even apart from these forms of secrecy, the metaphor of transparency is misleading, for it bespeaks an oversimplified view of nations. As novelists like Tolstoy or Virginia Woolf remind anyone tempted by such a view, not even the simplest aspects of an individual's life can be transparent, much less those of groups or entire nations. And secrecy about intentions— of government leaders as of all others—can never be fully dispelled. Forecasts of the course a nation will take are as chancy as ever. For all the facts at their disposal, understanding among governments remains meager.

In sum, although nations find it harder and harder to guard many military secrets, practices of secrecy flourish; and it will become increasingly difficult to verify and keep track of enemy weapons unless cooperative measures are agreed on. Technology, which has brought unprecedented means for probing secrets, has also provided new methods for shielding them. And the arms race spurs the search for more powerful means of both probing and shielding, just as it engenders ever more distorted forms of distrust and trust in uneasy bondage.

III

Viewed from the perspective of nations collectively, the interwoven spirals of distrust and secrecy are counterproductive and dangerously unstable. Spurring the arms race and impeding negotiations, they call for deescalation in their own right. Yet to policymakers advising nuclear powers the matter is less simple. They may see present levels of distrust and secrecy as the only reasonable attitude in the face of the threat of nuclear attack, though admittedly far from ideal. So long as the reasons for distrust are so compelling, they ask, what else can one do? Given the immense danger that nations must now contemplate, it is impossible simply to decide to be less distrustful, and it seems ill-advised to abandon the secrecy that is needed for defense.

But what if it is also the case, as I have argued, that negotiations to reduce the threat of nuclear attack substantially cannot succeed so long as nations labor with the present levels of distrust and secrecy? The nuclear predicament has been described as a Prisoner's Dilemma writ large: one where governments have to reach decisions governing collective survival without sufficient trust in one another to make the choices most likely to ensure such survival.[12] Must we then acknowledge a stalemate?

This would only be true if there were no chance of improving the degree to which governments could trust one another: if they were literally enclosed in cells and unable to communicate directly with one another, for instance, as the prisoners in the original dilemma, or if, able to communicate but not to trust in such communication, they resigned themselves to existing or even deteriorating levels of distrust.[13]

Such resignation would be premature. Since distrust grows through reciprocal and repeated actions, it stands to reason that it can also be cut back thus. Many nations, once bitter enemies, have conquered distrust of one another; and there have been periods in past decades where even the threat between nuclear powers has been cut back and distrust correspondingly diminished. SALT I and SALT II provided agreements to limit secrecy in ways that had this effect. There is always a risk of backsliding; and other elements of distrust can spur the arms race anew; but constant deterioration is not preordained. Once governments fully understand the harm done to their own as to other nations from policies that increase distrust, they can hardly ignore the need to reexamine those policies. And though it is hard for governments simply to decide to be less distrustful of others, it does lie within their power to work to inspire less distrust than they now do and to negotiate further steps to increase mutual confidence.

Instead of staying trapped in the spirals of distrust and secrecy as in that of the arms race, it is important to see that there are a great many avenues for piecemeal deescalation in all three. Much discussion has

12. See, e.g., Paul Watzlawick, *How Real Is Real?* (New York: Vintage Books, 1976), pp. 98–102; and J. L. Mackie, *Ethics: Inventing Right and Wrong* (Harmondsworth: Penguin Books, 1977), pp. 115–20. For a discussion of an economic model of the role of secrecy and information in an arms race between two world powers, see Martin C. McGuire, *Secrecy and the Arms Race* (Cambridge, Mass.: Harvard University Press, 1965); the author acknowledges, however, that his model gives little attention to irrationality in the arms race.

13. The limitations of a genuine Prisoner's Dilemma are hardly to be found in complex contexts of repeated interaction between innumerable individuals and agencies having intricate relationships to the two major blocs. For a criticism of the analogy between Prisoner's Dilemmas and the arms race, see Derek Parfit, *Reasons and Persons* (Oxford: Clarendon Press, 1984), pp. 56–90. See also Anatol Rapoport and Albert M. Chammah, *Prisoner's Dilemma* (Ann Arbor: University of Michigan Press, 1965).

centered on the third one alone; but if the three are linked, equal scrutiny should go to policies that might help reverse the first two.

Already nations have begun to negotiate increased mutual cooperation, notification of military maneuvers, and other "confidence-building measures," meeting in Stockholm since January 1984 for the purpose of reducing distrust. Similar efforts should be expanded to encompass more activities and more countries.

Such efforts to build confidence among nations are urgent. But it is if possible even more urgent to counteract government practices that undercut international cooperation directly: practices that erode or destroy what little trust still remains. Just how much easier it is to squander trust than to rebuild it has once again been made clear by the shooting down of KAL 007. Such acts destroy trust directly; secrecy erodes what remains more gradually.

For practices that squander trust thus, I propose the term "confidence-destroying measures." Some are directly connected with armaments policy— among them the refusals to abide by international law, the failure to respond to inquiries about apparent cheating on arms agreements, and the indiscriminate arms sales that do so much to prolong and to brutalize regional conflicts. Others undermine the trust needed for arms talks more insidiously. Propagating disinformation, aggressive name-calling, subversion, bribing public officials, and subsidizing terrorists may seem only remotely connected to arms negotiation, yet such acts debilitate its chances continuously. Only by recognizing the role of such practices in destroying confidence and in producing a vicious circle of imitation and retaliation can states break out of the stalemate.

Among such policies, few are as directly injurious to the communication between nations as the practice of "disinformation." The word is a neologism that stands for the spreading of false information not primarily to protect oneself but to discredit adversaries. Common in wartime and increasingly used by rival intelligence networks even in peacetime, it now flourishes in the media as governments try to influence public opinion against one another. When conflicting stories circulate, as about the flow of arms in Central America or the assassination attempt on Pope John Paul II, accusations of disinformation are often voiced only to be heatedly denied. In the face of such discordant accounts, suspicion is natural. The more difficult it is to be certain just whose story is false or where it originates, the more extensive the resulting distrust. And the more an agency becomes known for generating false information, the more often it will be suspected of having done so, however innocent it may be of having started a particular flurry of false rumors. Inevitably, the distrust of an agency colors the respect granted the pronouncements of the government it serves.

Aggressive language is similarly injurious to trust, both on the part of the domestic and international public and on the part of the governments that participate in such wars of words. In recent years, the intensity and violence of invective between government leaders have reached a new level of contemptuousness; threats and warlike propaganda are commonplace. If such language is taken seriously, it cannot help angering its intended targets and increasing distrust in the speaker's proclaimed desire for accommodation; if it is taken to be mere rhetoric for domestic consumption, it raises doubts about the speaker's sincerity, once again giving added cause for distrust.

When coordinated, propaganda, threats, disinformation, and invective can threaten the peace directly, as John Whitton and Arthur Larson have argued:

> Take a given clash of interests. Suppose that the nations on both sides of the dispute are relatively disarmed, and that they use all the means of communications at their disposal to soften and conciliate the controversy. War will probably be avoided. Take the same clash of interests, and suppose instead the both nations are armed to the teeth, and use every technique of modern mass communication to exaggerate the dispute, arouse hatreds and fears by false news and invented threats, and whip the people on both sides into a lather of war frenzy. The result will quite possibly be war.[14]

Both the spreading of false information and highly aggressive propaganda are regularly denounced in the United Nations; yet they continue unabated. Even when they do not reach the level of intensity envisioned by Whitton and Larson, they allow politicians to manipulate public opinion and to heighten distrust of domestic and foreign opponents. Such tactics also increase two of the most serious difficulties in arms talks: that of obtaining accurate information about one's adversary and that of conveying credible information about oneself.[15]

A number of other practices similarly debilitate negotiations by undermining confidence among nations in one another's desire for cooperation. Cutbacks in international exchanges and in athletic, scientific, and other meetings contribute, along with censorship and travel restrictions, to inhibiting the communication necessary to stem the present deteriorating relations. Excessive military secrecy adds to the likelihood of misjudgment, error, corruption, and abuse: something that gives adversaries as much cause for concern as it does allies and the home public since a misstep in one country can mean disaster for all.[16] Mutual secrecy also makes it easier to overestimate an adversary's military preparations in worst-case analyses. The actual breach of formal agreements is clearly highly damaging to the credibility of any country that takes such a step; but the stretching of many more and the refusal to explain whether there has been a breach erodes confidence in a manner sometimes equally debilitating. The flouting of international law by a state such as the Soviet Union or the United

14. John B. Whitton and Arthur Larson, *Propaganda: Toward Disarmament in the War of Words* (Dobbs Ferry, N.Y.: Oceana Publications, 1964), p. 1.

15. Russell Hardin, "Unilateral versus Mutual Disarmament," *Philosophy & Public Affairs* 12 (1983): 236–54, p. 236.

16. See my *Secrets*, chaps. 12, 13.

States opens the door to similar action on the part of all nations, large and small, that perceive some legitimate interest in, for example, violating the national sovereignty of a neighboring state or mining waterways to endanger international shipping. And efforts to "destabilize" governments by subsidizing terrorist groups or through financial manipulations are as destructive of confidence in the probity of a state as are similar measures to "stabilize" exploitative and brutal regimes.

The steps toward reforming these practices should therefore no longer be granted mere lip service. Some of them are so harmful even domestically or so injurious to a nation's reputation that they could be curtailed or discontinued unilaterally. In this category fall the various forms of censorship, the travel restrictions, and the excesses of scientific and other secrecy that drain the spirit of citizens even as they hamper international relations. Others, such as disinformation, do not lend themselves to negotiation; for how can governments negotiate the cessation of activities which they have carried out clandestinely and denied in public? Rather, being so harmful domestically and so damaging to the fragile system of international communication, such practices should simply be quietly terminated.

Still other policies that inspire distrust require negotiation, chief among them the many kinds of secrecy that governments now employ. Since secrecy tends to spread and to conceal wrongdoing, domestically as abroad, the general presumption should be in favor of openness. Scrutiny of weapons systems and defense policies from the point of view of the degree of secrecy, censorship, and clandestine operations they require or generate is also important from this point of view. Verification, wherever it is feasible, protects against incentives to cheat and thus against creating new reason for legitimate distrust. The advent of national and international technical means of surveillance has greatly facilitated the verification of certain treaty commitments. But unless special cooperative measures are instituted in time, new types of weapons will remain less verifiable by such means. And the means of surveillance themselves are hardly without costs. Some pose extensive threats to forms of privacy such as that of telephonic, computer, or postal communication and recordkeeping; many are capable of abuse and of assisting aggressive aims; and all generate renewed efforts at concealment on the part of those who wish to avoid exposure.

But while the effort should be one of deescalation, certain forms of secrecy will remain necessary for defense purposes; and a few that cut down on the risks of war or encourage the nonviolent resolution of conflicts may be preferable to all governments. So long as nuclear-armed submarines are in existence, for instance, secrecy regarding their exact location is at times a protection for all nations against the risk of attempts at a preemptive first strike. But even if such secrecy is collectively desirable, it carries risks that submarines will take advantage of their capacity to escape detection to engage in territorial violations and espionage and create dangerous confrontations far from their home base. It then becomes necessary to establish stand-off zones or other means whereby to prevent them from exploiting this form of secrecy.

A similar problem arises in diplomacy. It has long been recognized that a degree of secrecy in negotiations is helpful to all participants. Publicity tempts negotiators to "play to the galleries" and to please their constituents at the expense of the public good that agreement would represent. And when public exposure is selectively magnified by the media, biased public responses can damage negotiations long before they have been completed. At the same time, secret bargaining may allow negotiators to reach an accord with one another at the expense of persons or groups absent or to make secret deals never submitted to ratification. Once again, though a degree of secrecy is often needed, it is necessary to keep it to a minimum and to provide safeguards against its abuse.[17]

In negotiating the deescalation of practices of secrecy as with other policies that increase distrust, it is possible to propose guidelines for greater openness while setting forth specific exceptions where secrecy remains necessary and in turn specifying safeguards so that these exceptions do not increase the risks of war. There are precedents for such a process in the national legislation concerning secrecy and openness in countries such as Sweden (with its Freedom of the Press Act of 1766) and the United States (with its Freedom of Information Act of 1966).

But in these as in other nations the exception made for military secrecy is so vague that it allows a great many practices harmful to collective security. An international agreement could help reduce the amount of distrust and the propensity for secrecy that occasioned leaving the national legislation so permissive. If so, these exceptions should be further specified and provided with safeguards; this in turn could provide incentives to change on the part of the many countries which have no such laws at all, or which, having them, do not live up to them, or which, like Britain and Canada, still have official secrets acts denying citizens the right to access to government documents.

IV

> For it must still remain possible, even in wartime, to have some sort of trust in the attitude of the enemy, otherwise peace could not be concluded and the hostilities will turn into a war of extermination.

17. With respect to declaratory policy the role of secrecy is ambiguous. From the point of view of any one nuclear power, it may appear preferable to lock oneself into a particular stance—say, the announced intention to retaliate massively if attacked—and to make such an intention clear to adversaries so as to minimize misunderstanding. Such a posture is more plausible as a deterrent if one takes actors on all sides to be fully rational and if one discounts accidental ways in which nuclear war might begin. But considering such factors, is it then better to have a policy of not disclosing intentions? Of appearing unpredictable? Or of disclosing a rigid intention that one is prepared to countermand should the occasion so require?

The war of extermination of which Kant warned in "Perpetual Peace" now threatens every nation.[18] This common danger underscores the need for devoting the same scrutiny to political relations between nations that is already given to military policies. Confidence-destroying practices are problematic from both a moral and a strictly self-interested point of view. They cast doubt on a government's fidelity to commitments and to the standards of conduct that it invokes in judging the actions of other governments; they add to the pressures for increasingly catastrophic worst-case scenarios; and they undercut the minimum of trust needed for negotiating a stable peace. There is every reason, therefore, to seek to cut them back.

Efforts to do so will doubtless encounter powerful obstacles. The disparity between highly secretive and more open societies mentioned earlier reveals one of the greatest barriers to such cutbacks. For while excessive secrecy debilitates any society and prevents public debate about collective security and the role of confidence-destroying policies, it also helps unpopular governments stay in power and thus gives them a strong incentive to tighten rather than to relax their control: something which, in turn, invites adversaries to reciprocate. But even when government leaders perceive the collective emergency clearly enough to join in efforts to reduce secrecy and all confidence-destroying policies, they have to cope with strong domestic resistance, much as in the parallel attempts to reduce and to control armaments; for powerful vested interests benefit from these policies. A great many individuals gain their livelihood and their prestige from taking part in them. Entire agencies depend on them for continued existence; officials in many countries need them to stay in power; and all those who profit from the arms race have a stake in perpetuating the political obstacles to its reversal.

But while numerous and powerful, those who benefit from or otherwise promote the intertwined spirals of the arms race, distrust and secrecy, are hardly unanimous. Many—officials and citizens alike—feel trapped in the momentum of these spirals and go along simply because they see no way out. Increasing numbers of military personnel, scientists, and others who work on projects they see as contributing to the danger and brutality of war now consider conscientious refusal or changing careers as alternatives to mere acquiescence. Religious and professional groups support the search for such alternatives. Among those who would ordinarily dismiss such qualms, many now express fear for their own survival and for that of their children. Even the most hardheaded pro-

18. Immanuel Kant, "Perpetual Peace: A Philosophical Sketch," in *Kant's Political Writing*, ed. Hans Reiss (Cambridge: Cambridge University Press, 1970), pp. 93–130, p. 96. Kant noted that, the more nations rely on "dishonorable" means to guard against one another in wartime, the more easily they turn to them in peacetime as well in order to forestall or prepare for new wars. The time would come, he believed, when the threat would be so apparent to government leaders that they would agree to relinquish such methods or perish.

ponents of doing their job with no questions asked may hesitate once they see their children's future at stake.

If nations are serious about not foreclosing this future, then they must overcome the traditional shortsighted approaches not only to arms policy but also to diplomacy and to all practices that destroy confidence and cripple negotiations. Nothing guarantees that they will be able to cope in time with the current strains in a way that is not mutually destructive. Yet the very difficulties that confront governments should challenge them to question their instinctive resort to confidence-destroying policies in times of danger. Neither war nor politics can any longer be safely conducted by traditional means.

Strategists, Philosophers, and the Nuclear Question

Marc Trachtenberg

What should a symposium on ethics and strategy attempt to do? Should the goal simply be to lay down judgments about which strategies are "morally permissible" and which are not? Such an approach to the problem does not seem particularly fruitful: for judgments of this sort always depend on an appeal to some principle, generally rooted in some ancient tradition; but if a policy we believe in is inconsistent with that principle, why are we morally compelled to sacrifice the former instead of the latter? The conclusions reached are binding only on those who share the premises on which they are based; those who are convinced that the policy in question is right can simply reject these premises as the obsolete products of the prenuclear age.

The "strategists," of course, do not actually come out and say that the concerns of the moral philosophers are irrelevant. But they are aware that their basic assumptions about what makes for stability in the nuclear age contradict traditional principles about morality in warfare. The term "strategic stability" has referred, since the late 1950s, to a situation where neither superpower has any incentive to strike first with nuclear weapons; targeting strategic weapons might undermine an enemy's confidence in his ability to ride out a first strike and thus give him an incentive to preempt. To those who look at things from this perspective, it follows that the "best of all possible nuclear worlds" would be one where only cities were targeted, for in that case there would be no incentive—in fact there would be a tremendous disincentive—for either side to strike first, and thus a nuclear holocaust would be virtually out of the question.

Most of the strategists at the conference subscribed to the stability doctrine in one form or another. Since this theory is not consistent with traditional views about the desirability of aiming at military as opposed to civilian targets, those principles themselves had to be sacrificed. Thus Robert Art, one of the political scientists at Aspen, said in this connection that he was "willing to live in sin." What he meant, I think, was that in the context of the theory that he depended on, the principles of the philosophers had no real meaning, no moral salience, for him.

In fact, the strategists as a whole are not comfortable in the world of the moral philosophers. It strikes them as a strange place, where issues are painted in blacks and whites, where policies are either "permissible" or "impermissible." The choices are stark, the judgments absolute. The issue that preoccupies the philosophers is whether nuclear deterrence is right or wrong—whether "it is wrong to intend, even conditionally, to do that which it would be wrong to do."[1] This is perhaps not quite the right way to put the question: every circumstance is different, and no one can really see the future or tell for sure how he or she would react in extreme cases; intentions, therefore, are rarely rock solid; and deterrence consequently turns more on risk than on intent—the risk, for example, that we would be so carried away with rage following the destruction of our cities that we would pull the nuclear trigger ourselves. The question then would be whether it would be wrong to risk doing—if only because of the imperfect predictability of our own behavior—that which it would be wrong to do.

But however the question is defined, it is set up in such a way that it has a yes or no answer. The philosophers do not seem particularly concerned with questions of degree. They apply their yardstick and either the policy measures up or it does not. And if it falls short, as it does for many of them, it follows that deterrence has to be abandoned and replaced by a policy of no deterrence—that is, by what amounts in effect, and often quite explicitly, to a policy of unilateral nuclear disarmament.

At Aspen, I gave a talk criticizing the philosophers for taking an absolutist approach to issues that, because of the inescapability of the nuclear problem, were inherently relative in nature—that is, making the same kind of argument that I will be making in this essay. The most interesting response was from Gerald Dworkin who told a parable about another conference, held in 1860, on the problem of slavery in America. Not everyone was an abolitionist; there were those who argued that one had to weigh costs and benefits, that maybe the slave system could be softened, that the issue had to be viewed as political and not just moral in nature. The implication was that there was clearly something wrong with that line: some questions are so clear-cut that the moral issues involved have to be viewed as absolute. Slavery was one such question, and nuclear war was another.

No one today would defend slavery, of course; but the more I thought about it, the clearer it seemed that before the Civil War one should have indeed tried to balance all the relevant considerations: that the institution of slavery was not so absolute an evil that it was morally imperative to do whatever was necessary to eradicate it immediately, without regard to any other consideration. In fact, if it was obvious that it would take a war—as it turned out, a long and gruesome war—to abolish slavery, the suffering and anguish that that war would produce should certainly have

1. Jeff McMahan, "Deterrence and Deontology," in this volume, p. 143.

been taken into account. And one should have given some thought to what would happen to the ex-slaves, even in the event that the North were to win: if one could predict that there was a good chance that slavery would be replaced by another brutal and repressive system—by in fact the kind of system that took root in the South after Reconstruction— then this too should have been entered into the balance. And it also would have made sense to look at just how brutal the slave system was: there are different degrees of loathsomeness, and this could have made a difference in one's assessments. (Questions of degree are of course crucial if we are interested in striking a balance.) Finally, arguments about peaceful alternatives—the bidding up of the price of slaves by the federal government, for instance, to make the institution economically irrational in comparison with free labor—would certainly have had a place; historical experience—an analysis of the peaceful way slavery had in fact been ended in the British Empire is the most obvious case—might also have played a central role. Why shouldn't these things all be taken into account? Are we so convinced of the rightness of our personal moral values that we can turn a blind eye to the kinds of considerations that might moderate the force of our commitment? One wonders even whether it can ever be truly moral to simply refuse to weigh these sorts of factors seriously.

One can take the argument a step further by means of a hypothetical example. Suppose, in this case, that the Southerners had told the abolitionists that, if the North did come down to free the slaves, before they arrived the slaves would all be killed. Certainly at this point considerations other than the moral impermissibility of slavery would have to be taken into account. In such a case, an absolutist position—that the institution of slavery was so great an evil that it had to be rooted out without regard to consequence—reveals itself as inhuman and, indeed, as morally preposterous. There has to be some point where issues of balance become morally salient; and thus in general these basic moral issues have to be approached in nonabsolutist—and by that I mean more than just nondeontological—terms.

There are degrees of "moral unacceptability," and the process of judgment should be sensitive to this. In our everyday lives, we all take this for granted. I drive a car knowing there is a small but finite risk that I may kill some innocent pedestrian, due perhaps to some lapse of alertness on my part, and perhaps in some sense it is therefore wrong for me ever to drive. But doing this when the risk is low is not nearly as bad as doing it when, for some reason or other, the risk is high. It may be wrong to risk doing that which it would be wrong to do, but *how* wrong it is depends on the level of risk. Policies which are not tantamount to a ruling out of all nuclear options may be "impermissible" according to some moral standard or other; but they are hardly *as* "impermissible" by any reasonable standard as the actual pulling of the nuclear trigger, if that involved the slaughter of hundreds of millions of innocent people. To fail to recognize this simply strikes me as in itself a form of moral blindness.

We are condemned by circumstance, I think, to live in the moral twilight. If we try to escape, we risk doing more harm than good. If our hatred for nuclear war is so absolute that all other considerations are eclipsed, then we risk giving our adversaries a blank check, and this may draw them into the kinds of policies which we would view with great distaste. Suppose this led to a situation where, in desperation, we resorted to apocalyptic threats; but, having gone so far, our adversary may find it hard to pull back and might prefer to discount our threats on the basis of his prior appraisal of us. Major wars have come about in this way in the past. But this is just one of many ways in which the attempt to escape from the nuclear dilemma can be self-defeating. Such considerations are not morally compelling in themselves; but a sensitivity to such possibilities is essential if these issues are to be analyzed fairly—if the analysis, that is, is to be something more than a preaching to the converted, or a rationalization of one's own political biases.

If the issues of nuclear war are approached in absolutist terms, such considerations simply disappear from the analysis. But much of this has to do with the way the basic problem is structured. The odd thing here is that both philosophers and strategists define the central moral issue the same way: is deterrence right or wrong? It is just that their answers, by and large, happen to be different. According to the strategists, deterrence is right because it keeps the peace, and since peace, or at least nuclear peace, is the overriding goal, nuclear deterrence is fully justified.

But claims about deterrence being a pillar of peace, "an inextricable element of Europe's unprecedented stability,"[2] cannot be accepted uncritically. Why, in fact, would Europe be less stable if nuclear weapons had never existed? American power—in the sense of war-making potential, governed by a specific political intent, and not just forces-in-being—would still balance Soviet power, as it did in the immediate postwar period, before there were enough atomic bombs to be decisive militarily. Or to look at the issue from a somewhat different angle, if both Hitler and the British had had nuclear weapons before 1939, is it obvious that that would have made international politics in the 1930s appreciably more stable? Would Hitler have become more cautious, or would he have viewed the British fear of nuclear war as something that simply strengthened his hand and allowed him to proceed even more aggressively?

There is a certain tendency among some strategists to attribute too much to nuclear weapons. The argument, indeed, can be carried to the point where the strategist seems to be saying that we should be grateful that nuclear weapons exist. But claims of this sort tend, I think, to distort the terms of the debate. The real moral question is not whether nuclear weapons are good or bad. They exist and cannot be disinvented. The nuclear problem is therefore inescapable; the real moral issues have to

2. Josef Joffe, "Nuclear Weapons, No First Use, and European Order," in this volume, 233.

do with how we come to terms with this, with how we are to manage a problem that we can scarcely hope, in any ultimate sense, to resolve.

But does the notion of "deterrence" give us an adequate handle on all this? I want to argue, in fact, that the question of whether deterrence is good or bad does not capture the essence of the problem. For defining the issue in this way does not allow us to deal with what has to be our central concern—the problem of how to strike a balance between conflicting goals. Suppose, for example, we took the question seriously and answered it by saying simply that deterrence is good. But if some deterrence is good, more deterrence would be better; should we therefore try to make retaliation certain—should the use of nuclear weapons, in specific circumstances, be automatic? Or do we pay a rising price as we move along in this direction? If so—and most people would agree that at some point at least a certain price is exacted—how should costs be related to benefits? Where, in other words, should the balance be struck?

There is a need, therefore, to get away from a kind of analysis that directs our attention almost solely to the extremes of absolute deterrence or unilateral nuclear disarmament. Indeed, we need to make sure that we are asking the right questions—that we are framing the issues in such a way as to clarify and bring into focus the moral problems they involve. What are the trade-offs? What, if anything, do we lose when deterrence is made more absolute?

One of the basic problems here has to do with defining exactly what this price is. One should not assume too readily that it is simply an increase in the level of risk: risk in a particular crisis and overall risk are, of course, two different things for the obvious reason that crises are not purely random phenomena dealt out like hands in a game of cards. It is quite possible that a policy of increasing the level of risk if a crisis breaks out, by making escalation more automatic, would have the effect of making crises less likely to emerge in the first place. Thus the overall risk may go down. But even if this is the case, most people would still feel uneasy about too extreme a reliance on nuclear weapons. Therefore something other than the overall level of risk must be an operative consideration. What is it, and is it right to allow such factors to influence our policy in this area?

I was talking to a friend of mine, who happens to be an economist, about the doctrine of "strategic stability," or "mutual assured destruction," as it has bizarrely come to be called. Economists played a central role in the development of the idea, and one of the things that struck me as odd was that the use of analogues to everyday life, which was very characteristic of the analytical style of their strategic writings, was not in evidence in their discussion of "stability." And indeed such analogues would have been very strange. Should we design cars on purpose so that any serious collision would result in the death of both drivers, or structure our system of labor relations so that any strike would drive the company out of business and force the workers into prolonged unemployment?

If we did these things, people would probably drive more carefully and strikes would probably be much less frequent. Maybe even the overall number of highway fatalities would go down, or perhaps by some measure workers and employers would both be better off. But even if it could be shown that this kind of restructuring would have these kinds of effects, people would still be very reluctant to move in this direction.

To my surprise, he told me that there had been a study in one of the economics journals of the effect of seat belts on road safety that developed this kind of argument. Seat belts, the contention was, give a false sense of security, and thus lead to greater carelessness and more accidents than would otherwise be the case. It was not clear whether this was a tongue-in-cheek argument, designed to show just how pervasive the problem of trade-offs is. And it is right that we should be sensitized to the problem of unintended, indirect effects: given how complex human affairs are, such indirect effects are important in all areas of public policy. But the thing that interested me was that my visceral reaction to the argument about seat belts was independent of how well established its conclusions were—how valid the statistical analysis, how cogent the reasoning, and so on. No matter how solid the findings, I found it hard to imagine myself supporting a public policy of discouraging the use of seat belts.

In nuclear strategy as well, there is a similar visceral aversion to making retaliation too automatic that has nothing to do with any systematic calculation of the overall level of risk. It has to do instead, I think, with our distrust of our ability to plan in detail for future contingencies be-forehand—that is, with our desire to maintain some kind of control even in extreme circumstances. Perhaps it was also rooted in some vague sense that we need to hedge against the possible inadequacy of our own theories. Indeed, this aversion was even shared by those strategists who were most sensitive to the strategic advantages of automaticity of response—who understood, in other words, how control and initiative could be handicaps.

The point here is simply that for these issues to be well defined, we have to give some thought to exactly what it is that we are trying to balance. At the very least, this means we should try to get away from the kind of analysis that is not sensitive to the problem of trade-off at all—that is, from an approach that tends to draw our attention away from the kinds of problems we should be concerned with. The very concept of deterrence almost invariably conjures up images of crude threat making; in dwelling on it, we tend to lose sight of the more subtle ways in which power can, and I think should, be used.

Consider, for example, the case of West Berlin. How should Berlin be defended in the event its status is once again challenged? We can explicitly threaten that if the Soviets seize Berlin we would launch a nuclear attack against the USSR. We might, to enhance the credibility of this threat, take measures that would make such retaliation virtually automatic. Or we could say that we are not quite sure how we would react in such a case, but simply as a question of fact we recognize that a Soviet seizure of the city would unleash a semiuncontrollable chain of events that might well culminate in a nuclear holocaust. Or, at yet a further remove, we could say that a takeover would in no case be resisted militarily, but immediately West Germany would be armed with nuclear weapons, thus counting on basic Soviet anxieties about Germany to produce the desired dissuasive effect—this last option, of course, making sense only in a world where there is a finite risk that these nuclear weapons might eventually be used, for otherwise those Soviet anxieties would be nonexistent. Therefore, all of these alternatives depend on—indeed, consciously take advantage of—the risk of nuclear war. Are they thus all to be subsumed under the rubric of "deterrence"?

But there are important moral differences between these different policies, and these distinctions suggest issues which need to be explored. What is the moral difference, for example, between threat making and the conscious exploitation of nuclear risk, especially when that risk is viewed as inescapable? It is of basic moral importance that we define the issues in a way that allows us to *savor* such distinctions.

In the final analysis, this is because peace depends on the skill and subtlety with which power is handled. For in a world of sovereign states, where unresolved disputes can degenerate into armed conflict, the threat of war inevitably conditions political behavior—and thus power necessarily plays a central role in international politics. Peace therefore depends on a stable structure of power, and on the intelligent exercise of power. Peace, in other words, can depend on policies that accept a finite risk of war; and policies which try to rule out any such risk may disrupt the structure of power and thus lead to the very instability that their makers most fear.

This point of view implies that the exercise of power should be seen as normal and natural—that power is something to be exercised continuously and not just held in reserve for those occasions when moral issues are clear-cut. It follows, therefore, that the use of power should be subtle: not the kind of blatant threats, associated with the notion of deterrence, that are linked with the idea that the only function of power is to deal with "aggression" but, rather, the less risky measures which serve simply to condition an adversary's behavior. In the nuclear age, it is too dangerous in most cases to try to dictate the behavior of one's rival; but one should try to influence it by structuring the incentive system within which a rival operates.

In any event, our views on the general subject of war and peace— and thus our sense for what is wrong and what is right in the whole area of foreign and military policy—depend in a fundamental way on our theory of what makes for war or for international stability. The moral issues, that is, cannot be separated from the political ones, and issues of nuclear weapons policy cannot be treated in isolation from more general problems of international politics. Moreover, on those broader issues of war and peace, we are not simply free to choose whatever theory we happen to like: there are certain insights which are intellectually compelling.

One of these is that wars are *not,* as a rule, to be attributed to aggression. They are to be understood, in general, as the outcome of a political process unfolding over time and governed by a dynamic in which the amoral logic of power plays a central role. Indeed, judgments about right and wrong in international affairs are rarely clear-cut. This is true, to one degree or another, of practically every international conflict that I know anything about. But for present purposes I would like to consider only the two great crises of the nuclear age—the confrontations that brought the world closest to thermonuclear holocaust.

The Berlin Crisis of 1958–62 and the Cuban Missile Crisis are both thought of by most Americans, when they think about them at all, in terms of Soviet aggressiveness. The Soviets, it was certainly assumed at the time, were always probing for weakness, and Western policy was purely defensive in character. And yet it is abundantly clear—obvious even from the terms of the November 1958 Soviet "ultimatum" on Berlin— that what set off the Berlin Crisis was Soviet fear of West German acquisition of nuclear weapons, and it was very evident to any careful reader of the *New York Times* that Western policy as a whole was moving in that direction. Was it "legitimate" to allow West Germany, presumably a sovereign power, to acquire nuclear weapons? Or were Soviet anxieties "legitimate"—given that the Bonn government viewed itself as the only legitimate government for Germany as a whole, that West Germany had still not reconciled itself to the status quo in Europe, that it proposed to change it, in a phrase that the Soviets were always quoting, by building "positions of strength," that its army was led by veterans of Hitler's *Wehrmacht,* and so on? Was it therefore valid for the Soviets to apply pressure on Berlin as a way of giving point to their concerns?

Consider in comparison the American reaction in 1962 when the Soviet Union tried to place nuclear missiles in Cuba, condemned at the time as an unacceptable attempt to radically alter the status quo. But this was in many ways a less extreme provocation than what the Americans had intended to do with West Germany. Indeed, imagine what the American reaction would have been in 1962 if the Soviet Union had actually intended to turn control of their missiles over to Cuba; suppose also that the Cuban government still claimed large areas then under American control, and that only twenty years earlier a Cuban army had nearly conquered the United States and that veterans of that army occupied important positions within Cuba's armed forces. But the United States was willing in 1962 to take the world to the brink of war over much less.

This is not, however, an argument about American aggressiveness. One can easily describe the crises in a way that would imply that Soviet behavior was morally questionable without doing any violence to the facts. I put it this way only because it shows how one-sided, and indeed simplistic, our traditional assumptions about international politics have tended to be. The point, in other words, is merely that aggression is a difficult thing to define. There are other reasons for this as well. Judgments depend on values, and values are to a certain extent arbitrary. Nor are our values as a rule fully consistent with each other: we want other countries to be in charge of their own destinies, for example, but we also want them to be democracies just like us. Moreover, policy decisions are always made in the context of a particular structure of power; power has its own logic, and our judgments, whatever scheme of values we have, should be attuned to it.

If moral judgments, then, are difficult to make—if, as most professional historians believe, the allocation of blame is not an intelligent way of approaching the problem of war causation—then the whole concept of aggression, with all its moral overtones, it of limited utility. But if this is true, then the notion of deterrence is also of very limited value. For the two concepts are organically linked: it is aggression, and only aggression, that one seeks to deter.

If one approaches the problem of war and peace in less highly value-laden terms, then the exercise of power by an adversary is more likely to be treated as natural and not as "blackmail"; if moral judgments are viewed as relative, one is more likely to make the effort to see things from a rival's point of view; if one is not ashamed to use one's own power, one can exercise the kind of continuous influence that can conduce to mutual respect, to a real accommodation of interests, and thus to a stable international system. The real question, then, has to do not with whether, but rather with how, power is used; and I think it is clear that the more subtle the system is, the fewer rough edges it has, the more smoothly it is able to function. This means that a reliance on crude threats of war, held in reserve to deal with the most blatant acts of "aggression," is more dangerous than a policy which involves the manipulation of anxieties in a more indirect way. The West could derive greater leverage over Soviet behavior from a nonnuclear than from a nuclear West Germany, for the *threat* of allowing the West Germans to arm themselves with atomic weapons would vanish as soon as they acquired them; a policy of this sort thus tends to lead to tacit accommodations secured by implicit sanctions. In the late 1950s, however, the opportunity to work out such arrangements was sacrificed by a policy that viewed matters in more narrowly military terms—that is, which viewed deterrence as the be-all and end-all of strategy.

The line of argument I am trying to develop here is one that many people find hard to accept. And it is not really to be expected that anyone would accept this kind of reasoning simply on the basis of the few arguments I have just sketched out. What I do insist on, though, is that what I have been dealing with here are the right *questions*. We are all interested above all in peace; therefore we must try to understand what makes for war, and this involves coming to terms with how the international system works. We want to know what makes for a stable international system, and for a good foreign and military policy; and this means that we have to explore the relation between war and politics — that is, that we have to concern ourselves with such things as the political significance of the strategic balance and the role, if any, that arms races play in undermining stability.

But these, of course, are not the kinds of questions that can be handled by a purely abstract analysis. Our approach to the problem instead should be structured in such a way that the conclusions turn on the empirical evidence. A respect for hard evidence has to be at the core of serious thinking on the subject. Purely abstract reasoning, no matter how good it is in formal terms — and sometimes it is very good indeed — can only take us so far.

This sounds like it applies mainly to the moral philosophers, but actually I have the strategists in mind as well. In fact, I think the main criticism that can be directed against classic American strategic thought is that it was, at its core, excessively abstract in character. To Thomas Schelling, for example — in terms of pure intellectual power without any doubt the most impressive thinker in this school — history was like a great grab bag of facts that he could use to illustrate his theories. Approaching the problem on a highly abstract level, his analysis was not controlled and disciplined by the kind of sense for what is important and what is not that you develop when you have to think intensively about these issues in concrete contexts over a very long period of time. As a result he placed tremendous emphasis on the role of purely military factors in war causation. "The reciprocal fear of surprise attack" and "the dynamics of mutual alarm" are the kinds of phenomena he liked to talk about; but the effect of emphasizing such forms of interaction is that one tends to lose sight of the fact that international conflict is at its core a political and not a military phenomenon.

Today, however, strategists seem to be moving away from the old abstract approaches — after a brief period of astonishing productivity, the well had more or less run dry by the mid-1960s anyway — and toward a more empirically oriented style of analysis. But the philosophers, to judge from some of these essays, are still a little too cavalier, for my taste at least, about empirical matters. It certainly does not do any good simply to repeat old claims about how American military policy since 1945 "has been dominated by worst case reasoning," how therefore "the sky is the limit now when it comes to resources that might be expended on military preparations," and how all this has led to an arms race that has poisoned relations between the major powers.[3] The simple fact of the matter is that fiscal restraints are indeed still operative; it is clear, moreover, that we are devoting a much smaller share of our national income to military purposes than we are capable of doing, and indeed a smaller share than

    3. Jan Narveson, "Getting on the Road to Peace: A Modest Proposal," in this volume, p. 216; and Sissela Bok, "Distrust, Secrecy, and the Arms Race," in this volume, p. 341.

was the case during other peacetime periods in the past; and if policy were truly dominated by worst case reasoning, we would be spending much more on the military than we now are, we would have a serious civil defense system on at least the Swiss scale, we would never have signed the ABM treaty, and we would have been constantly reaching for a disarming first strike capability.

As for the point about the arms race leading to the deterioration of political relations, is it totally without relevance to note that U.S.-Soviet relations now, as unsatisfactory as they still are, are nevertheless much better than they were when the nuclear arms competition began thirty-five years ago? Aren't we entitled to ask for some empirical proof for the proposition that the U.S.-Soviet nuclear rivalry has been destabilizing? In fact, I cannot think of any important claim, in any area of thought, where the gap between intensity of conviction and the adequacy of the evidence and reasoning supporting it is as great as it is here: the assumption about the terribly destabilizing effects of the arms race and its corollary about the transcendant importance of arms control are for many people simply articles of faith; and one often has the sense that to question these beliefs in any way, even to say anything that suggests that they be obliged to undergo the same kind of intellectual scrutiny we try to subject our other political beliefs to, is in itself viewed as mildly immoral, or as at best betraying an insensitivity to the great moral issues of the nuclear age.

The basic problem, though, with the kind of approach that views the arms race as the central problem is its assumption that international politics is not about anything real: distrust is rooted in distrust, not in substantive differences of interest; the Cold War is at heart just a gigantic misunderstanding, artificially propelled by the dynamics of mutual suspicion. I wish it were true, and I can understand why people want to believe it is true. But I know it just is not. There is a political conflict at the heart of U.S.-Soviet tension. This is not to be overdefined as a conflict between a threatening Evil Empire and a beleaguered Free World but is rather to be understood in more classic terms as a rivalry between two very great powers whose interests do not coincide.

The role that military factors have played in U.S.-Soviet relations is of course a central issue, if only because of the implications it has concerning how we should direct our efforts. The view that the basic problem has to do with the internal dynamics of the military competition leads to the conclusion that arms control is of preeminent importance as an end in itself—that is, that peace and arms control are virtually synonymous. On the other hand, the idea that the political conflict is fundamental leads to the conclusion that a political accommodation is the essential goal and that both arms control and arms buildups are to be conceived as instruments of a broader policy—as incentives and disincentives that can be used by a policy aiming at a political settlement.

These issues are basic, but they are not beyond our intellectual reach. So much depends on the kind of questions we ask, the kind of standards we hold up for ourselves—indeed, on the kind of intellectual effort we are willing to make. We are dealing with great issues of policy here, but we all have our personal moral responsibilities as well; and in this context it would be an evasion if we allowed our efforts to be wasted on fruitless, or even counterproductive, lines of inquiry. If we are serious about this whole enterprise, we have to make sure that we have thought through exactly what it is that we are trying to do and whether we are going about it in the right way. And these problems of definition can be terribly difficult: the problems of nuclear strategy are often very puzzling, but the hardest problem of all is to figure out what the right questions are.

CONTRIBUTORS

ROBERT J. ART is Herter Professor of International Relations at Brandeis University and research associate at the Harvard Center for International Affairs. He is the author of *TFX Decision* and is currently writing two books: *NATO in the Era of Parity* and *Legislating Defense: Congress and National Security.*

SISSELA BOK is associate professor of philosophy and the history of ideas at Brandeis University. She is the author of *Lying: Moral Choice in Public and Private Life* and *Secrets: On the Ethics of Concealment and Revelation.*

THOMAS DONALDSON is associate professor of philosophy at Loyola University of Chicago. He has published a number of articles and books on ethics, including *Corporations and Morality* (Englewood Cliffs, N.J.: Prentice-Hall, Inc., 1982). He is general editor of a series of books on the subject of ethics, economics, and business published through the Notre Dame University Press.

GERALD DWORKIN is professor of philosophy at the University of Illinois at Chicago. His research interests include the philosophy of law, moral theory, and applied ethics. He is an associate editor of *Ethics.*

DAVID GAUTHIER is professor and chairman of the department of philosophy at the University of Pittsburgh. His recent publications focus on contractarian moral theory, both in historical perspective and treated systematically as a part of the theory of rational choice.

ROBERT E. GOODIN is senior lecturer in government at the University of Essex, an associate editor of *Ethics,* and the author of various articles and books, most recently *Political Theory and Public Policy* (Chicago: University of Chicago Press, 1982) and *Protecting the Vulnerable* (Chicago: University of Chicago Press, 1985).

COLIN GRAY is president of the National Institute for Public Policy in Fairfax, Virginia, and is a member of the General Advisory Committee on Arms Control and Disarmament of the U.S. Arms Control and Disarmament Agency. He is the author of *American Military Space Policy: The American Experience* (Lexington, Ky.: University Press of Kentucky, 1982).

RUSSELL HARDIN is professor of political science and philosophy and chair of the Committee on Public Policy Studies at the University of Chicago. He is the editor of *Ethics* and the author of *Collective Action* (1982). His current research is in the ethics and strategy of nuclear weapons policy and in rational choice and ethics. He is completing a book entitled *Morality within the Limits of Reason.*

JOSEF JOFFE is a senior associate of the Carnegie Endowment for International Peace and a professorial lecturer at the Johns Hopkins School of Advanced International Studies in Washington, D.C. He serves on the editorial board of the *Atlantic Quarterly* and has contributed many articles on international relations, strategy, and arms control to *Foreign Affairs, Foreign Policy,* and *Survival.* He is currently working on a book on European-American relations and completing a book on postwar German foreign policy.

367

GREGORY S. KAVKA is professor of philosophy at the University of California, Irvine, where he teaches political philosophy and ethics. He has published a series of papers on moral issues related to nuclear deterrence and is currently completing a book on Hobbesian moral and political philosophy.

KARL LAUTENSCHLÄGER evaluates future trends in international relations and evolving naval problems as part of long-range planning at the Los Alamos National Laboratory. He has taught courses in international politics, Asian history, and international security studies.

STEVEN LEE is assistant professor of philosophy at Hobart and William Smith Colleges. He has written on the ethics of nuclear deterrence and is coeditor, with Avner Cohen, of *Nuclear Weapons and the Future of Humanity: The Fundamental Questions* (Totowa, N.J.: Rowman & Allanheld, 1985). He has, in addition, published essays on social philosophy, philosophy of law, and action theory.

JEFF MCMAHAN is research fellow in philosophy at St. John's College, Cambridge University. He is the author of *British Nuclear Weapons: For and Against, Reagan and the World: Imperial Policy in the New Cold War* (London: Pluto Press, 1984), and various articles on moral philosophy, strategy, and politics, including one in *Dangers of Deterrence: Philosophers on Nuclear Strategy* (Boston: Routledge & Kegan Paul, 1984).

JOHN J. MEARSHEIMER is associate professor in the Political Science Department at the University of Chicago. He is the author of *Conventional Deterrence* (Ithaca, N.Y.: Cornell University Press, 1983), which won the 1983 Edgar S. Furniss award.

CHRISTOPHER W. MORRIS is currently professor of philosophy at the University of California at Riverside. He has published articles on natural rights, the ethics of redistribution, and rectificatory justice. He is currently working on a rational choice or contractarian account of the liberal state.

JAN NARVESON is professor of philosophy at the University of Waterloo in Ontario, Canada. He has published numerous articles on moral and social philosophy, a book *Morality and Utility,* and an anthology *Moral Issues* (Toronto: Oxford University Press, 1983). His current research interests center around the exploration of contractarianism.

GEORGE H. QUESTER is chairman of the Department of Government and Politics at the University of Maryland. His areas of interest include military strategy, American foreign policy, and international politics. He is the author of *American Foreign Policy: The Lost Consensus, Offense and Defense in the International System,* and *The Politics of Nuclear Proliferation,* along with a number of articles on international security issues. He is a member of the International Institute for Strategic Studies and the Council on Foreign Relations.

THEODORE ROSZAK is professor of History at California State University at Hayward. He is the author of many books on contemporary culture and politics.

MARC TRACHTENBERG is a professor in the History Department at the University of Pennsylvania.

ROBERT W. TUCKER is Edward B. Burling Professor of International Law and Diplomacy at the School of Advanced International Studies, Johns Hopkins University. He is also president and a trustee of the Lehrman Institute. He is the author of many books and articles, among the most recent of which are *The Fall of the First British Empire: Origins of the American Revolution* and *The Purposes of American Power.*

RICHARD H. ULLMAN is professor of international affairs at Princeton University. He first became involved with issues related to nuclear weapons as a member of the Policy Planning Staff in the Office of the Secretary of Defense. In recent years he has served as director of studies at the Council on Foreign Relations, as a member of the editorial board of the *New York Times,* and as editor of *Foreign Policy.*

RICHARD WASSERSTROM is professor of philosophy at the University of California, Santa Cruz. He has published numerous articles on ethics and social and political philosophy, including the morality of war.